COLLECTOR'S GUIDE TO

TRANSISTOR RADIOS

Second Edition

IDENTIFICATION & VALUES

Marty and Sue Bunis

COLLECTOR BOOKS

A Division of Schroeder Publishing Co., Inc.

The current values in this book should be used only as a guide. They are not intended to set prices, which vary from one section of the country to another. Auction prices as well as dealer prices vary greatly and are affected by condition as well as demand. Neither the Authors nor the Publisher assumes responsibility for any losses that might be incurred as a result of consulting this guide.

Searching for a Publisher?

We are always looking for knowledgeable people considered to be experts within their fields. If you feel that there is a real need for a book on your collectible subject and have a large comprehensive collection, contact COLLECTOR BOOKS.

On the Cover:
Mitsubishi 6X–870 "Elite," $125.00 – 150.00.

Cover design: Beth Summers
Book design: Michelle Dowling

Additional copies of this book may be ordered from:

COLLECTOR BOOKS
P.O. BOX 3009
Paducah, Kentucky 42003–3009
or
Marty & Sue Bunis
32 West Main Street
Bradford, New Hampshire 03221
(603) 938-5051

@ $16.95. Add $2.00 for postage and handling.

Printed by IMAGE GRAPHICS, INC., Paducah, Kentucky

DEDICATION

This book is dedicated to all the radio collectors who have so willingly shared their knowledge and expertise with us for the benefit of radio collectors everywhere.

ACKNOWLEDGMENTS

We extend our most sincere thanks to the following people, all of them avid transistor collectors, who provided many of the transistor radios, photographs, facts, and figures that made this book possible. We couldn't have done this without your help and generosity, and we thank you:

Walter Bernd, Dick and Kay Botzum, Bill Burkett, Bob Davidson, Al DeCristofano, Mervyn Ellsworth, Bob Evans, Jules Feir, Larry Gilbert, Bob Goad, Jon Hall, Rudi Herzog, Marvin Hess, Matt Householder, George Kaczowka, Al Manaster, John Miller, Kevin Moe, Tom Mooningham, Bill Overbeck, Bret Phillips, Bruce Phillips, David Polott, Robert Ross, Dan Steele, Franks Sykes, Enrico Tedeschi, John Treggiari, Michael Trocchia, Doug Warren, Gary Willoughby, Wally Worth.

Special thanks to Henry Bohlmann of Hamburg, Germany, who provided a wealth of information and pictures of German transistor radios.

Sincere thanks also to those who loaned transistor radio-related paper goods, catalogs, encouragement, and constructive suggestions. We appreciate your help and support.

INTRODUCTION

Welcome to the wonderful world of Transistor Radios!

If you have ever wished you could be in on the ground floor of collecting with an item that is still easy to find and usually affordable, but will certainly increase in demand and value in a relatively short time, now is the time to jump on the transistor radio bandwagon. Once viewed by vintage tube radio collectors as second-rate radios barely worth a glance, transistor radios are currently enjoying a rapidly growing popularity and have finally taken their rightful place in the world of radio collecting. They are plentiful and affordable, and there is still time to build a good collection before prices get too high. In the past year or two, as more and more people discover the fun, excitement, and nostalgia of collecting transistor radios, their popularity has grown at a fantastic rate.

There are several reasons for this recent surge of interest in transistor radio collecting.

1. **Price and availability.** As the older tube sets become harder to find and more expensive, more and more people begin to collect newer, more affordable radios, and transistors fill that bill perfectly. Many are still readily available at yard sales and flea markets for relatively low prices, making them a very attractive alternative to older, much more expensive and hard-to-find tube sets. Transistor radio prices will definitely go higher and now is a great time to buy.

2. **Style and size.** Take a look through the pictures in this book and notice the wonderful styling that is unique to transistor radios. What a change from the old boxy styles of tube table sets and consoles that take up so much space. Transistor radios are small, stylish eyecatchers that are easily displayed in very small spaces.

3. **Nostalgia and historical significance.** First introduced in 1954, transistor radios were an instant success. They were part of the new, exciting space age technology of the fifties and sixties, and many featured futuristic case designs or space age rocket names such as Vanguard, Satellite, Constellation, Galaxy, and Comet. Many of today's new collectors are attracted to transistor radios simply because they grew up with them and they have a nostalgic fondness for collectibles from the space age era.

EXPLANATION OF PRICING

Because transistor radio collecting is still relatively new, pricing is much more volatile than that of the older, more established tube sets, but since the publication of the first edition of *The Collector's Guide to Transistor Radios*, transistor radio pricing has begun to settle into an accepted norm. As you go through this new edition, you will find that prices are stable or lower on most of the easy to find sets, while the prices of some others, like the highly styled, early Japanese sets, have skyrocketed. Of course, beauty is in the eye of the beholder and we can't all afford to collect expensive radios, so we try to provide a complete range of transistors, priced accordingly, to benefit collectors with budgets and tastes of all kinds.

The pricing information in this book has been gathered from several sources — classified ads, radio meets, and most notably from a panel of "veteran" transistor radio collectors. Our pricing method is to gather as many prices as possible on each set, discard the high and low ends and average the remainder to arrive at a fairly current figure. Please note we have given almost all transistor radios in this book a price range, rather than a firm one figure dollar amount. Because so many transistor prices are still so variable, we feel a price range presents a much more realistic picture of true value. Also be aware that some models were made in various colors and some colors are more valuable than others. Bright colors like red or yellow should generally be valued at the high end of the range while the darker colors like black or brown will usually fall into the low end.

Most importantly, the primary factor in determining the value of a transistor radio is its condition. We have listed pricing that reflects sets in very good condition, using the following guidelines:

1. **Case condition.** One of the great pluses of collecting transistor radios is that they are still so relatively new that they are occasionally found in like-new condition or, better yet, mint in the original box with paperwork. Because most transistor radio collectors want a set to be as close to mint as possible, the condition of the case is of primary concern. As you use this book, keep in mind that the prices written here are for sets in very good condition with all parts intact and having no damage to the case. "No damage" is generally defined as no cracks or hairlines of any kind, no chips, no dents or heavy scratches (very light wear is acceptable), no deep gouge marks around the coin slot or the seams, no missing pieces (logos, battery doors, etc). We have not based our pricing on mint sets or those found mint with their original boxes and paperwork — pricing for sets in this pristine, original condition are generally higher than those listed here, usually by up to 100% or more, depending on the scarcity of the set.

2. **Electronically complete.** Transistor radio collectors are generally less concerned with whether a set works or not than they are with the condition and visual appeal of the case, so the chassis of the radio is generally a secondary concern. Although the set may not be working, all the electrical components should be intact and a minimal amount of repair would bring it to operating condition. Before purchasing a transistor radio, be sure to inspect the inside of the case for any unacceptable corrosion from battery leakage, and be sure to remove the batteries from transistor radios on display to prevent any future damage.

BASIC TRANSISTOR RADIO TERMS AND DESCRIPTIVE INFORMATION

1. **Model Numbers** — We have listed all model numbers in the most logical sequence. Within each company, you will find the numerical model numbers listed

first followed by any model numbers beginning with letters. One important point — sometimes, especially with very inexpensive Japanese transistor radios, the original box is the only source of the model number, as some of the cheap sets never had paper labels inside with model information. If you find a transistor radio at a flea market or yard sale, always be sure to ask if the seller has the box or any original paperwork — it never hurts to ask and you might end up with more than you bargained for!

2. **Description** — For each set we have included, whenever possible, a general description of the shape of the case (either vertical or horizontal), the material from which the case is made, the approximate date of manufacture, the number of transistors, placement and shape of the dial, knobs and grill, bands, power sources, and any other information important to identifying each set. The following terms are frequently used in the descriptions:

AC — Alternating Current

Airplane Dial — a dial which moves in a 360° circle.

AM — Amplitude Modulation

Bat — Battery

Billfold — A transistor radio in the shape of a folding billfold or wallet, usually with the dial, controls, and grill located on the inside of the case.

FM — Frequency Modulation

Horizontal — a transistor radio whose case is longer than it is high.

Hybrid — the term used for a small group of radios that contain both tubes and transistors. Hybrid radios are popular with both tube and transistor radio collectors because they represent the transitional period during the mid-1950s when radios were beginning to shift from tubes to transistors.

Leather/Leatherette — the word "leather" is used to describe those cases covered with leather-looking material. In some cases this material may actually be a man-made leatherette.

LW — Long Wave

Measurements — the approximate case measurements included in this book are listed by height first, followed by length, and then width. They do not include flexible or moving parts, such as swing handles or leather straps.

Micro — a very small, usually square transistor radio.

Slide Rule Dial — a rectangular dial, usually horizontal, which features a thin sliding indicator.

SW — Short Wave

Swing Handle — a dual-purpose handle (usually metal) that can be used in an upright position as a handle or in a lower, diagonal position as a stand.

Table — a general term used to describe a transistor radio that is a table-top model.

Telescoping Antenna — a sectional antenna that folds or telescopes into itself and/or the radio case. Note that some of the telescoping antennas listed here are of the built-in variety that telescope down flush with the case surface and some are of the screw-in kind which only telescope down to the height of their outside shell and must be attached or detached by hand. More often than not, the manually attached type of telescoping antenna is not found with the radio, as they are rather small and easily lost.

Thumbwheel Knob — a thin, round wafer-shaped knob with a serrated outer rim, easily tuned with one finger or thumb.

Vertical — a transistor radio whose case is higher than it is wide.

Watch Radio — a transistor radio that contains a watch face.

Year — We have tried to list the approximate year of manufacture for as many of the sets listed as possible. Please keep in mind that many manufacturers overlapped models from one year to the next and many popular models were made for a number of years.

3. **Pictures** — There may be a few pictures included here that show transistor radios with some slight case damage, but we have tried, to the best of our ability, to photograph only transistor radios that are as close to original as possible.

Keep in mind that this is a *guide* only and it was written to do just that — guide you with identification information and current pricing. Because there are so many variables to consider and because transistor radio prices are escalating rapidly, we make no guarantees that these prices are hard and fast, but we do recommend that you use your judgement when considering the purchase of a transistor radio. If it is in good condition, the price seems fair according to the book and you like it — buy it!

Feel free to write or call us at any time with anything you feel would be helpful for future transistor radio books. We are always happy to hear from other transistor radio collectors and we welcome your calls and letters. (If you write, please enclosed a self-addressed, stamped envelope for a reply.) To maintain accuracy, we only list a model number if we have actually seen the radio — either in person, or from a photograph or vintage company advertising — so we always welcome information from all sources.

Be sure to check the back of the book for current information on antique radio clubs throughout the country. Radio collecting is growing at a rapid pace and there are new clubs forming all the time. We recommend joining a club near you — it's a great way to meet others with the same interests.

If you would like to learn more about transistor radios send $1.00 (refundable toward a subscription) for a sample copy of the *Transistor Network* — a monthly newsletter featuring pictures, articles, and classified ads, all exclusively about transistor radios.

Marty & Sue Bunis
32 West Main Street
Bradford, NH 03221
Phone (603) 938-5051
Fax (603) 938-2430

Acme

Boy's Radio, vertical, 4x2½x1", plastic, two transistors, upper left front window dial with left side thumbwheel tuning, right side thumbwheel on/off/volume knob, round metal perforated grill area, made in Japan, AM, bat...........$45.00 – 55.00

CH-610 "Tops All," horizontal, 1962, six transistors, right front thumbwheel dial, upper right front thumbwheel on/off/volume knob, large perforated grill area, AM, bat...$25.00 – 35.00

CH-620 "Tops All," horizontal, 1961, six transistors, right front dial with right side thumbwheel tuning, right side thumbwheel on/off/volume knob, perforated grill area, swing handle, AM, bat ....$30.00 – 40.00

TR102 "Boy's Radio," "Deluxe," vertical, 4¼x2¾x1¼", plastic, two

transistors, upper front diamond shaped window dial with top thumbwheel tuning, lower textured and perforated metal grill area, made in Japan, AM, bat...........$50.00 – 60.00

Acopian

257P-E "Solar Radio," horizontal, 2¼x3⅛x1½", plastic snap-shut case, right front dial area with large rear tuning knob, lower left front solar cell, no speaker, earphone only, made in USA, AM ...$90.00 – 110.00

Admiral

4P21, horizontal, 1957, charcoal, four transistors, right front round dial knob over large perforated grill area, upper right front thumbwheel on/off/volume knob, chrome swing handle, AM, bat ....$50.00 – 60.00

4P22, horizontal, 1957, red, four transistors, right front round dial knob over large perforated grill area, upper right front thumbwheel on/off/volume knob, chrome swing handle, AM, bat ....$60.00 – 70.00

4P24, horizontal, 1957, tan, four transistors, right front round dial knob over large perforated grill area, upper right front thumbwheel on/off/volume knob, chrome swing handle, AM, bat ....**$50.00 – 60.00**

4P28, horizontal, 1957, turquoise, four transistors, right front round dial knob over large perforated grill area, upper right front thumbwheel on/off/volume knob, chrome swing handle, AM, bat ....**$60.00 – 70.00**

7L12, horizontal, 1956, holiday red, six transistors, world's first solar powered radio, runs on battery or on solar power when used with optional "Sun Power Pak," right side dial knob, left side on/off/volume knob, large front grill area with stylized "V," "orbiting electrons" emblem, top pop-up rotating antenna, AM, bat/solar powered.
radio only ....**$125.00 – 150.00**
w/Sun Power Pak..**$300.00 – 350.00**
w/Sun Power Pak and leather case ....**$500.00+**

7L14, horizontal, 1956, Arizona tan, six transistors, world's first solar powered radio, runs on battery or on solar power when used with optional "Sun Power Pak," right side dial knob, left side on/off/volume knob, large front grill area with stylized "V," "orbiting electrons" emblem, top pop-up rotating antenna, AM, bat/solar powered.
radio only ....**$125.00 – 150.00**
w/Sun Power Pak..**$300.00 – 350.00**
w/Sun Power Pak and leather case ....**$500.00+**

7L16, horizontal, 1956, tropic yellow, six transistors, world's first solar powered radio, runs on battery or on solar power when used with optional "Sun

Power Pak," right side dial knob, left side on/off/volume knob, large front grill area with stylized "V," "orbiting electrons" emblem, top pop-up rotating antenna, AM, bat/solar powered.
radio only ....**$125.00 – 150.00**
w/Sun Power Pak..**$300.00 – 350.00**
w/Sun Power Pak and leather case ....**$500.00+**

7L18, horizontal, 1956, turquoise, six transistors, world's first solar powered radio, runs on battery or on solar power when used with optional "Sun Power Pak," right side dial knob, left side on/off/volume knob, large front grill area with stylized "V," "orbiting electrons" emblem, top pop-up rotating antenna, AM, bat/solar powered.
radio only ....**$125.00 – 150.00**
w/Sun Power Pak..**$300.00 – 350.00**
w/Sun Power Pak and leather case ....**$500.00+**

7M11, horizontal, $3\frac{3}{8}$x$5\frac{7}{8}$x$1\frac{3}{4}$", 1958, ebony plastic, seven transistors, right front round dial knob over large metal perforated grill area, upper right front thumbwheel on/off/volume knob, swing handle, AM, bat ....**$40.00 – 50.00**

7M12, horizontal, $3\frac{3}{8}$x$5\frac{7}{8}$x$1\frac{3}{4}$", 1958, white and red plastic, seven transistors, right front round dial knob over large metal perforated grill area, upper right front thumbwheel on/off/volume knob, gold swing handle, AM, bat.........**$50.00 – 60.00**

7M14, horizontal, $3\frac{3}{8}$x$5\frac{7}{8}$x$1\frac{3}{4}$", 1958, white and tan plastic, seven transistors, right front round dial knob over large metal perforated grill area, upper right front thumbwheel on/off/volume knob, gold swing handle, AM, bat..........$40.00 – 50.00

7M16, horizontal, 3⅜x5⅞x1¾", 1958, white and yellow plastic, seven transistors, right front round dial knob over large metal perforated grill area, upper right front thumbwheel on/off/volume knob, gold swing handle, AM, bat..........$40.00 – 50.00

7M18, horizontal, 3⅜x5⅞x1¾", 1958, white and turquoise plastic, seven transistors, right front round dial knob over large metal perforated grill area, upper right front thumbwheel on/off/volume knob, gold swing handle, AM, bat..........$50.00 – 60.00

221, horizontal, 1958, black, six transistors, upper right front dial knob, upper left front on/off/volume knob, large perforated grill area with lower left stylized "A" logo, rotatable antenna in handle, AM, bat ....$35.00 – 45.00

227, horizontal, 1958, tan, six transistors, upper right front dial knob, upper left front on/off/volume knob, large perforated grill area with lower left stylized "A" logo, rotatable antenna in handle, AM, bat ....$35.00 – 45.00

228, horizontal, 1958, turquoise, six transistors, upper right front dial knob, upper left front on/off/volume knob, large perforated grill area with lower left stylized "A" logo, rotatable antenna in handle, AM, bat ....$35.00 – 45.00

231, horizontal, 1959, black, eight transistors, upper right front dial knob, upper left front on/off/volume knob, large perforated grill area with lower left stylized "A" logo, rotatable antenna in handle, AM, bat ....$35.00 – 45.00

237, horizontal, 1959, tan, eight transistors, upper right front dial knob, upper left front on/off/volume knob, large perforated grill area with lower left stylized "A" logo, rotatable antenna in handle, AM, bat ....$35.00 – 45.00

521, horizontal, 9x9½x3⅜", 1958, golden charcoal leatherette, six transistors, upper right front dial knob, upper left front on/off/volume knob, center grill cut-outs, dual speakers, rotatable antenna in handle, AM, bat..........$30.00 – 40.00

528, horizontal, 9x9½x3⅜", 1958, turquoise leatherette, six transistors, upper right front dial knob, upper left front on/off/volume knob, center grill cut-outs, dual speakers, rotatable antenna in handle, AM, bat..........$35.00 – 45.00

531, horizontal, 9x9½x3⅜", 1958, charcoal leatherette, eight transistors, upper right front dial knob, two upper left front knobs, center grill cut-outs, dual speakers, rotatable antenna in handle, AM, bat..........$30.00 – 40.00

537, horizontal, 9x9½x3⅜", 1958, tan leatherette, eight transistors, upper right front dial knob, two upper left front knobs, center grill cut-outs, dual speakers, rotatable antenna in handle, AM, bat.........$30.00 – 40.00

561 "Super 8," horizontal/table, 1959, black plastic, eight transistors, right front dial knob over wrap-around horizontal grill bars, two left front knobs, feet, AM, bat....................$10.00 – 20.00

561X "Super 8," horizontal/table, 1959, black plastic, eight transistors, right front dial knob over wrap-around horizontal grill bars, two left front knobs, feet, AM, bat....................$10.00 – 20.00

566 "Super 8," horizontal/table, 1959, gold plastic, eight transistors, right front dial knob over wrap-around horizontal grill bars, two left front knobs, feet, AM, bat..$10.00 – 20.00

566X "Super 8," horizontal/table, 1959, gold plastic, eight transistors, right front dial knob over wrap-around horizontal grill bars, feet, AM, bat.....$10.00 – 20.00

581, horizontal, 1959, ebony, five transistors, right front dial over large perforated grill area, upper right front thumbwheel knob, AM, bat...................$25.00 – 35.00

582, horizontal, 1959, red, five transistors, right front dial over large perforated grill area, upper right front thumbwheel knob, AM, bat...................$30.00 – 40.00

691 "Deluxe 5," horizontal, 1960, dove gray, five transistors, right front dial knob, left front on/off/volume

knob, lattice grill area, crown logo, AM, bat......................$20.00 – 30.00

692 "Deluxe 5," horizontal, 1960, coral, five transistors, right front dial knob, left front on/off/volume knob, center lattice grill area, crown logo, swing handle, AM, bat....................$20.00 – 30.00

703 "Super 7," horizontal, $3\%x5^{11}\!/_{16}x1^{13}\!/_{16}''$, 1960, white plastic, seven transistors, right front dial knob, left front on/off/volume knob, center lattice grill area, crown logo, swing handle, AM, bat....................$20.00 – 30.00

708 "Super 7," horizontal, $3\%x5^{11}\!/_{16}x1^{13}\!/_{16}''$, 1960, Nassau green plastic, seven transistors, right front dial knob, left front on/off/volume knob, center lattice grill area, crown logo, swing handle, AM, bat...............$20.00 – 30.00

711 "Imperial 8," horizontal, $3\%x$ $5^{11}\!/_{16}x1^{13}\!/_{16}''$, 1959, starlight black/white plastic, eight transistors, right front dial and lower knob, left front knob, lattice grill area, crown logo, swing handle, AM, bat......................$20.00 – 30.00

717 "Imperial 8," horizontal, $3\%x$ $5^{11}\!/_{16}x1^{13}\!/_{16}''$, 1959, Tahiti tan/white plastic, eight transistors, right front dial and lower knob, left front knob, center lattice grill area, crown logo, swing handle, AM, bat....................$20.00 – 30.00

739, horizontal, 1959, gray leather, five transistors, right front clear round dial knob over large lattice grill area, left front knob, crown logo, leather handle, AM, bat ....$15.00 – 20.00

739X, horizontal, 1959, gray leather, five transistors, right front clear round dial knob over large lattice grill area, left front knob, crown logo, leather handle, AM, bat ....$15.00 – 20.00

742, horizontal, 1959, red leather, seven transistors, right front clear round dial knob over large lattice grill area, left front knob, crown logo, leather handle, AM, bat ....$15.00 – 20.00

742X, horizontal, 1959, red leather, seven transistors, right front clear round dial knob over large lattice grill area, left front knob, crown logo, leather handle, AM, bat ....$15.00 – 20.00

743, horizontal, 1959, white leather, seven transistors, right front clear round dial knob over large lattice grill area, left front knob, crown logo, leather handle, AM, bat ....$15.00 – 20.00

743X, horizontal, 1959, white leather, seven transistors, right front clear round dial knob over large lattice grill area, left front knob, crown logo, leather handle, AM, bat ....$15.00 – 20.00

751, horizontal, 1959, black leather, eight transistors, right front oval window dial, left front knob, large center lattice grill area, crown logo, leather handle, AM, bat ....$15.00 – 20.00

751X, horizontal, 1959, black leather, eight transistors, right front oval window dial, left front knob, large center lattice grill area, crown logo, leather handle, AM, bat ....$15.00 – 20.00

757, horizontal, 1959, tan leather, eight transistors, right front oval window dial, left front knob, large center lattice grill area, crown logo, leather handle, AM, bat ....$15.00 – 20.00

757X, horizontal, 1959, tan leather, eight transistors, right front oval window dial, left front knob, large center lattice grill area, crown logo, leather handle, AM, bat ....$15.00 – 20.00

801, horizontal, $3\frac{3}{8} \times 5\frac{1}{2} \times 1\frac{5}{8}$", 1959, black plastic, eight transistors, right front round dial knob over large perforated grill area, upper right front thumbwheel on/off/volume knob, gold swing handle, AM, bat ....$25.00 – 35.00

802, horizontal, $3\frac{3}{8} \times 5\frac{1}{2} \times 1\frac{5}{8}$", 1959, red plastic, eight transistors, right front round dial knob over large perforated grill area, upper right front thumbwheel on/off/volume knob, gold swing handle, AM, bat ......$30.00 – 40.00

808, horizontal, $3\frac{3}{8} \times 5\frac{1}{2} \times 1\frac{5}{8}$", 1959, turquoise plastic, eight transistors, right front round dial knob over large metal perforated grill area, upper right thumbwheel on/off/volume knob, swing handle, AM, bat..............$30.00 – 40.00

811 "Super 8," horizontal/clock radio, 6¼x11x4", 1959, black back/white front plastic, eight transistors, right front round dial/left front round clock face over wraparound horizontal grill bars, feet, AM, bat.....................$10.00 – 20.00

811B "Super 8," horizontal/clock radio, 6¼x11x4", 1959, black back/white front plastic, eight transistors, right front round dial/left front round clock face over wraparound horizontal grill bars, feet, AM, bat.....................$10.00 – 20.00

816 "Super 8," horizontal/clock radio, 6¼x11x4", 1959, gold back/white front plastic, eight transistors, right front round dial/left front round clock face with wraparound horizontal grill bars, feet, AM, bat.....................$10.00 – 20.00

816B "Super 8," horizontal/clock radio, 6¼x11x4", 1959, gold back/white front plastic, eight transistors, right front round dial/left front round clock face with wraparound horizontal grill bars, feet, AM, bat.....................$10.00 – 20.00

909 "All World," horizontal, 1960, nine transistors, inner horizontal multi-band slide rule dial, perforated grill area, fold-down front, telescoping antenna, handle, nine bands, bat...................$60.00 – 75.00

PR277, vertical, 4x2½x1¼", plastic, solid state, upper right front window dial with thumbwheel tuning, left side thumbwheel on/off/volume knob, lower perforated plastic grill area, made in Hong Kong, AM, bat.....................$5.00 – 10.00

PRF111 "Islander," horizontal, black leatherette, right front vertical slide rule dial, two right thumbwheel knobs, large left perforated grill area, telescoping antenna, handle, AM/FM, bat........$10.00 – 15.00

Y701R, vertical, 4x2½x1¼", plastic, six transistors, upper right front circular window dial, lower vertical grill bars, left side strap, crown logo, AM, bat............$15.00 – 20.00

Y793 "Starlet," horizontal/clock radio, 1960, white, five transistors, right front dial/clock panel, left front lattice grill area with alarm/volume knob, crown logo, AM, bat.....................$10.00 – 15.00

Y797 "Starlet," horizontal/clock radio, 1960, tan, five transistors, right front dial/clock panel, left front lattice grill area with alarm/volume knob, crown logo, AM, bat......................$10.00 – 15.00

Y798 "Starlet," horizontal/clock radio, 1960, green, five transistors, right front dial/clock panel, left front lattice grill area with alarm/volume knob, crown logo, AM, bat......................$10.00 – 15.00

Y821 "Holiday," horizontal/clock radio, 1960, black & white, eight transistors, right front dial/clock panel, left front lattice grill area with alarm/volume knob, crown logo, AM, bat..............$10.00 – 15.00

Y822 "Holiday," horizontal/clock radio, 1960, coral & white, eight transistors, right front dial/clock panel, left front lattice grill area with alarm/volume knob, crown logo, AM, bat..............$10.00 – 15.00

Y909 "All World," horizontal, 10x12½x4⅝", 1961, falcon gray leatherette and metal, nine transistors, fold-down front with map and log book, inner horizontal multi-band slide rule dial, telescoping antenna, handle, nine bands, bat..................$75.00 – 90.00

Y2009 "Super 7," horizontal, 3½x5½x1¾", 1960, gray plastic, seven transistors, right front dial, left front on/off/volume knob over large lattice grill area, crown logo, AM, bat......................$15.00 – 25.00

Y2009X "Super 7," horizontal, 3½x5½x1¾", 1960, gray plastic, seven transistors, right front dial, left front on/off/volume knob over large lat-

tice grill area, crown logo, swing handle, AM, bat..................$15.00 – 25.00

Y2011 "Super 7," horizontal, 3½x5½ x1¾", 1960, black plastic, seven transistors, right front dial, left front on/off/volume knob over large lattice grill area, crown logo, swing handle, AM, bat ....$15.00 – 25.00

Y2011X "Super 7," horizontal, 3½x5½x1¾", 1960, black plastic, seven transistors, right front dial, left front on/off/volume knob over large lattice grill area, crown logo, swing handle, AM, bat..........$15.00 – 25.00

Y2012 "Super 7," horizontal, 3½x5½ x1¾", 1960, coral plastic, seven transistors, right front dial, left front on/off/volume knob over large lattice grill area, crown logo, swing handle, AM, bat ....$15.00 – 25.00

Y2012X "Super 7," horizontal, 3½x5½x1¾", 1960, coral plastic, seven transistors, right front dial, left front on/off/volume knob over large lattice grill area, crown logo, swing handle, AM, bat..........$15.00 – 25.00

Y2013 "Super 7," horizontal, 3½x5½ x1¾", 1960, white plastic, seven transistors, right front dial, left front on/off/volume knob over large lattice grill area, crown logo, swing handle, AM, bat..........$15.00 – 25.00

Y2013X "Super 7," horizontal, 3½x5½x1¾", 1960, white plastic, seven transistors, right front dial, left front on/off/volume knob over large lattice grill area, crown logo, swing handle, AM, bat..........$15.00 – 25.00

Y2018 "Super 7," horizontal, 3½x5½ x1¾", 1960, green plastic, seven transistors, right front dial, left front on/off/volume knob over large lattice grill area, crown logo, swing handle, AM, bat ....$15.00 – 25.00

Y2023 "Super 7," horizontal, 1960, white, seven transistors, off-center dial with right and left lattice grill areas, left front knob, crown logo, AM, bat ....$15.00 – 25.00

Y2027 "Super 7," horizontal, 1960, beige, seven transistors, off-center dial with right and left lattice grill areas, left front knob, crown logo, AM, bat ....$15.00 – 25.00

Y2028, "Super 7," horizontal, 1960, green, seven transistors, off-center dial with right and left lattice grill areas, left front knob, crown logo, AM, bat ....$15.00 – 25.00

Y2061 "Super 7," vertical, 4⅛x2⅝x1½", 1960, starlight black plastic, seven transistors, upper front off-center window dial with right side thumbwheel tuning, left side thumbwheel on/off/volume knob, lower lattice grill area, crown logo, rear fold-out stand, AM, bat ....$20.00 – 25.00

Y2063 "Super 7," vertical, 4⅛x2⅝x 1½", 1960, pearl white plastic, seven transistors, upper front off-center window dial with right side thumbwheel tuning, left side thumbwheel on/off/volume knob, lower lattice grill area, crown logo, rear fold-out stand, AM, bat ....$20.00 – 25.00

Y2067 "Super 7," vertical, 4⅛x2⅝x1½", 1960, Sahara beige plastic, seven transistors, upper front off-center window dial with right side thumbwheel tuning, left side thumbwheel on/off/volume knob, lower lattice grill area, crown logo, rear fold-out stand, AM, bat...............$20.00 – 25.00

Y2068 "Super 7," vertical, 4⅛x2⅝x1½", 1960, Nassau green plastic, seven transistors, upper front off-center window dial with right side thumbwheel tuning, left side thumbwheel on/off/volume knob, lower lattice grill area, crown logo, rear fold-out stand, AM, bat...............$20.00 – 25.00

Y2081 "Imperial 7," "Lancer," horizontal, 3½x5¾x1⅝", 1961, starlight black plastic, seven transistors, upper right front window dial, lower on/off/volume knob, horizontal front grill bars with crown logo inside large oval, swing handle, made in USA, AM, bat..........$20.00 – 30.00

Y2082 "Imperial 7," "Lancer," horizontal, 3½x5¾x1⅝", 1961, reef coral plastic, seven transistors, upper right front window dial, lower on/off/volume knob, horizontal front grill bars with crown logo inside large oval, swing handle, made in USA, AM, bat ....$20.00 – 30.00

Y2083 "Imperial 7," "Lancer," horizontal, 3½x5¾x1⅝", 1961, pearl white plastic, seven transistors, upper right front window dial, lower on/off/volume knob, horizontal front grill bars with crown logo inside large oval, swing handle, made in USA, AM, bat..........$20.00 – 30.00

Y2091 "Imperial 8," "Conqueror," horizontal, 3½x5⅞x1⅝", 1961, starlight black plastic, eight transistors, upper right front window dial, lower on/off/volume knob, large oval grill area with center crown logo, swing handle, made in USA, AM, bat ....$20.00 – 30.00

Y2093 "Imperial 8," "Conqueror," horizontal, 3½x5⅞x1⅝", 1961, pearl white plastic, eight transistors, upper right front window dial, lower on/off/volume knob, large oval grill area with center crown logo, swing handle, made in USA, AM, bat ....$20.00 – 30.00

Y2098 "Imperial 8," "Conqueror," horizontal, 3½x5⅞x1⅝", 1961, Nassau green plastic, eight transistors, upper right front window dial, lower on/off/volume knob, large oval grill area with center crown logo, swing handle, made in USA, AM, bat ....$20.00 – 30.00

Y2101 "Super 7," "Spartan," vertical, 7½x5⅝x2⅝", 1961, starlight black

plastic, seven transistors, upper right front window dial, left on/off/volume knob, large lower grill area with horizontal bars, crown logo, handle, AM, bat......................$15.00 – 25.00

Y2102 "Super 7," "Spartan," vertical, 7½x5⅝x2⅝", 1961, reef coral plastic, seven transistors, upper right front window dial, left on/off/volume knob, large lower grill area with horizontal bars, crown logo, handle, AM, bat ....$15.00 – 25.00

Y2108 "Super 7," "Spartan," vertical, 7½x5⅝x2⅝", 1961, Nassau green plastic, seven transistors, upper right front window dial, left on/off/volume knob, large lower grill area with horizontal bars, crown logo, handle, AM, bat......................$15.00 – 25.00

Y2119 "Deluxe 7," "Adventurer," horizontal, 5¼x9x2¾", 1962, dove gray leather, seven transistors, right front dial knob, left horizontal grill bars with on/off/volume knob, crown logo, leather handle, AM, bat.........$10.00 – 15.00

Y2127 "Imperial 8," "Olympian," horizontal, 5¼x9x2¾", 1959, Tahiti tan leather, eight transistors, right front round dial, left horizontal grill bars with on/off/volume knob, crown logo, leather handle, AM, bat ....$10.00 – 15.00

Y2127X "Imperial 8," "Olympian," horizontal, 5¼x9x2¾", 1959, Tahiti tan leather, eight transistors, right front round dial, left horizontal grill bars with on/off/volume knob, crown logo, leather handle, AM, bat ....$10.00 – 15.00

Y2129X "Imperial 8," horizontal, brown leather, right front round dial, left horizontal grill bars with on/off/volume knob, crown logo, leather handle, AM, bat ....$10.00 – 15.00

Y2137 "Clipper," horizontal, 5¼x9x 3¾", 1961, saddle tan leather, eight transistors, right front semicircular three band dial and three knobs, left horizontal grill bars with center crown logo, top rotary azimuth scale, leather handle, AM, SW, LW, bat ....$15.00 – 20.00

Y2137C "Clipper," horizontal, 1964, leather, eight transistors, right front semicircular three band dial and three knobs, left horizontal grill bars with center crown logo, top rotary azimuth scale, leather handle, AM, SW, LW, bat ....$15.00 – 20.00

Y2221 "Golden Eagle," vertical, 3⅜x2½x1", 1962, starlight black plastic, six transistors, upper right front circular window dial with right side thumbwheel tuning, left side thumbwheel on/off/volume knob, large lower perforated grill area, crown logo, AM, bat..........................$20.00 – 30.00

Y2223 "Golden Eagle," vertical, 3⅜x2½x1", 1962, bone white plastic, six transistors, upper right front circular window dial with right side thumbwheel tuning, left side thumbwheel on/off/volume knob, large lower perforated grill area, crown logo, AM, bat....................$20.00 – 30.00

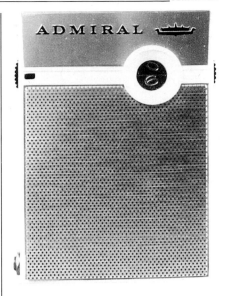

Y2223A "Golden Eagle," vertical, 3⅜x2½x1", 1962, white plastic, six transistors, upper right front circular window dial with right side thumbwheel tuning, left side thumbwheel on/off/volume knob, large lower perforated grill area, crown logo, AM, bat..$20.00 – 30.00

Y2226 "Golden Eagle," vertical, 3⅜x2½x1", 1962, harvest yellow plastic, six transistors, upper right front circular window dial with right side thumbwheel tuning, left side thumbwheel on/off/volume knob, large lower perforated grill area, crown logo, AM, bat..............$20.00 – 30.00

Y2229 "Golden Eagle," vertical, 3⅜x2½x1", 1962, jade blue plastic, six transistors, upper right front circular window dial with right side thumbwheel tuning, left side thumbwheel on/off/volume knob, large lower perforated grill area, crown logo, AM, bat..$20.00 – 30.00

Y2230 "Triumph," vertical, 1962, plastic, six transistors, small upper right front window dial with right side thumbwheel tuning, left side thumbwheel on/off/volume knob, lower grill area with concentric circles, crown logo, AM, bat.....**$5.00 – 10.00**

Y2231, vertical, 1962, black plastic, six transistors, small upper right front window dial with right side thumbwheel tuning, left side thumbwheel on/off/volume knob, lower grill area with concentric circles, crown logo, AM, bat.....**$5.00 – 10.00**

Y2231GPS, vertical, 1962, black plastic, six transistors, small upper right front window dial with right side thumbwheel tuning, left side thumbwheel on/off/volume knob, lower grill area with concentric circles, crown logo, AM, bat.....**$5.00 – 10.00**

Y2232, vertical, 1962, coral plastic, six transistors, small upper right front window dial with right side thumbwheel tuning, left side thumbwheel on/off/volume knob, lower grill area with concentric circles, crown logo, AM, bat.....**$5.00 – 10.00**

Y2232GPS, vertical, 1962, coral plastic, six transistors, small upper right front window dial with right side thumbwheel tuning, left side thumbwheel on/off/volume knob, lower grill area with concentric circles, crown logo, AM, bat.....**$5.00 – 10.00**

Y2238, vertical, 1962, green plastic, six transistors, small upper right front window dial with right side thumbwheel tuning, left side thumb-wheel on/off/volume knob, lower grill area with concentric circles, crown logo, AM, bat.....**$5.00 – 10.00**

Y2238GPS, vertical, 1962, green plastic, six transistors, small upper right front window dial with right side thumbwheel tuning, left side thumbwheel on/off/volume knob, lower grill area with concentric circles, crown logo, AM, bat .....**$5.00 – 10.00**

Y2252 "Wayfarer," vertical, 7½x5⅝x2⅝", 1962, shell coral plastic, seven transistors, upper right front dial knob, upper left front on/off/volume knob, lower grill area with horizontal bars, handle, AM, bat ....**$15.00 – 25.00**

Y2253 "Wayfarer," vertical, 7½x5⅝x2⅝", 1962, bone white plastic, seven transistors, upper right front dial knob, upper left front on/off/volume knob, lower grill area with horizontal bars, handle, AM, bat ....**$15.00 – 25.00**

Y2256 "Wayfarer," vertical, 7½x5⅝x2⅝", 1962, harvest yellow plastic, seven transistors, upper right front dial knob, upper left front on/off/volume knob, lower grill area with horizontal bars, handle, AM, bat ....**$15.00 – 25.00**

Y2271, vertical, 1963, black plastic, six transistors, upper right round dial knob over large front textured grill area, crown logo, AM, bat.............................**$15.00 – 20.00**

Y2271GPN "Comet," vertical, 3⅜x2½x1", 1963, starlight black plastic, six transistors, upper right round dial knob over large front textured grill area, crown logo, AM, bat ....$15.00 – 20.00

Y2272, vertical, 1963, red plastic, six transistors, upper right round dial knob over large front textured grill area, crown logo, AM, bat................$15.00 – 20.00

Y2272GPN "Comet," vertical, 3⅜x2½x1", 1963, ruby red plastic, six transistors, upper right round dial knob over large front textured grill area, crown logo, AM, bat................$15.00 – 20.00

Y2273, vertical, 1963, white plastic, six transistors, upper right round dial knob over large front textured grill area, crown logo, AM, bat................$15.00 – 20.00

Y2273GPN "Comet," vertical, 3⅜x2½x1", 1963, bone white plastic, six transistors, upper right round dial knob over large front textured grill area, crown logo, ΛM, bat................$15.00 – 20.00

Y2301GP, vertical, 1963, black plastic, six transistors, upper right front round window dial surrounded by star-shaped trim over large front perforated grill area, right side thumbwheel knob, crown logo, AM, bat................$20.00 – 30.00

Y2301GPN "Starfire," vertical, 3⅜x2½x1", 1963, starlight black plastic, six transistors, upper right front round window dial surrounded by star-shaped trim over large

front perforated grill area, right side thumbwheel knob, crown logo, AM, bat................$20.00 – 30.00

Y2301GPS, vertical, 1963, black plastic, six transistors, upper right front round window dial surrounded by star-shaped trim over large front perforated grill area, right side thumbwheel knob, crown logo, AM, bat................$20.00 – 30.00

Y2303GP, vertical, 1963, white plastic, six transistors, upper right front round window dial surrounded by star-shaped trim over large front perforated grill area, right side thumbwheel knob, crown logo, AM, bat................$20.00 – 30.00

Y2303GPN "Starfire," vertical, 3⅜x2½x1", 1963, bone white plastic, six transistors, upper right front round window dial surrounded by star-shaped trim over large front perforated grill area, right side thumbwheel knob, crown logo, AM, bat................$20.00 – 30.00

Y2303GPS, vertical, 1963, white plastic, six transistors, upper right front round window dial surrounded by star-shaped trim over large front perforated grill area, right side thumbwheel knob, crown logo, AM, bat................$20.00 – 30.00

Y2307GP, vertical, 1963, brown plastic, six transistors, upper right front round window dial surrounded by star-shaped trim over large front perforated grill area, right side thumbwheel knob, crown logo, AM, bat................$20.00 – 30.00

Y2307GPN "Starfire," vertical, 3⅜x2½x1", 1963, cinnamon brown plastic, six transistors, upper right front round window dial surrounded by star-shaped trim over large front perforated grill area, right side thumbwheel knob, crown logo, AM, bat .... $20.00 – 30.00

Y2307GPS, vertical, 1963, brown plastic, six transistors, upper right front round window dial surrounded by star-shaped trim over large front perforated grill area, right side thumbwheel knob, crown logo, AM, bat .... $20.00 – 30.00

Y2332, horizontal, 6x7½x2½", 1963, ruby red plastic, six transistors, right front round dial knob over large checkered grill area, lower right knob, crown logo, fold-down handle, AM, bat .... $15.00 – 20.00

Y2351, horizontal, 1963, starlight black leather, eight transistors, upper front horizontal dial, two knobs, large lower grill area with vertical bars, crown logo, leather handle, AM, bat .... $10.00 – 15.00

Y2351X, horizontal, 1963, black leather, eight transistors, upper front horizontal dial, two knobs, large lower grill area with vertical bars, crown logo, leather handle, AM, bat .... $10.00 – 15.00

Y2357X, horizontal, 1963, tan leather, eight transistors, upper front horizontal dial, two knobs, large lower grill area with vertical bars, crown logo, leather handle, AM, bat .... $10.00 – 15.00

Y2371 "All American," horizontal, 7¼x10⅛x3¾", 1963, chrome and ebony black leatherette, 11 transistors, upper left horizontal two-band slide rule dial, two knobs, large lower perforated grill area, telescoping antenna, handle, AM, FM, bat .... $15.00 – 20.00

Y2401GPN "Meteor," vertical, 3⅜x2½x1", 1963, starlight black plastic, six transistors, upper right front window dial over large textured grill area, right side thumbwheel knob, AM, bat .... $15.00 – 20.00

Y2402GPN "Meteor," vertical, 3⅜x2½x1", 1963, ruby red plastic, six transistors, upper right front window dial over large textured grill area, right side thumbwheel knob, AM, bat .... $15.00 – 20.00

Y2403GPN "Meteor," vertical, 3⅜x2½x1", 1963, bone white plastic, six transistors, upper right front window dial over large textured grill area, right side thumbwheel knob, AM, bat .... $15.00 – 20.00

Y2411GP, vertical, 1963, black plastic, eight transistors, large upper right front dial knob, left side thumbwheel on/off/volume knob, lower metal perforated grill area, crown logo, AM, bat .. $15.00 – 20.00

Y2411GPN "V.I.P.," vertical, 4⅜x2¾x1⅜", 1963, starlight black plastic, eight transistors, large upper right front dial knob, left side thumbwheel on/off/volume knob, lower metal perforated grill area, crown logo, AM, bat .. $15.00 – 20.00

**Y2413GP, vertical, 4⅜x2¾x1⅜",
1964, white plastic, eight transistors, large upper right front dial
knob, left side thumbwheel
on/off/volume knob, lower metal
perforated grill area, crown logo,
AM, bat.....................$15.00 – 20.00**

Y2413GPN "V.I.P.," vertical,
4⅜x2¾x1⅜", 1963, bone white plastic, eight transistors, large upper
right front dial knob, left side
thumbwheel on/off/volume knob,
lower metal perforated grill area,
crown logo, AM, bat..$15.00 – 20.00

Y2421GP, vertical, 1963, black plastic, eight transistors, upper front
horizontal slide rule dial with right
side thumbwheel tuning, large lower
perforated grill area with "starburst"
decoration, swing handle, crown
logo, AM, AC/bat .....$20.00 – 30.00

Y2421GPN "Starburst," vertical,
5⅞x3⅝x1½", 1963, black plastic,
eight transistors, upper front horizontal slide rule dial with right side
thumbwheel tuning, large lower
perforated grill area with "starburst"
decoration, swing handle, crown
logo, AM, AC/bat.....$20.00 – 30.00

Y2423GP, vertical, 1963, white plastic, eight transistors, upper front
horizontal slide rule dial with right
side thumbwheel tuning, large lower
perforated grill area with "starburst"
decoration, swing handle, crown
logo, AM, AC/bat .....$20.00 – 30.00

Y2423GPN "Starburst," vertical,
5⅞x3⅝x1½", 1963, white plastic,
eight transistors, upper front
horizontal slide rule dial with
right side thumbwheel tuning,
large lower perforated grill area
with "starburst" decoration,
swing handle, crown logo, AM,
AC/bat...................$20.00 – 30.00

Y2432 "Little Jewel," horizontal,
5¼x7¼x2⅜", 1963, ruby red plastic,
six transistors, upper right front
round dial knob, large lower grill
area, handle, crown logo, AM,
AC/bat....................$10.00 – 15.00

Y2433 "Little Jewel," horizontal,
5¼x7¼x2⅜", 1963, bone white plastic, six transistors, upper right front
round dial knob, large lower grill
area, handle, crown logo, AM,
AC/bat....................$10.00 – 15.00

Y2438 "Little Jewel," horizontal,
5¼x7¼x2⅜", 1963, Nassau green
plastic, six transistors, upper right
front round dial knob, large lower
grill area, handle, crown logo, AM,
AC/bat....................$10.00 – 15.00

Y2441 "Power Eight," horizontal, 5x7¼x3⅛", 1963, black leather, eight transistors, right front vertical dial and two knobs, left textured grill area with lower left crown logo, leather handle, AM, AC/bat.....................$10.00 – 15.00

Y2451 "Crest," horizontal, 4½x8x1⅞", 1963, jet black plastic, 10 transistors, two upper front horizontal slide rule dials – one AM, one FM – right and left thumbwheel knobs, lower textured grill area with lower right switch, telescoping antenna, swing handle, crown logo, AM, FM, AC/bat....................$15.00 – 20.00

Y2451N, horizontal, 1963, black plastic, 10 transistors, two upper front horizontal slide rule dials – one AM, one FM – right and left thumbwheel knobs, lower textured grill area with lower right switch, telescoping antenna, swing handle, crown logo, AM, FM, AC/bat ....$15.00 – 20.00

Y2461 "Galaxy," horizontal, 5x8x2", 1963, midnight black leather, 10 transistors, two upper front horizontal slide rule dials – one AM, one FM – lower textured grill area with lower right band switch, telescoping antenna, leather handle, crown logo, AM, FM, AC/bat....................$15.00 – 20.00

Y2461N, horizontal, 1963, black leather, 10 transistors, two upper front horizontal slide rule dials – one AM, one FM – lower textured grill area with lower right band

switch, telescoping antenna, leather handle, crown logo, AM, FM, AC/bat.....................$15.00 – 20.00

Y2531GP, vertical, 1965, black front/white back, 10 transistors, upper front horizontal two-band dial, large lower grill area, crown logo, telescoping antenna, swing handle, AM, FM, bat...............$10.00 – 15.00

Y2537GP, vertical, 1965, brown front/white back, 10 transistors, upper front horizontal two-band dial, large lower grill area, crown logo, telescoping antenna, swing handle, AM, FM, bat...............$10.00 – 15.00

Y2539GP, vertical, 1965, blue front/white back, 10 transistors, upper front horizontal two-band dial, large lower grill area, crown logo, telescoping antenna, swing handle, AM, FM, bat..$10.00 – 15.00

Y2557, horizontal, 5½x7½x3", 1964, tan leather, eight transistors, upper right front dial, large lower grill area with horizontal bars, crown logo, leather handle, AM, bat...............................$5.00 – 10.00

Y2577, horizontal, 1965, eight transistors, two upper front horizontal slide rule dials – one AM, one SW – large lower grill area with lower right AM/SW switch, telescoping antenna, handle, crown logo, AM, SW, bat....................$15.00 – 20.00

Y2587, horizontal, 1965, eight transistors, upper front horizontal two-band slide rule dial, large lower perforated grill area, telescoping antenna, leather handle, crown logo, AM, SW, bat......**$10.00 – 15.00**

YD101GP, vertical, 1965, nine transistors, upper front horizontal two-band slide rule dial, large lower perforated grill area, telescoping antenna, crown logo, AM, FM, bat......................**$10.00 – 15.00**

YD107GP, vertical, 1965, nine transistors, upper front horizontal two-band slide rule dial, large lower perforated grill area, telescoping antenna, crown logo, AM, FM, bat......................**$10.00 – 15.00**

YD109GP, vertical, 1965, nine transistors, upper front horizontal two-band slide rule dial, large lower perforated grill area, telescoping antenna, crown logo, AM, FM, bat......................**$10.00 – 15.00**

YD201GP, horizontal, 2¾x4¼x1", 1965, plastic, upper right front circular window dial with thumbwheel tuning, lower right circular on/off/volume window with thumbwheel knob, left lattice grill area, AM, bat............**$10.00 – 15.00**

YD242, horizontal, 5¾x7¼x2⅜", 1965, plastic, eight transistors, upper right front dial and on/off/volume knobs, large lower grill area with rectangular slots, fold-down handle, crown logo, made in Japan, AM, bat ....**$10.00 – 15.00**

YH331GP, vertical, leather, 10 transistors, upper front horizontal two-band slide rule dial, lower metal perforated grill area, tele-

scoping antenna, crown logo, AM/FM, bat..............**$10.00 – 15.00**

YH371GP, horizontal, 2⅜x3⅝x1⅛", plastic, eight transistors, upper right front round window dial over large lattice grill area, upper right side thumbwheel dial knob, lower right side thumbwheel on/off/volume knob, crown logo, made in Japan, AM, bat......................**$10.00 – 15.00**

YK201GP, horizontal, black plastic, eight transistors, upper right front round window dial with upper right side thumbwheel tuning, lower right side thumbwheel on/off/volume knob, large lattice grill area, crown logo, AM, bat............................**$10.00 – 15.00**

YK211GP "Caprice," vertical, black & white plastic, 10 transistors, upper right front window dial with right side thumbwheel tuning, left side thumbwheel on/off/volume knob, large lattice grill area, crown logo, AM, bat............**$10.00 – 15.00**

YK212GP "Caprice," vertical, red & white plastic, 10 transistors, upper right front window dial with right side thumbwheel tuning, left side thumbwheel on/off/volume knob, large lattice grill area, crown logo, AM, bat............**$10.00 – 15.00**

YK237 "Polaris," horizontal, beige & brown plastic, 10 transistors, upper right front dial knob, upper left front on/off/volume knob, large lattice grill area with lower right hi-lo switch, handle, crown logo, AM, bat..............**$10.00 – 15.00**

YK327 "Bolero," horizontal, brown & beige plastic, 12 transistors, upper front horizontal two-band slide rule dial, large lower grill area with lower right AFC/FM/AM switch, telescoping antenna, handle, AM, FM, bat.......$10.00 – 15.00

Advanco

802 "Super DeLuxe," vertical, 4¼x 2½x1⅜", plastic, eight transistors, upper right front window dial with thumbwheel tuning, left side thumbwheel on/off/volume knob, lower lattice grill area, made in Hong Kong, AM, bat ....$5.00 – 10.00

MT-608, horizontal, 2¾x4¼x1¼", plastic, six transistors, upper right

front square window dial surrounded by concentric squares, horizontal grill bars, top strap, made in Okinawa, AM, bat.....$10.00 – 15.00

AEG

Carina 61, horizontal, 1960, plastic, seven transistors, diagonally divided front with right round dial, top left thumbwheel on/ off/volume knob, vertical grill bars, made in West Germany, AM, LW, bat.....................$20.00 – 30.00

Carina 62, horizontal, 1961, plastic, seven transistors, upper front horizontal three-band slide rule dial with upper right front thumbwheel tuning, left side thumbwheel on/off/volume knob, perforated grill area, made in West Germany, AM, LW, SW, bat.......$30.00 – 40.00

Carina UKW 61, horizontal, 1960, plastic, eight transistors, upper front horizontal two-band slide rule dial with upper right front thumbwheel tuning, left side thumbwheel on/off/volume knob, two telescoping antennas, made in West Germany, AM, FM, bat..........................$30.00 – 40.00

Carina UKW 62, horizontal, 1961, plastic, eight transistors, upper front horizontal two-band slide rule dial with upper right front thumbwheel tuning, left side thumbwheel on/off/volume knob, telescoping antenna, made in West Germany, AM, FM, bat...............**$30.00 – 40.00**

Match II, horizontal, 1965, leather & plastic, eight transistors, horizontal slide rule dial with thumbwheel tuning, thumbwheel on/off/volume knob, strap, made in West Germany, AM, bat...........**$15.00 – 25.00**

Pico 61, horizontal, 1960, plastic, six transistors, upper right front window dial with right side thumbwheel tuning, top left thumbwheel on/off/volume knob, large metal perforated grill area, made in West Germany, AM, bat...............**$35.00 – 45.00**

Ticcolo 3461, horizontal/watch radio, 1963, plastic, six transistors, upper front horizontal two-band slide rule dial with right thumbwheel tuning, left thumbwheel on/off/volume knob, right watch face, left perforated grill area, made in West Germany, AM, LW, bat...............**$75.00 – 90.00**

Ticcolo 3561, horizontal/watch radio, 1964, plastic, six transistors, upper front horizontal two-band slide rule dial with right thumbwheel tuning, left thumbwheel on/off/volume knob, right watch face, left perforated grill area, made in West Germany, AM, LW, bat...............**$75.00 – 90.00**

Aimor

103, horizontal/travel clock radio, folding leather case, center dial and controls, left perforated grill area, right alarm clock face, AM, FM, bat.....................**$10.00 – 15.00**

Aircastle

TR1300, horizontal, 5¾x9⅛x2¾", leather, 13 transistors, upper front horizontal two-band slide rule dial, lower metal perforated grill area, two telescoping antennas, rear AC plug, leather handle, made in Japan, AM, FM, AC/bat........**$10.00 – 15.00**

Air Chief

3-V-80, horizontal, 1963, leather, six transistors, top dial and knob, large front grill area with rectangular cut-outs, leather handle, optional dashboard mounting bracket, AM, bat.....................**$10.00 – 15.00**

4-C-50 "Transiclock," horizontal/ clock radio, 1961, seven transistors, lower right front dial knob, upper right lattice grill area, left alarm clock face and on/off/volume knob, swing handle, AM, bat...........**$15.00 – 20.00**

4-C-55, horizontal, 1964, eight transistors, right front thumbwheel dial, large grill area with horizontal slots, handle, AM, bat........**$10.00 – 15.00**

4-C-66, horizontal, 1963, 10 transistors, right front thumbwheel dial, top left thumbwheel on/off/volume knob, large grill area with horizontal slots, handle, AM, bat..**$10.00 – 15.00**

4-C-69, horizontal, 1963, 14 transistors, upper front horizontal three-band slide rule dial, four knobs, large lower grill area, two telescoping antennas, handle, AM, FM, SW, bat...........**$15.00 – 25.00**

4-C-96, vertical, 1965, 10 transistors, upper front horizontal two-band slide rule dial, large lower grill area, telescoping antenna, left strap, AM, FM, bat.......**$5.00 – 10.00**

4-C-97, horizontal, 1965, 10 transistors, right front two-band thumbwheel dial, lower on/off/volume knob, upper AM/FM switch, large left grill area, telescoping antenna, AM, FM, bat...............**$10.00 – 15.00**

4-C-100, horizontal, 1965, 10 transistors, right front window dial with thumbwheel tuning, large perforated grill area, AM, bat..**$10.00 – 15.00**

4-C-101, vertical, 1965, 12 transistors, upper front round thumbwheel dial, lower perforated grill area, AM, bat...............**$5.00 – 10.00**

4-C-102, horizontal, 1965, leather, 12 transistors, right front two-band thumbwheel dial, large perforated grill area, telescoping antenna, handle, AM, FM, bat...................**$10.00 – 15.00**

_____

Airline

BR-1100A, horizontal, 3⅜x6¼x2", plastic, right front round brass dial, lower right thumbwheel on/off/volume knob, center grill area with vertical bars, AM, bat..$275.00 – 350.00

BR-1102A, horizontal, 3⅜x6¼x2", turquoise & white plastic, right front round brass dial, lower right thumbwheel on/off/volume knob, center grill area with vertical bars, AM, bat.................**$275.00 – 350.00**

GEN-1106A, horizontal, 1958, tan leather, right front tuning dial overlaps large grill area with circular cut-outs, leather handle, AM, bat............................**$35.00 – 45.00**

GEN-1112A, horizontal, 1958, tan, right front tuning dial overlaps large grill area with circular cut-outs, handle, AM, bat ....**$35.00 – 45.00**

GEN-1119A, vertical, 1968, plastic, seven transistors, upper right front window dial with right side thumbwheel tuning, left side on/off/volume knob, lower metal perforated grill area, AM, bat.........................**$10.00 – 15.00**

GEN-1120C, horizontal, 1959, eight transistors, upper right front dial knob, large lower grill area with lower left "M/W" logo, handle, AM, bat ....**$20.00 – 30.00**

GEN-1130A, horizontal, 1961, six transistors, diagonally divided front with right see-through panel, right window dial with right side thumbwheel tuning, right side thumbwheel on/off/volume knob, left metal perforated grill area, made in Japan, AM, bat...........**$35.00 – 50.00**

GEN-1131A, horizontal, 1961, six transistors, diagonally divided front with right see-through panel, right window dial with right side thumbwheel tuning, right side thumbwheel on/off/volume knob, left metal perforated grill area, AM, bat.............................$35.00 – 50.00

GEN-1136A, vertical, 4⅜x2⅝x1¼", plastic, six transistors, upper right front dial over horizontal grill bars, left circular on/off/volume window with left side thumbwheel knob, made in Taiwan, AM, bat.........$5.00 – 10.00

GEN-1136B, vertical, 4⅜x2⅝x1¼", plastic, six transistors, upper right front dial over horizontal grill bars, left circular on/off/volume window with left side thumbwheel knob, made in Taiwan, AM, bat ....$5.00 – 10.00

GEN-1156B, vertical, 4½x2½x1¼", plastic, seven transistors, upper right front window dial with right side thumbwheel tuning, upper left on/off/volume window with left side thumbwheel knob, lower metal perforated grill area, AM, bat............................$15.00 – 25.00

GEN-1176A, horizontal, plastic, eight transistors, upper right front window dial with right side thumbwheel tuning, right side thumbwheel on/off/volume knob, large front perforated grill area with decorative trim & center "M/W" logo, AM, bat.....................$25.00 – 35.00

GEN-1202A, horizontal, 1962, six transistors, vertically divided front, right oval window dial with right side thumbwheel tuning, right side thumbwheel on/off/volume knob, left grill area with "M/W" logo, AM, bat ....$25.00 – 35.00

GEN-1202B, horizontal, 1963, six transistors, vertically divided front, right oval window dial with right side thumbwheel tuning, right side thumbwheel on/off/volume knob, left grill area with "M/W" logo, AM, bat ....$25.00 – 35.00

GEN-1207A, horizontal, 1961, eight transistors, upper right front dial knob, large lower grill area with lower right on/off/volume knob and lower left "M/W" logo, handle, AM, bat ....$20.00 – 30.00

GEN-1208A "Eldorado," horizontal, 1962, six transistors, two right front window dials — one BC, one

SW — with right side thumbwheel tuning, lower right on/off/volume window with right side thumbwheel knob, left perforated grill area with upper left logo, telescoping antenna, AM, SW, bat........$30.00 – 45.00

GEN-1212A, horizontal, four transistors, right front round dial knob overlaps large perforated grill area, lower right side thumbwheel on/off/volume knob, lower left front "M/W" logo, AM, bat..............$25.00 – 35.00

GEN-1213A, vertical, 1963, six transistors, upper front thumbwheel dial, right thumbwheel on/off/volume knob, large lower perforated grill area, AM, bat .....$10.00 – 15.00

GEN-1214A, vertical, 1961, plastic, eight transistors, upper left dial knob over perforated front panel, lower right on/off/volume knob, metal swing handle, AM, bat.$25.00 – 35.00

GEN-1215A, vertical/billfold, 1962, folding billfold style, six transistors, inner right window dial with right side thumbwheel tuning, upper left thumbwheel on/off/volume knob, lower perforated grill area with "M/W" logo, AM, bat..$40.00 – 50.00

GEN-1218A, vertical, 1962, 10 transistors, upper left front round dial, lower perforated grill area with logo, AM, bat..............$10.00 – 15.00

GEN-1222A, horizontal, 1963, nine transistors, step-back upper front with horizontal two-band slide rule dial, large lower perforated grill area with right knob/left logo, tele-

scoping antenna, handle, AM, FM, bat..............................$15.00 – 20.00

GEN-1225A, vertical, 1963, six transistors, small upper front circular window dial with right side thumbwheel tuning, lower perforated grill area, AM, bat.............$10.00 – 15.00

GEN-1227A, horizontal, 1963, eight transistors, right front window dial and "M/W" logo over large perforated grill area, AM, bat..$15.00 – 20.00

GEN-1228A, vertical, 1963, eight transistors, upper left front round dial, lower lattice grill with logo, AM, bat.....................$10.00 – 15.00

GEN-1229A, horizontal, 1963, 10 transistors, upper right front round dial over large lattice grill area, lower left front knob, swing handle, AM, bat.....................$10.00 – 15.00

GEN-1231A, horizontal, 1963, nine transistors, upper front horizontal two-band slide rule dial, large lower perforated grill area with logo, telescoping antenna, handle, AM, FM, bat..............................$15.00 – 20.00

GEN-1232A, horizontal, 1964, 10 transistors, upper front horizontal three-band slide rule dial, large lower grill area with logo, telescoping antenna, handle, AM, FM, SW, bat..............................$10.00 – 15.00

GEN-1240A, vertical, 4¼x2⅝x1¼", 1964, plastic, six transistors, upper right front round window dial with right side thumbwheel tuning, upper left front round on/off/volume window with left side thumbwheel knob, lower metal perforated grill area with center "M/W" logo, made in Japan, AM, bat ....$10.00 – 15.00

GEN-1245A, horizontal, 1964, leather, eight transistors, upper right front round dial, lower on/off/volume knob, left grill area with horizontal bars, leather handle, AM, bat ....$5.00 – 10.00

GEN-1246A, horizontal, 1964, 10 transistors, upper front horizontal two-band slide rule dial, large lower perforated grill area with logo, telescoping antenna, handle, AM, FM, bat ....$10.00 – 15.00

GEN-1247A "Deluxe," horizontal, 1964, 10 transistors, upper front horizontal four-band slide rule dial, large lower perforated grill area, telescoping antenna, handle, AM, FM, 2SW, bat ....$15.00 – 25.00

GEN-1247B "Deluxe," horizontal, 1965, 10 transistors, upper front horizontal four-band slide rule dial, large lower perforated grill area, telescoping antenna, handle, AM, LW, 2SW, bat..............$15.00 – 25.00

GEN-1248A, horizontal, 1964, 12 transistors, upper front horizontal two-band slide rule dial, large lower perforated grill area, handle, AM, FM, bat......................$10.00 – 15.00

GEN-1249A, horizontal, 1964, 14 transistors, upper front horizontal three-band slide rule dial, large lower grill area, two telescoping antennas, handle, AM, FM, SW, bat...$10.00 – 15.00

GEN-1249C, horizontal, 1965, 13 transistors, upper front horizontal three-band slide rule dial, large lower grill area, two telescoping antennas, handle, AM, FM, SW, bat.......................$10.00 – 15.00

GEN-1253A, vertical, 4¼x2½x1¼", 1965, plastic, seven transistors, upper right front square window dial with right side thumbwheel tuning, upper left on/off/volume window with left side thumbwheel knob, lower metal perforated grill area with center "M/W" logo, AM, bat ..$10.00 – 15.00

GEN-1254A, horizontal, 1965, seven transistors, upper right front window dial with right side thumbwheel tuning, right side thumbwheel on/off/volume knob, large front perforated grill area with decorative trim and center "M/W" logo, AM, bat.............$25.00 – 35.00

GEN-1255A, horizontal, 1965, eight transistors, right front vertical slide rule dial with right side thumbwheel tuning, right side thumbwheel on/off/volume knob, left grill area with horizontal slots, AM, bat ....$10.00 – 15.00

GEN-1257A, horizontal, 1965, leather, eight transistors, right front vertical slide rule dial and three knobs, left grill area with horizontal bars, leather handle, AM, bat ....$5.00 – 10.00

GEN-1258A, horizontal, 1965, leather, 10 transistors, right front vertical slide rule dial and three knobs, left grill area with horizontal bars, leather handle, AM, bat.......$5.00 – 10.00

GEN-1259A, vertical, 1964, 10 transistors, upper front horizontal two-band slide rule dial with right side thumbwheel tuning, lower perforated grill area with center "M/W" logo, telescoping antenna, AM, FM, bat ....$10.00 – 15.00

GEN-1261A, horizontal, 1965, 17 transistors, upper front horizontal four-band slide rule dial, lower left grill area with logo, telescoping antenna, handle, AM, FM, SW, Marine, bat ....$15.00 – 20.00

GEN-1262A, horizontal, 1965, 15 transistors, upper front horizontal six-band slide rule dial, large lower grill area, telescoping antenna, handle, AM, FM, LW, 3SW, bat ....$20.00 – 25.00

GTI-1234A, horizontal, 1963, nine transistors, right front knobs and vertical four-band slide rule dial, left perforated grill area with logo, telescoping antenna, handle, AM, FM, 2SW, bat ....$15.00 – 20.00

GTM-1108A, horizontal, 1958, tan leather, five transistors, right front round dial knob, lower thumbwheel on/off/volume knob, left perforated grill area, leather handle, AM, bat ....$35.00 – 45.00

GTM-1109A, horizontal, 1958, white & turquoise plastic, seven transistors, right front round dial knob, lower thumbwheel on/off/volume knob, vertical grill bars, AM, bat ....$30.00 – 40.00

GTM-1200A, horizontal, 1960, nine transistors, upper front horizontal two-band slide rule dial, right knob, large lower grill area with "M/W" logo, telescoping antenna, AM, SW, bat ....$15.00 – 20.00

GTM-1201A, vertical, 1960, gray & white, seven transistors, lower front round dial over horizontal grill bars, right side on/off/volume knob, swing handle, AM, bat...........$20.00 – 30.00

GTM-1230A, horizontal, 1963, nine transistors, upper front horizontal two-band slide rule dial, large lower grill area with "M/W" logo, telescoping antenna, handle, AM, SW, bat ....$10.00 – 15.00

GTM-1233A, horizontal, 1963, leather, nine transistors, upper front horizontal three-band slide rule dial, top controls, large lower grill area, telescoping antenna, handle, AM, 2SW, bat ......$15.00 – 20.00

Aiwa

AR-102, horizontal, 1964, eight transistors, upper front horizontal four-band slide rule dial, large lower grill area, telescoping antenna, handle, AM, 3SW, bat..............$10.00 – 15.00

AR-111, horizontal, 1964, 11 transistors, upper front horizontal two-band slide rule dial, upper left knob, large lower four-section grill area with off-center knob, telescoping antenna, handle, AM, FM, bat...$15.00 – 20.00

AR-113, horizontal, 1964, 13 transistors, two upper front horizontal slide rule dials, pushbuttons, top control knobs, lower horizontal grill bars, telescoping antenna, handle, AM, FM, Marine, bat..$10.00 – 15.00

AR-115, horizontal, 1964, 12 transistors, large right front round two-band dial over horizontal grill bars, telescoping antenna, handle, AM, FM, bat.....................$10.00 – 15.00

AR-116, horizontal, 1965, leather, 12 transistors, upper front horizontal two-band slide rule dial, large lower grill area with vertical bars, telescoping antenna, leather handle, AM, FM, bat........$10.00 – 15.00

AR-122, horizontal, 1965, leather, 12 transistors, two upper front horizontal slide rule dials, large lower grill with vertical bars and left circular grill area, telescoping antenna, leather handle, AM, FM, SW, AC/bat...$15.00 – 20.00

AR-123, horizontal, 1965, 10 transistors, upper left front horizontal three-band slide rule dial, right side pushbuttons, large lower perforated grill area, telescoping antenna, handle, AM, FM, SW, bat..$10.00 – 15.00

AR-125, vertical, 1965, 10 transistors, upper front horizontal two-band slide rule dial, large lower grill area with horizontal bars, telescoping antenna, AM, FM, bat......$5.00 – 10.00

AR-666, vertical, plastic, six transistors, upper right front window dial with right side thumbwheel tuning, upper left front on/off/volume window with left side thumbwheel knob, large metal perforated grill area, AM, bat..............$5.00 – 10.00

AR-670, vertical, 1964, plastic, six transistors, upper right front window dial with right side thumbwheel tuning, left side thumbwheel on/off/volume knob, lower metal perforated grill area with center logo, AM, bat............$20.00 – 35.00

AR-751, vertical, 1965, seven transistors, upper front horizontal see-through dial, large lower grill area with horizontal bars, AM, bat ....$20.00 – 25.00

AR-752, vertical, 4½x3x1½", 1966, plastic, seven transistors, upper front horizontal slide rule dial with thumbwheel tuning, lower lattice grill area, AM, bat ....$5.00 – 10.00

AR-804, horizontal, 1964, eight transistors, upper front horizontal three-band slide rule dial, large lower grill area, telescoping antenna, handle, AM, 2SW, bat..............$15.00 – 20.00

AR-852, horizontal, 1964, eight transistors, right front round dial knob, top thumbwheel knob, left lattice grill with circular speaker area, AM, bat.............$20.00 – 30.00

AR-853, horizontal, 1964, plastic, eight transistors, right front round dial knob, top thumbwheel on/off/volume knob, left grill area with horizontal bars, AM, bat............$10.00 – 15.00

AR-854, horizontal, 1964, leather, eight transistors, right front circular two-band dial over vertical grill bars, telescoping antenna, leather handle, AM, SW, bat........$10.00 – 15.00

Akkord
Autotransistor Automatic, horizontal car/portable radio, 1964, metal & plastic, 12 transistors, made for use in or out of the car, top horizontal slide rule dial with top right dial knob, top left on/off/volume knob, four top pushbuttons, large metal lattice grill area, made in West Germany, AM, FM, LW, bat......$50.00 – 75.00

Autotransistor Automatic K, horizontal car/portable radio, 1964, metal & plastic, 12 transistors, made for use in or out of the car, top horizontal slide rule dial with top right dial knob, top left on/off/volume knob, four top pushbuttons, large metal lattice grill area, made in West Germany, AM, FM, SW, bat........$50.00 – 75.00

Jerry, horizontal, 1966, plastic, nine transistors, top horizontal three-band slide rule dial, upper right front dial knob, lower right front on/off/volume knob, large left grill area, made in West Germany, AM, FM, LW, bat................$20.00 – 30.00

Jerry K, horizontal, 1966, plastic, nine transistors, top horizontal three-band slide rule dial, upper right front dial knob, lower right front on/off/volume knob, large left grill area, made in West Germany, AM, FM, SW, bat.........$20.00 – 30.00

Peggie, horizontal, 1957, leather, five transistors, right round dial knob overlaps diagonally divided front, top thumbwheel on/off/volume knob, metal perforated grill area, leather handle, made in West Germany, AM, bat.....$25.00 – 35.00

Pippo a, horizontal, 1958, plastic, six transistors, upper right front window dial, step-back right side with upper thumbwheel tuning knob and lower switch, left side on/off/volume knob, left grill area with vertical bars, rear fold-out stand, made in West Germany, AM, LW, bat ....$30.00 – 40.00

U60-US "Pinguin," horizontal, 1961, leatherette case with rounded corners, upper front horizontal slide rule dial, pushbuttons, lower grill area with vertical bars, two telescoping antennas, handle, AM, FM, SW, bat.....................$30.00 – 40.00

UKW-Autotransistor, horizontal car/portable radio, 1963, metal & plastic, 12 transistors, made for use in or out of the car, top horizontal slide rule dial with top right dial knob, top left on/off/volume knob, three top pushbuttons, large metal lattice grill area, made in West Germany, AM, FM, bat ....$50.00 – 75.00

Aladdin
AL65, vertical, 3½x2¼x1", 1962, plastic, six transistors, small upper right front window dial with right side thumbwheel tuning, lower metal perforated grill area with center Aladdin's lamp logo, AM, bat.....................$100.00 – 125.00

AL80, vertical, 1962, eight transistors, upper right front window dial with right side thumbwheel tuning, top left thumbwheel on/off/volume knob, checkered grill area with center Aladdin's lamp logo, AM, bat.....................$60.00 – 75.00

Alaron
B-666 "Deluxe HiFi," vertical, 1963, six transistors, upper front window dial with right side thumbwheel tuning, top left thumbwheel on/off/volume knob, lower perforated grill area, AM, bat.....................$15.00 – 20.00

B-1066, vertical, 4⅝x3x1½", plastic, 10 transistors, upper front horizontal two-band slide rule dial with right side thumbwheel tuning, right side thumbwheel on/off/volume knob, lower lattice grill area, rear AM/FM switch, folding telescoping antenna, left side vinyl strap, made in Japan, AM, FM, bat.$5.00 – 10.00

DC3280 "Deluxe Eight," horizontal, 1964, nine transistors, upper front horizontal two-band slide rule dial with thumbwheel tuning, lower perforated grill area, telescoping antenna, AM, SW, bat..........$25.00 – 35.00

FAR-113, horizontal, 1964, 12 transistors, upper right front round three-band dial, pushbuttons, large left grill area, left side telescoping antenna, swing handle, AM, FM, SW, bat..$15.00 – 20.00

TR-709, vertical, 1964, seven transistors, upper right and left side thumbwheel knobs, large front perforated grill area with center logo, AM, bat......................$10.00 – 15.00

TRN-1210, horizontal, 1964, 12 transistors, right front window dial, right side knob, off-center grill area with horizontal slots, AM, bat........$5.00 – 10.00

TRN-DX, horizontal, 1963, eight transistors, right front airplane dial, two thumbwheel knobs, large left perforated grill area, AM, bat ...$10.00 – 15.00

UR-701, square, 1964, eight transistors, upper right front horizontal dial, two left thumbwheel knobs and one switch, large perforated grill area, AM, bat .....$15.00 – 20.00

Alco
Boy's Radio, horizontal, plastic, two transistors, right front thumbwheel dial knob, lower right side thumbwheel on/off/volume knob, large grill area with horizontal bars, made in Japan, AM, bat.......$45.00 – 55.00

Allied
24SC075, vertical, 1965, 10 transistors, upper right front window

dial, lower lattice grill area, AM, bat..............................$5.00 – 10.00

24SC080, vertical, 10 transistors, upper right front window dial with thumbwheel tuning, lower lattice grill area, AM, bat.......$5.00 – 10.00

TR-1053, vertical, 10 transistors, upper front horizontal slide rule dial with thumbwheel tuning, large lower grill area with vertical bars, AM, bat..............................$5.00 – 10.00

Alpha

M6M, horizontal, plastic, six transistors, large right front thumbwheel knob inside horseshoe-shaped dial scale, lower right front on/off/volume window with right side thumbwheel knob, large metal perforated grill area with lower left logo, AM, bat..............................$60.00 – 75.00

Q62, vertical, 1962, six transistors, upper right front round dial with thumbwheel tuning, left thumbwheel on/off/volume knob, lower perforated grill area with lower left logo, AM, bat...........$85.00 – 100.00

Ambassador
A-155, horizontal, 1965, 15 transistors, upper front horizontal five-band slide rule dial, large lower grill area, two telescoping

antennas, handle, AM, FM, 3SW, bat.............................$15.00 – 20.00

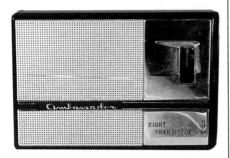

A-880, horizontal, 3⅛x4⅝x1⅜", **plastic, eight transistors, right front** **magnifying window dial with upper** **right side thumbwheel tuning,** **lower right side thumbwheel** **on/off/volume knob, left metal** **perforated grill area, made in** **Japan, AM, bat..........$20.00 – 25.00**

A-884, horizontal, 1965, eight transistors, right front window dial with upper right side thumbwheel tuning, lower right side thumbwheel on/off/volume knob, left perforated grill area with upper left logo, AM, bat ....$20.00 – 25.00

A-1064, horizontal, 1965, 10 transistors, right front window dial with thumbwheel tuning, left oval perforated grill area, strap, AM, bat ....$10.00 – 15.00

AE-10, horizontal, 4⅜x6⅞x2", solid state, upper right front round dial knob, lower on/off/volume knob, left metal perforated grill area with lower left logo, leather handle, made in Hong Kong, AM, AC/bat..........$5.00 – 10.00

FM-10, vertical, 1965, 10 transistors, upper front horizontal two-band

slide rule dial, right side thumbwheel knobs, lower grill area with horizontal slots, telescoping antenna, AM, FM, bat.........$15.00 – 20.00

Vanguard, horizontal, 5⅛x6⅜x2½", leather, right side dial knob, left side on/off/volume knob, front grill area with circular cut-outs, leather handle, made in USA, AM, bat ....$10.00 – 15.00

AMC

6TR-22, vertical, 3¾x2⅜x1⅛", six **transistors, upper right front win-** **dow dial with right side thumb-** **wheel tuning, large lower metal** **perforated grill area, made in** **Japan, AM, bat..........$10.00 – 15.00**

821 (TRB-821), horizontal, 2¾x4½x1⅜", plastic, eight transistors, upper front horizontal slide rule dial with right side thumbwheel tuning, right side thumbwheel on/off/volume knob, large metal perforated grill area, right side strap, made in Japan, AM, bat.............$20.00 – 25.00

American Supply Co.

61N25-07, vertical, 1961, moonstone plastic, six transistors, diagonally divided front, upper metal panel with right thumbwheel dial, left side thumbwheel on/off/volume knob, checkered grill area, AM, bat.................$20.00 – 25.00

61N29-07, vertical, 1961, black plastic, six transistors, diagonally divided front, upper metal panel with right thumbwheel dial, left side thumbwheel on/off/volume knob, checkered grill area, AM, bat.................$20.00 – 25.00

Americana

FC60, vertical, 4¼x2½x1¼", 1961, six transistors, upper right front window dial with right side thumbwheel tuning, top left thumbwheel on/off/volume knob, lower metal perforated grill area with vertical lines, AM, bat.............$25.00 – 30.00

FM-10, horizontal, 1963, 10 transistors, upper front horizontal two-band slide rule dial, lower perforated grill area with left H/L switch and right AM/FM switch, telescoping antenna, AM, FM, bat.................$20.00 – 25.00

FP62, vertical, 1962, eight transistors, upper front window dial with right side thumbwheel tuning, top left thumbwheel on/off/volume knob, lower perforated grill area, AM, bat ....$20.00 – 25.00

FP64, vertical, 1962, six transistors, upper right front window dial with thumbwheel tuning, lower perforat-

ed grill area, made in Japan, AM, bat ....$40.00 – 50.00

FP80, vertical, 1962, plastic, eight transistors, upper right front window dial with right side thumbwheel tuning, top left thumbwheel on/off/volume knob, lower metal perforated grill area, AM, bat.......$20.00 – 25.00

FP-861, vertical, 1962, eight transistors, upper checkered panel with right thumbwheel window dial, lower wrap-around metal perforated grill area with lower left logo, AM, bat ....$50.00 – 75.00

ST-6X "Wayfarer," vertical, 1962, six transistors, upper right front window dial with thumbwheel tuning, upper left thumbwheel on/off/volume knob, lower wrap-around perforated grill area with lower right logo, AM, bat ....$50.00 – 60.00

ST-6Z, vertical, 1962, six transistors, upper right front thumbwheel dial knob, lower perforated grill area with lower left logo, AM, bat ....$25.00 – 35.00

TP-7, horizontal, 1962, leather, seven transistors, upper right front dial knob, left grill with diamond-shaped cut-outs, leather handle, AM, bat ....$10.00 – 15.00

Amertone

6YR-19, vertical, 2⅞x2x⅞", plastic, six transistors, upper right front circular window dial with top right corner thumbwheel tuning, top left thumbwheel on/off/volume knob, rhinestone decoration on dial panel, lower metal perforated grill area, made in Japan, AM, bat............$25.00 – 35.00

Amico

Boy's Radio, horizontal/desk set, plastic, two transistors, two top right thumbwheel knobs, top left round checkered grill area, pen holder, made in Japan, AM, bat..........$35.00 – 45.00

Angel

ATR-23 "Boy's Radio," vertical, 4⅜x2⅝x1¼", plastic, two transistors, front see-through panel with window dial, top thumbwheel tuning, right side thumbwheel on/off/volume knob, lower metal perforated & textured grill area, made in Japan, AM, bat ....$50.00 – 60.00

Boy's Radio, vertical, 4¼x2⅝x1¼", plastic, two transistors, upper left front round dial knob, upper right front Angel logo, right thumbwheel on/off/volume knob, lower metal perforated grill area, made in Japan, AM, bat..........$50.00 – 60.00

Boy's Radio, vertical, 3½x2⅜x1⅛", plastic, two transistors, upper front window dial with top right

thumbwheel tuning, top left thumbwheel on/off/volume knob, lower metal perforated grill area with lower left Angel logo, made in Japan, AM, bat ....$45.00 – 55.00

Archer

2 transistor (no #), horizontal, 2⅝x4x1½", plastic, two transistors, large right front thumbwheel dial knob, large grill area with horizontal bars, AM, bat ....$45.00 – 55.00

AristoTone

HT-1244, vertical, 4¼x2⅝x1¼", plastic, 12 transistors, upper right front window dial with right side thumbwheel tuning, top left thumbwheel on/off/volume knob, lower metal perforated grill area, made in Japan, AM, bat ....$20.00 – 30.00

MT-601, vertical, plastic, six transistors, upper right front window dial with thumbwheel tuning, large lower metal perforated grill area, AM, bat ....$15.00 – 20.00

Arkay

TR-5, horizontal/kit radio, 3⅛x5½x1⅜", 1957, sold as a kit, plastic, five transistors, right front round dial, top thumbwheel on/off/volume knob, left checkered grill area, AM, bat ....$15.00 – 25.00

TR-6, horizontal/kit radio, 1957, sold as a kit, leatherette, six transistors, upper right and left front knobs, center grill area with cut-outs, handle, AM, bat..........$15.00 – 20.00

Artemis

ST-7EL, horizontal, 1961, seven

transistors, off-center two-band vertical dial, right side thumbwheel knobs, left front perforated grill area with lower left logo, AM, LW, bat ....$25.00 – 35.00

ST-8B, horizontal, 4⅝x5¾x2", **eight transistors, right front dial** **panel with decorative design,** **upper right quarter-round dial** **with lower tuning knob, lower right** **thumbwheel on/off/volume knob** **and BC/SW switch, left lattice grill** **area, handle, made in Japan, AM,** **SW, bat ....$50.00 – 65.00**

Artic

TR-100, horizontal, plastic, two transistors, large right front thumbwheel dial knob, lower right side thumbwheel on/off/volume knob, left grill area with horizontal bars, made in Japan, AM, bat ......$45.00 – 55.00

Arvin

60R19, horizontal, 1959, slate gray, four transistors, step-back top, large right front round dial with right thumbwheel on/off/volume knob, left grill area, swing handle, "A" logo, AM, bat.............$15.00 – 25.00

60R23, horizontal, 5x7¼x2¼", 1960, flame plastic, six transistors,

step-back top, large right front round dial over vertical grill bars, right thumbwheel on/off/volume knob, swing handle, "A" logo, AM, bat ....$15.00 – 25.00

60R25-11, compact style, 1½x4⅛x4⅛", plastic, looks like ladies' compact, front window dial with thumbwheel tuning, rear thumbwheel on/off/volume knob, top metal perforated grill area with floral design and center logo, vinyl wrist strap, made in Hong Kong, AM, bat ....$25.00 – 35.00

60R25-17, compact style, 1½x4⅛x 4⅛", plastic, looks like ladies' compact, front window dial with thumbwheel tuning, rear thumbwheel on/off/volume knob, top metal perforated grill area with floral design and center logo, vinyl wrist strap, made in Hong Kong, AM, bat..............$25.00 – 35.00

60R25-19, compact style, 1½x4⅛x4⅛", plastic, looks like ladies' compact, front window dial with thumbwheel tuning, rear thumbwheel on/off/volume knob, top metal perforated grill area with floral design and center logo, vinyl wrist strap, made in Hong Kong, AM, bat..............$25.00 – 35.00

60R28, horizontal, 5x7¼x2¼", 1960, sandstone plastic, six transistors, step-back top, large right front round dial over vertical grill bars, right thumbwheel on/off/volume knob, swing handle, "A" logo, AM, bat ....$15.00 – 25.00

60R29, horizontal, 5x7¼x2¼", 1960, gray plastic, six transistors, step-back top, large right front round dial over vertical grill bars, right thumbwheel on/off/volume knob, swing handle, "A" logo, AM, bat........$15.00 – 25.00

60R33, horizontal, 5x7¼x2⅝", 1959, flame, seven transistors, wedge-shaped case, large right front round dial, right thumbwheel on/off/volume knob, plastic perforated grill area, swing handle, "A" logo, AM, bat.............$20.00 – 30.00

60R35, horizontal, 5x7¼x2⅝", 1959, slate blue, seven transistors, wedge-shaped case, large right front round dial, right thumbwheel on/off/volume knob, plastic perforated grill area, swing handle, "A" logo, AM, bat.............$20.00 – 30.00

60R38, horizontal, 5x7¼x2⅝", 1959, taupe, seven transistors, wedge-shaped case, large right front round dial, right thumbwheel on/off/volume knob, plastic perforated grill area, swing handle, "A" logo, AM, bat.............$20.00 – 30.00

60R47, horizontal, 1960, white, seven transistors, upper front off-center thumbwheel dial, right thumbwheel on/off/volume knob, large grill area with horizontal bars and lower left "A" logo, metal handle, AM, bat.............$15.00 – 25.00

60R49, horizontal, 1960, black, seven transistors, upper front off-center thumbwheel dial, right thumbwheel on/off/volume knob, large grill area with horizontal bars and lower left "A" logo, metal handle, AM, bat.............$15.00 – 25.00

60R58, 1960, tan cowhide, seven transistors, upper right front round dial, left on/off/volume knob, lower checkered grill area, leather handle, AM, bat.........$10.00 – 20.00

60R69, vertical, 1960, black, six transistors, upper right front dial with right side thumbwheel tuning, left side thumbwheel on/off/volume knob, lower perforated grill area, AM, bat.............$10.00 – 15.00

61R13, vertical, 4x2¾x1¼", 1961, red plastic, six transistors, diagonally divided front, upper metal panel with right round dial knob, left side thumbwheel on/off/volume knob, lower checkered grill area, AM, bat.....................$20.00 – 30.00

61R16, vertical, 4x2¾x1¼", 1961, mint green plastic, six transistors, diagonally divided front, upper metal panel with right round dial knob, left side thumbwheel on/off/volume knob, lower checkered grill area, AM, bat.............$20.00 – 30.00

61R19, vertical, 4x2¾x1¼", 1961, black pearl plastic, six transistors, diagonally divided front, upper metal panel with right round dial knob, left side thumbwheel on/off/volume knob, lower checkered grill area, AM, bat..............$20.00 – 30.00

61R23, vertical, 4x2¾x1¼", 1961, sunset plastic, six transistors, diagonally divided front, upper metal panel with right round dial knob, left side thumbwheel on/off/volume knob, lower checkered grill area, AM, bat.............$20.00 – 30.00

61R26, vertical, 4x2¾x1¼", 1961, green plastic, six transistors, diagonally divided front, upper metal panel with right round dial knob, left side thumbwheel on/off/volume knob, lower checkered grill area, AM, bat.............$20.00 – 30.00

61R29, vertical, 4x2¾x1¼", 1961, black plastic, six transistors, diagonally divided front, upper metal panel with right round dial knob, left side thumbwheel on/off/volume knob, lower checkered grill area, AM, bat.............$20.00 – 30.00

61R35, vertical, 4⅛x2½x1⅜", 1961, ice blue plastic, seven transistors, upper right front window dial with right side thumbwheel tuning, left side thumbwheel on/off/volume knob, lower perforated grill area, made in USA, AM, bat.............$20.00 – 30.00

61R39, vertical, 4⅛x2½x1⅜", 1961, jet black plastic, seven transistors, upper right front window dial with right side thumbwheel tuning, left side

thumbwheel on/off/volume knob, lower perforated grill area, made in USA, AM, bat..............$20.00 – 30.00

61R48, vertical, 1961, leather and metal, seven transistors, upper right front dial with thumbwheel tuning, lower checkered grill area, leather buckle handle, AM, bat............................$15.00 – 20.00

61R58, horizontal, 6x8x3½", 1961, chestnut leather, eight transistors, upper front horizontal slide rule dial, lower metal perforated grill area, leather handle, AM, bat...................$10.00 – 20.00

61R61, vertical, 1963, six transistors, upper right front oversized round dial, lower textured grill area, crown logo, AM, bat..$15.00 – 20.00

61R64, vertical, 1963, six transistors, upper right front oversized round dial, lower textured grill area, crown logo, AM, bat..$15.00 – 20.00

61R65, vertical, 1963, six transistors, upper right front oversized round dial, lower textured grill area, crown logo, AM, bat..$15.00 – 20.00

61R69, vertical, 1963, six transistors, upper right front oversized round dial, lower textured grill area, crown logo, AM, bat..**$15.00 – 20.00**

61R79, vertical, 1963, six transistors, upper right front oversized round dial, lower textured grill area, crown logo, AM, bat..**$15.00 – 20.00**

61R89 "International II," horizontal, 9x11⅞x5¼", 1961, seven transistors, fold-up front with inner map, inner horizontal three-band slide rule dial, lower checkered grill area, telescoping antenna, handle, AM, SW, LW, bat........**$30.00 – 40.00**

61R95, vertical, 1963, six transistors, upper right front oversized round dial, lower textured grill area, crown logo, AM, bat..**$15.00 – 20.00**

61R99, vertical, 1963, six transistors, upper right front oversized round dial, lower textured grill area, crown logo, AM, bat..**$15.00 – 20.00**

62R09, vertical, 1962, five transistors, upper right front dial with right side thumbwheel tuning, left side thumbwheel on/off/volume knob, vertical grill bars, AM, bat.......**$10.00 – 15.00**

62R13, vertical, 1962, sunset plastic, six transistors, upper right front dial with right side thumbwheel tuning, left side thumbwheel on/off/volume knob, textured grill area with crown logo, AM, bat..**$10.00 – 15.00**

62R16, vertical, 1962, green plastic, six transistors, upper right front dial with right side thumbwheel tuning,

left side thumbwheel on/off/volume knob, textured grill area with crown logo, AM, bat..**$10.00 – 15.00**

62R19, vertical, 1962, black plastic, six transistors, upper right front dial with right side thumbwheel tuning, left side thumbwheel on/off/volume knob, textured grill area with crown logo, AM, bat..**$10.00 – 15.00**

62R23, vertical, 1962, sunset plastic, six transistors, upper right front dial with right side thumbwheel tuning, left side thumbwheel on/off/volume knob, textured grill area with crown logo, AM, bat...$10.00 – 15.00

62R26, vertical, 1962, green plastic, six transistors, upper right front dial with right side thumbwheel tuning, left side thumbwheel on/off/volume knob, textured grill area with crown logo, AM, bat..**$10.00 – 15.00**

62R29, vertical, 1962, black plastic, six transistors, upper right front dial with right side thumbwheel tuning, left side thumbwheel on/off/volume knob, textured grill area with crown logo, AM, bat..**$10.00 – 15.00**

62R35, vertical, 1962, blue, seven transistors, upper right front window dial with right side thumbwheel tuning, left side thumbwheel on/off/volume knob, perforated grill area, crown logo, AM, bat....**$10.00 – 15.00**

62R39, vertical, 1962, charcoal, seven transistors, upper right front window dial with right side thumbwheel tuning, left side thumbwheel on/off/volume knob, perforated grill area, crown logo, AM, bat....**$10.00 – 15.00**

62R48, vertical, 6¼x3½x2", 1962, chestnut leather with metal trim, eight transistors, upper right front round dial with thumbwheel tuning, lower metal perforated grill area, leather buckle handle, AM, bat...............**$10.00 – 20.00**

62R49, vertical, 6¼x3½x2", 1962, black leather with metal trim, eight

transistors, upper right front round dial with thumbwheel tuning, lower metal perforated grill area, leather buckle handle, AM, bat...........................$10.00 – 20.00

62R59, horizontal, 1962, leather, eight transistors, upper front horizontal slide rule dial, lower perforated grill area, leather handle, AM, bat.....................**$10.00 – 15.00**

62R65, vertical, 1962, six transistors, upper right front oversized round dial, lower textured grill area, crown logo, AM, bat.......................**$15.00 – 20.00**

62R69, vertical, 1962, six transistors, upper right front oversized round dial, lower textured grill area, crown logo, AM, bat..**$15.00 – 20.00**

62R98, horizontal, 1962, 12 transistors, two upper front round dials — one AM, one FM — lower perforated grill area with right thumbwheel knobs, upper switch, telescoping antenna, handle, AM, FM, bat.....**$15.00 – 20.00**

63R38, vertical, 1963, leather, seven transistors, upper front horizontal slide rule dial with right side thumbwheel tuning, left side thumbwheel on/off/volume knob, lower perforated grill area, crown logo, AM, bat.............**$10.00 – 15.00**

63R58, horizontal, 6½x8½x3¾", 1963, brown leather, nine transistors, upper front horizontal slide rule dial, pushbutton dial light, large lower perforated grill area, leather handle, AM, bat.................**$10.00 – 15.00**

63R88, horizontal, 1963, nine transistors, upper front horizontal three-band slide rule dial, large lower perforated grill area, telescoping antenna, handle, AM, FM, SW, bat......................$15.00 – 20.00

63R98, horizontal, 1963, nine transistors, upper front horizontal four-band slide rule dial, large lower perforated grill area, telescoping antenna, handle, AM, FM, 2SW, bat......................$15.00 – 20.00

64R03, vertical, 1964, six transistors, upper right front window dial with right side thumbwheel tuning, top left thumbwheel on/off/volume knob, large perforated grill area w/vertical lines, AM, bat ....$10.00 – 20.00

64R29, horizontal, 1964, white front/charcoal back, eight transistors, upper right front window dial with right side thumbwheel tuning, lower right front on/off/volume window with right side thumbwheel knob, large left perforated grill area, AM, bat ....$10.00 – 20.00

64R38, vertical, 4¼x2¾x1½", 1964, walnut leather, eight transistors, upper front horizontal slide rule dial with thumbwheel tuning, left side thumbwheel on/off/volume knob, large lower metal perforated grill area, detachable braided leather strap, AM, bat ....$10.00 – 20.00

64R78, horizontal, 1964, 10 transistors, two upper front round dials, AM/FM switch, left thumbwheel on/off/volume knob,

lower perforated grill area, telescoping antenna, handle, AM, FM, bat.....................$15.00 – 20.00

65R03, vertical, 1965, seven transistors, upper right front window dial with right side thumbwheel tuning, large lower perforated grill area, crown logo, AM, bat..$10.00 – 15.00

65R03-1, vertical, 1965, seven transistors, upper right front window dial with right side thumbwheel tuning, large lower perforated grill area, crown logo, AM, bat...$10.00 – 15.00

65R29, vertical, 1965, eight transistors, upper right front window dial with thumbwheel tuning, large lower perforated grill area, crown logo, AM, bat ....$5.00 – 10.00

65R58, horizontal, 1965, brown leather, ten transistors, upper front horizontal slide rule dial, large lower grill area, leather handle, AM, bat ....$10.00 – 15.00

65R69, vertical, 1965, nine transistors, upper front horizontal two-band slide rule dial, lower grill area with horizontal bars, telescoping antenna, AM, FM, bat....$10.00 – 15.00

65R79, horizontal, 1965, nine transistors, right front vertical two-band slide rule dial, large left grill area, telescoping antenna, handle, AM, FM, bat.....................$10.00 – 15.00

65R98, horizontal, 6½x9x3", 1965, 12 transistors, two upper front round dials, large lower grill area with two right thumbwheel knobs, telescoping antenna, handle, AM, FM, bat......................**$10.00 – 15.00**

66R29, vertical, 4⅜x2¾x1½", black plastic, eight transistors, upper right front window dial with right side thumbwheel tuning, left side thumbwheel on/off/volume knob, large metal perforated grill area, made in Hong Kong, AM, bat..**$10.00 – 15.00**

66R39, vertical, 1966, 10 transistors, upper right front window dial, left side thumbwheel knob, large lower perforated grill area, crown logo, AM, bat......................**$10.00 – 15.00**

66R58, horizontal, 6x7¾x3", 1966, leather, eight transistors, upper front horizontal slide rule dial, large lower plastic grill area, leather handle, AM, bat..........$5.00 – 10.00

66R69, horizontal, 1966, 10 transistors, upper right front horizontal two-band slide rule dial, lower switches and tuning knob, vertical grill bars, telescoping antenna, handle, AM, FM, bat ....**$10.00 – 15.00**

66R78, horizontal, 1966, 10 transistors, two upper front dials, thumbwheel on/off/volume knob, three

switches, perforated grill area, telescoping antenna, handle, crown logo, AM, FM, bat .....**$15.00 – 20.00**

67R09, vertical, 4⅛x2⅝x1⅜", 1967, six transistors, diagonally divided front, upper right front thumbwheel dial, left side thumbwheel on/off/volume knob, lower checkered grill area, made in Hong Kong, AM, bat ....$20.00 – 25.00

67R19, vertical, 1967, six transistors, upper right front dial with right side thumbwheel tuning, left side thumbwheel on/off/volume knob, textured grill area with crown logo, AM, bat......................**$10.00 – 15.00**

67R29, vertical, 1967, eight transistors, upper right front window dial with right side thumbwheel tuning, left side thumbwheel on/off/volume knob, large metal perforated grill area, crown logo, AM, bat.....**$10.00 – 15.00**

67R32, vertical, 1967, 10 transistors, upper right front window dial with right side thumbwheel tuning, left side thumbwheel on/off/volume knob, large metal perforated grill area, crown logo, AM, bat.....**$10.00 – 15.00**

68R05, vertical, 1968, six transistors, upper right front window dial with right side thumbwheel tuning, left side thumbwheel on/off/volume knob, lower textured grill area, crown logo, AM, bat..**$10.00 – 15.00**

68R38, vertical, 1968, 10 transistors, upper right front window dial, left side thumbwheel knob, large lower perforated grill area, crown logo, AM, bat.................**$10.00 – 15.00**

77R19, vertical, 4½x2¾x1½", 1966, plastic, nine transistors, upper front horizontal two-band slide rule dial, lower perforated grill area, telescoping antenna, AM, FM, bat.................**$10.00 – 15.00**

77R29, horizontal, 1966, nine transistors, right front vertical two-band slide rule dial, two knobs, large left perforated grill area, telescoping antenna, handle, crown logo, AM, FM, bat.................**$10.00 – 15.00**

86R29, vertical, 4⅝x2⅞x1⅝", 10 transistors, black plastic, upper front horizontal three-band slide rule dial with right side thumbwheel tuning, right side thumbwheel on/off/volume knob, large lower metal perforated grill area with lower right logo, telescoping antenna, rear SW/AM/FM switch, made in Japan, AM, FM, SW, bat........**$15.00 – 20.00**

2598, horizontal, 1960, white and charcoal, six transistors, center front round dial over horizontal

grill bars, lower left knob, AM, bat.............................**$15.00 – 20.00**

3588, horizontal, 1959, ivory and gray, six transistors, lower left front horizontal slide rule dial, three lower right front knobs, large upper grill area with center logo, feet, AM, bat......................**$15.00 – 20.00**

7595, horizontal, 5x7⅜x2⅝", 1959, two-tone case, four transistors, large right front dial with thumbwheel knob, left lattice grill area, swing handle, AM, bat........**$25.00 – 35.00**

8576, vertical, 6¼x3x1½", 1958, available in ebony or turquoise, five transistors, upper right front round brass dial knob, lower perforated random patterned grill area, rear combination belt clip/stand, AM, bat..........................**$175.00 – 200.00**

8584, horizontal, 8¾x11⅛x2½", 1959, available in red or blue, five transistors, upper right front thumbwheel dial, upper left thumbwheel on/off/volume knob, lower grill area with horizontal bars, rotatable antenna in handle, AM, bat..**$35.00 – 45.00**

9562, horizontal, 8⅝x11⅜x3⅞", 1957, available in British tan or alligator, seven transistors, top raised horizontal slide rule dial adjusts for visibility from front or back, two top knobs, large front perforated grill area with brass trim, fold-down handle, made in USA, AM, bat.........**$45.00 – 55.00**

9574, horizontal, 8⅜x10¾x3½", 1958, available in white or tan molded case, six transistors, right and left side control knobs, large front lattice grill area with lower right "starburst" emblem, handle, AM, bat......................$40.00 – 50.00

9574-P, horizontal, 8⅜x10¾x3½", 1956, available in white or tan molded case, six transistors, right and left side control knobs, large front lattice grill area with lower right "starburst" emblem, handle, AM, bat......................$40.00 – 50.00

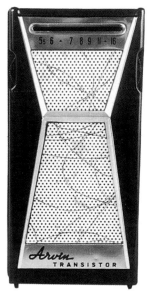

9577, vertical, 6⅜x3x1½", 1957, available in ebony, pink, or white plastic, six transistors, upper front horizontal slide rule dial with right side thumbwheel tuning, left side thumbwheel on/off/volume knob, lower "hourglass" shaped random patterned grill, rear combination belt clip/stand, AM, bat .....$125.00 – 150.00

9594, horizontal, 1960, six transistors, upper front thumbwheel dial,

right front thumbwheel on/off/volume knob, left and lower grill area with horizontal bars and "starburst" logo, AM, bat..............$30.00 – 40.00

9595, horizontal, 5x7⅜x2¾", available in white, gray, or charcoal wedge-shaped plastic case, seven transistors, large right front round dial over random patterned grill area, right thumbwheel knob, swing handle, AM, bat........$35.00 – 45.00

9598, horizontal, 1960, seven transistors, upper front horizontal three-band slide rule dial, large lower checkered grill area, telescoping antenna, handle, AM, SW, LW, bat......................$15.00 – 25.00

Astrotone
99-3513L, vertical, 1965, nine transistors, upper right front window dial with thumbwheel tuning, large lower grill area with horizontal bars, AM, bat..............$5.00 – 10.00

Atkins
61N39-11, vertical, 1964, available in blue or black, seven transistors, upper right front window dial with thumbwheel tuning, left side thumbwheel on/off/volume knob, lower perforated grill area, AM, bat............................$10.00 – 15.00

61N59-11, horizontal, 1964, black leather, eight transistors, upper front horizontal slide rule dial, large lower grill area, leather handle, AM, bat..................$5.00 – 10.00

Aud-ion

Boy's Radio, vertical, 4¼x2⅝x1⅜", plastic, two transistors, upper front round dial, upper right front thumbwheel on/off/volume knob, lower wedge-shaped metal perforated grill with V-shaped lines, made in Japan, AM bat...........$50.00 – 60.00

Boy's Radio, vertical, 4x2½x1", plastic, two transistors, upper right front window dial with right side thumbwheel tuning, lower round metal perforated grill area, made in Japan, AM, bat...........$45.00 – 55.00

Audition

1069, vertical, plastic, six transistors, upper front see-through panel with V-shaped dial window, top thumbwheel tuning, upper right front thumbwheel on/off/volume knob,

lower metal grill area with vertical slots, AM, bat.........$125.00 – 150.00

1410, vertical, 4¼x2¾x1¼", plastic, 10 transistors, upper front "cat's eye" dial inside oval metal perforated grill area, right side thumbwheel tuning knob, left side thumbwheel on/off/volume knob, made in Okinawa, AM, bat............$20.00 – 30.00

Boy's Radio, vertical, plastic, two transistors, upper right front window dial with right side thumbwheel tuning, upper left front on/off/volume window, lower metal perforated grill area, made in Japan, AM, bat.........$50.00 – 60.00

Aud-I-Tone

Boy's Radio, vertical, 4x2⅜x1¼", plastic, two transistors, upper right front wedge shaped window dial with thumbwheel tuning, thumbwheel on/off/volume knob, metal perforated grill area, made in Japan, AM, bat...........$50.00 – 60.00

Automatic

APT-6227 "Tom Thumb," horizontal car/portable radio, 2½x8x6¾", plastic, front horizontal slide rule dial, two knobs, pushbuttons, top and bottom metal perforated grill areas, made for use in or out of the car, swing handle, made in Japan, AM..............................$50.00 – 75.00

P-990, horizontal, 6½x9¼x3", 1962, leather, two top control knobs, large front grill area with rectangular cut-outs, leather handle, made in USA, bat................$15.00 – 25.00

PTR-15B, horizontal, 1958, leather, upper right front dial knob, upper left front on/off/ volume knob, large grill area with rectangular cut-outs, handle, AM, bat............$15.00 – 25.00

TT 600 "Tom Thumb," horizontal/hybrid, 3¾x5⅞x1⅞", 1955, two-tone plastic, right front round dial knob, top right thumbwheel on/off/volume knob, left checkered grill area, fold-down handle, AM, bat................$150.00 – 175.00

Avis
AS-615 "Hi-Fi," vertical, plastic with metal front panel, six transistors, upper right front window dial with right side thumbwheel tuning, left side thumbwheel on/off/volume knob, lower grill area with vertical slots, AM, bat.............$35.00 – 45.00

Barlow

6T-180, vertical, 4¼x2¾x1¼", plastic, six transistors, upper see-through dial with top thumbwheel tuning knob, right side thumbwheel on/off/volume knob, lower metal perforated grill area, AM, bat...$100.00 – 125.00

Baylor
6YR-15A, vertical, 1962, plastic, six transistors, upper right front thumbwheel dial, upper left front thumbwheel on/off/volume knob, lower round perforated grill area, AM, bat...................$85.00 – 100.00

H501 "Hi-Fi," horizontal, 5⅜x9¾x2", plastic, eight transistors, upper front horizontal two-band slide rule dial, three upper right front thumbwheel

knobs, large metal perforated grill area, right side band switch, telescoping antenna, two speakers, AM, SW, bat ....$35.00 – 50.00

Bell

2 transistor (no #), vertical, 3¾x2¼x1", plastic, two transistors, upper right front window dial with right side thumbwheel tuning, thumbwheel on/off/volume knob, round checkered grill area, lower left front logo, made in Japan, AM, bat ....$40.00 – 50.00

Bell Kamra

KTC-62, horizontal/camera radio, plastic, six transistors, right front window dial with right side thumbwheel tuning, right side thumbwheel on/off/volume knob, center round metal perforated grill area, left front camera, made in Japan, AM, bat ....$75.00 – 100.00

Bendix

420 "Navigator," horizontal, 5⅛x7⅞x2⅜", nine transistors, upper front horizontal three-band slide rule dial, upper right front tuning knob, lower metal perforated grill area, lower right front band switch, international code printed on top of handle, made in Japan, AM, Beacon, Marine ....$65.00 – 80.00

Benida

6TR-270, vertical, plastic, six transistors, upper left front thumbwheel dial knob, right front on/off/volume window with right side thumbwheel knob, metal textured and perforated grill area, AM, bat ....$85.00 – 100.00

PR-1161, vertical, 4x2½x1⅛", plastic, six transistors, upper left front window dial with right side thumbwheel tuning, right side thumbwheel on/off/volume knob, metal perforated grill area with vertical lines and lower right logo, made in Japan, AM, bat...........$25.00 – 35.00

Blaupunkt

22503 "Lido," horizontal, 1963, nine transistors, upper front horizontal three-band slide rule dial, upper right and left thumbwheel knobs, lower grill area with horizontal bars, telescoping antenna, handle, AM, FM, SW, bat ....$35.00 – 45.00

Derby DeLuxe, horizontal car/portable radio, 7⅝x10¾x2⅞", made for use in or out of the car, top controls, large front grill area with vertical bars, handle, made in Germany.................. $45.00 – 60.00

Bon

Boy's Radio "Hi-Fi Tone," vertical, 4⅛x2½x1¼", plastic, two transistors, upper right front window dial with right side thumbwheel tuning, left side thumbwheel on/off/volume knob, lower front round metal perforated grill area, made in Japan, AM, bat ....$45.00 – 55.00

Bradford

AR-121, vertical, 1965, 10 transistors, step-back top with thumbwheel controls, horizontal two-band slide rule dial, lower grill area with vertical bars, telescoping antenna, AM, FM, bat...............$10.00 – 15.00

AR-857, horizontal, 1964, eight transistors, step-back top with thumbwheel controls, large right front round dial, left grill area, handle, AM, bat...............$10.00 – 15.00

P100, horizontal, 1965, leather, 10 transistors, right front window dial, left grill area with horizontal bars, leather handle, AM, bat...............$5.00 – 10.00

TR-1626, vertical, 4x2½x1¼", 1963, plastic, six transistors, upper right front window dial with right side thumbwheel tuning, left side thumbwheel on/off/volume knob, metal perforated grill area with raised vertical bar, AM, bat.......$55.00 – 75.00

Braun

T3, horizontal, 1958, plastic, six transistors, right front round dial, left side thumbwheel on/off/volume knob, left grill area with circular cut-outs, made in West Germany, AM, LW, bat...............$35.00 – 50.00

T4, horizontal, 1959, plastic, seven transistors, right front window dial with right side thumbwheel tuning, left side thumbwheel on/off/volume knob, left round grill area with circular cut-outs, made in West Germany, AM, LW, SW, bat.....................$35.00 – 50.00

T-23, horizontal, plastic, upper front horizontal multi-band slide rule dial, lower grill area with horizontal bars, two top thumbwheel knobs, five top pushbuttons, leather handle, bat....$35.00 – 45.00

T31, horizontal, 1960, plastic, seven transistors, right front round dial, left side thumbwheel on/off/volume knob, left grill area with circular cut-outs, made in West Germany, AM, bat.....$35.00 – 45.00

T41, horizontal, 1962, plastic, seven transistors, right front almost semi-circular dial with right side thumbwheel tuning, left side thumbwheel on/off/volume knob, left round grill area with circular cut-outs, made in West Germany, AM, SW, bat ....$50.00 – 75.00

T52, horizontal car/portable radio, 1961, plastic, nine transistors, made for use in or out of the car, top three-band horizontal slide rule dial, three top knobs, three top pushbuttons for bands, front lattice grill area, telescoping antenna, handle, made in West Germany, AM, FM, LW, bat ....$75.00 – 100.00

T520, horizontal car/portable radio, 1962, plastic, nine transistors, made for use in or out of the car, top three-band horizontal slide rule dial, three top knobs, three top pushbuttons for bands, front lattice grill area, telescoping antenna, handle, made in West Germany, AM, FM, LW, bat ....$75.00 – 100.00

T580, horizontal car/portable radio, 1963, plastic, 11 transistors, made for use in or out of the car, top three-band horizontal slide rule dial, three top knobs, four top pushbuttons for bands, front lattice grill area, telescoping antenna, handle, made in West Germany, AM, FM, LW, bat ....$75.00 – 100.00

Bresco

**6YR-15A, vertical, $3\frac{1}{2}$x$2\frac{1}{4}$x1",
plastic, six transistors, upper right front thumbwheel dial, upper left front thumbwheel on/off/volume knob, lower round perforated grill area, made in Japan, AM, bat ..$85.00 – 100.00**

Browni

10NR-103 "Hi-Fi," horizontal, $4\frac{1}{2}$x$8\frac{5}{8}$x$2\frac{1}{4}$", plastic, 10 transistors, large right front thumbwheel dial, top left thumbwheel on/off/volume knob, large metal grill area with vertical slots, pull-up handle, made in Japan, AM, bat............$25.00 – 35.00

702, vertical, $4\frac{1}{2}$x$2\frac{5}{8}$x$1\frac{1}{4}$", plastic, solid state, upper right front round thumbwheel dial, upper left front round thumbwheel on/off/volume knob, lower grill area with horizontal bars, made in Hong Kong, AM, bat ....$5.00 – 10.00

G-803, horizontal, 3x$4\frac{1}{2}$x$1\frac{1}{4}$", plastic, eight transistors, right front window dial with right side thumbwheel tuning, right side thumb-wheel on/off/volume knob, large front metal grill area with upper perforations and lower horizontal slots, AM, bat.............$20.00 – 30.00

YTR-603, vertical, 4x2½x1⅛", plastic, six transistors, upper front window dial with right side thumbwheel tuning, right side thumbwheel on/off/volume knob, lower circular metal perforated grill area, made in Japan, AM, bat.............$25.00 – 35.00

Buick

981970 "Trans-Portable," horizontal/auto radio, 3½x7x1½", 1958, metal, designed to be used as a car radio as well as a portable, right front dial over lattice grill area with left Buick logo, left side auto plug, AM....$100.00 – 125.00

Bulova

250 Series/plastic case, vertical, 5x3x1¼", plastic, identical to Regency TR-1 except no earphone jack, upper right front round brass dial knob, upper left front thumbwheel on/off/volume knob, lower perforated grill area, AM, bat
black......................$300.00 – 350.00
white ....$400.00 – 450.00

250 Series/leather case, vertical, 5⅛x3⅜x1⅜", leather, same chassis and dial knob as Regency TR-1, upper right front round brass dial knob, upper left front thumbwheel on/off/volume knob, lower woven cloth grill area, leather strap, AM, bat ....$450.00 – 500.00

260 Series, horizontal, 1957, leather, six transistors, upper right front

round dial knob with scalloped edge, right side thumbwheel knob, left grill area with square cut-outs, leather handle, AM, bat.........$40.00 – 50.00

270, horizontal, 1957, leather, right front round dial knob, left plastic three dimensional checkered grill area, crown and shield logo, leather handle, AM, bat........$35.00 – 45.00

278, horizontal, 1958, leather, four transistors, right front round dial knob, right side thumbwheel knob, left plastic three-dimensional checkered grill area, crown and shield logo, leather handle, AM, bat.............................$35.00 – 45.00

290, horizontal, 3x6x1⅝", plastic, right front round tuning knob in crescent-shaped dial area, right side thumbwheel on/off/volume knob, large checkered grill, AM, bat.............................$50.00 – 65.00

290P, horizontal, 3⅛x6x1¼", plastic, right front round tuning knob in crescent-shaped dial area, right side thumbwheel on/off/volume knob, large checkered grill, AM, bat..................$50.00 – 65.00

620, horizontal, 3x6x1½", plastic, right front round thumbwheel dial knob over large crescent-shaped checkered grill area with crown and shield logo, swing handle, AM, bat....................$80.00 – 100.00

622, vertical, plastic, six transistors, upper right front window dial with right side thumbwheel tuning, left side thumbwheel on/off/volume knob, lower metal perforated and textured grill area with lower right logo, AM, bat..............$25.00 – 35.00

640 Series, horizontal, 3x6x2", plastic, right front round dial w/center crest, right side thumbwheel on/off/volume knob, large grill area with metal filigreed design, AM, bat.......$75.00 – 100.00

660 Series, vertical, 5¾x3¾x1¾", 1959, plastic, eight transistors, upper right front window dial with right side thumbwheel tuning, upper left front on/off/volume window with left side thumbwheel knob, lower metal grill area with raised diamond-shaped cut-outs, swing handle, AM, bat................$65.00 – 85.00

670, vertical, 3⅜x2⅜x1", plastic, six transistors, metal front panel with

upper right thumbwheel dial and upper left "starburst" decoration with rhinestone, top left switch, lower perforated grill area, AM, bat............................$50.00 – 65.00

672, vertical, 3⅜x2⅜x1", 1962, plastic, six transistors, metal front panel with upper right thumbwheel dial and upper left "starburst" decoration with rhinestone, left side thumbwheel volume knob, top left switch, lower perforated grill area, made in Japan, AM, bat...........$50.00 – 65.00

685, vertical, 1962, four transistors, upper right front round dial knob, lower grill area with oval-shaped cut-outs, swing handle, AM, bat.....................$20.00 – 35.00

740 Series "Super 6," vertical, six transistors, upper right front thumbwheel dial, left side thumbwheel on/off/volume knob, lower metal perforated grill area with vertical lines and lower left logo, AM, bat.............................$35.00 – 45.00

742 "Super 6," vertical, 1962, six transistors, upper right front thumbwheel dial, lower metal perforated grill area with vertical lines and lower left logo, AM, bat ....$35.00 – 45.00

750 Series, vertical, 4x2½x1⅛", **plastic, upper left front window** **dial with top thumbwheel tuning,** **right side thumbwheel on/off/vol-** **ume knob, metal front panel with** **textured and perforated grill area,** **AM, bat**....................$15.00 – 20.00

782, horizontal, 1962, seven transistors, upper front horizontal two-band slide rule dial with thumbwheel tuning, top left thumbwheel knob, large lower perforated grill area with lower left logo, two switches, telescoping antenna, AM, SW, bat ...$25.00 – 35.00

792 "Super Transistor 7," horizontal, 3⅛x4¾x1", 1962, plastic, seven transistors, upper right front horizontal dial with thumbwheel tuning, right side thumbwheel on/off/volume knob, large metal perforated grill area with

lower right logo, made in Japan, AM, bat ....$25.00 – 35.00

820 "Scout," vertical, 4¼x2⅝x1⅛", plastic, six transistors, upper right front window dial, lower metal textured grill area with horizontal slots and lower right logo, made in Japan, AM, bat...........$15.00 – 20.00

830 Series—832/833/836, verti- **cal/watch radio, 3¾x2½x1¼",** 1963, plastic, six transistors, upper right front window dial with right side thumbwheel tuning, upper left front watch face, lower metal perforated grill area, rear fold-out stand, AM, bat ....$75.00 – 90.00

840 Series, horizontal/travel watch radio, 3½x5x1½", metal and leatherette folding case, seven transistors, inner metal panel with right round dial, left round watch face, center perforated grill area, AM, bat ....$30.00 – 40.00

862, horizontal, 1963, nine transistors, upper front horizontal two-band slide rule dial with thumbwheel tuning, left thumb-wheel volume knob, top pushbuttons, large lower perforated grill area, telescoping antenna, handle, AM, FM, bat...............$30.00 – 40.00

870, vertical, 3x2x1", 1963, plastic, six transistors, upper right front thumbwheel dial with V-shaped cut-out, lower metal perforated grill area with vertical bars, AM, bat...$20.00 – 30.00

872, vertical, 1963, six transistors, upper right front thumbwheel dial with V-shaped cut-out, lower metal perforated grill area with vertical bars, AM, bat.............$20.00 – 30.00

882, horizontal, 1963, seven transistors, upper front horizontal two-band slide rule dial, large lower perforated grill area, telescoping antenna, AM, SW, bat........................$25.00 – 35.00

890 Series, horizontal, 3⅛x4⅞x1", plastic, upper left front horizontal slide rule dial with right side thumbwheel tuning, right side thumbwheel on/off/volume knob, large perforated grill area, AM, bat.....................$35.00 – 45.00

892, horizontal, 1963, seven transistors, upper left front horizontal slide rule dial with right side thumbwheel tuning, right side thumbwheel on/off/volume knob, large lower perforated grill area, AM, bat.....................$35.00 – 45.00

1042, horizontal, 1965, 12 transistors, upper front horizontal three-band slide rule dial, large lower perforated grill area, tele-

scoping antenna, handle, AM, FM, SW, bat.............$15.00 – 20.00

1060 Series "Epic," vertical, eight transistors, upper front window dial with right side thumbwheel tuning, right side thumbwheel on/off/volume knob, lower round metal perforated grill area, AM, bat............................$10.00 – 15.00

1130, vertical, 1964, upper front oval window dial with right side thumbwheel tuning, lower perforated grill area, AM, bat.............$10.00 – 15.00

1420, horizontal, eight transistors, upper right front window dial with right side thumbwheel tuning, right side thumbwheel on/off/volume knob, large grill area with vertical bars, AM, bat.............$10.00 – 15.00

7866, horizontal, 3½x6x1¾", 1962, seven transistors, upper front horizontal two-band slide rule dial with thumbwheel tuning, top left thumbwheel knob, large lower perforated grill area with lower left logo, two switches, telescoping antenna, AM, SW, bat.............$30.00 – 40.00

Calrad

60A183, vertical, 1960, six transistors, upper left front window dial with left side thumbwheel tuning, right side thumbwheel on/off/volume knob, lower perforated grill area with geometric design, AM, bat.........................$100.00 – 125.00

Cameo

61N29-03, vertical, 1963, black plastic, six transistors, diagonally divided front, upper metal panel with right round dial knob, left side thumbwheel on/off/volume knob, lower checkered grill area, AM, bat ....$20.00 – 25.00

64N06-03, vertical, 1964, six transistors, upper right front round window dial with thumbwheel tuning, top left thumbwheel on/off/volume knob, large perforated grill area, AM, bat ....$10.00 – 15.00

64N09-03, vertical, 1964, six transistors, upper right front window dial with thumbwheel tuning, top left thumbwheel on/off/volume knob, large perforated grill area with vertical lincs, AM, bat ....$10.00 – 15.00

Candle

2 Transistor (no #), vertical, 4³⁄₈x2³⁄₄x1³⁄₈," plastic, two transistors, step-back top, upper right front thumbwheel dial knob, upper left front thumbwheel on/off/volume knob, lower checkered grill area with center crest, made in Japan, AM, bat..........$75.00 – 85.00

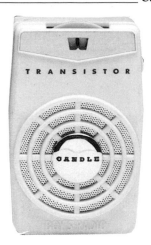

Boy's Radio, vertical, plastic, two transistors, upper front window dial with top thumbwheel tuning, thumbwheel on/off/volume knob, lower round perforated grill area with concentric circles and center Candle nameplate, AM, bat....$50.00 – 60.00

PTR-62B, vertical, plastic, six transistors, upper right front thumbwheel dial, upper left front thumbwheel on/off/volume knob, lower metal perforated grill area with vertical lines, AM, bat ....$20.00 – 30.00

PTR-85C, vertical, 4¹⁄₂x2³⁄₄x1⁷⁄₈", 1963, plastic, eight transistors, step-down top, upper front window dial with upper right thumbwheel tuning, upper left thumbwheel on/off/volume knob, lower metal perforated grill area, made in Japan, AM, bat..............$40.00 – 60.00

PTR-100, horizontal, 3¹⁄₈x5¹⁄₄x1³⁄₈", plastic, 10 transistors, upper right front window dial with top thumbwheel tuning, left side thumbwheel on/off/volume knob, large metal perforated grill area with lower left logo, made in Japan, AM, bat ....$30.00 – 40.00

PTR-605, vertical, plastic, six transistors, upper right front window dial with right side thumbwheel tuning, left side thumbwheel on/off/volume knob, metal textured and perforated grill area, candle logo, AM, bat..............................$75.00 – 85.00

Capehart

T6-202 "Incomparable," vertical, 1961, six transistors, upper front panel with crown logo and half circle window dial, large lower perforated grill area with horizontal slots and lower left crown logo, AM, bat.................$100.00 – 125.00

T6-203 "Incomparable," vertical, 1961, six transistors, upper right front window dial with thumbwheel tuning, upper left front on/off/volume window, lower perforated grill area with horizontal slots and lower left crown logo, AM, bat ....$35.00 – 50.00

T7-S200 "Incomparable," horizontal, 1961, seven transistors, two right front horizontal dials with thumbwheel tuning, left perforated grill area with lower crown logo, telescoping antenna, AM, SW, bat.....................$45.00 – 65.00

T8-201 "Incomparable," vertical, 4⅜x2⅞x1¼", 1961, eight transistors, upper right front round dial with thumbwheel tuning, upper left front thumbwheel knob, lower perforated grill area with horizontal slots and lower left

logo, swing handle, made in Japan, AM, bat .....$100.00 – 125.00

Capri

KR-6TS35, vertical, 4¼x2½x1¼", plastic, six transistors, upper left front round dial with left side thumbwheel tuning, upper right front on/off/volume window with right side thumbwheel knob, metal perforated grill area, swing handle, made in Japan, AM, bat...$100.00 – 125.00

Captain

YT-781 "Deluxe," horizontal 3⅛x5½x1½", plastic with metal front panel, eight transistors, right front window dial with right side thumbwheel tuning, right side thumbwheel on/off/volume knob, left front grill area with horizontal bars, made in Japan, AM, bat ....$20.00 – 30.00

Casey

010, vertical, 3¾x2¾x1½", plastic, solid state, upper right front window dial with top right thumbwheel tuning, top left thumbwheel on/off/volume knob, large lower grill area with horizontal bars, braided strap, made in Hong Kong, AM, bat.**$5.00 – 10.00**

CBS Columbia

TR261, horizontal, 10½x13x6¼" (without stand), wood with brass trim, horizontal two-sided top dial, two top knobs, brass handle, front and rear cloth grill areas, radio snaps off metal stand for use as a table model, made in USA, AM, bat.
radio only ....**$45.00 – 55.00**
w/metal stand ....**$65.00 – 75.00**

Champion

TR-600 "Boy's Radio," vertical, 4x2⅜x1⅛", plastic, two transistors, upper right front window dial with right side thumbwheel tuning, left side thumbwheel on/off/volume knob, circular metal perforated grill area with center crest logo, optional external speaker available, made in Japan, AM, bat.
radio only ....**$50.00 – 60.00**
w/optional speaker ..**$85.00 – 100.00**

Champtone

Boy's Radio "Super," vertical, 4x2½x1⅛", plastic, two transistors, upper front window dial with left side thumbwheel tuning, right side thumbwheel on/off/volume knob, lower round metal perforated grill area, made in Japan, AM, bat ....$45.00 – 55.00

Channel Master

6252A, horizontal, 7x9⅛x4", leatherette, 13 transistors, upper front horizontal three-band slide rule dial, lower metal perforated grill area with four knobs, telescoping antenna, handle, AM, two Police, bat ....**$15.00 – 20.00**

6459 "Signal Seeker," horizontal, 10 transistors, plastic with metal trim, left front round dial, left top manual thumbwheel tuning knob, right top automatic tuning button, right front perforated grill area, bat..........................**$35.00 – 50.00**

6461 "Maverick," vertical, 4⅛x2⅜x1⅜", plastic, eight transistors, upper right front round window dial with right side thumbwheel tuning, left side thumbwheel on/off/volume knob, lower metal perforated grill area, made in Hong Kong, AM, bat...........$10.00 – 15.00

6463, horizontal/table, 5½x13x4¼", plastic, nine transistors, right front vertical two-band slide rule dial, three right front knobs, large left grill area with vertical bars, telescoping antenna, fold-down handle, feet, AM, FM.......$10.00 – 15.00

6467A "Maverick," vertical, 4x2½x1⅜", plastic, six transistors, upper right front round window dial with right side thumbwheel tuning, left side thumbwheel on/off/volume knob, lower metal perforated grill area, made in Hong Kong, AM, bat...........$10.00 – 15.00

6474, horizontal, 1965, six transistors, upper right front window dial with right side thumbwheel tuning, right side thumbwheel on/off/volume knob, large left metal perforated grill area, AM, bat..$10.00 – 15.00

6475, vertical, 1965, eight transistors, upper right front round two-band dial with thumbwheel tuning, telescoping antenna, AM, FM, bat...................$15.00 – 20.00

6476 "VHF Monitor," horizontal, 1965, nine transistors, upper front horizontal two-band slide rule dial, large lower grill area with horizontal slots, telescoping antenna, AM, VHF, bat....................$15.00 – 20.00

6477, horizontal, 1965, nine transistors, upper front horizontal two-band slide rule dial, large lower perforated grill area with lower left logo, AM, FM, bat.....$15.00 – 20.00

6479, horizontal, 1965, available in red or black, 14 transistors, upper front horizontal two-band slide rule dial, large lower grill area, telescoping antenna, AM, FM, bat....................$15.00 – 20.00

6500, horizontal, 1960, ivory, six transistors, right front round dial over horizontal grill bars, lower right on/off/volume knob, pull-up handle, feet, AM, bat........................$10.00 – 15.00

6501, horizontal, 3x4¾x1¼", 1959, available in maroon or black, six transistors, upper right front window dial with right side thumbwheel tuning, lower right front on/off/volume window with right side thumbwheel knob, left perforated grill area with logo, AM, bat..............$45.00 – 55.00

6502 (revised), vertical, 4x2½x1¼", 1964, plastic, six transistors, metal front panel, upper right front window dial with right side thumbwheel tuning, left side thumbwheel on/off/volume knob, lower perforated grill area with lower left logo, made in Hong Kong, AM, bat..............$15.00 – 20.00

6503, vertical, 4¼x2½x1⅜", 1960, plastic, five transistors, upper right front window dial with right side thumbwheel tuning, left front on/off/volume window with left side thumbwheel knob, lower metal perforated grill area, made in Japan, AM, bat...........$40.00 – 50.00

6505 "Cordless," 5x10¼x4¾", 1962, caramel and white two-tone plastic, five transistors, upper right front horizontal slide rule dial, large lower checkered grill area with two knobs, fold-down handle, AM, bat.....................$20.00 – 30.00

6506, horizontal, 3x6x1¾", 1960, available in red or black plastic, six transistors, right front dial with thumbwheel tuning, left metal perforated grill area with upper left logo, made in Japan, AM, bat ....$25.00 – 35.00

6506A, horizontal, 3x6x1¾", 1960, plastic, six transistors, right front dial with thumbwheel tuning, right side thumbwheel on/off/volume knob, left perforated grill area with upper left logo, made in Japan, AM, bat ....$25.00 – 35.00

6507, horizontal, 1960, antique ivory and tan two-tone plastic, six transistors, upper right front horizontal two-band slide rule dial, large lower checkered grill area with two knobs and switch, telescoping antenna, fold-down handle, feet, AM, SW, bat.......$20.00 – 30.00

6508 (revised), vertical, 4¼x2½x1½", 1964, plastic, eight transistors, upper

left front round window dial, right side thumbwheel knob, lower metal perforated grill area with center logo, AM, bat..............$10.00 – 15.00

6509, vertical, 3¾x2¼x1", 1960, available in red or black plastic, six transistors, upper front window dial with right side thumbwheel tuning, right side thumbwheel on/off/volume knob, lower metal perforated grill area with center logo, swing handle, made in Japan, AM, bat.........$25.00 – 35.00

6510, horizontal, 5¾x12¾x5", 1960, caramel and white two-tone plastic, six transistors, upper right front horizontal slide rule dial, large lower checkered grill area with two knobs and switch, fold-down handle, feet, AM, bat ......$20.00 – 30.00

6511, horizontal, 6⅛x12¼x5", 1960, Nile green plastic, six transistors, diagonally divided front with upper right see-through slide rule dial and left horizontal grill bars, two knobs, switch, feet, made in Japan, AM, bat ....$20.00 – 30.00

6512, horizontal, 3⅜x6⅛x1⅞", 1960, plastic, eight transistors, right front panel with two-sided rectangular window dial and lower switch, two right side thumbwheel knobs, left perforated grill area with upper left logo, telescoping antenna, made in Japan, AM, SW, bat....$35.00 – 50.00

6512-2, horizontal, 1960, available in red or black plastic, eight transistors, right front panel with two-sided rectangular window dial and lower switch, two right side thumbwheel knobs, left perforated grill area with upper left logo, telescoping antenna, AM, SW, bat.........$35.00 – 50.00

6514, horizontal, 3½x6¼x1¾", 1960, plastic, eight transistors, right front panel with two-sided rectangular window dial and lower switch, two right side thumbwheel knobs, left perforated grill area with upper left logo, telescoping antenna, made in Japan, AM, Marine, bat.........$35.00 – 50.00

6515 "Super Fringe," horizontal, 4½x8½x1¾", 1960, available in red or black plastic, eight transistors, right front dial with right side thumbwheel tuning, right side thumbwheel on/off/volume knob, left metal perforated grill area, AM, bat....................$25.00 – 35.00

6515-A "Super Fringe," horizontal, 4¼x8½x1¾", plastic, eight transistors, right front dial with thumbwheel tuning, left metal perforated grill area, AM, bat.....$25.00 – 35.00

6516, vertical, 1960, available in red or black plastic, seven transistors, upper front window dial with right side thumbwheel tuning, right side thumbwheel on/off/volume knob, lower metal perforated grill area with center logo, swing handle, AM, bat.............................$25.00 – 35.00

6517, horizontal, 1960, black, six transistors, upper front horizontal two-band slide rule dial with thumbwheel tuning, top right on/off/volume knob, large lower metal perforated grill area with BC/LW switch, AM, LW, bat ....$20.00 – 30.00

6518, horizontal, 5½x9½x2¼", 1960, available in red or black plastic, 14 transistors, upper right front horizontal two-band slide rule dial with thumbwheel tuning, thumbwheel on/off/volume knob, large lower metal perforated grill area, two top telescoping antennas, made in Japan, AM, FM, bat.......$20.00 – 30.00

6518A, horizontal, 5½x9½x2¼", 14 transistors, upper right front horizontal two-band slide rule dial with thumbwheel tuning, thumbwheel on/off/volume knob, left side band switch, large lower metal perforated grill area, two top telescoping antennas, made in Japan, AM, FM, bat....................$20.00 – 30.00

6519, horizontal, 1960, available in red or black plastic, 10 transistors, upper right front horizontal three-band slide rule dial with thumbwheel tuning, right side knob, large lower metal perforated grill area, telescoping antenna, battery test meter, pushbutton dial light, AM, LW, Marine, bat.........$20.00 – 30.00

6520, horizontal, 1960, cream and caramel two-tone plastic, eight transistors, upper right front horizontal slide rule dial, large lower checkered grill area with two knobs and switch, fold-down handle, feet, AM, bat.............................$20.00 – 30.00

6521, horizontal/clock radio, 1960, black and chrome, seven transistors, low rectangular radio with center front horizontal slide rule dial and four knobs, top right and left perforated grill areas with center raised alarm clock, telescoping antenna, AM, SW, bat ....$20.00 – 30.00

6522, horizontal, 1963, 10 transistors, right front oval two-band dial, left checkered grill area, four knobs, two telescoping antennas, feet, AM, FM, bat ......$15.00 – 20.00

6523 "Trans-World," horizontal, 1960, available in red or black plastic, 10 transistors, upper right front horizontal three-band slide rule dial, right side knob, large lower metal perforated grill area, telescoping antenna, battery test meter, pushbutton dial light, AM, 2SW, bat ....$30.00 – 40.00

6524, horizontal, 1960, available in red or black plastic, nine transistors, upper front horizontal two-band slide rule dial, right side thumbwheel knob, large lower metal perforated grill area with AM/FM switch, two telescoping antennas, fold-down handle, AM, FM, bat ..$15.00 – 25.00

6527, vertical, 4¼x2½x1¼", 1960, available in red/ivory or black/ivory

plastic, six transistors, upper right front window dial with right side thumbwheel tuning, left side thumbwheel on/off/volume knob, lower lattice grill area, AM, bat.$10.00 – 15.00

6528, horizontal, 1960, available in red/ivory or black/ivory plastic, six transistors, upper right front window dial with thumbwheel tuning, large lower lattice grill area, AM, bat.............................$15.00 – 20.00

6528A, horizontal, 3x5¼x1½", **1960, plastic, six transistors, upper** **right front window dial with thumb-** **bwheel tuning, large lower lattice** **grill area with vertical bars, AM,** **bat..........................$15.00 – 20.00**

6550 "Swing-Along," portable **radio/phono, 4x9x9½", 1962,** **ivory and caramel plastic with bas-** **ketweave trim, left front round dial** **over perforated grill area, five**

pushbuttons, volume knob, inner top record player with unseen tone arm that plays from underneath the record, inner bottom record storage, flexible plastic handle, AM, bat ....$45.00 – 55.00

6560, horizontal, 1965, eight transistors, right front vertical slide rule dial, two knobs, large left perforated grill area, fold-down handle, AM, bat ....$10.00 – 15.00

6561, horizontal, 1965, six transistors, upper right front round window dial with right side thumbwheel tuning, right side thumbwheel on/off/volume knob, lower horizontal grill bars, AM, bat....$5.00 – 10.00

6562, horizontal, 6¼x10¼x3⅝", 1965, six transistors, right front round dial overlaps vertical grill bars, lower left logo, lower right knob, feet, handle, made in Japan, AM, bat ....$10.00 – 15.00

Charmy

Boy's Radio, vertical, 3⅞x2½x1⅛", plastic, two transistors, upper left front window dial with left side thumbwheel tuning, right side thumbwheel on/off/volume knob, circular metal perforated grill area, made in Japan, AM, bat ....$45.00 – 55.00

Claricon

46-070 "Hi-Fidelity," horizontal, 1965, eight transistors, right front round dial and on/off/volume knob, left perforated grill area, leather handle, AM, bat ....$10.00 – 15.00

46-090, horizontal, 1965, 12 transistors, right front round two band dial and two knobs, left perforated grill area, telescoping antenna in handle, AM, FM, bat.$10.00 – 15.00

TR605 "VI," vertical, 1964, six transistors, upper right front window dial with right side thumbwheel tuning, lower grill area with horizontal slots, AM, bat..$15.00 – 20.00

Clarion

77A, auto/portable radio, 2½x5⅞x8¾", plastic/metal, seven transistors, made to use in or out of the car, front horizontal slide rule dial, right and left knobs, top grill area, AM, bat..........$85.00 – 100.00

Columbia

400B, vertical, 1960, black, four transistors, upper right front window dial with thumbwheel tuning, upper left front on/off/volume window with thumbwheel knob, lower circular grill area with vertical bars, AM, bat.......$45.00 – 55.00

400G, vertical, 1960, gray, four transistors, upper right front window dial with thumbwheel tuning, upper left front on/off/volume window with thumbwheel knob, lower circular grill area with vertical bars, AM, bat.......$45.00 – 55.00

400R, vertical, 1960, red, four transistors, upper right front window dial with thumbwheel tuning, upper left front on/off/volume window with thumbwheel knob, lower circular grill area with vertical bars, AM, bat.......$45.00 – 55.00

600BX, vertical, 4x2½x1¼", 1960, black plastic, six transistors, upper right side thumbwheel dial, upper left side thumbwheel on/off/volume knob, lower circular metal perforated grill area, made in Japan, AM, bat.....................$25.00 – 35.00

600G, vertical, 4x2½x1¼", 1960, green plastic, six transistors, upper right side thumbwheel dial, upper left side thumbwheel on/off/volume knob, lower circular metal perforated grill area, made in Japan, AM, bat...........$25.00 – 35.00

610G "Transistor Convertible," horizontal portable w/speaker box, 1960, gray, six transistors, portable radio unit has right front dial with thumbwheel tuning and left perforated grill area, radio slides into speaker box for use as a table model, AM, bat.
radio only ....$60.00 – 85.00
w/speaker box ......$125.00 – 150.00

610R "Transistor Convertible," horizontal portable with speaker

box, 1960, red, six transistors, portable radio unit has right front dial with thumbwheel tuning and left perforated grill area, radio slides into speaker box for use as a table model, AM, bat.
radio only ....$60.00 – 85.00
w/ speaker box .....$125.00 – 150.00

C-605, horizontal, 1962, available in tan or brown leather, five transistors, right side dial knob, left side on/off/volume knob, large front grill area with cut-outs, handle, AM, bat............................$10.00 – 15.00

C-615 "Triumph III," horizontal, 6½ x9x3¼", 1961, plastic leatherette, nine transistors, right front round three-band dial over large metal perforated grill area, four pushbuttons, right side telescoping antenna, handle, made in West Germany, AM, FM, SW, bat...............$35.00 – 45.00

Columbia Records

TR-1000, vertical, 1958, available in saddle tan, rawhide or cordovan leather, six transistors, lift-up top with clasp, inner top right thumbwheel dial and left thumbwheel volume knob, outer front perforated grill area, strap handle, AM, bat............................$35.00 – 45.00

Comet

Boy's Radio, vertical, 4x2¼x1⅛", plastic, two transistors, upper left front wedge shaped dial cut-out with top thumbwheel tuning, top right thumbwheel on/off/volume knob, lower round metal perforated grill area, swing handle, made in Japan, AM, bat...........$55.00 – 65.00

Commodore

610A "HiFi," vertical, 3⅞x2⅝x1⅛", plastic, six transistors, upper right front window dial with right side thumbwheel tuning, left side thumbwheel on/off/volume knob, lower metal grill area with horizontal slots, made in Japan, AM, bat..............$10.00 – 15.00

660, vertical, plastic, upper front quarter-round window dial with thumbwheel tuning, left thumbwheel on/off/volume knob, lower metal perforated grill area with center crest, AM, bat.....$85.00 – 100.00

777, square, 2½x2⅜x1", plastic, eight transistors, right side tuning and on/off/volume knobs, metal front panel with center round perforated grill area, left side key chain, made in Okinawa, AM, bat.......$35.00 – 50.00

TW-60, vertical, 4x2⅝x1⅛", plastic, six transistors, upper right front window dial with right side thumbwheel tuning, left side thumbwheel on/off/volume knob, large checkered grill area, right side vinyl strap, made in Okinawa, AM, bat ....$5.00 – 10.00

TW-66, vertical, 3⅞x2⅝x1⅛", plastic, six transistors, upper right front round window dial with right side thumbwheel tuning, upper left front round on/off/volume window with left side thumbwheel knob, lower lattice grill area, made in Okinawa, AM, bat ...$5.00 – 10.00

**TW-100, vertical, 4½x2¾x1⅜",
plastic, 10 transistors, upper right
front window dial with right side
thumbwheel tuning, left side
thumbwheel on/off/volume knob,
lower lattice grill area, made in Taiwan, AM ....$5.00 – 10.00**

TW-140, vertical, 4½x2¾x1⅜", plastic, 14 transistors, upper right window dial with right side
thumbwheel tuning, left side thumbwheel on/off/volume knob, lattice grill area, made in Okinawa,
AM, bat ....$5.00 – 10.00

YTR-601, vertical, 3¾x2½x1⅛",
plastic, six transistors, upper right
front thumbwheel dial knob, left
side thumbwheel on/off/volume
knob, large front textured and perforated grill area, made in Japan,
AM ....$35.00 – 45.00

Computron
540 "AA Mark II," horizontal,
2¼x4⅜x1⅛", plastic/metal, top horizontal dial and two knobs, front

grill area with horizontal bars, vinyl
strap, made in Hong Kong, AM, bat
$10.00 – 15.00

Consul Deluxe
HT-6023, vertical, 4⅛x2⅝x1¼", plastic,
six transistors, upper front horizontal
dial with right side thumbwheel tuning, left side thumbwheel on/off/vol-
ume knob, lower metal perforated
grill area, rear fold-out stand, made in
Japan, AM ....$30.00 – 40.00

**Boy's Radio, vertical, 3¾x2½x1⅜",
plastic, two transistors, upper right
front window dial with right side
thumbwheel tuning, left side thumbwheel on/off/volume knob, lower
round grill area with vertical bars
plus an inner circular and V-shaped
design, two molded rear feet, made
in Japan, AM, bat ....$75.00 – 100.00**

Continental
160, vertical, 1959, six transistors, upper left front round dial, upper right
front round on/off/volume knob,
lower rectangular perforated grill
area, center front raised "V," swing
handle, AM, bat..........$50.00 – 75.00

MB-7, horizontal, 1961, eight transistors, upper front horizontal three-band slide rule dial with thumbwheel tuning, lower perforated grill area with right knob, telescoping antenna, swing handle, AM, 2SW, bat.............$30.00 – 45.00

SW-7, horizontal, 4¼x7x2", 1959, two-tone blue, seven transistors, upper front horizontal three-band slide rule dial with thumbwheel tuning, lower perforated grill area with right knob, swing handle, AM, 2SW, bat........................$30.00 – 45.00

TFM-1064, horizontal, 4x7⅜x2", 1964, 10 transistors, right front two band dial with thumbwheel tuning, upper left thumbwheel on/off/volume knob, upper right AM/FM switch, left side high/low tone switch, large oval perforated grill area, telescoping antenna, made in Japan, AM, FM, bat ...$25.00 – 35.00

TFM-1086, horizontal, 1964, 10 transistors, top horizontal two-band slide rule dial with thumbwheel tuning, three pushbuttons, large front perforated grill area, telescoping antenna, strap, AM, FM, bat......$15.00 – 20.00

TFM-1087 "Dual Power," horizontal, 1964, leather, 10 transistors, right front dial with thumbwheel tuning, upper right AM/FM switch, lower right thumbwheel on/off/volume knob, large left perforated grill area, telescoping antenna, leather handle, AM, FM, AC/bat........$15.00 – 20.00

TFM-1088, vertical, 1965, nine transistors, upper right front round two-band dial, lower perforated grill area, telescoping antenna, AM, FM, bat.....................$10.00 – 15.00

TFM-1090, horizontal, 1964, 10 transistors, right front two-band dial with thumbwheel tuning, large grill area, telescoping antenna, handle, AM, FM, bat.$10.00 – 15.00

TFM-1124, horizontal, 8½x12¼x3¾", 1962, black plastic, 11 transistors, upper front horizontal two-band dial with right tuning knob and left tone/volume knobs, large lower grill area, dual speakers, telescoping antenna, AM, FM, bat/optional AC adaptor......................$20.00 – 25.00

TFM-1150-B, horizontal, 5½x9½x2⅝", 1962, 11 transistors, upper front horizontal three-band slide rule dial, large lower perforated grill area, two telescoping antennas, AM, FM, SW, optional AC adaptor/bat.$20.00 – 25.00

TFM-1155, horizontal, 1964, 11 transistors, upper front horizontal two-band slide rule dial, lower grill area with horizontal bars, telescoping antenna, handle, AM, FM, bat ....$10.00 – 15.00

TFM-1200, horizontal, 7½x9¼x3", 1965, 12 transistors, upper front horizontal two-band slide rule dial, three knobs, large lower grill area, telescoping antenna, handle, AM, FM, bat......................$10.00 – 15.00

TFM-1365, horizontal, 1964, 13 transistors, upper front horizontal three-band slide rule dial, two left front thumbwheel knobs, two right side knobs, large lower perforated grill area, two telescoping antennas, handle, AM, FM, SW, bat.$10.00 – 15.00

TR-100, vertical, 4⅛x2½x1¼", 1959, two-tone blue, four transistors, upper front window dial with right side thumbwheel tuning, upper left front volume window with left side thumbwheel knob, lower round perforated grill area, swing handle, AM, bat......................$45.00 – 55.00

TR-150, horizontal, 3x5½x1½", 1959, available in red or ebony, four transistors, right front dial with right side thumbwheel tuning, lower right volume window with right side thumbwheel knob, left crisscross grill area, "CMC" logo, AM, bat......................$55.00 – 75.00

TR-182, horizontal, 2½x4½x1¼", 1959, available in black or ivory plastic, six transistors, right front window dial with right side thumbwheel tuning, right side thumbwheel on/off/volume knob, large front perforated grill area with upper left logo, AM, bat..............$25.00 – 40.00

TR-200, vertical, 4x2⅜x1¼", 1959, available in ivory or gray plastic, six transistors, upper right front wedge-shaped dial area with thumbwheel tuning, upper left front on/off/volume window with left side thumbwheel knob, lower perforated grill area, AM, bat..............$35.00 – 50.00

TR-208, vertical, 1959, four transistors, upper front window dial with right side thumbwheel tuning, diagonally divided front with left checkered grill area, AM, bat........$35.00 – 50.00

TR-215, horizontal, 4⅛x5¾x1¼", 1960, available in black or ivory/gray plastic, six transistors, center front vertical dial with upper right thumbwheel tuning, lower right thumbwheel on/off/volume knob, left perforated grill area, AM, bat............................$45.00 – 60.00

TR-300, horizontal, 2¾x4¾x1¼", 1959, eight transistors, right front vertical slide rule dial with right side thumbwheel tuning, lower right on/off/volume window with right side thumbwheel knob, left perforated grill area, AM, bat....................$40.00 – 55.00

TR-613, vertical, 1964, six transistors, upper front window dial with right side thumbwheel tuning, top left thumbwheel on/off/volume knob, lower perforated grill area, AM, bat......................$10.00 – 15.00

TR-630, desk set/radio, 1¾x7½x4", 1962, combination pen holder/radio, available in ebony or ivory, seven transistors, front horizontal slide rule dial with thumbwheel tuning, thumbwheel on/off/volume knob, top grill area with diagonal bars, pen holder, AM, bat..$20.00 – 30.00

TR-632, vertical, 1961, six transistors, upper front window dial with thumbwheel tuning, lower perforated grill area with lower left logo, AM, bat ....$125.00 – 150.00

TR-652, vertical, 3⅞x2⅝x1¼", plastic, six transistors, upper front window dial with top right thumbwheel tuning, top left thumbwheel on/off/volume knob, lower metal perforated grill area, swing handle, made in Japan, AM ...$65.00 – 80.00

TR-660, vertical, 4x2⅝x1⅛", plastic, six transistors, upper right front window dial with right side thumbwheel tuning, lower metal perforated grill area, made in Okinawa, AM ....$10.00 – 15.00

TR-682, vertical, 4¼x2½x1¼", 1962, plastic, six transistors, center front window dial with top thumbwheel tuning, upper right front thumbwheel on/off/volume knob, lower metal perforated grill area with vertical bars, AM, bat .....$75.00 – 90.00

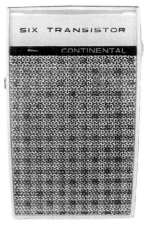

TR-683, vertical, 3⅞x2½x1", 1962, plastic, six transistors, upper left front

window dial with right side thumbwheel tuning, right side thumbwheel on/off/volume knob, large lower plaid metal perforated grill area, made in Japan, AM ......$40.00 – 50.00

TR-716, square, 1965, seven transistors, right side dial and on/off/volume knobs, front perforated grill area with center logo, left side strap, AM, bat............$30.00 – 40.00

TR-751, vertical, 1961, seven transistors, upper front horizontal two-band slide rule dial with right side thumbwheel tuning, right side thumbwheel on/off/volume knob, lower recessed circular perforated grill area, telescoping antenna, AM, SW, bat....................$30.00 – 40.00

TR-801, horizontal, 3x5x1½", 1961, eight transistors, available in red, gray, or ivory plastic, upper front horizontal slide rule dial with right side thumbwheel tuning, lower right front on/off/volume window with right side thumbwheel knob, large perforated chrome grill area, AM, bat ....$30.00 – 40.00

TR-814, vertical, 1964, plastic, eight transistors, upper front round window dial with right side thumbwheel tuning, left side thumbwheel on/off/volume knob, lower metal perforated grill area, AM, bat........................$5.00 – 10.00

TR823 "Globemaster," horizontal, 9x10½x2⅝", 1962, eight transistors, upper front horizontal four-band slide rule dial, large lower grill area with three knobs, telescoping antenna, handle, AM, foreign, 2SW, bat..............**$20.00 – 30.00**

TR-862, vertical, 1964, eight transistors, upper right front window dial with thumbwheel tuning, lower metal grill area with horizontal slots, AM, bat.............**$10.00 – 15.00**

TR-875, horizontal, 1964, eight transistors, upper front horizontal three-band wrap-over slide rule dial, large lower perforated grill area, telescoping antenna, AM, 2SW, bat....................**$15.00 – 20.00**

TR-884, vertical, 4¼x2½x1¼", 1962, eight transistors, upper front window dial with right side thumbwheel tuning, right side thumbwheel on/off/volume knob, large lower perforated grill area, AM, bat....................**$10.00 – 15.00**

TR-1066, horizontal, 5x9x2¾", 1964, leather, 10 transistors, upper right front dial with thumbwheel tuning, lower right front thumbwheel on/off/volume knob, large center grill area with horizontal slots, leather handle, BC, AC/bat.............**$10.00 – 15.00**

TR-1067, horizontal, 3½x6⅝x1⅝", 1965, ten transistors, right front window dial over large metal perforated grill area, right side thumbwheel tuning and thumbwheel on/off/volume knobs, made in Japan, AM, bat.............**$35.00 – 45.00**

TR-1085, vertical, 4½x2¾x1¼", 1964, 10 transistors, upper front window dial with thumbwheel tun-

ing, large lower perforated grill area with center "starburst" logo, made in Okinawa, AM, bat..**$10.00 – 15.00**

_____

Coronado

43-9900, vertical, 3¾x2¼x1", 1960, six transistors, upper front see-through panel, upper right front window dial with right side thumbwheel tuning, upper left front volume window with thumbwheel knob, lower perforated grill area, made in Japan, AM, bat.........**$75.00 – 100.00**

43-9902, horizontal, 1960, six transistors, right front wedge-shaped window dial with right side thumbwheel tuning, right side thumbwheel on/off/volume knob, large perforated grill area, AM, bat .**$55.00 – 70.00**

RA44-9914A, vertical, 1963, six transistors, upper right front window dial with right side thumbwheel tuning, lower perforated grill area, AM, bat....................**$15.00 – 20.00**

RA44-9915A, horizontal, 1963, seven transistors, upper front thumbwheel dial, left and lower grill area with horizontal bars and lower left logo, swing handle, AM, bat.............**$15.00 – 25.00**

RA48-9898A, horizontal, 1959, leather, four transistors, upper right front dial knob, upper left front on/off/volume knob, center grill area with cut-outs, leather handle, AM, bat .... $25.00 – 35.00

RA48-9903A "66," horizontal, 1960, six transistors, upper right front round dial, lower on/off/volume knob, left and lower horizontal bars, fold-down handle, AM, bat .... $15.00 – 25.00

RA48-9905A "88," horizontal, 1960, eight transistors, upper right front round dial, lower on/off/volume knob, left and lower horizontal bars, crown logo, fold-down handle, AM, bat .... $15.00 – 25.00

RA50-9900A, vertical, 1960, six transistors, large upper right front window dial with right side thumbwheel tuning, upper left front volume window with thumbwheel knob, lower perforated grill area, AM, bat .... $75.00 – 100.00

RA50-9902A, horizontal, 1960, six transistors, right front wedge-shaped window dial with right side thumbwheel tuning, right side thumbwheel on/off/volume knob, large perforated grill area, AM, bat .... $55.00 – 70.00

RA60-9899A, vertical, 1962, seven transistors, upper front window dial with right front thumbwheel tuning, left front thumbwheel on/off/volume knob, lower metal perforated wrap-around grill area, top and side metal trim, AM, bat ... $35.00 – 45.00

RA60-9917A, horizontal/watch radio, 1963, seven transistors, upper right

front horizontal slide rule dial with right side thumbwheel tuning, lower right watch face over large perforated grill area, AM, bat.. $60.00 – 75.00

RA60-9922A, vertical, 1964, six transistors, upper front horizontal slide rule dial with right side thumbwheel tuning, left thumbwheel on/off/volume knob, lower perforated grill area, AM, bat .... $10.00 – 15.00

RA60-9925A, vertical, 1964, six transistors, upper left front window dial with thumbwheel tuning, right and lower checkered grill area, AM, bat .... $5.00 – 10.00

RA60-9930B, vertical, 4¼x2⅝x1⅜", **1965, plastic, eight transistors, upper** **front window dial with thumbwheel** **tuning, large lower perforated grill** **area with lower crown logo, made in** **Japan, AM .... $10.00 – 15.00**

RA60-9940A, horizontal, 1964, 12 transistors, right front round dial, right side knob, left grill area, crown logo, AM, bat.. $15.00 – 20.00

RA60-9941A, horizontal, 1964, eight transistors, right front round dial, lower right knob, large left perforated grill area with center crown logo, handle, AM, bat........$10.00 – 15.00

RA60-9943A, horizontal, 1964, 12 transistors, upper front horizontal two-band slide rule dial, large lower grill area, telescoping antenna, handle, AM, FM, bat.$10.00 – 15.00

Coronet

Boy's Radio, vertical, 4x2½x1¼", **plastic, two transistors, upper** **right front "crown" window dial** **with right side thumbwheel tun-** **ing, left front on/off/volume win-** **dow with left side thumbwheel** **knob, metal perforated grill area,** **telescoping antenna, made in Ja-** **pan, AM, bat ....$50.00 – 60.00**

STP-502, desk set/radio, 1962, combination pen holder/radio, two transistors, two right front thumbwheel knobs, left grill area with vertical bars, pen holder, made in Japan, AM..................$25.00 – 35.00

STR-601, horizontal, 1962, two transistors, right dial over large front grill area with vertical bars, left front on/off/volume knob, feet, made in Japan, AM....$30.00 – 40.00

Corvair

8P23, vertical, 4¼x2½x1¼", plastic, eight transistors, upper left front round window dial with left side thumbwheel tuning, right side thumbwheel on/off/volume knob, metal perforated grill area, made in Hong Kong, AM, bat.$10.00 – 15.00

10PL62, horizontal, 1964, leather, 10 transistors, right front round dial, left grill area, leather handle, AM, bat ....$5.00 – 10.00

10SK63, vertical, 1964, 10 transistors, upper left front round window dial with thumbwheel tuning, lower grill area with horizontal bars, AM, bat ....$10.00 – 15.00

Cosmos B

Boy's Radio, vertical, 4x2½x1¼", plas- **tic, two transistors, upper left front** **dial knob, upper right side thumb-** **wheel on/off/volume knob, metal tex-**

tured and perforated grill area, made in Japan, AM.................$50.00 – 60.00

Crest

IV, vertical, 1962, four transistors, upper right front round dial with right side thumbwheel tuning, lower perforated grill area with lower left logo, AM, bat............$75.00 – 100.00

Crestline

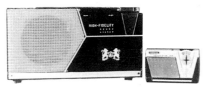

6T-220, horizontal portable with speaker box, radio measures 2⅞x4⅝x1⅜", plastic, six transistors, portable radio unit has upper right front dial with thumbwheel tuning, upper left front thumbwheel on/off/volume knob, lower metal perforated grill area, radio slides into speaker box for use as a table model, made in Japan, AM, bat. radio only ....$75.00 – 100.00 with speaker box...$125.00 – 150.00

6T-280, vertical, plastic, six transistors, upper right front see-through dial panel with top thumbwheel tuning, left side thumbwheel on/off/volume knob, metal perforated grill area, AM............................$100.00 – 125.00

Crosley

JM-8BG "Musical Memories," book shaped hybrid novelty, 7x4½x2", 1956, leather covered "book," three subminiature tubes and two transistors, outside book spine reads "Musical Memories," inner metal panel with dial, on/off/volume knob and perforated grill area, AM, bat.........................$125.00 – 150.00

JM-8BK "Enchantment," book shaped hybrid novelty, 7x4½x2", 1956, leather covered "book," three subminiature tubes and two transistors, outside book spine reads "Enchantment," inner metal panel with dial, on/off/volume knob and perforated grill area, AM, bat..................$125.00 – 150.00

JM-8BN "As You Like It," book shaped hybrid novelty, 7x4½x2", 1956, leather covered "book," three subminiature tubes and two transistors, outside book spine reads "As You Like It," inner metal panel with dial, on/off/volume knob and perforated grill area, AM, bat..................$125.00 – 150.00

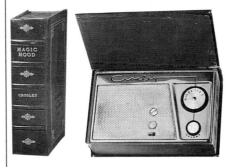

JM-8GN "Magic Mood," book shaped hybrid novelty, 7x4½x2", 1956, leather covered "book," three subminiature tubes and two transistors, outside book spine reads "Magic Mood," inner metal panel with dial, on/off/volume knob and perforated grill area, AM, bat ....$125.00 – 150.00

JM-8WE "Treasure Island," book shaped hybrid novelty, 7x4½x2", 1956, leather covered "book," three subminiature tubes and two transistors, outside book spine reads "Treasure Island," inner metal panel with dial, on/off/volume knob and perforated grill area, AM, bat...........................$125.00 – 150.00

Crown

TR-9, horizontal, 1965, leather, nine transistors, upper right front dial knob, lower right on/off/volume knob, left grill area with horizontal slots, handle, AM, bat..............$5.00 – 10.00

TR-333, vertical, 1959, three transistors, upper front see-through panel, upper right front round dial with right side thumbwheel tuning, left side thumbwheel on/off/volume knob, lower perforated wraparound grill area, crown logo, AM, bat...........................$125.00 – 150.00

TR-400, horizontal, 2⅞x4⅞x1½", 1959, available in red, black, or blue, four transistors, right front see-through panel, right front dial with right side thumbwheel tuning, lower right side thumbwheel on/off/volume knob, left lattice grill area, swing handle, AM, bat........$90.00 – 120.00

TR-555, vertical, 1960, five transistors, upper front see-through panel with window dial, right side thumbwheel tuning knob, right side thumbwheel on/off/volume knob, lower metal perforated grill area, lower right crown logo, AM, bat.......................$175.00 – 200.00

TR-610 "Super Six," horizontal, 3¾x6¼x2", 1959, available in gray, blue, turquoise, black, or white, six transistors, right front round dial with arrow pointer, lower right side thumbwheel knob, left perforated grill area, swing handle, made in Japan, AM, bat..........$45.00 – 60.00

TR-666, horizontal, 1959, six transistors, right front see-through panel, right front dial with right side thumbwheel tuning, lower right side thumbwheel on/off/volume knob, diagonally divided front with left perforated grill area, AM, bat......................$100.00 – 125.00

TR-670, vertical, 1960, seven transistors, small upper front diamond-shaped window dial with thumbwheel tuning, lower perforated grill area with horizontal slots and lower left crown logo, AM, bat....$55.00 – 70.00

TR-680, vertical, 3½x2½x1", plastic, six transistors, upper front window dial with thumbwheel tuning, lower metal perforated grill area, AM, bat..............................$25.00 – 35.00

TR-750, horizontal, 1961, seven transistors, two right front window dials – one broadcast, one shortwave, right side thumbwheel tuning, lower right front thumbwheel on/off/volume knob, left perforated grill area with lower crown logo, telescoping antenna, AM, SW, bat............$55.00 – 70.00

TR-770R, vertical, plastic, seven transistors, left front vertical dial panel over large metal perforated grill area with lower left logo, two right side thumbwheel knobs, rechargeable, AM......$30.00 – 40.00

TR-777, vertical, 1960, seven transistors, upper front see-through panel with window dial, right side thumbwheel tuning knob, left side thumbwheel on/off/volume knob, lower perforated grill area with lower left crown logo, AM, bat....................$175.00 – 200.00

TR-800, horizontal, 1960, eight transistors, right front see-through panel with vertical slide rule dial, upper right front thumbwheel tuning knob, lower right front thumbwheel on/off/volume knob, left circular perforated grill area, lower left crown logo, swing handle, AM, bat..........................$100.00 – 125.00

TR-802, horizontal, 4½x6¾x1¾", plastic, eight transistors, upper front horizontal two-band slide rule dial, right front thumbwheel tuning and on/off/volume knobs, metal grill area with horizontal slots and lower left logo, telescoping antenna, made in Japan, AM, SW.......$65.00 – 80.00

TR-820, horizontal, 1959, four transistors, right front round dial, lower right thumbwheel on/off/volume knob, left checkered grill area, swing handle, AM, bat..........$50.00 – 65.00

TR-830, horizontal, 1959, four transistors, right front round dial over horizontal grill bars, lower right thumbwheel on/off/volume knob, AM, bat.....................$40.00 – 50.00

TR-860, horizontal flashlight/radio, 2½x5½x1⅛", eight transistors, two right side knobs, left side flashlight, front rectangular perforated grill area, AM.....................$15.00 – 25.00

TR-875, horizontal, 1960, eight transistors, upper front horizontal two-band slide rule dial, right side knobs, large perforated grill area with lower left crown logo, telescoping antenna, AM, SW, bat...............$50.00 – 60.00

TR-999 "Super 9," vertical, 1961, nine transistors, upper front see-through panel with window dial, right side thumbwheel tuning knob, right side thumbwheel on/off/volume knob, lower perforated grill area with horizontal slots and left crown logo, AM, bat.....................$175.00 – 200.00

TRF-1000, horizontal, 1965, 13 transistors, upper right front horizontal three-band slide rule dial, large lower grill area, two telescoping antennas, handle, AM, FM, SW, bat.............................$15.00 – 20.00

TRF-1600R, horizontal, 1965, nine transistors, upper front horizontal two-band slide rule dial, upper left thumbwheel on/off/volume knob, lower right front AM/FM switch, center grill area with cut-outs, telescoping antenna, AM, FM, bat/rechargeable.................$15.00 – 20.00

TRF-1700, horizontal, 1965, 14 transistors, off-center vertical three-band slide rule dial, right knobs, left perforated grill area, telescoping antenna, handle, AM, FM, SW, bat ....$15.00 – 20.00

TRF-1800, vertical, 1965, nine transistors, upper front horizontal two-band slide rule dial, large lower perforated grill area, telescoping antenna, AM, FM, bat.$10.00 – 15.00

Daltone
Royal 400, vertical, plastic, two transistors, upper front see-through panel, rounded top right corner, upper right front dial knob, left side thumbwheel on/off/volume knob, metal perforated grill area, made in Japan, AM ...$50.00 – 60.00

Dansette
60, horizontal/table, 8½x18x5¼", wood case, large front woven grill area with center round dial and two knobs, metal legs, MW, LW, bat ....$30.00 – 40.00

Daylite

TN-603, vertical, 3⅞x2⅜x1", plastic, six transistors, upper front see-through panel with large dial numer-

als and right round pointer area, right side thumbwheel tuning knob, left side thumbwheel on/off/volume knob, lower metal perforated grill area with lower left logo, made in Japan, AM ....$90.00 – 110.00

Delco

989131 "Trans-Portable," auto/portable radio, 2x4¼x6¾", 1958, plastic and metal, designed to be used as a car radio as well as a portable, chrome front with horizontal dial and horizontal grill bars, two knobs, swing handle, AM ..$100.00 – 125.00

989172 "Trans-Portable," auto/portable radio, 3¾x6⅞x1¼", 1959, plastic and metal, designed to be used as a car radio as well as a portable, chrome front panel with right round dial and left horizontal grill bars, right side chrome handle, made in USA, AM ..$100.00 – 125.00

Delmonico
6TRS, horizontal, 2½x4½x1¼", plastic, right front window dial with thumbwheel tuning, large metal grill area with vertical slots and horizontal bars, AM, bat.$20.00 – 25.00

7TA-2, horizontal, 1963, seven transistors, upper right front horizontal two-band slide rule dial, upper left thumbwheel on/off/ volume knob, large perforated grill area, telescoping antenna, AM, SW, bat..............$30.00 – 40.00

7TH-1, horizontal, 1963, seven transistors, right round two-band dial over large lattice front panel with left round speaker area, tele-scoping antenna, handle, AM, SW, bat............................$15.00 – 20.00

7YR707, square, 1965, seven transis-tors, right side dial and on/off/vol-ume knobs, front circular grill area with center logo, left side chain, AM, bat......................$30.00 – 40.00

8TR8, horizontal, 1965, eight tran-sistors, upper right front window dial with thumbwheel tuning, top thumbwheel on/off/volume knob, front oval perforated grill area, AM, bat..............................$15.00 – 20.00

9FM190, horizontal, 1965, nine transistors, upper front horizontal two-band slide rule dial, large lower perforated grill area with lower right logo, telescoping antenna, handle, AM, FM, bat.$10.00 – 15.00

10TR10, horizontal, 1965, 10 tran-sistors, upper right front window dial with thumbwheel tuning, top thumbwheel on/off/volume knob, front oval perforated grill area, AM, bat.............................$15.00 – 20.00

AW6000 "International," 1965, 12 transistors, inner horizontal six-band slide rule dial, large lower grill area, fold-up front, two tele-scoping antennas, handle, AM, FM, 3SW, LW, bat..............$50.00 – 65.00

TR-7C, horizontal/watch radio, 1963, seven transistors, upper right front horizontal slide rule dial with thumbwheel tuning, lower right front watch face over perforated grill area, AM, bat.....$50.00 – 65.00

TRS-6, horizontal, 1959, six transis-tors, right front window dial with right side thumbwheel tuning over large grill area with vertical slots, lower right side thumbwheel on/off/ volume knob, AM, bat.$20.00 – 30.00

Delta

3 transistor (no #), square, plastic, three transistors, upper left front thumbwheel dial, top right thumb-wheel on/off/volume knob, no built-in speaker, earphone only, AM ....$80.00 – 95.00

Deluxe

2 transistors (no #) (two versions), horizontal, 2⅝x4x1⅜", plastic, two transistors, large right front tuning knob, lower right side thumbwheel on/off/volume knob, left grill area with either horizontal bars or triangular cut-outs, made in Japan, AM ....$50.00 – 65.00

Boy's Radio, vertical, 4x2½x1⅛",
plastic, upper front see-through
panel with right round dial, top
right thumbwheel tuning knob, top
left thumbwheel on/off/volume
knob, lower metal textured and
perforated grill area, made in
Japan, AM, bat..........$50.00 – 60.00

G-601, horizontal, plastic, "mother-of-pearl" right front panel with thumbwheel dial knob, top thumbwheel on/off/volume knob, left metal perforated grill area with upper left globe logo, AM, bat ....$65.00 – 80.00

Dewald

K-544 "Tuckaway," horizontal, 3½x5⅞x2¼", 1957, leather, four transistors, right front round dial knob inside horseshoe-shaped tuning area, upper thumbwheel on/off/volume knob, left grill area with diamond cut-outs and perforations, leather handle, made in USA, AM, bat ....$50.00 – 65.00

K-544A, horizontal, 3½x5⅞x2¼", 1957, leather, four transistors, right

front round dial knob inside horse-shoe-shaped tuning area, upper thumbwheel on/off/volume knob, left grill area with diamond cut-outs and perforations, leather handle, AM, bat ....$50.00 – 65.00

K-701 "Playmate," horizontal, 7x8¾x3½", 1955, plastic, six transistors, lower front round dial knob, right side on/off/volume knob, upper vertical grill bars, pull-up handle, made in USA, AM, bat ....$225.00 – 275.00

K-701A, horizontal, 7x8¾x3½", 1956, plastic, six transistors, lower front round dial knob, right side on/off/volume knob, upper vertical grill bars, pull-up handle, AM, bat ....$225.00 – 275.00

K-701B, horizontal, 7x8¾x3½", 1956, plastic, six transistors, lower front round dial knob, right side on/off/volume knob, upper vertical grill bars, pull-up handle, made in USA, AM, bat ....$225.00 – 275.00

K-702B, horizontal, 1957, leather, six transistors, lower front round dial knob, right side on/off/volume knob, upper grill with cut-outs, leather handle, AM, bat .....$50.00 – 65.00

L-414, horizontal, 1958, leather, three transistors, right side dial and on/off/volume knobs, large front grill area with vertical cut-outs, leather pull-up handle, AM, bat..............**$40.00 – 50.00**

L-546, horizontal, 1959, leather, four transistors, right front round dial knob overlaps grill area with rectangular cut-outs, top thumbwheel on/off/volume knob, leather handle, AM...**$50.00 – 65.00**

L-703, horizontal, 1958, leather, six transistors, right side dial knob, left side on/off/volume knob, large front grill area with cut-outs, leather handle, AM, bat..........**$30.00 – 40.00**

Diplomat

HT-6088 **"HiFi,"** **vertical, 3½x2⅝x1¼", plastic, six transistors, upper right front window dial with thumbwheel tuning, lower metal perforated grill area, made in Japan, AM**..............**$45.00 – 55.00**

Domex

Boy's Radio "Skylark," vertical, 3⅝x2½x1¼", plastic, two transistors, upper front window dial with top right thumbwheel tuning, top left thumbwheel on/off/volume knob, lower metal textured and perforated grill area, made in Japan, AM.................**$45.00 – 55.00**

Ducretet Thomson

TR-854, horizontal, 8x12½x4", leatherette on wood, upper front horizontal slide rule dial, large lower metal perforated grill area with horizontal bar and center logo, one left side knob, two right side knobs, handle, bat.....**$25.00 – 35.00**

Dumont

900, horizontal, 1963, available in ebony or gray, nine transistors, three decorative front panels made up of concentric rectangles, right front window dial with thumbwheel tuning, swing handle, AM, bat.**$30.00 – 40.00**

1210, horizontal, 1957, available in green, red, or tan leather, six transistors, upper right front dial knob, lower right on/off/volume knob, left grill area with diamond cut-outs, leather strap, AM, bat.**$30.00 – 40.00**

Echo

2 transistor (no #), vertical, 4¼x2⅝x1⅜", plastic, two transistors, upper front round dial knob, upper right front thumbwheel on/off/volume knob, lower wedge-shaped metal textured and perforated grill area, made in Japan, AM, bat ....**$50.00 – 75.00**

TRK-225, vertical, plastic, six transistors, large upper front dial knob, upper left front thumbwheel on/off/volume knob, lower metal wedge-shaped grill area with horizontal rows of perforations, AM.............................$50.00 – 75.00

Eden

TR-600, vertical, plastic with metal front panel, six transistors, upper left front window dial with left side thumbwheel tuning, upper right front thumbwheel on/off/volume knob, lower perforated grill area with lower left logo, AM......$25.00 – 35.00

Eico

RA-6, horizontal, 1960, leather, six transistors, available as a kit or completely assembled, right side dial knob, left side on/off/volume knob, large front grill area with cut-outs, leather handle, AM, bat............$10.00 – 15.00

Electra

MTR-716 "Pee Wee 7," vertical, 2⅝x1⅝x⅞", plastic, seven transistors, upper right front window dial with right side thumbwheel tuning, right side thumbwheel on/off/volume knob, large metal perforated grill area, made in Japan, AM, bat....................$40.00 – 50.00

Electro Brand

637, vertical, plastic, upper right front dial with red disk, left and lower perforated grill area, top right vinyl strap, AM ...$5.00 – 10.00

1466, vertical, 4¾x3x1¼", plastic with wood-grained front panel, 14 transistors, upper right front round window dial with right side thumbwheel tuning, lower round "sunburst" grill area, made in Taiwan, AM, bat......................$5.00 – 10.00

Electronics Guild

E1000, horizontal/clock radio, 1964, six transistors, right front window dial with upper and lower perforated grill areas, left alarm clock face, AM, AC ....$10.00 – 15.00

Elgin

R-800, vertical, 1964, 10 transistors, upper front horizontal dial with thumbwheel tuning, large lower perforated grill area, AM, bat........$10.00 – 15.00

R-1000, horizontal, 3¼x5⅝x1⅞", 1964, plastic, 10 transistors, upper front horizontal dial, right tuning and on/off/volume knobs, left metal textured and perforated grill area, made in Japan, AM.....**$10.00 – 15.00**

R-1000B, horizontal, 1964, 10 transistors, upper front horizontal dial, right tuning and on/off/volume knobs, left perforated grill area, AM, bat ....**$10.00 – 15.00**

R-1000C, horizontal, 1964, 10 transistors, upper front horizontal dial, right tuning and on/off/volume knobs, left perforated grill area, AM, bat ....**$10.00 – 15.00**

R-1110, horizontal, 3¼x5¾x1⅞", 1964, 10 transistors, upper front horizontal dial, right tuning and on/off/volume knobs, left metal perforated grill area, AM, bat ....$10.00 – 15.00

R-1200, horizontal, 1964, 10 transistors, upper front horizontal dial, right tuning, on/off/volume and fine tuning knobs, left perforated grill area, handle, AM, bat .**$10.00 – 15.00**

R-1400, vertical, 6⅛x3½x1¾", 1965, plastic, 12 transistors, upper front horizontal two-band slide rule dial, lower perforated grill area, three knobs and AM/FM selector switch, telescoping antenna, made in Japan, AM, FM, bat ......**$10.00 – 15.00**

R-1500, horizontal, 1964, 11 transistors, upper front horizontal two-band slide rule dial, lower perforated grill area, two telescoping antennas, handle, AM, FM, bat ....**$10.00 – 15.00**

R-1600 "Commander," horizontal, 1965, 11 transistors, upper front horizontal three-band slide rule dial, lower perforated grill area, two telescoping antennas, handle, AM, FM, SW, bat ....**$15.00 – 20.00**

R-1700, horizontal, 1965, 15 transistors, upper front horizontal five-band slide rule dial, large lower two section perforated grill area, telescoping antenna, handle, AM, FM, 2SW, LW, bat ,............**$20.00 – 25.00**

R-2100, vertical, 5¾x5¼x3⅛", leather, 10 transistors, upper front horizontal dial, two right knobs and treble/bass switch, lower metal perforated two-tone grill area, fold-down handle, AM .....$10.00 – 15.00

R-2400, vertical, 3½x2⅜x1¼", plastic, upper front wood-grained panel with round two-band dial, lower metal perforated grill area, telescoping antenna, made in Japan, AM, FM, bat..............$10.00 – 15.00

TR-4, vertical, 3¾x2⅜x1⅛", plastic, upper front see-through panel with right round dial, right side thumbwheel tuning knob, upper left front on/off/volume window with left side thumbwheel knob, lower metal perforated grill area, made in Japan, AM..................$65.00 – 80.00

Emerson

31P56, horizontal, 3½x6¾x1½", plastic, eight transistors, right front dial with thumbwheel tuning, upper right thumbwheel on/off/volume knob, large left metal perforated grill area with upper left G clef logo, right side strap, AM, bat.....................$15.00 – 20.00

31P58 "Gemini," vertical, 5⅞x3⅝x1⅜", plastic, eight transistors, upper right front oval dial panel with center window dial, two right side thumbwheel knobs, large

lower metal perforated grill area, made in Japan, AM ...$20.00 – 30.00

31P61, horizontal, 5¼x9x2½", leather, nine transistors, upper front horizontal two-band slide rule dial, lower grill area, right tuning and volume knobs, telescoping antenna, handle, AM, FM, bat..$10.00 – 15.00

31P65, vertical, plastic, 12 transistors, upper front horizontal two-band dial, three lower knobs and band switch, large metal perforated grill area with lower left G clef logo, telescoping antenna, left side vinyl strap, AM, FM............$10.00 – 15.00

555 "All-American," horizontal, 3½x6x2", 1959, plastic, four transistors, right front dial with center G clef logo and right side thumbwheel tuning, right side thumbwheel on/off/volume knob, left lattice grill area, "see-through" back, made in USA, AM, bat........$50.00 – 75.00

555V "All-American," horizontal, 3½x6x2", 1959, plastic, four transistors, right front dial with center G clef logo and right side thumbwheel tuning, right side thumbwheel on/off/volume knob, left lattice grill area, AM, bat......$50.00 – 75.00

707, vertical, 4⅛x2½x1¼", 1962, plastic, eight transistors, upper front window dial with top thumbwheel tuning, right side thumbwheel on/off/volume knob, lower metal perforated grill area, made in USA, AM, bat............$45.00 – 60.00

808, vertical, 1962, plastic, eight transistors, front window dial with top thumbwheel tuning, right side thumbwheel on/off/volume knob, large front metal perforated grill area, AM, bat.............$25.00 – 35.00

838, horizontal/hybrid, 3¾x6⅜x1½", 1955, plastic, three tubes and two transistors, right front round dial, upper right thumbwheel on/off/vol-

ume knob, left checkered grill area with lower left G clef logo, fold-down handle, AM, bat......$125.00 – 150.00

842, horizontal, 7x9½x3¾", 1956, leather, six transistors, large center front round dial knob over grill cut-outs, left side on/off/volume knob, leather handle, AM, bat ....$35.00 – 45.00

843 "Transistor III," horizontal/hybrid, 7¼x9½x3¼", leather, tubes and transistors, large top dial knob, top left thumbwheel on/off/volume knob, front metal perforated grill area with lower right G clef logo, swing handle, AM ......$40.00 – 60.00

844, horizontal, 1956, available in gray, green, maroon, or tan leather, six transistors, right front dial knob, left front volume knob, center hourglass-shaped grill with center G clef logo, rotatable handle, AM ....$35.00 – 45.00

847, horizontal, 9¾x10x3½", 1956, available in red, blue, green, or ginger plastic, six transistors, center front hourglass-shaped checkered grill area with center window dial, right and left front knobs, top "Miracle Wand" antenna in rotatable handle, AM, bat ....$50.00 – 75.00

849, horizontal, 3½x5¾x1½", 1955, plastic, right hourglass-shaped panel with window dial over large front checkered grill area, right side thumbwheel tuning knob, AM, bat ....$150.00 – 175.00

855, horizontal, 1956, available in red, blue, champagne, cinnamon, or cordovan leather, six transistors, large center front round dial knob over grill cut-outs, top left thumbwheel on/off/volume knob, leather handle, AM, bat........$35.00 – 45.00

856, horizontal/hybrid, 3¾x6⅛ x1½", plastic, tubes and transistors, right front round dial knob, upper right thumbwheel on/off/ volume knob, left checkered grill area, pull-up handle, made in USA, AM, bat................$125.00 – 150.00

868, horizontal, 9¾x10⅛x3⅜", 1957, available in burgundy, yellow, or beige plastic, four transistors, upper center front dial, upper left on/off/volume knob, lower grill area with horizontal bars and G clef logo, top "Miracle Wand" rotatable antenna in handle, AM, bat ....$50.00 – 75.00

869, horizontal, 9¾x10⅛x3⅜", 1957, available in navy or ivory plastic, four transistors, upper center front dial, upper left on/off/volume knob, lower grill area with horizontal bars and G clef logo, top "Miracle Wand" rotatable antenna in handle, AM, bat.....$50.00 – 75.00

880, vertical, 1962, eight transistors, front window dial with top thumbwheel tuning, right side thumbwheel on/off/volume knob, lower metal perforated grill area, AM, bat.....................$35.00 – 45.00

888 (no name), vertical, 6½x4x2", plastic, eight transistors, upper front round dial knob, large lower metal perforated grill area with V-shaped top and lower right G clef logo, left front on/off/volume knob, swing handle, AM, bat........$100.00 – 125.00

888 "Atlas," vertical, 6½x4x2", 1960, plastic, eight transistors, upper front round dial knob, left front on/off/volume knob, lower metal perforated random-patterned grill area with V-shaped top, swing handle, AM, bat ....$75.00 – 100.00

888 "Explorer," vertical, 6½x4x2", 1960, available in white, green, ebony, red, turquoise, or gray plastic, eight transistors, upper front dial with top thumbwheel tuning, diagonally divided lower front with upper checkered plastic panel and lower metal perforated grill area, left front on/off/volume knob, swing handle, made in USA, AM, bat..............$90.00 – 110.00

888 "Galaxy," vertical/Seattle World's Fair commemorative model, 1963, available in ebony, green, white, red, turquoise, or charcoal plastic, eight transistors, upper front window dial with thumbwheel tuning, right side thumbwheel on/off/volume knob, lower lattice grill area, AM, AC/bat..............$35.00 – 45.00

888 "Pioneer," vertical, 6½x4x2", 1958, plastic, eight transistors, upper front round dial knob, large lower metal perforated grill area with V-shaped top, crisscross

design and lower right G clef logo, left front on/off/volume knob, swing handle, made in USA, AM, bat..............$75.00 – 90.00

888 "Satellite," vertical, 1958, available in oyster white or autumn brown leather, eight transistors, upper front round dial knob, left front on/off/volume knob, lower grill area with random-patterned circular cut-outs of varying sizes, leather handle, AM, bat..............$125.00 – 150.00

888 "Titan," vertical, 6x3¾x1¾", 1963, available in ebony, green, white, red, turquoise, or charcoal plastic, eight transistors, off-center oval dial area with center window dial, top thumbwheel tuning knob, right side thumbwheel on/off/volume knob, large front perforated grill area, AM, AC/bat..............$65.00 – 80.00

888 "Transtimer," horizontal/clock radio, 7x8⅝x3⅜", 1958, saddle tan leather, eight transistors, front cover unsnaps and folds back to form easel, inner lower left round dial, lower right round metal perforated grill, upper round clock face, leather handle, made in USA, AM, bat..............$75.00 – 100.00

888 "Transtimer II," horizontal/clock radio, 7x8⅝x3⅜", 1959, available in black or tan leather, eight transistors, front cover unsnaps and folds back to form easel, inner lower left round dial, lower right round metal perforated grill, upper round clock face, leather handle, AM, bat..............$75.00 – 100.00

888 "Vanguard," vertical, 6½x4x2", 1958, available in white, green, ebony, red, or turquoise plastic, eight transistors, futuristic front case design with upper round dial knob, left front on/off/volume knob, lower grill area with random-pattern cut-outs, rocket logo, made in USA, AM, bat....................$85.00 – 115.00

899 "Mercury," vertical, 1964, available in ebony, green, white, red, turquoise, or charcoal plastic, eight transistors, upper front window dial with top thumbwheel tuning, right side thumbwheel on/off/volume knob, lower lattice grill area, G clef logo, AM, bat.............$35.00 – 50.00

911 "Eldorado," horizontal, 4¼x6¾x2", 1960, available in ebony, charcoal gray, coral, ivory, gold, or turquoise plastic, nine transistors, right front window dial with right side thumbwheel tuning over large checkered grill area, right side on/off/volume knob, swing handle, made in USA, AM, bat.............................$30.00 – 40.00

977 "Falcon," horizontal, 3¾x6x2", 1961, plastic, seven transistors, right front dial over horizontal grill bars, right side thumbwheel on/off/volume knob, AM, bat ...$25.00 – 35.00

988 "Rambler," vertical, 6½x4x2", 1960, available in white, green, ebony, red, or turquoise plastic, eight transistors, upper front dial with top thumbwheel tuning, lower horizontal grill bars, left front on/off/volume knob, swing handle, made in USA, AM, bat.............$60.00 – 75.00

991, horizontal, 5¾x8½x3¼", 1963, available in brown, ebony, or charcoal gray leather, nine transistors, upper left front horizontal slide rule dial, lower lattice grill area, right side knob, leather handle, AM, bat.....................$10.00 – 15.00

999 "Champion," 1958, plastic, four transistors, upper front round dial knob over checkered grill area, upper right thumbwheel on/off/volume knob, AM, bat........$150.00 – 175.00

Empire

2 transistor (no #), horizontal, 2⅝x4x1⅛", plastic, two transistors, large right front dial knob, lower right side thumbwheel on/off/volume knob, left grill area with horizontal bars, made in Japan, AM ....$40.00 – 50.00

Encore

Boy's Radio, vertical, 4x2½x1", plastic, two transistors, upper left front window dial with thumbwheel tuning, lower round metal perforated grill area, AM, bat .....**$45.00 – 55.00**

TR8A7 "High Fidelity," vertical, 4½x2⅝x1⅜", plastic, eight transistors, upper left front thumbwheel dial knob over large metal perforated grill area, right side thumbwheel on/off/volume knob, AM ....**$25.00 – 35.00**

Essex

Boy's Radio, vertical, 4¼x2⅝x1¼", plastic, two transistors, upper right front window dial with right side thumbwheel tuning, left side thumbwheel on/off/volume knob, lower lattice grill area, made in Japan, AM, bat ....**$25.00 – 35.00**

TR-6K, vertical, six transistors, upper right front window dial with thumbwheel tuning, lower perforated grill area, made in Taiwan, AM, bat ....**$5.00 – 10.00**

TR-10P "Super DeLuxe," horizontal, 1964, 10 transistors, right front window

dial with right side thumbwheel tuning, right side thumbwheel on/off/volume knob, large left perforated grill area, AM, bat ....**$10.00 – 15.00**

Ever-Play

100 "Rechargeable," horizontal, 4⅛x8¾x2", 1963, plastic, nine transistors, rechargeable, upper front horizontal two-band slide rule dial, recessed right front with thumbwheel knobs, upper left battery/tuning indicator, large metal perforated grill area, left side telescoping antenna, right side pull-out handle, AM, FM, AC/bat ....**$25.00 – 35.00**

1836A "Rechargeable," vertical, 1963, six transistors, upper left front round window dial with right side thumbwheel tuning, right side on/off/volume knob, metal perforated grill area, lower right side recharger plug, AM, bat.....................**$25.00 – 35.00**

2836A "Rechargeable," vertical, 1963, eight transistors, upper front horizontal slide rule dial with right side thumbwheel tuning, lower perforated grill area with lower right logo, AM, AC/bat .....**$25.00 – 35.00**

PR-1266 "Rechargeable," vertical, 4⅜x2¾x1⅜", plastic, six transistors, upper left front round window dial with right side thumbwheel tuning, right side on/off/volume knob, metal perforated grill area, lower right side recharger plug-in, made in Japan, AM, bat ......**$25.00 – 35.00**

Excel

6T-2 "Aristocrat," horizontal, 1959, six transistors, right front see-through dial with right side thumbwheel tuning, lower right side thumbwheel on/off/volume knob, left checkered grill area, AM, bat .....**$90.00 – 110.00**

Executive

CPR-7 "The Executive Desk Radio," horizontal desk set/radio, 1964, seven transistors, top left thumbwheel knobs and perforated grill area, two pen holders, AM, bat..............................**$25.00 – 35.00**

Faircrest

1094, vertical, 1965, 10 transistors, upper right front window dial, lower lattice grill area, AM, bat...**$5.00 – 10.00**

1670, vertical, 1965, six transistors, upper right front window dial, lower grill area with horizontal bars, AM, bat ....**$5.00 – 10.00**

2091, horizontal, 1965, 10 transistors, upper front horizontal two-band slide rule dial, large lower perforated grill area with lower right AM/FM switch, telescoping antenna, AM, FM, bat ....**$10.00 – 15.00**

Falcon

6THK, vertical, 4x2½x1¼", 1964, plastic, six transistors, upper right front diamond shaped window dial with right side thumbwheel tuning, left side thumbwheel on/off/volume knob, lower metal perforated grill area, made in Hong Kong, AM, bat ....**$15.00 – 20.00**

8THK "DeLuxe," vertical, eight transistors, upper right front diamond shaped window dial with right side thumbwheel tuning, left

side thumbwheel on/off/volume knob, lower metal perforated grill area with center diamond shaped logo, AM, bat.............**$15.00 – 20.00**

Firestone

4-C-29, horizontal/hybrid, 3¾x 5⅞x1⅞", 1955, plastic, tubes and transistors, right front round dial knob, top right thumbwheel on/off/volume knob, left checkered grill area, fold-down handle, AM........................**$250.00 – 300.00**

4-C-33, horizontal, 9x6⅛x2⅞", 1958, leather, six transistors, upper right front dial knob, upper left front on/off/volume knob, center rectangular grill cut-outs, leather handle, AM, bat ....**$15.00 – 25.00**

4-C-34, horizontal, 1957, British tan leather, seven transistors, top horizontal slide rule dial, right and left knobs, large front lattice grill area, handle, AM, bat ....**$30.00 – 40.00**

4-C-36, horizontal, 1959, six transistors, top right dial, top left on/off/volume knob, large front grill area with horizontal bars and lower right logo, pull-up handle, AM, bat......**$25.00 – 35.00**

4-C-40, horizontal, plastic, step-down top with thumbwheel tuning knob, lower front on/off/volume knob, right and left circular grill areas with horizontal bars, twin speakers, swing handle, AM, bat ....$50.00 – 65.00

4-C-42, horizontal, 4x6¾x2", plastic, step-down top with thumbwheel tuning knob, large lower grill area with horizontal bars, on/off/volume knob, and "F" logo, swing handle, made in USA, AM......$40.00 – 50.00

Four Star (****)

Boy's Radio, vertical, 4x2¼x1⅛", plastic, two transistors, upper left front wedge shaped dial cut-out with top thumbwheel tuning, top right thumbwheel on/off/volume knob, round metal perforated grill area, swing handle, made in Japan, AM ....$55.00 – 65.00

NR-23 "Boy's Radio," vertical, 4x2½x1⅜", plastic, two transistors, rounded upper right corner, upper

right front dial knob, left side thumbwheel on/off/volume knob, lower metal textured and perforated grill area with lower left logo, made in Japan, AM ...$50.00 – 60.00

Fuji Denki

TRB-611, vertical, 1962, six transistors, upper right front thumbwheel dial, left side on/off/volume knob, lower perforated grill area with lower left logo, AM, bat..$45.00 – 60.00

TRS-701, horizontal, 1962, upper front horizontal slide rule dial with thumbwheel tuning, large lower perforated grill area with MW/SW switch, telescoping antenna, AM, SW, bat....................$20.00 – 30.00

Fujitone

Boy's Radio, vertical, 4x2½x1", plastic, two transistors, upper left front window dial with left side thumbwheel tuning, rear volume control, round metal perforated grill area, made in Japan, AM, bat ....$50.00 – 60.00

Futura

2 transistor (no #), vertical, 3¾x2¼x1¼", plastic, two transistors, upper front dial knob, upper right front thumbwheel on/off/volume knob, lower vertical bars, no speaker, earphone-only, made in USA, AM, bat ....$75.00 – 85.00

366, vertical, 1963, six transistors, upper right front thumbwheel dial, lower perforated grill area, AM, bat ....$40.00 – 50.00

Gala

TR-824, vertical, 4¼x2½x1¼", 1965,

eight transistors, upper front window dial with thumbwheel tuning, large lower textured and perforated grill area, AM, bat......**$10.00 – 15.00**

Galaxie

FT-881, vertical, 4¼x2⅝x1¼", plastic, eight transistors, upper front window dial with right side thumbwheel tuning, left side thumbwheel on/off/volume knob, lower perforated grill area, made in Ryukyu, AM, bat ....**$15.00 – 25.00**

Galaxy

ST-620, vertical, plastic, six transistors, upper left front window dial inside oversized "6," two right side thumbwheel knobs, metal perforated grill area with scalloped edge, AM, bat.....................**$60.00 – 75.00**

General

8GA 701F, horizontal, plastic, 10 transistors, slanted top with horizontal two-band dial, right top thumbwheel tuning knob, left top thumbwheel

on/off/volume knob, large lower metal perforated grill area with lower left logo and lower right switch, telescoping antenna, made in Japan, AM, FM...............................**$30.00 – 40.00**

General Electric

7-2705C, vertical, 4x2½x1¼", plastic, upper right front round window dial with right side thumbwheel tuning, left checkered grill area, top left strap, AM, bat.**$5.00 – 10.00**

7-2753D "76," vertical/Bicentennial radio, 4x2½x1¼", 1976, red, white, and blue plastic, upper right front window dial with right side thumbwheel tuning, left side thumbwheel on/off/volume knob, metal perforated grill painted with red, white, and blue "76," braided strap, made in Hong Kong, AM, bat ....**$15.00 – 20.00**

675, horizontal, 3⅛x5½x1½", 1955, ebony plastic, five transistors, GE's first commercially produced transistor radio, right front round dial with brass knob, top thumbwheel on/off/volume knob, left checkered grill area, made in USA, AM, bat.................$75.00 – 100.00

676, horizontal, 3⅛x5½x1½", 1955, ivory plastic, five transistors, GE's first commercially produced transistor radio, right front round dial with brass knob, top thumbwheel on/off/volume knob, left checkered grill area, made in USA, AM, bat.................$100.00 – 125.00

677, horizontal, 3⅛x5½x1½", 1955, red plastic, five transistors, GE's first commercially produced transistor radio, right front round dial with brass knob, top thumbwheel on/off/volume knob, left checkered grill area, made in USA, AM, bat.................$125.00 – 150.00

678, horizontal, 3⅛x5½x1½", 1955, aqua plastic, five transistors, GE's first commercially produced transistor radio, right front round dial with brass knob, top thumbwheel on/off/volume knob, left checkered grill area, made in USA, AM, bat.................$125.00 – 150.00

C2418A "Disneyland," horizontal/clock radio, 6x10¾x5¼", white plastic, both right and left front panels feature Disney characters, right front round dial with Tinkerbell pointer, left alarm clock face, AM, AC.................$50.00 – 75.00

C2418A "Mickey Mouse," horizontal/clock radio, 6x10¾x5¼", white plastic, right front round dial with 3-D Mickey head pointer over horizontal bars, left alarm clock face with other Disney characters, AM, AC.................$50.00 – 75.00

C2419A "Disneyland," horizontal/clock radio, 6x10¾x5¼", yellow plastic, both right and left front panels feature Disney characters, right front round dial with Tinkerbell pointer, left alarm clock face, AM, AC.................$50.00 – 75.00

C2419A "Mickey Mouse," horizontal/clock radio, 6x10¾x5¼", yellow plastic, right front round dial with 3 D Mickey head pointer over horizontal bars, left alarm clock face with other Disney characters, AM, AC.................$50.00 – 75.00

C-2450A "Micro Electronic," radio with clock/recharger/speaker unit, 1⅛x3¼x2¼" (radio only), 1966, plastic, radio has front slide rule dial with two right side thumbwheel knobs and a top metal perforated grill area, radio fits into clock/recharger/speaker base for use as a table set, AM, bat.
radio alone ....$25.00 – 30.00
radio with base ....$50.00 – 60.00

CT455A, horizontal/clock radio, 1960, six transistors, right front round dial knob over large perforated grill area, left alarm clock face, AM, bat ....$10.00 – 20.00

KT-1P-2751C, vertical, 4x2½x1¼", plastic, upper right front window dial with right side thumbwheel tuning, left side thumbwheel on/off/volume knob, front perforated grill area and right vertical panel with six stars, braided strap, made in Hong, Kong, AM, bat.......................$10.00 – 20.00

P710A, horizontal, 1958, ebony plastic, four transistors, right front round dial knob with "bubble" magnifier, center on/off/volume knob, left lattice grill area, AM, bat ....$30.00 – 40.00

P711A, horizontal, 3½x6⅜x1⅝", 1957, turquoise plastic, four transistors, right front round dial knob with "bubble" magnifier, center on/off/volume knob, left lattice grill area, AM, bat .....$30.00 – 40.00

P711C, horizontal, 3½x6⅜x1⅝", 1957, turquoise plastic, four transistors, right front round dial knob with "bubble" magnifier, center on/off/volume knob, left lattice grill area, AM, bat .....$30.00 – 40.00

P715-D, horizontal, 3½x6⅝x1½," 1958, metal and leatherette, six transistors, right front round dial, center on/off/volume knob, left metal perforated grill area, pull-up handle, AM, bat ....$30.00 – 40.00

P716B, horizontal, 3½x6⅝x1½," 1958, metal and leatherette, six transistors, right front round dial, center on/off/volume knob, left metal plaid perforated grill area, pull-up handle, AM, bat.........$30.00 – 40.00

P716D, horizontal, 3½x6⅝x1½," 1958, metal and leatherette, six tran-

sistors, right front round dial, center on/off/volume knob, left metal plaid perforated grill area, pull-up handle, AM, bat.........$30.00 – 40.00

P720, horizontal, 9½x6⅝x3½", ginger leather, six transistors, right side dial knob, left side on/off/volume knob, front grill area with circular cut-outs, leather handle, AM.....$10.00 – 15.00

P720B, horizontal, 9½x6⅝x3½", ginger leather, six transistors, right side dial knob, left side on/off/volume knob, front grill area with circular cut-outs, leather handle, AM ......$10.00 – 15.00

P721, horizontal, 9½x6⅝x3½", champagne leather, six transistors, right side dial knob, left side on/off/volume knob, front grill area with circular cut-outs, leather handle, AM...............$10.00 – 15.00

P721B, horizontal, 9½x6⅝x3½", champagne leather, six transistors, right side dial knob, left side on/off/volume knob, front grill area with circular cut-outs, leather handle, AM...............$10.00 – 15.00

P725A, horizontal, 1958, brown plastic with brown handle, six transistors, right side dial knob, left side on/off/volume knob, large front perforated grill area, fold-down handle, AM, bat ....$15.00 – 25.00

P725B, horizontal, 1958, brown plastic, six transistors, right side dial knob, left side on/off/volume knob, large front perforated grill area, fold-down handle, AM, bat ....$15.00 – 25.00

P726A, horizontal, 6x9¼x2½", 1958, turquoise plastic with white handle, six transistors, right side dial knob, left side on/off/volume knob, large front metal perforated grill area, fold-down handle, made in USA, AM, bat ....$15.00 – 25.00

P726B, horizontal, 6x9¼x2½", 1958, turquoise plastic with white handle, six transistors, right side dial knob, left side on/off/volume knob, large front metal perforated grill area, fold-down handle, made in USA, AM, bat ....$15.00 – 25.00

P740A, vertical, 1965, eight transistors, upper right front window dial with thumbwheel tuning, lower metal perforated grill area, AM, bat ....$10.00 – 15.00

P745A, horizontal, 3½x6⅝x1⅞", 1958, ebony plastic, five transistors, right front round dial knob, upper right thumbwheel on/off/volume knob, left grill area with vertical bars, made in USA, AM, bat...........$20.00 – 30.00

P745B, horizontal, 3½x6⅝x1⅞", 1958, ebony plastic, five transistors, right front round dial knob, upper right thumbwheel on/off/ volume knob, left grill area with vertical bars, made in USA, AM, bat ....$20.00 – 30.00

P746A, horizontal, 3½x6⅝x1⅞", 1958, antique white & turquoise plastic, five transistors, right front round dial knob, upper right thumbwheel on/off/volume knob, left grill area with vertical bars, AM, bat.....................$20.00 – 30.00

P746B, horizontal, 3½x6⅝x1⅞", 1958, antique white & turquoise plastic, five transistors, right front round dial knob, upper right thumbwheel on/off/volume knob, left grill area with vertical bars, made in USA, AM, bat.............$20.00 – 30.00

P750A, horizontal, 1958, ginger leather, six transistors, right side dial knob, left side on/off/volume knob, front plastic lattice grill area, leather handle, AM, bat ....$10.00 – 15.00

P755A, horizontal, 1959, gray plastic, five transistors, upper right front round dial knob, left thumbwheel on/off/volume knob, random pattern metal perforated grill area, pull-up handle, AM, bat ....$10.00 – 20.00

P760A, horizontal, 7¼x9⅜x2¾", 1958, beige and white plastic, five transistors, right side dial knob, left side on/off/volume knob, front lattice grill area, handle, AM, bat...$15.00 – 20.00

P761A, horizontal, 7¼x9⅜x2¾", 1958, green and white plastic, five transistors, right side dial knob, left side on/off/volume knob, front lattice grill area, handle, AM, bat...$15.00 – 20.00

P765A, horizontal, 3½x6⅞x1⅜", 1957, metal and leatherette, six transistors, right front round dial, center on/off/volume knob, left metal perforated grill area, pull-up handle, rechargeable, AM, bat...**$30.00 – 40.00**

P765B, horizontal, 3½x6⅞x1⅜", 1957, metal and leatherette, six transistors, right front round dial, center on/off/volume knob, left metal perforated grill area, pull-up handle, rechargeable, AM, bat...**$30.00 – 40.00**

P766A, horizontal, 3½x6⅞x1⅜", 1958, metal and leatherette, six transistors, right front round dial, center on/off/volume knob, left metal perforated grill area, pull-up handle, rechargeable, AM, bat...**$30.00 – 40.00**

P770A, horizontal, 6½x8⅞x3⅛", 1959, antique white plastic, seven transistors, upper right front round dial, upper left thumbwheel on/off/volume knob, large lower grill area, handle, AM, bat....................**$15.00 – 25.00**

P771A, horizontal, 6½x8⅞x3⅛", 1959, green plastic, seven transistors, upper right front round dial, upper left thumbwheel on/off/volume knob, large lower grill area, handle, AM, bat ....**$15.00 – 25.00**

P776A, horizontal, 1959, leather, seven transistors, upper right front round dial, upper left on/off/volume knob, lower grill area with horizontal bars, top right pushbutton, leather handle, AM, bat...........**$10.00 – 15.00**

P776B, horizontal, 6½x9½x3", 1959, leather, seven transistors, upper right front round dial, upper

left on/off/volume knob, lower plastic grill area with horizontal bars, top right pushbutton, leather handle, AM, bat ....**$10.00 – 15.00**

P780 "Cross-Country," horizontal, 1960, ginger plastic and chrome, eight transistors, upper front horizontal slide rule dial, two knobs, large lower lattice grill area, leather handle, AM, bat ....**$15.00 – 25.00**

P780A, horizontal, 1960, ginger plastic and chrome, eight transistors, upper front horizontal slide rule dial, two knobs, large lower lattice grill area, leather handle, AM, bat ....**$15.00 – 25.00**

P780B, horizontal, 1960, ginger plastic and chrome, eight transistors, upper front horizontal slide rule dial, two knobs, large lower lattice grill area, leather handle, AM, bat ....**$15.00 – 25.00**

P780E, horizontal, 8x10⅞x4⅛", plastic and chrome, eight transistors, upper front horizontal slide rule dial, two knobs, large lower lattice grill area, leather handle, AM, bat ....**$15.00 – 25.00**

P780H "Long Range," horizontal, 1965, plastic and chrome, nine transistors, upper front horizontal slide rule dial, two knobs, large lower lattice grill area, leather handle, AM, bat...............**$15.00 – 25.00**

P785A, horizontal, 3¼x6⅛x1⅞", 1959, black & white plastic, seven transistors, upper right front horizontal slide rule dial with right side thumbwheel tuning, lower right side on/off/volume knob, large grill area with circular cut-outs, AM, bat................$20.00 – 30.00

P786A, horizontal, 3¼x6⅛x1⅞", 1959, antique white plastic, seven transistors, upper right front horizontal slide rule dial with right side thumbwheel tuning, lower right side on/off/volume knob, large grill area with circular cut-outs, AM, bat................$20.00 – 30.00

P787A, horizontal, 3¼x6⅛x1⅞", 1959, blue & white plastic, seven transistors, upper right front horizontal slide rule dial with right side thumbwheel tuning, lower right side on/off/volume knob, large grill area with circular cut-outs, AM, bat................$20.00 – 30.00

P790A, horizontal, 1960, plastic, six transistors, right front round dial knob, lower right thumbwheel on/off/volume knob, left grill area with circular cut-outs, right side curves in, AM, bat.....$30.00 – 40.00

P790B, horizontal, 3¼x5⅝x1½", 1960, white and black plastic, six transistors, right front round dial knob, lower right thumbwheel on/off/volume knob, left grill area with circular cut-outs, right side curves in, made in USA, AM, bat...............$30.00 – 40.00

P791A, horizontal, 1960, plastic, six transistors, right front round dial knob, lower right thumbwheel on/off/volume knob, left grill area with circular cut-outs, right side curves in, AM, bat.....$30.00 – 40.00

P791B, horizontal, 3¼x5⅝x1½", 1960, turquoise and white plastic, six transistors, right front round dial knob, lower right thumbwheel on/off/volume knob, left grill area with circular cut-outs, right side curves in, made in USA, AM, bat...............$30.00 – 40.00

P795, horizontal, 6x8⅝x2⅞", 1958, black leather, right side dial knob, left side on/off/volume knob, front white plastic lattice grill area, leather handle, AM, bat.........$15.00 – 20.00

P795A, horizontal, 1958, black leather, right side dial knob, left side on/off/volume knob, front plastic lattice grill area, leather handle, AM, bat...............$15.00 – 20.00

P795B, horizontal, 1958, black leather, right side dial knob, left side on/off/volume knob, front plastic lattice grill area, leather handle, AM, bat...............$15.00 – 20.00

P796A, horizontal, 1958, pastel blue leather, right side dial knob, left side on/off/volume knob, front plastic lattice grill area, leather handle, AM, bat...............$15.00 – 20.00

P796B, horizontal, 1958, pastel blue leather, right side dial knob, left side on/off/volume knob, front plastic lattice grill area, leather handle, AM, bat...............$15.00 – 20.00

P797, horizontal, 6x8⅝x2⅞", 1958, beige leather, right side dial knob, left side on/off/volume knob, front cocoa plastic lattice grill area, leather handle, AM, bat..........$15.00 – 20.00

P797A, horizontal, 1958, light beige leather, right side dial knob, left side on/off/volume knob, front plastic lattice grill area, leather handle, AM, bat................$15.00 – 20.00

P979B, horizontal, 1958, light beige leather, right side dial knob, left side on/off/volume knob, front plastic lattice grill area, leather handle, AM, bat................$15.00 – 20.00

P798, horizontal, 6x8⅝x2⅞", 1958, burgundy leather, right side dial knob, left side on/off/volume knob, front white plastic lattice grill area, leather handle, AM, bat..........$15.00 – 20.00

P798C, horizontal, 1962, leather, right side dial knob, left side on/off/volume knob, front plastic lattice grill area, leather handle, AM, bat......................$15.00 – 20.00

P800A, horizontal, 3½x6¼x1¾", 1959, five transistors, right front round dial knob with "bubble" magnifier, center on/off/volume knob, left lattice grill area, made in USA, AM, bat............$30.00 – 40.00

P805, horizontal, 4¾x7x2¼", 1959, antique white plastic, five transistors, upper right front round dial knob, left thumbwheel on/off/volume knob, random pattern metal perforated grill area, pull-up handle, AM, bat................$10.00 – 20.00

P805A, horizontal, 4¾x7x2¼", 1959, white plastic, five transistors, upper right front round dial knob, left thumbwheel on/off/volume knob, random pattern metal perforated grill area, pull-up handle, made in USA, AM, bat..............$10.00 – 20.00

P806, horizontal, 4¾x7x2¼", 1959, blue plastic, five transistors, upper right front round dial knob, left thumbwheel on/off/volume knob, random pattern metal perforated grill area, pull-up handle, AM, bat.............$10.00 – 20.00

P806A, horizontal, 4¾x7x2¼", 1959, blue plastic, five transistors, upper right front round dial knob, left thumbwheel on/off/volume knob, random pattern metal perforated grill area, pull-up handle, AM, bat............................$10.00 – 20.00

P807, horizontal, 4⅝x7⅛x2⅜", 1961, black plastic, five transistors, upper right front round dial knob, left thumbwheel on/off/volume knob, gold woven grill area, pull-up handle, AM, bat ....$10.00 – 20.00

P807A, horizontal, 4⅝x7⅛x2⅜", 1961, black plastic, five transistors, upper right front round dial knob, left thumbwheel on/off/volume knob, woven grill area, pull-up handle, AM, bat................$10.00 – 20.00

P807B, horizontal, 4⅝x7⅛x2⅜", 1961, plastic, five transistors, upper right front round dial knob, left thumbwheel on/off/volume knob, woven grill area, pull-up handle, AM, bat ....**$10.00 – 20.00**

P807C, horizontal, 4⅝x7⅛x2⅜", 1961, black plastic, five transistors, upper right front round dial knob, left thumbwheel on/off/volume knob, woven grill area, pull-up handle, AM, bat ....$10.00 – 20.00

P807E, horizontal, 4⅝x7⅛x2⅜", 1961, black plastic, five transistors, upper right front round dial knob, left thumbwheel on/off/volume knob, woven grill area, pull-up handle, AM, bat ....**$10.00 – 20.00**

P807H, horizontal, 4⅝x7⅛x2⅜", 1961, black plastic, five transistors, upper right front round dial knob, left thumbwheel on/off/volume knob, woven grill area, pull-up handle, AM, bat ....**$10.00 – 20.00**

P807J, horizontal, 4⅝x7⅛x2⅜", 1961, black plastic, five transistors, upper right front round dial knob, left thumbwheel on/off/volume knob, woven grill area, pull-up handle, AM, bat ....**$10.00 – 20.00**

P808, horizontal, 4⅝x7⅛x2⅜", 1961, white plastic, five transistors,

upper right front round dial knob, left thumbwheel on/off/volume knob, gold woven grill area, pull-up handle, AM, bat ....**$10.00 – 20.00**

P808A, horizontal, 4⅝x7⅛x2⅜", 1961, white plastic, upper right front round dial knob, left thumbwheel on/off/volume knob, woven grill area, pull-up handle, AM, bat ....**$10.00 – 20.00**

P808C, horizontal, 4⅝x7⅛x2⅜", 1961, white plastic, five transistors, upper right front round dial knob, left thumbwheel on/off/volume knob, woven grill area, pull-up handle, AM, bat ....**$10.00 – 20.00**

P808E, horizontal, 4⅝x7⅛x2⅜", 1961, white plastic, five transistors, upper right front round dial knob, left thumbwheel on/off/volume knob, woven grill area, pull-up handle, AM, bat ....**$10.00 – 20.00**

P808H, horizontal, 4⅝x7⅛x2⅜", 1961, white plastic, five transistors, upper right front round dial knob, left thumbwheel on/off/volume knob, woven grill area, pull-up handle, AM, bat ....**$10.00 – 20.00**

P808J, horizontal, 4⅝x7⅛x2⅜", 1961, white plastic, five transistors, upper right front round dial knob, left thumbwheel on/off/volume knob, woven grill area, pull-up handle, AM, bat ....**$10.00 – 20.00**

P809, horizontal, 4⅝x7⅛x2⅜", 1961, olive green plastic, five transistors, upper right front round dial knob, left thumbwheel on/off/volume knob, gold woven grill area, pull-up handle, AM, bat ....$10.00 – 20.00

P809C, horizontal, 4⅝x7⅛x2⅜", 1961, green plastic, five transistors, upper right front round dial knob, left thumbwheel on/off/volume knob, woven grill area, pull-up handle, AM, bat..............$10.00 – 20.00

P809E, horizontal, 4¾x7x2¼", 1961, green plastic, five transistors, upper right front round dial knob, left thumbwheel on/off/volume knob, woven grill area, pull-up handle, AM, bat..............$10.00 – 20.00

P810A, horizontal, 6¾x8x2⅜", 1963, nutmeg leather and chrome, five transistors, right front dial, left thumbwheel on/off/volume knob, large metal perforated grill area, metal handle, made in USA, AM, bat............$10.00 – 15.00

P811A, horizontal, 6¾x8x2⅜", 1963, pearl white leather and chrome, five transistors, right front dial, left thumbwheel on/off/volume knob, large metal perforated grill area, metal handle, AM, bat ....$10.00 – 15.00

P815A, horizontal, 3⅜x6x1⅞", 1961, plastic, seven transistors, upper right front horizontal slide rule dial with right side thumbwheel tuning, lower right side on/off/volume knob, left checkered grill area, AM, bat ....$20.00 – 25.00

P820, vertical, 4¾x3x1⅜", 1961, black and white plastic, six transistors, upper front horizontal slide rule dial with right side thumbwheel tuning, right side thumbwheel on/off/vol-

ume knob, lattice grill area, made in USA, AM, bat ....$10.00 – 15.00

P820A, vertical, 4¾x3x1⅜", 1961, black and white plastic, six transistors, upper front horizontal slide rule dial with right side thumbwheel tuning, right side thumbwheel on/off/volume knob, lattice grill area, made in USA, AM, bat ....$10.00 – 15.00

P821, vertical, 4¾x3x1⅜", 1961, blue and white plastic, six transistors, upper front horizontal slide rule dial with right side thumbwheel tuning, right side thumbwheel on/off/volume knob, lattice grill area, made in USA, AM, bat ....$10.00 – 15.00

P821A, vertical, 4¾x3x1⅜", 1961, blue and white plastic, six transistors, upper front horizontal slide rule dial with right side thumbwheel tuning, right side thumbwheel on/off/volume knob, lattice grill area, made in USA, AM, bat ....$10.00 – 15.00

P825, vertical, 4x2⅞x1⅛", 1961, desert green & sand plastic, upper right front round dial with right side thumbwheel tuning, upper left front thumbwheel on/off/volume knob, lower grill area with circular cut-outs, swing handle, made in USA, AM, bat............**$20.00 – 25.00**

P825A, vertical, 4x2⅞x1⅛", 1961, plastic, upper right front round dial with right side thumbwheel tuning, upper left front thumbwheel on/off/volume knob, lower grill area with circular cut-outs, swing handle, made in USA, AM, bat......................**$20.00 – 25.00**

P826, vertical, 4x2⅞x1⅛", 1961, black & white plastic, upper right front round dial with right side thumbwheel tuning, upper left front thumbwheel on/off/volume knob, lower grill area with circular cut-outs, swing handle, made in USA, AM, bat............**$20.00 – 25.00**

P826A, vertical, 4x2⅞x1⅛", 1961, black & white plastic, upper right front round dial with right side thumbwheel tuning, upper left front thumbwheel on/off/volume knob, lower grill area with circular cut-outs, swing handle, made in USA, AM, bat............**$20.00 – 25.00**

P830A, vertical, 4¾x2¾x1¼", 1960, charcoal plastic, six transistors, upper front horizontal slide rule dial with right side thumbwheel tuning, right side thumbwheel on/off/volume knob, lower perforated grill area, rear metal fold-out stand, AM, bat..........**$20.00 – 30.00**

P830C, vertical, 4¾x2¾x1¼", 1960, charcoal plastic, six transistors,

upper front horizontal slide rule dial with right side thumbwheel tuning, right side thumbwheel on/off/volume knob, lower perforated grill area, rear metal fold-out stand, AM, bat..........**$20.00 – 30.00**

P830E, vertical, 4¾x2¾x1¼", 1960, charcoal plastic, six transistors, upper front horizontal slide rule dial with right side thumbwheel tuning, right side thumbwheel on/off/volume knob, lower perforated grill area, rear metal fold-out stand, AM, bat..........**$20.00 – 30.00**

P831A, vertical, 4¾x2¾x1¼", 1960, blue plastic, six transistors, upper front horizontal slide rule dial with right side thumbwheel tuning, right side thumbwheel on/off/volume knob, lower perforated grill area, rear metal fold-out stand, AM, bat.....................**$20.00 – 30.00**

P831C, vertical, 4¾x2¾x1¼", 1960, blue plastic, six transistors, upper front horizontal slide rule dial with right side thumbwheel tuning, right side thumbwheel on/off/volume knob, lower perfo-

rated grill area, rear metal fold-out stand, AM, bat.........$20.00 – 30.00

P835 "Super 6," horizontal, 6x8x3", 1961, saddle brown leatherette, six transistors, upper right front dial knob, lower on/off/volume knob, left silver textured grill area, handle, AM, bat...............$15.00 – 20.00

P840, horizontal, 6⅛x8½x3⅛", 1961, saddle brown leatherette, seven transistors, upper right front dial, lower on/off/volume knob, left chrome grill area with oval cut-outs, leather handle, AM, bat.........$15.00 – 20.00

P840A, horizontal, 6⅛x8½x3⅛", 1961, leatherette, seven transistors, upper right front dial, lower on/off/volume knob, left chrome grill area with oval cut-outs, leather handle, AM, bat........$15.00 – 20.00

P845A, horizontal, 1963, eight transistors, slanted top, right front vertical dial with thumbwheel tuning, thumbwheel on/off/volume knob, large perforated grill area, handle, AM, bat.....................$15.00 – 20.00

P850B, vertical, 3½x2⅜x1", 1962, black plastic and metal, six transistors,

upper right front round dial with right side thumbwheel tuning, left front thumbwheel on/off/volume knob, lower perforated grill area, top ring handle, AM, bat...$25.00 – 35.00

P850C, vertical, 3½x2⅜x1", 1962, black plastic and metal, six·transistors, upper right front round dial with right side thumbwheel tuning, left front thumbwheel on/off/volume knob, lower perforated grill area, top ring handle, made in USA, AM, bat.............$25.00 – 35.00

P850D, vertical, 3½x2⅜x1", 1962, black plastic and metal, six transistors, upper right front round dial knob, left front thumbwheel on/off/volume knob, lower perforated grill area, top ring handle, made in USA, AM, bat.........$25.00 – 35.00

P850E, vertical, 3½x2⅜x1", 1962, plastic and metal, six transistors, upper right front round dial knob, left front thumbwheel on/off/volume knob, lower perforated grill area, top ring handle, AM, bat.............................$25.00 – 35.00

P851C, vertical, 3½x2⅜x1", 1962, white plastic and metal, six transistors, upper right front round dial with right side thumbwheel tuning, left front thumbwheel on/off/volume knob, lower perforated grill area, top ring handle, made in USA, AM, bat.............$25.00 – 35.00

P851D, vertical, 3½x2⅜x1", 1962, white plastic and metal, six transistors, upper right front round dial knob, left front thumbwheel on/off/volume knob, lower perforated grill area, top ring handle, AM, bat ....$25.00 – 35.00

P855, horizontal, 5⅛x9x2⅜", 1964, black plastic, eight transistors, right front round dial, upper left thumbwheel on/of/volume knob, perforated grill area, fold-down handle, AM, bat ....$10.00 – 15.00

P855A, horizontal, 5⅛x9x2⅜",1964, eight transistors, right front round dial, upper left thumbwheel on/off/volume knob, perforated grill area, fold-down handle, AM, bat...$10.00 – 15.00

P856, horizontal, 5⅛x9x2⅜", 1964, gray plastic, eight transistors, right front round dial, upper left thumbwheel on/off/volume knob, perforated grill area, fold-down handle, AM, bat ....$10.00 – 15.00

P856A, horizontal, 1964, eight transistors, right front round dial, upper left thumbwheel on/off/volume knob, perforated grill area, fold-down handle, made in USA, AM, bat ....$10.00 – 15.00

P860 "Sportmate," vertical, 6½x4⅛x1⅞", 1963, ginger plastic, eight transistors, slanted upper front with horizontal dial, thumbwheel tuning and on/off/volume knobs, lower perforated grill area with center rifle logo, AM, bat.$10.00 – 15.00

P860A "Sportmate," vertical, 6½x4⅛x1⅞", 1963, ginger plastic, eight transistors, slanted upper front with horizontal dial, thumbwheel tuning and on/off/volume knobs, lower

perforated grill area with center rifle logo, AM, bat ....$10.00 – 15.00

P860E "Sportmate," vertical, 6½x4⅛x1⅞", 1963, plastic, eight transistors, slanted upper front with horizontal dial, thumbwheel tuning and on/off/volume knobs, lower perforated grill area with center rifle logo, AM, bat.....$10.00 – 15.00

860F "Sportmate," vertical, 6½x4⅛x1⅞", 1963, plastic, eight transistors, slanted upper front with horizontal dial, thumbwheel tuning and on/off/volume knobs, lower perforated grill area with center rifle logo, AM, bat.....$10.00 – 15.00

P865, horizontal, 1961, black & chrome, 11 transistors, upper front horizontal two-band slide rule dial, two knobs, large lower lattice grill area, telescoping antenna, handle, AM, FM, bat...............$20.00 – 25.00

P865A, horizontal, 1961, 11 transistors, upper front horizontal two-band slide rule dial, two knobs, large lower lattice grill area, telescoping antenna, handle, AM, FM, bat............................$20.00 – 25.00

P870 "General," horizontal, 2¼x7¼x6¼", 1961, black, eight transistors, has bottom clip-stand for use as a portable or car radio, front double-sided horizontal slide rule dial, two knobs, top perforated grill area, telescoping antenna, strap, AM, bat...........$15.00 – 20.00

P870A, horizontal, 2¼x7¼x6¼", 1961, eight transistors, has bottom clip-stand for use as a portable or car radio, front double-sided horizontal slide rule dial, two knobs, top perforated grill area, telescoping antenna, strap, AM, bat ....$15.00 – 20.00

P875, horizontal, 6¼x8½x3½", 1963, black leather, eight transistors, upper right front dial, lower on/off/volume knob with bass/treble switch, left chrome grill area with oval cut-outs, pushbutton dial light, leather handle, made in USA, AM, bat ....$15.00 – 20.00

P875A, horizontal, 6¼x8½x3½", 1963, leather, eight transistors, upper right front dial, lower on/off/volume knob with bass/treble switch, left chrome grill area with oval cut-outs, pushbutton dial light, leather handle, made in USA, AM, bat ....$15.00 – 20.00

P875D, horizontal, 6¼x8½x3½", 1963, leather, eight transistors, upper right front dial, lower on/off/volume knob with bass/treble switch, left chrome grill area with oval cut-outs, pushbutton dial light, leather handle, made in USA, AM, bat...............$15.00 – 20.00

P880, horizontal, 7x10x3⅛", 1964, honey beige & white, five transis-

tors, right side dial knob, left side on/off/volume knob, large front grill area with upper left logo, AM, AC/bat.....................$15.00 – 20.00

P881, horizontal, 7x10x3⅛", 1964, ebony & white, five transistors, right side dial knob, left side on/off/volume knob, large front grill area with upper left logo, AM, AC/bat.....................$15.00 – 20.00

P885B, vertical, 3⅞x2⅝x1⅛", 1963, six transistors, upper right front round dial knob, upper left front thumbwheel on/off/volume knob, lower grill area with horizontal bars, AM, bat ....$5.00 – 10.00

P885W, vertical, 3⅞x2⅝x1⅛", 1963, black, six transistors, upper right front round dial knob, upper left front thumbwheel on/off/volume knob, lower grill area with horizontal bars, AM, bat ....$5.00 – 10.00

P891A, horizontal, 1965, eight transistors, upper right front dial, two upper left front knobs, large grill area, handle, AM, bat ....$10.00 – 15.00

P905A, horizontal, 1963, black, seven transistors, lower right front window dial with right side thumbwheel tuning, large perforated grill area, swing handle, AM, bat ....$15.00 – 20.00

P911A, vertical, 1963, plastic, upper right front thumbwheel dial, large lower metal perforated grill area, AM, bat ....$10.00 – 15.00

P911D, vertical, 1963, plastic, upper right front thumbwheel dial, large lower metal perforated grill area, AM, bat............**$10.00 – 15.00**

P911J, vertical, 1963, plastic, upper right front thumbwheel dial, large lower metal perforated grill area, AM, bat......................**$10.00 – 15.00**

P915A, vertical, 1963, plastic, eight transistors, upper right front thumbwheel dial, lower metal perforated grill area, AM, bat.....**$10.00 – 15.00**

P915C, vertical, 1963, plastic, eight transistors, upper right front thumbwheel dial, lower metal perforated grill area, AM, bat.....**$10.00 – 15.00**

P915E, vertical, 1963, plastic, eight transistors, upper right front thumbwheel dial, lower metal perforated grill area, AM, bat.....**$10.00 – 15.00**

P916C, vertical, 1963, plastic, eight transistors, upper right front thumbwheel dial, lower metal perforated grill area, AM, bat.....**$10.00 – 15.00**

P916E, vertical, 4¾x3⅛x1⅜", 1963, plastic, eight transistors, upper right front thumbwheel dial, left side thumbwheel on/off/volume knob, lower metal perforated grill area, AM, bat............**$10.00 – 15.00**

P917C, vertical, 1963, plastic, eight transistors, upper right front thumbwheel dial, lower metal perforated grill area, AM, bat.....**$10.00 – 15.00**

P920A "Long Range," horizontal, 4⅞x8x2¾", 1965, leather, 10 transistors, center front vertical slide rule dial, two right thumbwheel knobs and one tone switch, left metal perforated grill area, leather handle, AM, bat......................**$10.00 – 15.00**

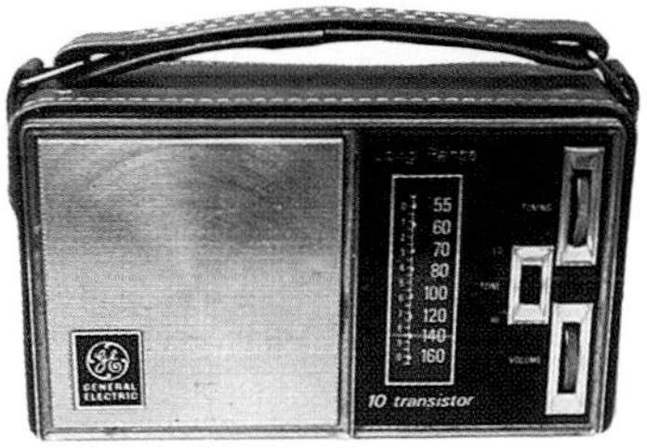

P920B "Long Range," horizontal, 4⅞x8x2¾", 1965, leather, 10 transistors, center front vertical slide rule dial, two right thumbwheel knobs and one tone switch, left metal perforated grill area, leather handle, AM, bat........$10.00 – 15.00

P926, horizontal, 5½x8⅝x3", 1964, charcoal brown, eight transistors, large right front round two-band dial, two upper left front knobs, large grill area with horizontal bars, telescoping antenna, handle, BC, SW, bat......................**$10.00 – 15.00**

P930, horizontal, 6½x9¼x3⅛", 1964, black, eight transistors, upper left front horizontal three-band slide rule dial, large lower perforated grill area, telescoping antenna, handle, AM, 2SW, bat.......**$15.00 – 20.00**

P930A, horizontal, 6½x9¼x3⅛", 1964, eight transistors, upper left front horizontal three-band slide rule dial, large lower perforated grill area, telescoping antenna, handle, AM, 2SW, bat......**$15.00 – 20.00**

P940, horizontal, 5¼x8½x2½", 1964, brown, 13 transistors, right front two-band dial, two right side knobs, large front perforated grill area with AM/FM and tone switches, telescoping antenna, handle, AM, FM, bat..............$10.00 – 15.00

P940C, horizontal, 5¼x8½x2½", 1964, 13 transistors, right front two-band dial, two right side knobs, large front perforated grill area with AM/FM and tone switches, telescoping antenna, handle, AM, FM, bat.....................$10.00 – 15.00

P943C, horizontal, 1965, 14 transistors, right front two-band dial, two right side knobs, large front perforated grill area with AM/FM and AFC switches, telescoping antenna, handle, AM, FM, bat..$10.00 – 15.00

P945B, vertical, 4½x3x1¼", 1965, plastic, upper right front oval window dial with right side thumbwheel tuning, left side thumbwheel on/off/volume knob, lower horizontal grill bars, AM, bat....$5.00 – 10.00

P955A, horizontal, 1963, seven transistors, upper front horizontal slide rule dial, two knobs, hi/lo switch, large lower perforated grill area, handle, AM, bat.........$10.00 – 15.00

P965A, vertical, 1965, leather, 10 transistors, upper front horizontal two-band slide rule dial, lower perforated grill area, telescoping antenna, leather handle, AM, SW, bat..............................$10.00 – 15.00

P968A, vertical, 1965, leather, 10 transistors, upper front horizontal two-band slide rule dial, lower per-

forated grill area, telescoping antenna, leather handle, AM, SW, bat..............................$10.00 – 15.00

P970A, horizontal, 1964, 14 transistors, upper left front round two-band dial, three knobs, two switches, large lower perforated grill area, telescoping antenna, AM, FM, bat.....................$10.00 – 15.00

P975A, vertical, 1964, 15 transistors, upper front horizontal two-band slide rule dial, lower metal perforated grill area with lower right logo, telescoping antenna, leather handle, AM, FM, bat........$10.00 – 15.00

P975B, vertical, 1964, 15 transistors, upper front horizontal two-band slide rule dial, lower metal perforated grill area with lower right logo, telescoping antenna, leather handle, AM, FM, bat ....$10.00 – 15.00

P990A "World Monitor," horizontal, 8½x12x4¾", 1965, leather, 17 transistors, upper front horizontal five-band slide rule dial, large lower perforated grill area, telescoping antenna, leather handle, AM, FM, 2SW, LW, bat ....$15.00 – 20.00

P990C "World Monitor," horizontal, 8½x12x4¾", 1965, leather, 17 transistors, upper front horizontal five-band slide rule dial, large lower metal perforated grill area, two telescoping antennas, rear log pouch, leather handle, AM, FM, 2SW, LW, bat ....$15.00 – 20.00

P995B, vertical, plastic, seven transistors, upper right front thumbwheel dial, large lower metal perforated grill area, AM, bat ....$5.00 – 10.00

P1700A, vertical, 1965, 10 transistors, upper right front window dial with thumbwheel tuning, lower metal perforated grill area, AM, bat............$10.00 – 15.00

P1701A, vertical, 1965, plastic, 10 transistors, upper right front window dial with thumbwheel tuning, lower metal perforated grill area, AM, bat............$10.00 – 15.00

P1710C, vertical, 4¼x2¾x1¼", 1965, plastic, upper front large round dial knob, right side thumbwheel on/off/volume knob, lattice grill area with lower left logo, AM, bat............$5.00 – 10.00

P1730B, vertical, 4½x2⅝x1¼", plastic, eight transistors, upper front round dial, right side thumbwheel on/off/volume knob, lower metal perforated grill area, AM, bat ....$10.00 – 15.00

P1740 "Micro Electronic," radio with clock/recharger/speaker unit, 1⅛x3¼x2¼" (radio only), 1966, plastic, radio has front slide rule dial with two right side thumbwheel knobs and a top metal perforated grill area, radio fits into clock/recharger/speaker base for use as a table set, AM, bat.
radio only ....$25.00 – 30.00
radio with base ....$50.00 – 60.00

P1757, vertical, 4x2½x1½", plastic, upper right front window dial with right side thumbwheel tuning, left side thumbwheel on/off/volume knob, lower horizontal grill bars, braided strap, made in Hong Kong, AM, bat ....$5.00 – 10.00

P1758, vertical, 4x2½x1½", plastic, upper right front window dial with right side thumbwheel tuning, left side thumbwheel on/off/volume knob, lower horizontal grill bars, braided strap, made in Hong Kong, AM, bat ....$5.00 – 10.00

P1761, horizontal, 2¾x4½x1¼", plastic, upper right front round dial with right side thumbwheel tuning, right side thumbwheel on/off/volume knob, metal perforated grill area, AM, bat ....$15.00 – 20.00

P1791E, vertical, plastic, large upper front round two-band dial, lower grill area with horizontal bars, telescoping antenna, left side strap, AM, FM, bat ......$5.00 – 10.00

P1805A, horizontal, 4½x6¾x2⅛", plastic, nine transistors, upper front horizontal slide rule dial, lower metal perforated grill area, left side thumbwheel knob, handle, AM, bat.......................$10.00 – 15.00

P1818B, horizontal, 5x7x2½", 1965, plastic, 10 transistors, upper right

front round two-band dial, lower AM/FM switch, horizontal grill bars, fold-down handle, AM, FM, bat...............................$5.00 – 10.00

P1821L, horizontal, 4½x6¾x2⅛", plastic, 11 transistors, upper front horizontal two-band slide rule dial, lower metal perforated grill area with right FM/AM switch and left logo, left side thumbwheel knob, telescoping antenna, handle, AM/FM, bat ....$15.00 – 20.00

P1871A, horizontal, 4¾x6¾x2½", plastic, eight transistors, right front round dial knob, left front thumbwheel on/off/volume knob, lower metal textured and perforated grill area, fold-down handle, AM, bat..$10.00 – 15.00

P2750D, vertical, 4x2⅞x1¼", plastic, upper right front window dial with right side thumbwheel tuning, large left front checkered grill area, left side strap, AM, bat.......$5.00 – 10.00

P2790F, vertical, 4x2½x1⅜", plastic, solid state, upper right front window dial with right side thumbwheel tuning, left side thumbwheel on/off/volume knob, large grill area with horizontal bars, left side braided strap, made in Hong Kong, AM, bat ....$5.00 – 10.00

P8501, vertical, 3½x2⅜x1", 1961, black plastic and metal, six transistors, upper right front round dial with right side thumbwheel tuning, left front thumbwheel on/off/volume knob, lower perforated grill area, top ring handle, AM, bat .... **$25.00 – 35.00**

P8511, vertical, 3½x2⅜x1", 1961, white plastic and metal, six transistors, upper right front round dial with right side thumbwheel tuning, left front thumbwheel on/off/volume knob, lower perforated grill area, top ring handle, AM, bat .... **$25.00 – 35.00**

P9001, horizontal, 1962, plastic, seven transistors, upper right front horizontal slide rule dial with right side thumbwheel tuning, lower right side on/off/volume knob, left checkered grill area, AM, bat....... **$20.00 – 30.00**

P9001A, horizontal, 1962, white plastic, seven transistors, upper right front horizontal slide rule dial with right side thumbwheel tuning, lower right side on/off/volume knob, left checkered silver grill area, AM, bat............. **$20.00 – 30.00**

P9011, horizontal, 1962, plastic, seven transistors, upper right front horizontal slide rule dial with right side thumbwheel tuning, lower right side on/off/volume knob, left checkered grill area, AM, bat ...... **$20.00 – 30.00**

P9011A, horizontal, 1962, honey beige plastic, seven transistors, upper right front horizontal slide rule dial with right side thumbwheel

tuning, lower right side on/off/volume knob, left checkered gold grill area, AM, bat............. **$20.00 – 30.00**

S-15, horizontal/kit radio, 4½x7½x2⅜", 1963, sold as a kit, leather, upper right front round dial, left front thumbwheel on/off/volume knob, center grill area with circular cut-outs, handle, AM, bat .... **$10.00 – 15.00**

Genie
Boy's Radio, vertical, 3⅞x2½x1⅛", plastic, two transistors, upper front window dial with left side thumbwheel tuning, right side thumbwheel on/off/volume knob, lower round metal perforated grill area, made in Japan, AM, bat........... **$45.00 – 55.00**

Global
GFM-931, horizontal, 4x6¾x1½", plastic, 10 transistors, finished on both sides, top wrap-over see-through two-band dial, lower metal perforated grill area with logo, top left telescoping antenna, AM, FM, bat........................... **$30.00 – 40.00**

GR-5T6, horizontal, 2½x4⅛x1¼", plastic, six transistors, right front see-through panel with window dial, right side thumbwheel tuning, upper right front thumbwheel on/off/volume knob, left grill area with horizontal bars, made in Japan, AM, bat..........$65.00 – 85.00

GR-201 "Boy's Radio," horizontal, 2½x4x1¼", plastic, two transistors, right front see-through panel with window dial, right side thumbwheel tuning, upper right front thumbwheel on/off/volume knob, left grill area with horizontal bars, made in Japan, AM, bat.......$65.00 – 85.00

GR-711, vertical, 3¾x2¾x1", plastic, six transistors, upper front see-through panel with V-shaped window dial, right side thumbwheel tuning, left side thumbwheel on/off/volume knob, lower metal perforated grill area, swing handle, made in Japan, AM, bat ....$100.00 – 125.00

GR-823, horizontal, 2⅞x7⅞x1¾", plastic, eight transistors, two upper front horizontal slide rule dials — one AM, one SW — lower metal perforated grill area with logo, BC/SW switch, made in Japan, AM, SW, bat..............$25.00 – 35.00

GR-900, vertical, 4½x3x1¼", 1963, plastic, nine transistors, upper front see-through panel with half-round dial and large "9," right side thumbwheel tuning, right side thumbwheel on/off/volume knob, lower metal textured and perforated grill area with logo, made in Japan, AM, bat ......$125.00 – 150.00

GR-920, horizontal, 1965, 10 transistors, upper front horizontal two-band slide rule dial, right side thumbwheel knobs, horizontal grill bars, telescoping antenna, AM, FM, bat ....$15.00 – 20.00

GRC-715, horizontal/clock radio, 3⅝x6¼x1¾", plastic, eight transis-

tors, upper front slanted horizontal slide rule dial with upper right front thumbwheel tuning knob, upper left front thumbwheel on/off/volume knob, lower metal textured and perforated grill area with left alarm clock face, made in Japan, AM, bat........$80.00 – 100.00

Global Imperial

HT-8054, vertical, 4¼x2½x1¼", plastic, eight transistors, metal front, upper right window dial with right side thumbwheel tuning, top left thumbwheel on/off/volume knob, lower grill area with horizontal slots, AM, bat........$10.00 – 20.00

Globe

Boy's Radio, vertical, 3½x2½x1¼", plastic, two transistors, upper front window dial with top right thumbwheel tuning, top left thumbwheel on/off/volume knob, lower metal textured and perforated grill area, made in Japan, AM, bat............$45.00 – 55.00

Gloria

Boy's Radio, vertical, 3¾x2½x1¼", plastic, two transistors, upper right front window dial with right side thumbwheel tuning, left side thumbwheel on/off/volume knob, round grill area with segmented horizontal bars, AM, bat.............$40.00 – 50.00

GMK

TN-201, vertical, 4x2½x1⅜", plastic, two transistors, rounded upper right corner, upper right front dial knob, left side thumbwheel on/off/volume knob, lower grill area with horizontal bars, made in Japan, AM, bat.........$50.00 – 60.00

Golden Shield

3500, vertical, 4x2⅜x1⅛", plastic, six transistors, upper right front round dial area with center gold shield and right side thumbwheel tuning, upper left front thumbwheel on/off/volume knob over-laps large metal perforated grill area, AM, bat.............$25.00 – 35.00

3608, vertical, 1961, plastic, six transistors, upper right front round dial area with center gold shield and right side thumbwheel tuning, upper left front thumbwheel on/off/volume knob overlaps large metal perforated grill area, AM, bat.................$25.00 – 35.00

7040, horizontal, 3½x6x1½", plastic, upper front horizontal two-band slide rule dial, upper right front thumbwheel tuning knob, upper left front thumbwheel on/off/volume knob, large perforated grill area with gold logo, telescoping antenna, AM, Marine, bat.................$30.00 – 40.00

7109 "Ten Power," horizontal, 3¾x 6⅛x1¾", plastic, eight transistors, right front dial with right side thumbwheel tuning, lower right front on/off/volume window with

right side thumbwheel knob, large left metal perforated grill area, shield logo, made in Japan, AM, bat.............................$25.00 – 35.00

7186, vertical, plastic, six transis-tors, step-back top, upper left front window dial over large grill area with horizontal bars, upper left thumbwheel tuning, right side thumbwheel on/off/volume knob, AM, bat......................$10.00 – 20.00

7210, vertical, 4⅛x2½x1¼", plastic, six transistors, upper right front round dial with right side thumbwheel tun-ing, left side thumbwheel on/off/vol-ume knob, lower metal perforated grill area, shield logo, made in Japan, AM, bat.........................$15.00 – 25.00

7309 "Personal," vertical, plas-tic, six transistors, upper right front window dial with right side thumbwheel tuning, upper left front golden shield logo, lower metal perforated grill area, AM, bat.........................$15.00 – 25.00

Gold-Tone

2 transistor (no #), horizontal, 2¾x4x1¼", plastic, two transistors, large right front dial knob, lower right side thumbwheel on/off/volume knob, left front grill area with horizontal bars, made in Japan, AM, bat....................$45.00 – 55.00

Boy's Radio, vertical, plastic, two transistors, upper left front window dial with left side thumbwheel tuning, right side thumbwheel on/off/volume knob, lower round metal perforated grill area, AM, bat.........$45.00 – 55.00

Boy's Radio, horizontal/table, 4½x6½x4¼", plastic, two transistors, upper right front dial, lower on/off/volume knob, left checkered grill area, feet, made in Japan, AM, bat....................$40.00 – 50.00

Grace II
Boy's Radio, vertical, 4x2⅝x1¼", plastic, two transistors, upper right

front window dial with right side thumbwheel tuning, left side thumbwheel on/off/volume knob, lower lattice grill area, made in Japan, AM, bat..........$55.00 – 65.00

Graetz
40 F "Flirt," horizontal, 1965, plastic, six transistors, upper right front window dial with right side thumbwheel tuning, lower right side thumbwheel on/off/volume knob, large left metal perforated grill area, strap, made in West Germany, AM, bat......................$45.00 – 55.00

40 H "Flirt," vertical, 1966, plastic, six transistors, upper right front window dial with right side thumbwheel tuning, top thumbwheel on/off/volume knob, lower metal perforated grill area, strap, made in West Germany, AM, bat............$35.00 – 45.00

41 C "Grazia," horizontal, 1965, plastic, nine transistors, two right front vertical slide rule dials with right side thumbwheel tuning, top thumbwheel on/off/volume knob, left metal perforated grill area, pull-up handle, made in West Germany, AM, FM, bat....$20.00 – 30.00

41 F "Grazia," horizontal, 1966, plastic, nine transistors, upper front horizontal two-band slide rule dial, right side on/off/volume knob, large lower metal perforated grill area, handle, made in West Germany, AM, FM, bat....$20.00 – 30.00

42 F "Flip," vertical, 1966, plastic, 10 transistors, upper front horizontal two-band slide rule dial with right side thumbwheel tuning, right side thumbwheel on/off/volume knob, lower metal perforated grill area, left side strap, made in West Germany, AM, FM, bat.............$25.00 – 35.00

42 H "Flip," vertical, 1966, plastic, eight transistors, upper front horizontal two-band slide rule dial with right side thumbwheel tuning, right side thumbwheel on/off/volume knob, lower metal perforated grill area, left side strap, made in West Germany, AM, FM, bat ....$25.00 – 35.00

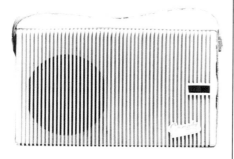

830 "Susi," horizontal, 1959, plastic, six transistors, right front window dial over large grill area with vertical bars, right side thumbwheel tuning knob, left side thumbwheel on/off/volume knob, rear AM/LW switch, handle, made in West Germany, AM, LW, bat....$20.00 – 30.00

1131 "Grazia," horizontal, 1961, soft plastic, nine transistors, top two-band slide rule dial with right side thumbwheel tuning, left side thumbwheel on/off/volume knob, padded front, long strap contains FM antenna, made in West Germany, AM, FM, bat.........$25.00 – 35.00

Grand Prix

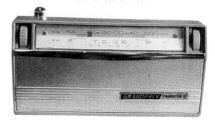

GP-901, horizontal, 3¼x6⅝x1¾", plastic, nine transistors, upper front horizontal two-band dial, upper right thumbwheel tuning knob, right side band switch, upper left thumbwheel on/off/volume knob, lower metal perforated grill area, telescoping antenna, made in Japan, bat.................$20.00 – 30.00

HR-22, vertical, 3¾x2⅜x1¼", plastic, six transistors, upper right front window dial with right side thumbwheel tuning, upper left front on/off/volume window with left side thumbwheel knob, lower metal grill area with horizontal slots, made in Japan, AM, bat......................$15.00 – 20.00

Grundig

Micro-Boy, horizontal portable with optional speaker box, 1960, plastic, six transistors, portable radio unit has upper right front round dial with right side thumbwheel tuning, upper left front thumbwheel on/off/volume knob, metal perforated grill area, radio slides into speaker box for use as a table model, made in West Germany, AM, bat. radio only ....$60.00 – 85.00
with speaker box ...$125.00 – 150.00

Micro-Boy 201, horizontal portable with optional speaker box, radio

measures 3x4⅝x1⅜", 1961, plastic, six transistors, portable radio unit has upper right front round two-band dial with right side thumbwheel tuning, upper left front thumbwheel on/off/volume knob, metal perforated grill area, radio slides into speaker box for use as a table model, made in West Germany, AM, LW, bat.
radio only ....$60.00 – 85.00
with speaker box ...$125.00 – 150.00

Micro-Boy 202, horizontal, 1962, plastic, six transistors, top horizontal wrap-over two-band dial with right side thumbwheel tuning, right side thumbwheel on/off/volume knob, lower metal perforated grill area, made in West Germany, AM, LW, bat................$30.00 – 40.00

Micro-Boy 204, horizontal, 1964, plastic, six transistors, top horizontal wrap-over two-band dial with right side thumbwheel tuning, right side thumbwheel on/off/volume knob, lower metal perforated grill area, made in West Germany, AM, LW, bat................$30.00 – 40.00

Micro-Boy 400, vertical, 4¾x3x1", plastic & metal, upper front horizontal slide rule dial with right side thumbwheel tuning, left side thumbwheel on/off/volume knob, lower perforated grill area, bat...........$20.00 – 30.00

Micro-Transistor-Boy 59, horizontal portable with optional speaker box, 1959, plastic, six transistors, portable radio unit has upper right front round dial with right side thumbwheel tuning, upper left

front thumbwheel on/off/volume knob, metal perforated grill area, radio slides into speaker box for use as a table model, made in West Germany, AM, bat.
radio only ....$60.00 – 85.00
with speaker box ...$125.00 – 150.00

Mini-Boy, horizontal portable with optional speaker box, 1960, plastic, six transistors, front diagonally divided with brass trim, right side see-through window dial with thumbwheel tuning, lower right front thumbwheel on/off/volume knob, left painted perforated grill area, rear fold-out stand, radio slides into speaker box for use as a table model, made in West Germany, AM, bat.
radio only ....$50.00 – 75.00
with speaker box ...$110.00 – 135.00

Mini-Boy Transistor 200, horizontal portable with optional speaker box, 2½x4⅛x1", 1961, plastic, six transistors, front diagonally divided with brass trim, right side see-through window dial with thumbwheel tuning, lower right front thumbwheel on/off/volume knob, left painted perforated grill area, rear fold-out stand, radio slides into speaker box for use as a table model, made in West Germany, AM, bat.
radio only ....$50.00 – 75.00
with speaker box...$110.00 – 135.00

Ocean-Boy 204, horizontal, 1965, 17 transistors, right front vertical six-band slide rule dial and nine pushbuttons, left grill area with horizontal bars, telescoping antenna, handle, LW, MW, 3SW, FM, bat............................$40.00 – 50.00

Prima-Boy, horizontal, 1961, plastic, nine transistors, top horizontal wrap-over three-band dial with right front thumbwheel tuning, upper left front thumbwheel on/off/volume knob, large metal perforated grill area with four horizontal bars, telescoping antenna, plastic handle, made in West Germany, AM, FM, LW, bat......................$25.00 – 30.00

Prima-Boy 201, horizontal, 1962, plastic, nine transistors, top horizontal wrap-over three-band dial with right front thumbwheel tuning, upper left front thumbwheel on/off/volume knob, large metal perforated grill area with four horizontal bars, telescoping antenna, plastic handle, made in West Germany, AM, FM, LW, bat................................$25.00 – 30.00

Prima-Boy 201E, horizontal, 1962, plastic, nine transistors, top horizontal wrap-over three-band dial with right front thumbwheel tuning, upper left front thumbwheel on/off/volume knob, large metal perforated grill area with four horizontal bars, telescoping antenna, handle, made in West Germany, AM, FM, SW, bat ....$25.00 – 35.00

Prima-Boy 203, horizontal, 1963, plastic, nine transistors, top horizontal wrap-over three-band dial with right

front thumbwheel tuning, upper left front thumbwheel on/off/volume knob, large metal perforated grill area with four horizontal bars, telescoping antenna, plastic handle, made in West Germany, AM, FM, LW, bat................................$25.00 – 35.00

Prima-Boy 204, horizontal, 1964, plastic, nine transistors, three top horizontal dials with top right thumbwheel tuning, top left thumbwheel on/off/volume knob, four top pushbuttons, front perforated grill area, telescoping antenna, plastic handle, made in West Germany, AM, FM, SW, bat..............................$25.00 – 35.00

Solo-Boy 201, horizontal portable with optional speaker box, radio measures 2⅛x3⅛x1", 1961, plastic, six transistors, portable radio unit has upper right front horizontal slide rule dial with thumbwheel tuning, lower left front on/off/volume window with right side thumbwheel knob, metal perforated grill area, radio slides into wedge-shaped speaker box with brass foot for use as a table model, made in West Germany, AM, bat.
radio only ....$55.00 – 75.00
with speaker box...$150.00 – 175.00

Taschen-Transistor-Boy, vertical, 1958, plastic, six transistors, upper left front window dial with thumbwheel tuning, upper right front on/off/volume window, lower metal grill area, metal swing handle, made in West Germany, AM, bat.............$40.00 – 50.00

Taschen-Transistor-Boy 59, vertical, 1959, plastic, six transistors, upper left front window dial with thumbwheel tuning, upper right front on/off/volume window, lower metal grill area, metal swing handle, made in West Germany, AM, bat.............$40.00 – 50.00

Teddy-Boy II/59E, horizontal, 1961, eight transistors, rounded case with top three band slide rule dial, pushbuttons, and two knobs, large front lattice area, two telescoping antennas, AM, FM, SW, bat.............$30.00 – 40.00

Transistor-Box, horizontal, 1958, leather, six transistors, right side dial knob, left side on/off/volume knob, large front grill area with rectangular cut-outs & center logo, leather handle, made in West Germany, AM, bat ....$30.00 – 40.00

Transistor-Box 59, horizontal, 1959, leather, six transistors, right side dial knob, left side on/off/volume knob, large front grill area with rectangular cut-outs & center logo, leather handle, made in West Germany, AM, bat ....$30.00 – 40.00

Transonette 89 "Black Magic Standard," horizontal/table, 1963, nine transistors, lower front horizontal two-band slide rule dial, large upper lattice grill area with three right

pushbuttons, two telescoping antennas, AM, FM, bat..$15.00 – 20.00

Transonette 99U, horizontal/table, 1964, nine transistors, lower front horizontal four-band slide rule dial, large upper lattice grill area with seven right pushbuttons, telescoping antenna, AM, FM, LW, SW, bat.............$20.00 – 25.00

Transworld Ambassador, horizontal, upper front horizontal four-band dial with right thumbwheel tuning, upper left front thumbwheel on/off/volume knob, lower grill area with horizontal bars and lower right logo, top pushbuttons, two telescoping antennas, handle, AM, FM, SW, LW, bat........$25.00 – 35.00

Transworld Junior, horizontal, 6¼x10¾x3¾", 1961, eight transistors, upper right front round three-band dial overlaps horizontal grill bars, thumbwheel knobs, three pushbuttons, telescoping antenna, handle, AM, FM, SW, bat.$20.00 – 30.00

Halex

Boy's Radio, vertical, 4¼x2⅝x1⅜", plastic, two transistors, upper left front thumbwheel dial, upper

115

right thumbwheel on/off/volume knob, lower metal textured and perforated grill area with center vertical nameplate, made in Japan, AM, bat ....$55.00 – 65.00

Hallicrafters

TR-88, horizontal, 1958, leather, six transistors, upper left front dial knob, upper right front on/off/volume knob, lower grill area with rectangular cut-outs, leather handle, AM, bat ....$30.00 – 40.00

Hamilton

YT-161, vertical, 4x2½x1¼", plastic, six transistors, upper right thumbwheel dial knob, left on/off/volume window with left side thumbwheel knob, lower metal perforated grill area, AM, bat..............$25.00 – 35.00

Harlie

Boy's Radio, vertical, 4x2½x1", plastic, two transistors, upper left front window dial with left side thumbwheel tuning, right side thumbwheel on/off/volume knob, round metal perforated grill area, made in Japan, AM, bat ....$45.00 – 55.00

TR-661, vertical, plastic, six transistors, upper left front window dial with left side thumbwheel tuning, lower round metal perforated grill area, swing handle, AM, bat ....$30.00 – 40.00

Harpers

2TP-110, vertical, 3¼x2¼x1¼", plastic, large front round dial, top on/off/switch, no speaker, earphone is wired in, no volume control, made in Japan, AM, bat........$75.00 – 85.00

547F, horizontal, plastic, diagonally divided front with right round dial and left horizontal grill bars, lower perforated horizontal panel, AM, bat.............................$25.00 – 35.00

GK-200, horizontal, 1962, eight transistors, upper front horizontal two-band slide rule dial with thumbwheel tuning, left on/off/volume window, lower perforated grill area, top pushbutton, telescoping antenna, AM, SW, bat........$30.00 – 40.00

GK-631, vertical, 1962, plastic, six transistors, upper front wedge-shaped window dial with right side**

thumbwheel tuning, left side thumbwheel on/off/volume knob, lower chrome grill area with horizontal slots, AM, bat.........$100.00 – 125.00

GK-900, vertical, 4⅜x2⅞x1⅛", plastic, nine transistors, upper front window dial with right side thumbwheel tuning, left side thumbwheel on/off/volume knob, lower chrome grill area with horizontal slots, AM, bat..........$85.00 – 100.00

Heathkit
GR-151A, horizontal, 6½x8⅛x3¼", leather, six transistors, lower right front dial knob, lower left front on/off/volume knob, large grill area with circular cut-outs, leather handle, AM, bat ....$10.00 – 15.00

XR-1, horizontal/kit radio, 8x9x3¾", 1957, gray plastic, six transistors, right & left side knobs, large front metal perforated grill area, upper front built-in handle, AM, bat.....................$10.00 – 15.00

XR-1L, horizontal/kit radio, 7¼x9½x4", 1958, leather, six transis-

tors, right & left side knobs, large front grill area with cut-outs, leather handle, AM, bat.........$10.00 – 15.00

XR-1P, horizontal/kit radio, 7¼x9½x4", 1958, two-tone blue plastic, six transistors, right & left side knobs, large front grill area with horizontal bars, pull-out handle, AM, bat...............$15.00 – 20.00

XR-2L, horizontal/kit radio, 7x10x3⅝", 1960, leather and plastic, six transistors, wedge-shaped case with side knobs, large front grill area with lower right logo, handle, AM, bat ....$10.00 – 15.00

XR-2P, horizontal/kit radio, 7x10x3⅝", 1960, plastic, six transistors, wedge-shaped case with side knobs, large front grill area with lower right logo, handle, AM, bat ....$10.00 – 15.00

Hemisphere
AM-6T4, vertical, 1964, six transistors, upper right front window dial with right side thumbwheel tuning, left side thumbwheel on/off/volume knob, perforated grill area, AM, bat.....................$10.00 – 15.00

AM-8T4, vertical, 1964, eight transistors, upper right front window dial with right side thumbwheel tuning, upper left front on/off/volume window with left side thumbwheel knob, perforated grill area, AM, bat.......................$10.00 – 15.00

Hi-Delity

6T-330, vertical, plastic, six transistors, upper front see-through plastic panel with large thumbwheel dial knob, left side thumbwheel on/off/volume knob, metal perforated grill area, AM, bat...$100.00 – 125.00

7TA-1X, horizontal, 1964, eight transistors, right front two-band window dial with right side thumbwheel tuning, lower right thumbwheel on/off/volume knob, left grill area with horizontal bars, telescoping antenna, AM, SW, bat......................$75.00 – 95.00

7TA-1Y, horizontal, 1964, eight transistors, right front two-band window dial with right side

thumbwheel tuning, lower right thumbwheel on/off/volume knob, left grill area with horizontal bars, telescoping antenna, AM, SW, bat......................$75.00 – 95.00

8T-888, horizontal, 3⅝x6x1⅜", 1963, plastic, eight transistors, upper right front dial with right side thumbwheel tuning, lower right front on/off/volume window with right side thumbwheel knob, left metal perforated grill area, made in Japan, AM, bat......................$30.00 – 40.00

CFM-3-1200S, horizontal, 1964, 10 transistors, upper front horizontal three-band slide rule dial, large lower grill area with right and left switches, telescoping antenna, AM, FM, SW, bat ....$20.00 – 25.00

CFM-1200S, horizontal, 1964, 10 transistors, upper front horizontal two-band slide rule dial, large lower grill area with right and left switches, telescoping antenna, AM, FM, bat.............................$20.00 – 25.00

N-601, horizontal, 1963, six transistors, upper right front window dial with right side thumbwheel tuning, lower right side thumbwheel on/off/volume knob, large grill area with vertical slots, AM, bat ....$10.00 – 15.00

N-801, horizontal, 1964, eight transistors, upper right front window dial with right side thumbwheel tuning, lower right side thumbwheel on/off/volume knob, large grill area with vertical slots, AM, bat...........................$10.00 – 15.00

PT-600, horizontal, 3⅜x5x1½", plastic, six transistors, right front round dial knob, top thumbwheel on/off/volume knob, metal perforated front panel with left horseshoe-shaped grill area, made in Japan, AM, bat.........$35.00 – 45.00

SR-H600 "HiFidelity," horizontal, 1964, eight transistors, upper front horizontal four-band slide rule dial, lower perforated grill area, telescoping antenna, handle, AM, 3SW, bat............................$20.00 – 25.00

STH-601, horizontal, 1963, six transistors, diagonally divided front with right globe dial and left grill area, two knobs, base, handle, AM, bat............................$20.00 – 30.00

Hi-Lite
STW-6, horizontal/clock radio, 1964, six transistors, lower front horizontal slide rule dial under center clock face, right and left grill areas, telescoping antenna, AM, bat.........$10.00 – 15.00

Hilton
2 transistor (no #), vertical, plastic, two transistors, upper front window dial with top thumbwheel tuning, right side thumbwheel on/off/volume knob, lower round grill area with concentric circles and center

metal nameplate, made in Japan, AM, bat.....................$50.00 – 60.00

Prince "Boy's Radio," vertical, plastic, two transistors, upper front window dial with right side thumbwheel tuning, lower round metal perforated grill area, made in Japan, AM, bat.........$45.00 – 55.00

TR8A7 "High Fidelity," vertical, 4⅜x2¾x1⅜", plastic, eight transistors, upper left front round dial knob over large metal perforated grill area, right side thumbwheel on/off/volume knob, made in Japan, AM, bat..........$20.00 – 25.00

TR108, vertical, 4⅜x2¾x1⅜", plastic, 10 transistors, upper left front round dial knob over large metal perforated grill area with lower right logo, right side thumbwheel on/off/volume knob, made in Japan, AM, bat.............$20.00 – 25.00

Hitachi
KH-903, horizontal, 5⅞x9⅞x3", 1964, nine transistors, upper front

horizontal two-band slide rule dial, two knobs, large lower grill area with horizontal bars, telescoping antenna, handle, AM, FM, bat ....$15.00 – 20.00

KH-915, horizontal, 1963, nine transistors, right front FM window dial with right side thumbwheel tuning, lower right side thumbwheel on/off/volume knob, left circular checkered grill area, telescoping antenna, FM, bat ......$20.00 – 25.00

KH-960H "Hiphonic," horizontal, 1965, available in black or beige, nine transistors, top horizontal two-band slide rule dial, right side controls, large front perforated grill area with lower left logo, telescoping antenna, AM, FM, bat ....$20.00 – 25.00

KH-1000H "Hiphonic," horizontal, 1965, 10 transistors, top horizontal two-band slide rule dial, two lower right front switches, front grill area with horizontal slots, telescoping antenna, AM, FM, bat....$20.00 – 25.00

KH-1002S "Hiphonic," horizontal, 10 transistors, upper front horizontal three-band slide rule dial with right thumbwheel tuning, upper left front thumbwheel on/off/volume knob, lower grill area with horizontal bars, top pushbuttons, telescoping antenna, handle, FM, SW, MW, bat ....$15.00 – 20.00

KH-1005, horizontal, 6¼x9⅜x2¾", 1963, 10 transistors, upper front horizontal two-band slide rule dial with right thumbwheel tuning, upper left front thumbwheel

on/off/volume knob, lower grill area with horizontal bars and lower right logo, four top pushbuttons, telescoping antenna, handle, AM, FM, bat......................$20.00 – 25.00

KH-1007M, horizontal, 10 transistors, upper front horizontal four-band slide rule dial, lower grill area with horizontal bars and three thumbwheel knobs, top pushbuttons, telescoping antenna, handle, AM, FM, SW, MW, bat................$20.00 – 25.00

T-728, horizontal/clock radio, 1963, seven transistors, right front dial, left alarm clock face, center perforated grill area with logo, AM, bat ....$10.00 – 15.00

TH-600 "Hiphonic," vertical, 1964, plastic, six transistors, upper left front window dial, right side thumbwheel on/off/volume knob, large round metal protruding perforated grill area with movable outer ring used for tuning, top vinyl strap, AM, bat ....$35.00 – 45.00

TH-620, vertical, 4⅛x2½x1⅛", plastic, six transistors, upper right front

horseshoe-shaped dial with right side thumbwheel tuning, left side thumbwheel on/off/volume knob, lower metal perforated grill area, made in Japan, bat....**$25.00 – 35.00**

TH-621, vertical, 4½x2¾x1¼", 1959, six transistors, upper left front round dial knob, upper right front thumbwheel on/off/volume knob, lower grill area with vertical bars, top strap, AM, bat.....**$65.00 – 85.00**

TH-627R, vertical, 4x2⅜x1", 1960, six transistors, upper front window dial with right side thumbwheel tuning, large lower perforated grill area with center logo, AM, bat...**$20.00 – 25.00**

TH-610, vertical, 1964, six transistors, upper front window dial with right side thumbwheel tuning, large lower perforated grill area with lower right logo, AM, bat..............**$10.00 – 15.00**

TH-650, vertical, 1963, available in black or white plastic, six transistors, upper front window dial with right side thumbwheel tuning, right side thumbwheel on/off/volume knob, large lower perforated grill area, AM, bat.............**$10.00 – 15.00**

TH-660, vertical, 4x2½x1⅛", 1962, six transistors, available in black, red, or beige plastic, front window dial with right side thumbwheel tuning, right side thumbwheel on/off/volume knob, large front perforated grill area with center logo, AM, bat.............**$30.00 – 40.00**

TH-666, vertical, 4x2¼x1¼", 1959, available in red/gray, gold/black,

or pearl/white plastic, six transistors, upper front see-through panel with right dial, right side thumbwheel tuning, upper left front volume window with left side thumbwheel on/off/volume knob, metal perforated grill area, could be used with optional speaker box model #ES-90H, AM, bat.
radio only.................**$75.00 – 90.00**
with speaker box ...**$125.00 – 150.00**

TH-666R, vertical, 4x2¼x1¼", plastic, six transistors, upper front see-through panel with right dial, right side thumbwheel tuning, upper left front volume window with left side thumbwheel on/off/volume knob, metal perforated grill area, AM, bat.............................**$75.00 – 90.00**

TH-667, horizontal, 4¼x6¾x1¾", 1960, available in pale pink, light blue, or mint green plastic, six transistors, recessed right front with thumbwheel tuning and on/off/volume knobs, large checkered front grill area with upper left logo, made in Japan, AM, bat.......**$65.00 – 80.00**

TH-680, vertical, 1965, available in black or ivory plastic, six transistors, upper front round dial with right side thumbwheel tuning, left side thumbwheel on/off/volume knob, large perforated grill area, AM, bat.....................**$20.00 – 25.00**

TH-759, horizontal, 3⅜x5¾x1⅜", 1962, available in red, beige, or black plastic, seven transistors, top horizontal slide rule dial with right front thumbwheel tuning, left front thumbwheel on/off/volume knob, large metal perforated grill area with lower left logo, AM, bat ...**$35.00 – 45.00**

TH-812, horizontal, 1964, leather, eight transistors, upper front horizontal slide rule dial, large lower grill area with right tuning and volume knobs, leather handle, AM, bat ....**$10.00 – 15.00**

TH-812R, horizontal, 6½x10x4½", 1964, leather, eight transistors, upper front horizontal slide rule dial, large lower grill area with right tuning and volume knobs, leather handle, AM, bat ....**$10.00 – 15.00**

TH-831, vertical, plastic, solid state, upper front horizontal slide rule dial, right and left side knobs, lower grill area with horizontal bars, top vinyl strap, AM, bat ...**$15.00 – 20.00**

TH-841, horizontal, 3¾x6¼x1½", 1964, plastic, eight transistors, top horizontal slide rule dial with right side thumbwheel tuning, lower right side thumbwheel on/off/volume knob, large front metal perforated grill area with lower right logo, AM, bat ....**$25.00 – 35.00**

TH-848, horizontal, 1964, available in red, black, or beige plastic, eight transistors, upper right front window dial with right side thumbwheel tuning, lower right front volume window with right side thumbwheel knob, large front grill area with lower left tone switch, AM, bat ....**$15.00 – 25.00**

TH-853, horizontal, 4x6⅞x1¾", available in ivory, red, green, or yellow

plastic, solid state, top slanted slide rule dial with right side tuning knob and left side on/off/volume knob, front horizontal grill bars, right side AC plug-in, braided strap, made in Taiwan, AM, AC/bat ..**$15.00 – 20.00**

TH-862, horizontal, 2¾x4½x1¼", 1960, available in coral, black, or gray plastic, eight transistors, right front window dial with right side thumbwheel tuning, lower right front on/off/volume window with right side thumbwheel knob, large metal perforated grill area with upper right logo, AM, bat ....**$30.00 – 40.00**

TH-862R "Marie," horizontal, 2¾x 4½x1¼", 1959, plastic, eight transistors, right front window dial with right side thumbwheel tuning, lower right front on/off/volume window with right side thumbwheel knob, large metal perforated grill area with upper right logo, AM, bat ....**$30.00 – 40.00**

TH-890 "Hi-Phonic," horizontal, 1965, eight transistors, upper right front window dial with right side thumbwheel tuning, lower right front on/off/volume window with right side thumbwheel knob, large front perforated grill area, AM, bat ....**$10.00 – 15.00**

WH-761, vertical, 4½x2¾x1⅛", 1960, seven transistors, two upper front window dials — one SW, AM — with right side thumbwheel tuning, lower perforated grill area with lower right logo, AM, SW, bat .....**$50.00 – 65.00**

WH-761M, vertical, 1961, seven transistors, two upper front window dials

— one Marine, one AM — with right side thumbwheel tuning, lower perforated grill area with lower right logo, AM, Marine, bat ....$50.00 – 65.00

WH-761MB, vertical, 4½x2¾x1⅛", 1962, seven transistors, two upper front window dials — one Marine, one AM — with right side thumbwheel tuning, lower perforated grill area with lower right logo, AM, Marine, bat ....$50.00 – 65.00

WH-761SB, vertical, 1962, seven transistors, two upper front window dials — one shortwave, one AM — with right side thumbwheel tuning, lower perforated grill area with lower right logo, AM, SW, bat ....$50.00 – 65.00

WH-761SW, vertical, 4½x2¾x1⅛", 1962, seven transistors, two upper front window dials — one SW, one AM — with right side thumbwheel tuning, lower perforated grill area with lower right logo, AM, SW, bat.............$50.00 – 65.00

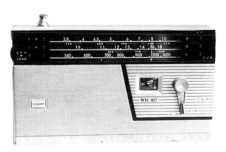

WH-817 "Peggy," horizontal, 4¾x8x2", 1962, plastic, eight transistors, upper front horizontal three-band slide rule dial with two right side thumbwheel tuning knobs, left side thumbwheel on/off and tone knobs, lower perforated

grill area with left dial lamp button and right band switch, telescoping antenna, made in Japan, AM, 2SW, bat...........................$30.00 – 45.00

WH-822 "Kelly," horizontal, 3¾x6x 1¾", 1959, available in black, coral, or gray plastic, eight transistors, top horizontal two-band dial with upper right front thumbwheel tuning, upper left front thumbwheel on/off/volume knob, large metal perforated grill area with lower right logo, AM, SW, bat .....$25.00 – 35.00

WH-822H, horizontal, 3¾x6x1¾", 1964, plastic, eight transistors, top horizontal two-band dial with upper right front thumbwheel tuning, upper left front thumbwheel on/off/volume knob, large metal perforated grill area with lower right logo, AM, SW, bat .....$25.00 – 35.00

WH-822M, horizontal, 3¾x6x1¾", 1959, plastic, eight transistors, top horizontal two-band dial with upper right front thumbwheel tuning, upper left front thumbwheel on/off/ volume knob, large metal perforated grill area with lower right logo, AM, Marine, bat........$25.00 – 35.00

WH-822MB, horizontal, 3¾x6x1¾", 1960, two-tone gray plastic, eight transistors, top horizontal two-band dial with upper right front thumbwheel tuning, upper left front thumbwheel on/off/volume knob, large metal perforated grill area with lower right logo, AM, Marine, bat.$25.00 – 35.00

WH-822SW, horizontal, 3¾x6x1¾", 1960, black plastic, eight transistors, top horizontal two-band dial with upper right front thumbwheel tuning, upper left front thumbwheel on/off/volume knob, large metal perforated grill area with lower right logo, AM, SW, bat ......$25.00 – 35.00

WH-829, horizontal, 3½x6⅛x1½", 1962, available in red, beige, or black plastic, eight transistors, top horizontal two-band slide rule dial with upper right front thumbwheel tuning, lower right front thumbwheel fine tuning knob, upper left front thumbwheel on/off/volume knob, large perforated grill area, telescoping antenna, AM, SW, bat ....$20.00 – 30.00

WH-829M, horizontal, 1963, eight transistors, top horizontal two-band slide rule dial with upper right front thumbwheel tuning, lower right front thumbwheel fine tuning knob, upper left front thumbwheel on/off/volume knob, large perforated grill area, telescoping antenna, AM, Marine, bat ..$20.00 – 30.00

WH-999 "Hiphonic," horizontal, 1965, nine transistors, upper front horizontal three-band slide rule dial, lower left lattice grill area and right band switch, light button, telescoping antenna, AM, 2SW, bat....................$25.00 – 35.00

XH-1500, horizontal, 6¼x9½x3", 1961, plastic, 15 transistors, upper front horizontal two-band illuminated slide rule dial, large lower perforated grill area, two top knobs and four pushbuttons, two telescoping antennas, handle, AM, FM, bat.............................$20.00 – 30.00

Hit Parade

2 transistors (no #), horizontal, 2⅛x3¾x1", plastic, two transistors, front off-center round dial knob, right side switch, no speaker, earphone only, made in USA, AM, bat....................$80.00 – 95.00

Hobby

Boy's Radio, vertical, plastic, two transistors, upper right front window dial with right side thumbwheel tuning, left side thumbwheel on/off/volume knob, lower grill area with vertical bars, AM, bat................$50.00 – 60.00

Hoffman

709X "Solar," horizontal, 3x5x1¾", 1963, available in black, beige, or ivory plastic, nine transistors, upper front horizontal slide rule dial with right side thumbwheel tuning, lower right side thumbwheel on/off/volume knob, perforated grill area with lower left logo, top solar panel, AM, bat..........................$100.00 – 150.00

719 "Solar," horizontal, 1963, seven transistors, right front round dial, large perforated grill area, top solar panel, AM, bat.......$100.00 – 150.00

727, vertical, 4x2½x1¼", six transistors, upper front window dial with right side thumbwheel tuning, left side thumbwheel on/

off/volume knob, lower metal perforated grill area, made in Japan, AM, bat......................$30.00 – 40.00

727X, vertical, 1963, six transistors, upper front window dial with right side thumbwheel tuning, left side thumbwheel on/off/volume knob, lower metal perforated grill area, AM, bat.....................$20.00 – 25.00

729, horizontal, 1964, 12 transistors, upper front horizontal two-band slide rule dial, large lower perforated grill area, two telescoping antennas, handle, AM, FM, bat.........................$10.00 – 15.00

759, horizontal, 1964, 14 transistors, upper front horizontal two-band slide rule dial, large lower perforated grill area, two telescoping antennas, handle, AM, FM, bat...$10.00 – 15.00

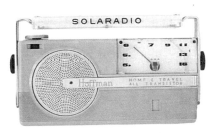

BP411 "Solaradio," "Home & Travel," horizontal, 4¼x8¾x1⅜", plastic, upper right front see-through dial area with top thumbwheel tuning, upper left front on/off/volume window with top left knob, left front round metal perforated grill area, rear brass fold-out stand, handle, made in USA, AM, bat ....$600.00+

BP706 "Trans Solar," horizontal, 3⅞x6¼x2", 1959, mocha plastic,

six transistors, right front dial knob, lower right side thumbwheel on/off/volume knob, left metal perforated grill area, top solar panel, rear batt/solar switch, swing handle, made in USA, AM, bat......................$250.00 – 300.00

BP707, vertical, plastic, seven transistors, upper right side thumbwheel dial knob with front wedge shaped indent, upper left front on/off/volume window with left side thumbwheel knob, metal perforated grill area with lower left logo, swing handle, AM, bat...............$45.00 – 55.00

BP709XS "Solar," horizontal, 3x5x 1¾", plastic, nine transistors, upper front horizontal slide rule dial with right side thumbwheel tuning, lower right side thumbwheel on/off/volume knob, metal perforated grill area with lower left logo, top solar panel, AM, bat.......$100.00 – 150.00

CP706 "Trans Solar," horizontal, 3⅞x 6¼x2", 1959, espresso plastic, six transistors, right front dial knob, lower right side thumbwheel on/off/volume knob, left metal perforated grill area, top solar panel, rear batt/solar switch, swing handle, made in USA, AM, bat.....................$250.00 – 300.00

EP706 "Trans Solar," horizontal, 3⅞x 6¼x2", 1959, espresso plastic, six transistors, right front dial knob, lower right side thumbwheel on/off/volume knob, left metal perforated grill area, top solar panel, rear batt/solar switch, swing handle, made in USA, AM, bat.....................$250.00 – 300.00

KP411 "Solaradio," "Home & Travel," horizontal, 4¼x8¾x1⅜", plastic, upper right front see-through dial area with top thumbwheel tuning, upper left front on/off/volume window with top left knob, left front round metal perforated grill area, rear brass fold-out stand, handle, made in USA, AM, bat ......$600.00+

KP706 "Trans Solar," horizontal, 3⅞ x6¼x2", 1959, ebony plastic, six transistors, right front dial knob, lower right side thumbwheel on/off/volume knob, left metal perforated grill area, top solar panel, rear batt/solar switch, swing handle, made in USA, AM, bat.....................$200.00 – 225.00

KP707, vertical, 1962, seven transistors, upper right front round dial knob with wedge-shaped opening, left side thumbwheel on/off/volume knob, lower metal perforated grill area with lower left logo, swing handle, AM, bat ....$45.00 – 55.00

KP-709X-CD "Solar," horizontal, 1964, plastic, nine transistors, upper

front horizontal slide rule dial with right side thumbwheel tuning, lower right side thumbwheel on/off/volume knob, perforated grill area with lower left logo, top solar panel, AM, bat...........................$100.00 – 150.00

KP-709XS "Solar," horizontal, 3⅛x5¼x1⅝", plastic, nine transistors, upper front horizontal slide rule dial with right side thumbwheel tuning, lower right side thumbwheel on/off/volume knob, perforated grill area with lower left logo, top solar panel, made in Japan, AM, bat ......$100.00 – 150.00

OP706 "Trans Solar," horizontal, 3⅞x6¼x2", 1959, oyster white plastic, six transistors, right front dial knob, lower right side thumbwheel on/off/volume knob, left metal perforated grill area, top solar panel, rear batt/solar switch, swing handle, made in USA, AM, bat.......$250.00 – 300.00

OP708, horizontal, 1962, eight transistors, upper front horizontal slide rule dial with right side thumbwheel tuning, lower right side thumbwheel on/off/volume knob, perforated grill area with lower left logo, AM, bat..............$30.00 – 40.00

OP-709XS "Solar," horizontal, 1963, nine transistors, upper front horizontal slide rule dial with right side thumbwheel tuning, lower right side thumbwheel on/off/volume knob, perforated grill area with lower left logo, top solar panel, AM, bat......**$100.00 – 150.00**

PP706 "Trans Solar," horizontal, 3⅞x 6¼x2", 1959, pink plastic, six transistors, right front dial knob, lower right side thumbwheel on/off/volume knob, left metal perforated grill area, top solar panel, rear batt/solar switch, swing handle, made in USA, AM, bat ....**$400.00 – 450.00**

RP706 "Trans Solar," horizontal, 3⅞x 6¼x2", 1959, red plastic, six transistors, right front dial knob, lower right side thumbwheel on/off/volume knob, left metal perforated grill area, top solar panel, rear batt/solar switch, swing handle, made in USA, AM, bat..................**$400.00 – 450.00**

T-P411 "Solaradio," "Home & Travel," horizontal, 4¼x8¾x1⅜", plastic, upper right front see-through dial area with top thumbwheel tuning, upper left front on/off/volume window with top left knob, left front round metal perforated grill area, rear brass fold-out stand, handle, made in USA, AM, bat ....$600.00+

TP706 "Trans Solar," horizontal, 3⅞x 6¼x2", 1959, turquoise plastic, six transistors, right front dial knob, lower right side thumbwheel on/off/volume knob, left metal perforated grill area, top solar panel, rear batt/solar switch, swing handle, made in USA, AM, bat ......**$300.00 – 350.00**

Holiday

HS921 "Super DX," vertical, 4¼x2½x1¼", plastic, nine transistors, upper right front window dial with right side thumbwheel tuning, left side thumbwheel on/off/volume knob, metal front panel with vertical grill slots, AM, bat.......**$15.00 – 20.00**

ST-600, horizontal, 3⅜x5x1½", plastic, six transistors, right front round dial knob, top thumbwheel on/off/volume knob, left horseshoe-shaped grill area with rectangular cut-outs, made in Japan, AM, bat .... **$35.00 – 45.00**

TS-190, horizontal, plastic, upper front horizontal multi-band slide rule dial, large lower metal perforated grill area, handle, bat..**$15.00 – 20.00**

Honey Tone

2 transistor (no #), vertical, 3½x2⅜x1", plastic, two transistors, upper right front thumbwheel dial knob, upper left front thumbwheel on/off/volume knob, large metal grill area with horizontal slots, AM, bat.....**$50.00 – 60.00**

8TP-412, vertical, 1963, plastic, eight transistors, upper front window dial with right side thumbwheel tuning, large lower perforated grill area with center logo, swing handle, AM, bat ....**$40.00 – 50.00**

601, vertical, plastic, six transistors, upper front window dial with right side thumbwheel tuning, left side thumbwheel on/off/volume knob, lower round metal perforated grill area, AM, bat.............**$45.00 – 55.00**

604, vertical, 1963, six transistors, upper front horizontal slide rule dial with right side thumbwheel tuning, left side thumbwheel on/off/volume knob, large perforated grill area, AM, bat........................**$15.00 – 20.00**

FR-601, vertical, 1962, six transistors, upper front window dial with right side thumbwheel tuning, left side thumbwheel on/off/volume knob, lower round perforated grill area, swing handle, AM, bat.**$40.00 – 50.00**

KTF-102G, horizontal, 1963, 11 transistors, upper front horizontal double slide rule dial, large lower perforated grill area with three knobs, telescoping antenna, handle, AM, FM, bat ....**$10.00 – 15.00**

TN-201 "Boy's Radio," vertical, 4x2½x1⅜", plastic, two transistors, rounded upper right corner, upper right front dial knob, left side thumbwheel on/off/volume knob, lower metal textured and perforated

grill area with lower left logo, made in Japan, AM, bat.......$50.00 – 60.00

TR-801 "All Wave Super," horizontal, 1963, eight transistors, upper front horizontal two-band slide rule dial, lower right thumbwheel knobs, large perforated grill area, AM, SW, bat...............$20.00 – 25.00

Hudson
T.S.-10, vertical, 4¼x2⅝x1¼", plastic, 10 transistors, upper front dial, right side thumbwheel on/off/volume knob, lower lattice grill area, made in USA, AM, bat........$10.00 – 15.00

Hy-Lite
E164, vertical, 4⅝x2¾x1¼", plastic, solid state, upper right front round window dial with right side thumbwheel tuning, upper left front round on/off/volume window with left side thumbwheel knob, lower checkered grill area, made in Hong Kong, AM, bat.............$5.00 – 10.00

I.D.A.

NTR-800, horizontal, 2⅞x4⅞x1¼", plastic, eight transistors, upper front horizontal two-band slide rule dial with right side thumbwheel tuning, right side thumbwheel on/off/volume knob, lower metal perforated grill area with lower right band switch, made in Japan, bat......$25.00 – 35.00

Imperial

Boy's Radio, vertical, 4x2½x1⅛", plastic, two transistors, upper right front window dial with right side thumbwheel tuning, left side thumbwheel on/off/volume knob, lower metal textured and perforated grill area, crown logo, made in Japan, AM, bat..........$35.00 – 45.00

GK-600 "Hi-Fi," vertical, 1963, six transistors, upper front window dial with side thumbwheel tuning, large lower grill area with horizontal slots, AM, bat.............$15.00 – 20.00

International
A9101, vertical, 4⅝x3x1¼", plastic, nine transistors, upper front see-through panel with window dial, right side thumbwheel tuning, left side thumbwheel on/off/volume knob, lower metal textured and perforated grill area, rear fold-out stand, made in Japan, AM, bat ....$100.00 – 125.00

Invicta
8PK1, vertical, 1965, eight transistors, upper front window dial with

side thumbwheel tuning, large lower grill area, AM, bat........$5.00 – 10.00

10PK1, vertical, 1965, 10 transistors, upper front window dial with side thumbwheel tuning, large lower perforated grill area, AM, bat..............................$5.00 – 10.00

TR-222, horizontal, plastic, six transistors, right front see-through panel with half-round dial, right side thumbwheel tuning, right side thumbwheel on/off/volume knob, large left metal perforated grill area with upper logo, AM, bat.....................$75.00 – 100.00

ITT

600, vertical, 1963, six transistors, upper front horizontal slide rule dial with thumbwheel tuning, large lower perforated grill area with center "6" logo, AM, bat..$45.00 – 55.00

615, vertical, 4x2⅝x¾", 1963, plastic, six transistors, upper left front window dial with top left thumbwheel tuning, top right thumbwheel on/off/volume knob, large metal perforated grill area with lower right logo, metal back, AM, bat..............................$15.00 – 20.00

628, horizontal, 2¾x4¼x1", 1963, leatherette and metal, six transistors, right front round window dial with right side thumbwheel tuning, lower

right side thumbwheel on/off/volume knob, large front metal perforated grill area with "star" emblem, left side strap, AM, bat......$30.00 – 40.00

631, vertical, 1963, six transistors, upper front window dial with right side thumbwheel tuning, right side thumbwheel on/off/volume knob, lower perforated grill area, AM, bat............................$15.00 – 20.00

731, horizontal, 1963, seven transistors, upper right front horizontal dial with right side thumbwheel tuning, large perforated grill area with lower right logo, AM, bat.....$25.00 – 35.00

871, vertical, 1963, eight transistors, upper front horizontal slanted two-band slide rule dial with right side thumbwheel tuning, large lower perforated grill area, telescoping antenna, AM, SW, bat..........$20.00 – 25.00

881, horizontal, 3½x6¼x1⅜", 1963, eight transistors, upper front horizontal two-band slide rule dial with right side thumbwheel tuning, left side thumbwheel on/off/volume knob, large metal perforated grill, right battery/tuning indicator window, rear band switch, made in Japan, AM, Marine, bat.$25.00 – 35.00

881-S, horizontal, 1963, eight transistors, upper front horizontal two-band slide rule dial with thumbwheel tuning, large perforated grill area, right battery/tuning indicator window, AM, SW, bat................$25.00 – 35.00

1005, horizontal, 1963, nine transistors, upper front horizontal three-band slide rule dial, large lower perforated grill area, telescoping antenna, handle, AM, Marine, SW, bat.............................$15.00 – 20.00

1011, horizontal, 1963, 10 transistors, upper front horizontal two-band slide rule dial, large lower perforated grill area with lower left logo, right and left side knobs, top pushbuttons, telescoping antenna, handle, AM, FM, bat..$20.00 – 25.00

6409-A "Super-Sensitivity," vertical, 9x4½x1⅞", plastic, nine transistors, left front vertical slide rule dial, three front thumbwheel knobs, metal perforated grill area, handle, AM, bat.....................$10.00 – 15.00

6409-F, horizontal, 1964, nine transistors, off-center vertical two-band dial with thumbwheel tuning, large front perforated grill area with lower left logo, telescoping antenna, handle, AM, FM, bat..$10.00 – 15.00

6509, vertical, 1964, nine transistors, two upper front dials – one AM, one

FM – lower perforated grill area with lower right logo, telescoping antenna, AM, FM, bat$10.00 – 15.00

_____

Jade

101, vertical, 4¼x2⅝x1⅜", plastic, 10 transistors, upper right front window dial with right side thumbwheel tuning, left side thumbwheel on/off/volume knob, metal perforated grill area, left side braided strap, made in Hong Kong, AM, bat............................$5.00 – 10.00

163, vertical, plastic, six transistors, upper right front window dial with right side thumbwheel tuning, top left thumbwheel on/off/volume knob, lower checkered grill area, AM, bat....................$5.00 – 10.00

171, vertical, plastic, seven transistors, upper right front window dial with right side thumbwheel tuning, large lower grill area with horizontal bars, left side strap, AM, bat..$5.00 – 10.00

J-142, horizontal, 3⅜x5⅞x1½", plastic, 14 transistors, upper right front round window dial with top right thumbwheel tuning, large lower metal perforated grill area, right side strap, made in Okinawa, AM, bat ....$10.00 – 15.00

J-162, vertical, plastic, six transistors, upper right front round window dial with right side thumbwheel tuning, left side thumbwheel on/off/volume knob, lower grill area with horizontal bars, AM, bat ....$5.00 – 10.00

J-1188, vertical, 4⅜x2¾x1¼", plastic, eight transistors, upper right front round window dial with right side thumbwheel tuning, left side thumbwheel on/off/volume knob, large grill area with vertical bars, made in Hong Kong, AM, bat .$10.00 – 15.00

_____

Jaguar

6T-250, vertical, 1960, six transistors, upper front see-through panel

with right dial, top thumbwheel tuning, left front volume window with left side thumbwheel knob, lower metal perforated grill area, made in Japan, AM, bat ......$150.00 – 175.00

9FM-T2024, horizontal, 4¼x6½x2", plastic, nine transistors, two upper front horizontal dials – one AM, one FM – right side thumbwheel dial knob, left side thumbwheel on/off/volume knob, large metal perforated grill area, telescoping antenna, rear band switch, made in Japan, AM, FM, bat ...$25.00 – 35.00

T2010, vertical, 3⅝x2⅜x1", plastic, six transistors, upper front window dial with right side thumbwheel tuning, left side thumbwheel on/off/volume knob, large metal perforated grill area, made in Japan, AM, bat...........$25.00 – 35.00

_____

Jeb

6YR-15A, vertical, plastic, six transistors, upper right see-through dial win-

dow with right side thumbwheel tuning, upper left see-through on/off/volume window with left side thumbwheel knob, lower round metal perforated grill area, AM, bat .....$85.00 – 100.00

Jefferson-Travis

JT-D210, vertical, 1961, four transistors, upper right front round dial knob, upper left thumbwheel on/off/volume knob, lower perforated grill area with lower left logo, AM, bat ....$30.00 – 40.00

JT-E212, horizontal, 1961, five transistors, right front window dial with right side tuning, lower right recessed thumbwheel on/off/volume knob, large perforated grill area, AM, bat ....$25.00 – 30.00

JT-F211, vertical, 3¾x2¾x1", 1961, plastic, six transistors, upper front horizontal slide rule dial with right side tuning knob, left side on/off/volume knob, large lower textured and perforated grill area with lower left logo, made in Japan, AM, bat ....$20.00 – 30.00

JT-G104, horizontal, 1961, plastic with chrome trim, seven transistors, upper front horizontal two-band slide rule dial with right side thumbwheel tuning, top left thumbwheel on/off/volume knob, horizontal grill bars, telescoping antenna, AM, SW, bat ....$45.00 – 60.00

JT-G200, vertical, 4½x2¾x1¼", plastic, seven transistors, upper front rectangular two-band window dial with right side thumbwheel tuning, upper left front volume window with left side thumbwheel knob, metal perforated grill area with lower left logo, AM, SW, bat .....$15.00 – 20.00

JT-G204 "Long Distance," vertical, 1961, seven transistors, upper front see-through panel, top right thumbwheel dial knob, top left thumbwheel on/off/volume knob, lower perforated grill area, swing handle, AM, bat ....$115.00 – 135.00

JT-H105, horizontal, 1961, eight transistors, upper front horizontal three-band slide rule dial with thumbwheel tuning, large lower perforated grill area with lower left logo, right side switch, telescoping antenna, AM, 2SW, bat ....$25.00 – 35.00

JT-H204 "Deluxe 8," vertical, 1961, plastic, eight transistors, upper front see-through panel, top right thumbwheel dial knob, top left thumbwheel on/off/volume knob, lower metal perforated grill area, swing handle, AM, bat .....$115.00 – 135.00

Jetstream

JK29B-63A, vertical, 4¼x2½x1¼", plastic, 14 transistors, upper right front window dial with right side thumbwheel tuning, left side thumbwheel on/off/volume knob, large metal perforated grill area, made in Hong Kong, AM, bat..$15.00 – 20.00

Jewel

T.S.-10, vertical, 5¾x3½x1¾", 1965, plastic, 10 transistors, upper left front dial knob, upper right front volume knob, large lower lattice grill area with lower left logo, swing handle, made in USA, AM, bat .... **$15.00 – 20.00**

Super-Eighty, vertical, 5¾x3½x1¾", plastic, eight transistors, upper right front dial knob, upper left front on/off/volume knob, lower grill area with horizontal bars, swing handle, made in USA, AM, bat.**$20.00 – 25.00**

Juliette

AA-64, horizontal, 2¾x4½x1¼", 1968, plastic, six transistors, upper right front diamond-shaped window dial, top thumbwheel on/off/volume knob, left perforated grill area with lower left logo, AM, bat ....**$10.00 – 15.00**

AB-81, vertical, 4½x2½x1½", 1968, plastic, eight transistors, upper front window dial with thumbwheel tuning, lower grill area with vertical bars, AM, bat ....**$5.00 – 10.00**

AB-121, vertical, 4½x2½x1½", 1968, plastic, 12 transistors, upper right front thumbwheel dial knob, upper left front thumbwheel on/off/volume knob, lower lattice grill area, AM, bat ....**$5.00 – 10.00**

ABH-108, horizontal, 2¾x4½x1½", 1968, plastic, eight transistors, upper right front thumbwheel dial knob, lower right side thumbwheel on/off/volume knob, left grill area, AM, bat ....**$5.00 – 10.00**

AK-8, vertical, 4¼x2⅝x1⅜", plastic, eight transistors, upper right front window dial with right side thumbwheel tuning, top left thumbwheel on/off/volume knob, horizontal grill bars with lower left logo, made in Hong Kong, AM, bat ....**$5.00 – 10.00**

AK-140, vertical, 4½x2½x1¼", 1968, plastic with metal front, upper right front window dial with right side thumbwheel tuning, top left thumbwheel on/off/volume knob, lower grill area with nine circular cutouts, AM, bat ....**$15.00 – 20.00**

AK-661, vertical, 4½x2½x1¼", 1968, plastic, six transistors, upper right front window dial with right side thumbwheel tuning, top left thumbwheel on/off/volume knob, lower perforated grill area with lower left logo, bat ....**$10.00 – 15.00**

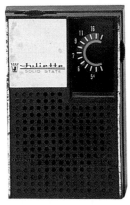

APR-256, vertical, plastic, upper right front semicircular dial with right side thumbwheel tuning, top left thumbwheel on/off/volume knob, lower perforated grill area, AM, bat ....**$5.00 – 10.00**

APR-306, vertical, 4¼x2⅝x1¼", plastic, solid state, upper right front window dial with right side thumbwheel tuning, top left thumbwheel on/off/volume knob, horizontal grill bars, made in Hong Kong, AM, bat ....**$5.00 – 10.00**

AT-65, vertical, 4½x2⅛x1⅜", 1965, six transistors, upper right front window dial with right side thumbwheel tuning, top left thumbwheel on/off/volume knob, horizontal grill bars, AM, bat ....**$5.00 – 10.00**

AT-85, vertical, 4¼x2⅛x1⅜", 1965, eight transistors, upper right front window dial with right side thumbwheel tuning, top left thumbwheel

on/off/volume knob, horizontal grill bars with lower left logo, AM, bat ....**$5.00 – 10.00**

AT-105, vertical, 4½x2⅛x1⅜", 1965, 10 transistors, upper right front window dial with right side thumbwheel tuning, top left thumbwheel on/off/volume knob, horizontal grill bars with lower left logo, AM, bat ..**$5.00 – 10.00**

CLA-1020, lamp/radio, 9x8x7½", 1968, plastic, five transistors, horizontal slide rule dial, top right clock face, top left high intensity lamp, AM, AC ....**$15.00 – 25.00**

DTF-150, horizontal, 6x8¾x2½", 1965, 15 transistors, two off-center round dials — one AM, one FM — left perforated grill area with lower left logo, three right knobs, telescoping antenna, handle, AM, FM, bat/AC...................**$10.00 – 15.00**

LR-57, lamp/radio, 1968, available in ivory, gold, or turquoise plastic, seven transistors, lamp shade folds up for use as a high intensity lamp or down for use as a night light, circular tuning, side thumbwheel knobs, base, AM, AC..**$25.00 – 35.00**

SH-516, vertical, 4⅝x2¾x1½", plastic, 16 transistors, upper right front circular window dial with right side thumbwheel tuning, top left thumbwheel on/off/volume knob, recessed circular metal perforated grill area, made in Hong Kong, AM, bat ....**$10.00 – 15.00**

TR-10M, square, micro, 2¼x2x1⅛", 1968, plastic, 10 transistors, two right side knobs, front grill area with center logo, left side chain, AM, bat .... $30.00 – 40.00

TR-91M, horizontal, micro, 1⅞x2⅛ x⅞", 1968, nine transistors, two top knobs, front grill area with horizontal bars and center logo, left side chain, AM, bat .... $35.00 – 45.00

TR-777, square, micro, 2¾x2¼x1", 1968, plastic, seven transistors, two right side knobs, front grill area with crossed bars and center logo, left side strap, AM, bat ..... $30.00 – 40.00

TR-888, square, micro, 2¾x2¼x1¼", 1968, available in black, white, red, green, or gold plastic, eight transistors, two right side knobs, front grill area with crossed bars and center logo, left side chain, AM, bat ... $30.00 – 40.00

Jupiter

Boy's Radio, radio/watch, 2¼x1¾x¾" (watch only), plastic watch/metal band, two transistors, top dial knob with center compass, no speaker, earphone only, radio turns on when earphone is

plugged into watch "stem," made in Japan, AM, bat .... $125.00 – 150.00

5T-210, horizontal, plastic, five transistors, large right front dial knob, upper left front thumbwheel on/off/volume knob, lower checkered grill area with lower left logo, AM, bat .... $30.00 – 40.00

6T-330, horizontal, 3⅝x2⅜x1", plastic, six transistors, upper front see-through panel with large thumbwheel dial knob, lower textured grill area, made in Japan, AM, bat .... $100.00 – 125.00

Kalimar

9TL-432S, horizontal, 4¾x8⅜x1¾", plastic, nine transistors, upper front horizontal two-band slide rule dial with upper right front thumbwheel tuning, upper left front thumbwheel on/off/volume knob, lower metal perforated grill area with two switches, top right band switch, telescoping antenna, bat .... $25.00 – 35.00

Kensington

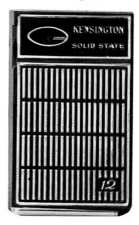

5026, vertical, plastic, 12 transistors, upper left front oval window dial with left side thumbwheel tuning, lower grill area with vertical bars, AM, bat..............$5.00 – 10.00

5037, vertical, 6⅞x4¾x2⅝", leatherette, 15 transistors, upper left front dial, right front on/off/volume knob, lower metal perforated grill area, handle, made in Japan, AM, bat........$5.00 – 10.00

HT-1268, vertical, 4¼x2½x1¼", plastic, 10 transistors, upper front window dial with right side tuning, top left thumbwheel on/off/volume knob, large metal perforated grill area, AM, bat.....$10.00 – 15.00

MT-601, vertical, 4¼x2½x1⅛", plastic, six transistors, upper right front window dial with right side thumbwheel tuning, large lower perforated grill area, made in Japan, AM, bat..............$10.00 – 15.00

Kent

600, vertical, 4¼x2⅝x1¼", plastic,

six transistors, upper right front window dial with right side thumbwheel tuning, top left thumbwheel on/off/volume knob, lower metal perforated grill area with horizontal & vertical lines, made in Japan, AM, bat.....................$10.00 – 15.00

TR-605, vertical, 1965, six transistors, upper right front window dial with right side thumbwheel tuning, left side thumbwheel on/off/volume knob, large perforated grill area, AM, bat.............$10.00 – 15.00

Boy's Radio, vertical, plastic, two transistors, upper left front dial knob, upper right side thumbwheel on/off/volume knob, lower metal textured and perforated grill area, AM, bat....................$50.00 – 60.00

Boy's Radio, vertical, 4⅛x2⅝x1¼", plastic, two transistors, top left thumbwheel dial knob, top right thumbwheel on/off/volume knob, large lower metal perforated grill area with lower right logo, left side horizontal telescoping antenna, made in Japan, AM, bat ....$50.00 – 60.00

Keroy

Boy's Radio, vertical, 4x2½x1⅛", plastic, two transistors, upper front window dial with left side thumbwheel tuning, right side thumbwheel on/off/volume knob, lower round metal perforated grill area, made in Japan, AM, bat ....$45.00 – 55.00

King

Boy's Radio, vertical, 4⅛x2½x1¼", plastic, two transistors, upper front see-through panel with right quarterround window dial, right side thumbwheel tuning, left side thumbwheel on/off/volume knob, lower metal perforated grill area, made in Japan, AM, bat ....$50.00 – 60.00

Knight

KN-2400, horizontal, 1964, nine transistors, top horizontal fourband slide rule dial, pushbuttons and knobs, large front grill area with horizontal bars, two telescop-

ing antennas, handle, AM, FM, 2SW, bat.....................$20.00 – 25.00

Y-262, square/kit radio, 4x3¾x1¾", 1961, leatherette, two transistors, upper right front dial knob, upper left front on/off/volume knob, no speaker, earphone-only, AM, bat..........................$65.00 – 75.00

Y-766, horizontal/kit radio, 3⅜x7½x1¾", plastic, five transistors, right front dial knob overlaps horizontal grill bars, left side pull-out handle, AM, bat ....$10.00 – 15.00

Kobe Kogyo

KT-1000, horizontal, 3⅝x6¼x1¼", plastic, eight transistors, two upper front horizontal slide rule dials – one AM, one LW – two lower right thumbwheel knobs, left metal perforated grill area,

top directional aerial, AM, LW,
bat ....$25.00 – 35.00

Kowa

KT-31, vertical, 1960, three transistors, upper right front diamond-shaped window dial with right side thumbwheel tuning, upper left front diamond-shaped volume window with left side thumbwheel knob, lower perforated grill area, AM, bat ....$75.00 – 95.00

KT-62A, horizontal, 1961, six transistors, upper right front window dial with right side thumbwheel tuning, lower right side thumbwheel on/off/ volume knob, large left perforated grill area, AM, bat ......$30.00 – 40.00

KT-63, vertical, 4⅛x2⅜x1¼", 1961, plastic, six transistors, upper window dial with upper right dial knob, top left thumbwheel on/off/volume knob, large lower metal perforated grill area, telescoping antenna, swing handle, made in Japan, AM, bat ....$35.00 – 45.00

KT-66, vertical, 4⅛x2⅝x1¼", 1961, plastic, six transistors, upper front window dial with upper right thumbwheel tuning, upper left thumbwheel on/off/volume knob, lower metal textured and perforated grill area, swing handle, made in Japan, AM, bat ....$35.00 – 45.00

KT-67, vertical, 1961, six transistors, upper right front window dial with top right thumbwheel tuning, top left thumbwheel on/off/volume knob, lower round perforated grill area, AM, bat ....$60.00 – 75.00

KT-91, vertical, 1962, plastic, nine transistors, upper front see-through panel, window dial with large sunburst pattern, right side thumbwheel tuning, left side thumbwheel on/off/volume knob, lower metal perforated grill area, AM, bat ....$175.00 – 200.00

KTC-62A "Ramera," horizontal/ camera radio, 1959, available in black, red, blue, and white plastic, six transistors, right front window dial with right side thumbwheel tuning, right side thumbwheel on/off/volume knob, center round perforated grill area, left front camera, AM, bat.............$75.00 – 100.00

KTF-1, horizontal, 7¾x9¼x3¼", 1961, plastic, 11 transistors, top horizontal two-band slide rule dial, lower checkered grill area, AM/FM switch, two telescoping antennas, handle, AM, FM, bat ....$30.00 – 40.00

KTS-1B, horizontal, 1961, eight transistors, top horizontal two-band slide rule dial with right tuning and left volume knobs, large lower perforated grill area, telescoping antenna, AM, SW, bat ...**$20.00 – 30.00**

Koyo

KR-6TZ2, horizontal, plastic, lower right front window dial with right side thumbwheel tuning, upper right front on/off/volume window with right side thumbwheel knob, large left grill area, AM, bat ....$10.00 – 15.00

KTR834, horizontal, 1965, eight transistors, upper front horizontal two-band slide rule dial with thumbwheel tuning, large lower perforated grill area with lower right logo, telescoping antenna, AM, SW, bat ....**$15.00 – 20.00**

KTR-1031, horizontal, 3⅝x6⅝x1⅛", 1965, 10 transistors, plastic, center front vertical slide rule dial with top thumbwheel tuning, top thumbwheel on/off/volume knob, twin speakers with right and left circular perforated grill areas, made in Japan, AM, bat..........**$20.00 – 30.00**

Kroy

T-880, square, 2⅝x2⅝x1¼", plastic, eight transistors, upper right side dial knob, lower right side on/off/vol-

ume knob, front metal perforated grill area, left side vinyl strap, made in Japan, AM, bat........**$20.00 – 30.00**

T-1001, vertical, 4½x2⅝x1⅜", plastic, 10 transistors, upper right front half-round dial with right side thumbwheel tuning, left side thumbwheel on/off/volume knob, lower horizontal grill bars, AM, bat ....**$5.00 – 10.00**

T-1010, horizontal, 10 transistors, right front vertical two-band slide rule dial with right side thumbwheel tuning, left grill area with horizontal bars, telescoping antenna, AM, FM, bat........**$10.00 – 15.00**

Lafayette

17-0101, vertical, 4x2⅝x1¼", 1965, plastic, six transistors, upper right front window dial with right side thumbwheel tuning, left side thumbwheel on/off/volume knob, textured grill area, made in Okinawa, AM, bat ....**$5.00 – 10.00**

17-0102, vertical, 1965, 10 transistors, upper front round dial, right thumbwheel knob, lower grill area, AM, bat ....**$10.00 – 15.00**

17G0104, horizontal, 1965, 15 transistors, upper front horizontal three-band slide rule dial, large lower grill area with lower left logo, four right knobs, two telescoping antennas, handle, AM, FM, SW, bat..............**$10.00 – 15.00**

17G6905L, vertical, 1965, nine transistors, upper right front window dial with right side thumbwheel tuning, large lower grill area with horizontal bars, AM, bat.....**$5.00 – 10.00**

FS-91, vertical, 4½x2⅞x1⅛", 1961, plastic, nine transistors, upper front see-through panel with quarter-round dial, right side thumbwheel tuning, left side thumbwheel on/off/volume knob, metal perforated grill area, rear fold-out stand, made in Japan, AM, bat...................**$175.00 – 200.00**

FS-93, horizontal, 1962, nine transistors, upper front horizontal three-band slide rule dial with right thumbwheel tuning, left thumbwheel on/off/volume knob, upper right band-select window, lower right switches, perforated grill area, telescoping antenna, AM, Weather, Marine, bat................**$25.00 – 35.00**

FS-110, vertical, 4⅝x2¾x1⅜", 1958, plastic, six transistors, large upper left front dial, upper right front thumbwheel on/off/volume knob, lower perforated grill area with lower right logo, AM, bat.....**$45.00 – 60.00**

FS-112, vertical, 1959, six transistors, top thumbwheel dial with see-through window, right front thumbwheel on/off/volume knob, lower perforated grill area, AM, bat........................**$115.00 – 135.00**

FS-129, horizontal, 1963, 10 transistors, right front vertical slide rule dial with lower right side thumbwheel tuning, upper right side thumbwheel on/off/volume knob, left perforated grill area, AM, bat....................**$10.00 – 15.00**

FS-200, horizontal, 1960, six transistors, right front window dial with right side thumbwheel tuning, lower right side thumbwheel on/off/volume knob, perforated grill arca, AM, bat...**$90.00 – 110.00**

FS-204, vertical, 1961, four transistors, upper left front round window dial with top thumbwheel tuning, top right thumbwheel on/off/volume knob, lower perforated grill arca, AM, bat............**$45.00 – 55.00**

FS-206, vertical, 4x2½x1¼", plastic, six transistors, upper front window dial with right side thumbwheel tuning, left side thumbwheel on/off/volume knob, lower round perforated grill area, AM, bat ....**$30.00 – 40.00**

FS-223, horizontal, 1962, seven transistors, upper front horizontal two-band slide rule dial with thumbwheel tuning, lower left perforated grill area, lower right "star" emblem, telescoping antenna, AM, SW, bat.....................**$30.00 – 40.00**

FS-230, vertical, plastic, upper right front thumbwheel dial knob, upper left front thumbwheel on/off/volume knob, metal grill panel with round perforated grill area, AM, bat............$40.00 – 50.00

FS-235, vertical, 1963, six transistors, upper front window dial with thumbwheel tuning, lower perforated grill area, AM, bat......$25.00 – 35.00

FS-238, horizontal/desk set radio, 1964, seven transistors, left front horizontal dial with two thumbwheel knobs and perforated grill area, two penholders, AM, bat....................$15.00 – 25.00

FS-243, vertical, 1963, six transistors, upper front window dial with thumbwheel tuning, lower round perforated grill area, swing handle, AM, bat.....................$30.00 – 40.00

FS-244, horizontal, 1963, eight transistors, upper front horizontal two-band slide rule dial with thumbwheel tuning, large lower perforated grill area, AM, SW, bat........$10.00 – 15.00

FS-245, horizontal, 1963, 10 transistors, raised center top with horizontal two-band slide rule dial and three pushbuttons, two top knobs, large lower perforated grill area, two telescoping antennas, handle, AM, FM, bat...............$25.00 – 35.00

FS-248, vertical, 1963, six transistors, upper front window dial with thumbwheel tuning, lower perforated grill area with center "L" logo, AM, bat.....................$10.00 – 15.00

FS-251, horizontal, 1963, 12 transistors, upper front horizontal three-band slide rule dial, lower perforated grill area, telescoping antenna, handle, AM, FM, SW, bat..$15.00 – 20.00

FS-252, horizontal, 1963, 12 transistors, upper left front horizontal four-band slide rule dial, four pushbuttons, lower grill area with two knobs, telescoping antenna, handle, AM, 3SW, bat......$15.00 – 20.00

FS-253, horizontal, 1963, eight transistors, upper front horizontal dial with thumbwheel tuning, center front horizontal cut-outs, lower perforated grill area, AM, bat...........................$15.00 – 20.00

FS-258, horizontal, 1964, leather, nine transistors, right front dial knob and left front on/off/volume knob over horizontal grill bars, leather handle, AM, bat.........$10.00 – 15.00

FS-280, horizontal, 1965, 10 transistors, three right front vertical slide rule dial scales with thumbwheel tuning, large left grill area with vertical bars, telescoping antenna, AM, SW, LW, bat ....$10.00 – 15.00

FS-284L, horizontal, 1964, 10 transistors, upper right front horizontal slide rule dial with thumbwheel tuning, left round metal perforated grill area, AM, bat .....$20.00 – 25.00

FS-305, horizontal, 1965, nine transistors, upper front horizontal two-band slide rule dial with right thumbwheel tuning, left thumbwheel volume knob, right VHF/MW switch, perforated grill area, telescoping antenna, AM, Aviation, bat.........$10.00 – 15.00

KT-68A, vertical/kit radio, 3½x2½x1¼", 1956, plastic, two transistors, two top knobs, no speaker, car phone-only, AM, bat....$40.00 – 50.00

KT-116, vertical/kit radio, 4⅛x2⅝x1", 1957, plastic, three transistors, upper left front dial knob, upper right front on/off knob, no speaker, earphone-only, AM, bat..............$60.00 – 75.00

TR-1645, vertical, 1965, six transistors, step-back top, upper left front window dial with thumbwheel tuning over horizontal grill bars, right side thumbwheel on/off/volume knob, AM, bat..............$5.00 – 10.00

TR-1660, vertical, 1964, six transistors, upper right front window dial with right side thumbwheel tuning, lower horizontal grill bars, AM, bat ....$5.00 – 10.00

TR-1948, vertical, 1964, nine transistors, upper right front window dial with right side thumbwheel tuning, lower horizontal grill bars, AM, bat ....$5.00 – 10.00

TR-2051, horizontal, 1964, 10 transistors, right front vertical two-band slide rule dial, large left grill area with horizontal bars, telescoping antenna, AM, FM, bat....$10.00 – 15.00

TR-3047, horizontal, 1964, 10 transistors, three right front vertical slide rule dial scales, large left grill area with vertical bars, telescoping antenna, AM, SW, LW, bat...$10.00 – 15.00

Lamie

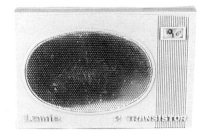

TR-263 "Boy's Radio," horizontal, 2½x3⅞x1", plastic, two transistors, upper right front window dial with right side thumbwheel tuning, right side thumbwheel on/off/volume knob, large oval perforated grill area, made in Japan, AM, bat..............................$60.00 – 75.00

Lark

TR-107 "Boy's Radio," vertical, plastic, one transistor, upper front window dial with thumbwheel tuning, no speaker, earphone-only, made in Japan, AM, bat...........$80.00 – 95.00

Lefco

6YR-15A, vertical, 3½x2¼x1", 1961, plastic, six transistors, upper right

front see-through dial window with thumbwheel knob, upper left front see-through on/off/volume window with thumbwheel knob, lower round metal perforated grill area, made in Japan, AM, bat.......... 85.00 – 100.00

Lido

TR-270, vertical, 4⅜x3x1¼", plastic, two transistors, upper front see-through panel, right front semicircular dial with right side thumbwheel tuning, left side thumbwheel on/off/volume knob, lower grill area with vertical slots, swing handle, made in Japan, AM, bat ....$150.00 – 175.00

Lincoln

24SC054, horizontal, 1965, 10 transistors, right front vertical two-band slide rule dial with thumbwheel tuning, large left grill area with horizontal bars, telescoping antenna, AM, FM, bat...............$10.00 – 15.00

24SC079, vertical, 1965, eight transistors, upper front horizontal slide rule dial with thumbwheel tuning, lower perforated grill area, AM, bat.....................$10.00 – 15.00

L640, vertical, 1963, six transistors, upper right front round dial knob, upper left front volume window with top thumbwheel knob, lower perforated grill area, AM, bat.................$100.00 – 125.00

TR-970, vertical, 6x4x2", 1963, plastic, nine transistors, top of case arches backwards, upper front horizontal three-band slide rule dial with right side thumbwheel tuning, left side thumbwheel volume and tone knobs, lower metal perforated grill area, telescoping antenna, swing handle, SW, LW, MW, bat........$55.00 – 65.00

TR-1055 "Duo Fi," horizontal, 1965, leather, 10 transistors, upper right front window dial, left grill area with cut-outs, H/L switch, leather handle, AM, bat.................$10.00 – 15.00

TR-1844, horizontal, 1964, leather, eight transistors, upper right front window dial, left grill area with circular cut-outs, leather handle, AM, bat..............................$5.00 – 10.00

TR-1946, vertical, 1964, nine transistors, upper right front window dial with thumbwheel tuning, large lower grill area with vertical bars, AM, bat.......................$5.00 – 10.00

TR-3047, horizontal, 1964, 10 transistors, three right front vertical slide rule dial scales, large left grill area with vertical bars, telescoping antenna, AM, SW, LW, bat...$10.00 – 15.00

TR-3422, horizontal, 1963, 14 transistors, upper front horizontal three-band slide rule dial, large lower grill area, thumbwheel knobs, three telescoping antennas, handle, AM, FM, SW, bat ....$20.00 – 25.00

TR-4016, horizontal, 1963, ten transistors, upper front horizontal four-band slide rule dial, large lower grill area, thumbwheel knobs, telescoping antenna, handle, AM, 2SW, LW, bat....................$20.00 – 25.00

Linmark

T-25 "Boy's Radio," vertical, 1959, plastic, two transistors, upper front see-through panel, window dial with thumbwheel tuning, thumbwheel on/off/volume knob, large lower perforated grill area, AM, bat ....$75.00 – 95.00

T-40, vertical, 1960, four transistors, upper left front round window dial with top thumbwheel tuning, top right thumbwheel on/off/volume knob, lower perforated grill area with vertical lines, AM, bat..**$35.00 – 45.00**

T-61, vertical, 1959, six transistors, left front rectangular window dial with top thumbwheel tuning, top right thumbwheel on/off/volume knob, lower round perforated grill area, AM, bat ....**$35.00 – 45.00**

T-62, vertical, 1960, six transistors, upper front thumbwheel dial with see-through window, upper right front thumbwheel on/off/volume knob, lower perforated grill area, AM, bat ....**$115.00 – 135.00**

T-63, vertical, 1960, six transistors, right front window dial with right side thumbwheel tuning, diagonally divided front, perforated grill area with diagonal lines, AM, bat.**$95.00 – 110.00**

T-80, vertical, 1960, eight transistors, upper right front window dial with right side thumbwheel tuning, upper left front thumbwheel on/off/volume knob, lower grill area with horizontal slots, swing handle, AM, bat ....**$125.00 – 140.00**

<hr />

Lloyd's

6K87B, square, 2½x2½x1¼", plastic, six transistors, upper right side dial knob, lower right side on/off/volume knob, front grill area, left side vinyl strap, AM, bat ...**$35.00 – 45.00**

6K89B, horizontal, 1¾x2⅛x1", nine transistors, top right dial knob, top center on/off/volume knob, front grill area with horizontal bars, left side chain & fob, made in Japan, AM, bat ....**$40.00 – 50.00**

6K98B, horizontal, 2¾x4⅜x1⅛", **plastic, 12 transistors, upper right** **front round window dial with right** **side thumbwheel tuning, lower** **right side thumbwheel on/off/vol-** **ume knob, left grill area with hori-** **zontal bars, AM, bat..$10.00 – 15.00**

8R-202A "Super Het," horizontal, 1964, eight transistors, upper front horizontal two-band slide rule dial with thumbwheel tuning, large lower perforated grill area with lower right switch, AM, SW, bat ....**$15.00 – 20.00**

10R-200A3, horizontal, 1964, 10 transistors, lower front horizontal three-band slide rule dial, large upper grill area with horizontal bars, four push-buttons, telescoping antenna, handle, AM, 2SW, bat ......**$20.00 – 25.00**

10R-303A, horizontal, 1964, 10 transistors, upper right front horizontal three-band slide rule dial with thumbwheel tuning, left perforated grill area, four top pushbuttons, telescoping antenna, handle, AM, 2SW, bat.............**$15.00 – 20.00**

108MB "Super Deluxe," horizontal, 1964, 10 transistors, three upper front horizontal slide rule dials, large lower perforated grill area, two speakers, telescoping antenna, AM, 2SW, bat ....$20.00 – 25.00

TF-58, horizontal, 1964, 10 transistors, upper front horizontal two-band slide rule dial with thumbwheel tuning, large lower grill area, telescoping antenna, handle, AM, FM, bat.$10.00 – 15.00

TF-97, vertical, 4¾x3x1¼", 1965, nine transistors, the upper front horizontal AM dial forms a right angle in the upper left corner with the left side vertical FM dial, large grill area, telescoping antenna, right side strap, AM, FM, bat ....$20.00 – 25.00

TF-110, vertical, 6x4¼x2¼", 1964, 10 transistors, upper front horizontal two-band slide rule dial, lower perforated grill area, telescoping antenna, handle, AM, FM, bat ..$10.00 – 15.00

TF-311, horizontal, 5½x8½x2½", 1965, 10 transistors, two upper front round dials and three knobs, lower grill area with horizontal bars and center logo, telescoping antenna, handle, AM, FM, SW, bat.........................$15.00 – 20.00

TF-911, horizontal, 1964, nine transistors, upper right front round two-band dial with top right thumbwheel tuning, off-center top thumbwheel on/off/volume knob, lower AM/FM switch, left grill area with horizontal slots, telescoping antenna, AM, FM, bat.........$10.00 – 15.00

TF-912, horizontal, 3¾x6⅜x1¾", 1965, plastic, nine transistors, upper right front round dial with top right thumbwheel tuning, off-

center top thumbwheel on/off/volume knob, lower AM/FM switch, left grill area with horizontal bars, telescoping antenna, right side vinyl strap, made in Japan, AM, FM, bat..........................$10.00 – 15.00

TF-990L, horizontal, 4x6½x1¾", 1965, leather, nine transistors, off-center vertical two-band slide rule dial, two right knobs and AM/FM switch, left perforated grill area, telescoping antenna, handle, AM, FM, bat......................$10.00 – 15.00

TR-6KA, vertical, 1964, six transistors, upper front round window dial with right side thumbwheel tuning, lower grill area with vertical slots, AM, bat............$10.00 – 15.00

TR-6KB, horizontal, 2⅞x4⅜x1¼", 1965, six transistors, upper right front window dial with right side thumbwheel tuning, lower right side thumbwheel on/off/volume knob, horizontal grill bars, AM, bat.............................$10.00 – 15.00

TR-6L, vertical, 4¼x2¾x1¼", 1964, six transistors, upper left front window dial with top thumbwheel tun-

ing, upper right front thumbwheel on/off/volume knob, lower perforated grill area, made in Ryukyus, AM, bat.....................$10.00 – 15.00

TR-6P, vertical, 1965, six transistors, upper right front round window dial with thumbwheel tuning, large lower grill area with horizontal bars, right side strap, AM, bat........$5.00 – 10.00

TR-6T, vertical, 1964, six transistors, upper right front round window dial with thumbwheel tuning, large lower grill area with horizontal bars, right side strap, AM, bat........$5.00 – 10.00

TR-8KA, vertical, 1964, eight transistors, upper right front window dial with right side thumbwheel tuning, upper left front on/off/volume window with left side thumbwheel knob, large grill area with horizontal slots, AM, bat ....$10.00 – 15.00

TR-8KB, horizontal, 2⅞x4⅜x1¼", 1965, eight transistors, upper right front window dial with right side thumbwheel tuning, lower right side thumbwheel on/off/volume knob, horizontal grill bars, AM, bat..................$10.00 – 15.00

TR-8L, vertical, 1964, eight transistors, upper left front window dial with top left thumbwheel tuning, upper right thumbwheel on/off/volume knob, lower perforated grill area, AM, bat...............$20.00 – 25.00

TR-10K, horizontal, 2⅞x4⅜x1¼", 1965, 10 transistors, upper right front window dial with right side thumbwheel tuning, lower right side thumbwheel on/off/volume

knob, horizontal grill bars, top right strap, AM, bat.....$5.00 – 10.00

TR-10L, horizontal, 1964, leather, 10 transistors, upper left round dial, two right knobs, large lower grill area with horizontal bars and center logo, leather handle, AM, bat.............................$10.00 – 15.00

TR-10N, vertical, 6x4⅛x1⅞", 1965, 10 transistors, upper right front window dial, upper left front knob, large lower grill area with horizontal bars, pull-up handle, AM, bat..............$5.00 – 10.00

TR-12L, horizontal, 12 transistors, upper right front round window dial with right side thumbwheel tuning, right side thumbwheel on/off/volume knob, front grill area with horizontal bars, AM, bat...$10.00 – 15.00

TR-71, micro, 1965, seven transistors, two right side knobs, front grill area with center logo, left side chain with fob, AM, bat.......$25.00 – 35.00

TR-86L, horizontal, 5x9x2", 1965, leather, eight transistors, right front thumbwheel dial, top left thumbwheel on/off/volume knob, horizontal grill bars, handle, AM, bat.............................$10.00 – 15.00

TR-89L, horizontal, 1964, leather, eight transistors, right front thumbwheel dial, upper left on/off/volume knob, large grill area with horizontal slots, leather handle, AM, bat.....................$10.00 – 15.00

TR-800, horizontal, plastic, eight transistors, step-back top with upper right thumbwheel dial knob, upper left thumbwheel on/off/volume knob, large front oval perforated grill area with center oval logo, handle, AM, bat...............**$30.00 – 40.00**

TRA-10, vertical, 4⅝x3⅝x1⅝", 1965, 10 transistors, upper right front round dial with right side thumbwheel tuning, lower grill area, top rectangular handle, AM, bat...................**$10.00 – 15.00**

Boy's Radio, vertical, 4⅛x2½x1¼", plastic, two transistors, upper right front window dial with right side thumbwheel tuning, left side thumbwheel on/off/volume knob, lower metal perforated grill area, made in Japan, AM, bat.........$35.00 – 45.00

Loewe Opta
Dandy 5900, vertical, 1960, plastic, six transistors, upper right front thumbwheel dial knob, upper left front thumbwheel on/off/volume knob, large lower metal perforated grill area with lower right logo, made in West Germany, AM, bat ...**$35.00 – 45.00**

Luxy 5910, horizontal, 1960, plastic, six transistors, upper front horizontal two-band slide rule dial with thumbwheel tuning, thumbwheel on/off/volume knob, large lower grill area with horizontal bars, made in West Germany, AM, LW, bat...................**$30.00 – 40.00**

Maco
AB-100, vertical, 1960, six transistors, right window dial with right side thumbwheel tuning, upper right front thumbwheel on/off/volume knob, lower perforated grill area with lower left logo, AM, bat...................**$20.00 – 30.00**

AB-175, horizontal, 3¾x6½x1¾", seven transistors, upper front horizontal two-band slide rule dial with right thumbwheel tuning, top left thumbwheel on/off/volume knob, right side band switch, large perforated grill area with lower left logo, telescoping antenna, AM, SW, bat...................$20.00 – 30.00

AB-175M, horizontal, 1962, seven transistors, upper front horizontal two-band slide rule dial with right thumbwheel tuning, top left thumbwheel on/off/volume knob, right side band switch, large perforated grill area with lower left logo, telescoping antenna, AM, SW, bat...................**$20.00 – 30.00**

T-16, horizontal, 1960, six transistors, upper right front dial with right side thumbwheel tuning, lower right front on/off/volume window with right side thumbwheel knob, left perforated grill area with lower left logo, AM, bat ...... **$60.00 – 75.00**

Magnavox

2AM-70, vertical, 1964, seven transistors, upper off-center window dial with right side thumbwheel tuning, right side thumbwheel on/off/volume knob, lower perforated grill area with lower left logo, AM, bat .... **$15.00 – 20.00**

2-AM-80, vertical, 4⅛x2½x1", 1963, plastic, eight transistors, upper front window dial with right side thumbwheel tuning, right side thumbwheel on/off/volume knob, large metal perforated grill area with lower right logo, made in Japan, AM, bat .... **$20.00 – 25.00**

2AM081, vertical, 4⅜x2⅝x1½", plastic, eight transistors, upper front horizontal slide rule dial with right side thumbwheel tuning, right side thumbwheel on/off/volume knob, metal perforated grill area with lower right logo, made in Japan, AM, bat .... **$10.00 – 15.00**

2-AM-802, horizontal, 3x4¾x1½", plastic, eight transistors, upper front horizontal slide rule dial, large lower metal perforated grill area with right thumbwheel tuning and volume knobs, AM, bat .... **$10.00 – 15.00**

2-AM-811, vertical, eight transistors, upper right front dial knob, left side

thumbwheel on/off/volume knob, left vertical grill area with vertical bars, right side strap. AM, bat .... **$10.00 – 15.00**

AM-2, horizontal, 3⅜x5¾x1¾", 1956, plastic, Magnavox's first transistor radio, large upper right front round dial, lower right front on/off/volume window with right side thumbwheel knob, large metal perforated grill area, AM, bat...**$125.00 – 150.00**

AM-5, horizontal, 3⅜x5¾x1¾", 1957, plastic, large upper right front round dial, lower right front on/off/volume window with right side thumbwheel knob, large metal perforated grill area, AM, bat.....**$75.00 – 100.00**

AM-22, horizontal, 2¾x4¼x1", 1960, plastic, six transistors, upper right front window dial with right side thumbwheel tuning, lower right front thumbwheel on/off/volume knob, left metal perforated grill area, AM, bat .....**$35.00 – 45.00**

AM-23, vertical, 4⅛x2⅝x1¼", 1960, plastic, six transistors, upper left front round dial knob, right side thumbwheel on/off/volume knob, lower metal perforated grill area, telescoping antenna, made in Japan, AM, bat..............**$45.00 – 60.00**

AM-60, vertical, 4⅛x2⅝x1", 1961, plastic, six transistors, upper front round dial with right side thumb-wheel tuning, right side thumb-wheel on/off/volume knob, lower metal textured and perforated grill area, rear fold-out stand, made in Japan, AM, bat...........$25.00 – 35.00

AM-61, vertical, 1965, plastic, six transistors, upper front horizontal slide rule dial with right side thumbwheel tuning, right side thumbwheel on/off/volume knob, lower metal perforated grill area with lower right logo, AM, bat ....$15.00 – 20.00

AM-62, vertical, 1963, upper front dial with right side thumbwheel tuning, right side thumbwheel on/off/volume knob, lower metal perforated grill area with lower left logo, AM, bat.............$20.00 – 30.00

AM-64, horizontal, 3¼x6x1¾", 1963, plastic, six transistors, right front vertical slide rule dial with right side thumbwheel tuning, right side thumbwheel on/off/volume knob, large grill area with horizontal slots, AM, bat........$15.00 – 20.00

AM-80, vertical, 4⅛x2½x1", 1961, plastic, eight transistors, upper front window dial with right side thumbwheel tuning, right side thumbwheel on/off/volume knob, large metal textured and perforated grill area with lower right logo, rear fold-out stand, AM, bat .....$15.00 – 25.00

AM-81, vertical, 4⅜x2⅝x1½", plastic, eight transistors, upper front horizontal slide rule dial with right side thumbwheel tuning, right side thumbwheel on/off/volume knob, metal perforated grill area with lower right logo, made in Japan, AM, bat..............................$15.00 – 20.00

AM-82 "Envoy," horizontal, 1964, leather, eight transistors, off-center vertical slide rule dial, two right knobs, left perforated grill area with lower left logo, handle, AM, bat..............................$10.00 – 15.00

AM-83 "Safari," horizontal, 6x8x 3¾", 1964, leather, eight transistors, upper front horizontal slide rule dial, two right knobs, lower perforated grill area with lower left logo, handle, AM, bat ....$10.00 – 15.00

AM-85, horizontal, 4¼x7¼x1¾", 1963, plastic, eight transistors, right front dial with thumbwheel tuning, right thumbwheel on/off/volume knob, left perforated grill area with left logo, AM, bat ......$20.00 – 25.00

AM-801, vertical, 4½x2⅝x1¼", plastic, large upper front round dial with right side thumbwheel tuning, right side thumbwheel on/off/volume knob, lower metal perforated grill area with lower right logo, made in Japan, AM, bat............$15.00 – 20.00

AM-805, square, 2⅛x2⅛x⅞", seven transistors, two right side knobs, large front metal perforated grill area with lower logo, made in Japan, AM, bat ....$25.00 – 30.00

AT-61, horizontal/table, 5⅞x10⅝x4⅝", 1961, available in black, light green, or sand plastic, six transistors, upper right front horizontal slide rule dial, large lower grill area with logo and two knobs, rear hand-hold, made in Japan, AM, bat..............$15.00 – 20.00

AW-24, horizontal, 1960, seven transistors, upper front horizontal two-band slide rule dial with top thumbwheel tuning, top thumbwheel on/off/volume knob, metal perforated grill area with lower right logo, telescoping antenna, AM, SW, bat .....$20.00 – 25.00

AW-88 "Constellation," horizontal, 1964, leather, eight transistors, upper front horizontal three-band slide rule dial, four right knobs, left metal perforated grill area with lower left logo, top knob, handle, AM, SW, LW, bat ....$15.00 – 20.00

AW-100 "Intercontinental," horizontal, 8x12x5⅛", 1958, leatherette, eight transistors, upper front horizontal four-band slide rule dial, large lower metal perforated grill area with large dial knob and three smaller knobs, telescoping antenna, handle, bat............$110.00 – 135.00

FM-90, horizontal, 1962, 10 transistors, upper front horizontal two-band slide rule dial with upper right front thumbwheel tuning, upper left front thumbwheel on/off/volume knob, top pushbuttons, perforated grill area with lower left logo, two telescoping antennas, handle, AM, FM, bat ....$25.00 – 35.00

FM-91, horizontal, 8½x10¼x3¾", 1965, 10 transistors, upper left front horizontal two-band slide rule dial, two upper right knobs and one switch, lower grill area with lower left logo, telescoping antenna, handle, AM, FM, bat........$15.00 – 20.00

FM-92, vertical, 1965, nine transistors, two upper front window dials – right AM, left FM – large perforated grill area with lower right logo, telescoping antenna, AM, FM, bat.................$10.00 – 15.00

FM-95 "Constellation," horizontal, 1963, nine transistors, upper front horizontal three-band slide rule dial, four right knobs, large grill area with lower left logo, two telescoping antennas, handle, AM, FM, SW, bat.....................$20.00 – 25.00

FM-97 "Celestial," horizontal, 1963, nine transistors, upper front horizontal four-band slide rule dial, four right knobs, large grill area with lower left logo, telescoping antenna, handle, AM, FM, 2SW, bat........$20.00 – 30.00

Majestic

FX-408, horizontal, plastic, 11 transistors, upper front horizontal two-band slide rule dial with upper right thumbwheel tuning, left thumbwheel on/off/volume knob, right FM/AM switch, lower metal perforated grill area with lower right bird logo, AM, FM, bat......$15.00 – 20.00

Super Eighty, vertical, 5¾x3½x 1½", plastic, upper right front dial knob, upper left front on/off/volume knob, lower horizontal grill

bars, swing handle, made in USA, AM, bat.....................$20.00 – 30.00

6G780, vertical, plastic, six transistors, upper left front round dial, right side thumbwheel on/off/volume knob, metal perforated grill area with lower right bird logo, AM, bat...............................$35.00 – 45.00

Mantola

M4D, vertical, 5x3x1¼", plastic, four transistors, similar to the Regency TR-4, large upper right front round brass dial knob with orbiting electrons, upper left thumbwheel on/off/volume knob, lower perforated grill area, AM, bat.....................$325.00 – 375.00

Mark VII

Boy's Radio, vertical, 4x2½x1", plastic, two transistors, upper left front window dial with left side thumbwheel tuning, right side thumbwheel on/off/volume knob, round

153

metal perforated grill area, made in Japan, AM, bat...........**$40.00 – 50.00**

Mars

Boy's Radio, vertical, 3⅞x2½x1⅛", plastic, two transistors, upper front window dial with left side thumbwheel tuning, rear thumbwheel on/off/volume knob, lower metal textured and perforated grill area, rear fold-out stand, made in Japan, AM, bat......................**$45.00 – 55.00**

Marvel

6YR-05, vertical, 3⅞x2⅜x1¼", 1961, six transistors, upper right front round dial with right side thumbwheel tuning, upper left front on/off/volume window with left side thumbwheel knob, lower perforated grill area, made in Japan, AM, bat......................**$65.00 – 75.00**

6YR-15A, vertical, 3½x2¼x1", 1961, plastic, six transistors, upper right front see-through dial window with thumbwheel knob, upper left front see-through on/off/volume window

with thumbwheel knob, lower round metal perforated grill area, made in Japan, AM, bat.........$85.00 – 100.00

6YR-20, vertical, plastic, six transistors, upper left front window dial with right side thumbwheel tuning, right side thumbwheel on/off/volume knob, large metal perforated grill area, AM, bat.....$30.00 – 40.00

8YR-10A, vertical, 1962, plastic, eight transistors, upper front horizontal slide rule dial with right side thumbwheel tuning, right side thumbwheel on/off/volume knob, lower round metal perforated grill area, AM, bat.............**$35.00 – 45.00**

TR-21 "Boy's Radio," vertical, 3½x2½x1¼", plastic, two transistors, upper front window dial with top right thumbwheel tuning, top left thumbwheel on/off/volume knob, lower metal textured and perforated grill area, made in Japan, AM, bat...........................**$45.00 – 55.00**

Mascot

RE-60, vertical, 1965, six transistors,

upper right front window dial with right side thumbwheel tuning, lower vertical grill bars, right side strap, AM, bat.............$5.00 – 10.00

Mascot II

2 transistor (no #), vertical, 4⅛x2⅝x1½", plastic, two transistors, upper front window dial with top thumbwheel tuning, right side thumbwheel on/off/volume knob, lower round grill area with concentric circles and center round nameplate, made in Japan, AM, bat..............$50.00 – 60.00

TR2 "II," vertical, plastic, upper right front thumbwheel dial knob, upper left front thumbwheel on/off/volume knob, lower metal perforated grill area, made in Japan, AM, bat..............$20.00 – 30.00

Master-Craft

TF-810, horizontal, 1⅜x6½x2⅜", leather/plastic/metal, eight transistors, concave front, left horizontal slide rule dial with thumbwheel tuning, thumbwheel on/off/volume knob, right side braided strap, made in Hong Kong, AM, bat..............$20.00 – 25.00

Masterwork

M2100TR "Galaxy III," horizontal, 1963, nine transistors, upper front horizontal three-band slide rule dial, top pushbuttons and thumbwheel knobs, lower checkered grill area, telescoping antenna, handle, AM, FM, SW, bat.......$20.00 – 25.00

M2810, horizontal, 1964, 10 transistors, upper front horizontal two-band

slide rule dial, top left thumbwheel on/off/volume knob, large lower perforated grill area, telescoping antenna, AM, FM, bat.....$10.00 – 15.00

M2812, horizontal, 1965, leather, eight transistors, upper left front horizontal slide rule dial, two right knobs, large lower perforated grill area, leather handle, AM, bat..............$5.00 – 10.00

M2815, horizontal, 1964, 10 transistors, two right front round dials — one AM, one FM — left perforated grill area, telescoping antenna, handle, AM, FM, bat.......$15.00 – 20.00

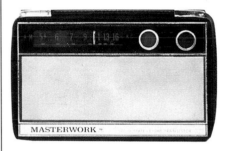

M2850, horizontal, leatherette, eight transistors, upper left front horizontal slide rule dial, two right knobs, large lower perforated grill area, handle, AM, bat..$5.00 – 10.00

M3102, horizontal, 4x4½x1⅛", leatherette, upper left front hori-

zontal two-band slide rule dial with upper right thumbwheel tuning, right side thumbwheel on/off/volume knob, two switches, lower metal perforated grill area, telescoping antenna, vinyl strap, AM, FM, bat....................$10.00 – 15.00

Matsushita

DT-495, horizontal/table, 5¾x10⅜x3½", 1962, six transistors, upper right front thumbwheel dial knob, lower right on/off/volume knob, left grill area with horizontal bars and lower left logo, AM, bat ....$20.00 – 25.00

T-7, vertical, 3¾x2½x1⅛", plastic, seven transistors, upper front horizontal slide rule dial with right side thumbwheel tuning, right side thumbwheel on/off/volume knob, lower metal grill area with horizontal slots, rear fold-out stand, made in Japan, AM, bat ......$25.00 – 35.00

T-13, vertical, 1961, six transistors, upper front horizontal slide rule dial with right side thumbwheel tuning, upper left thumbwheel on/off/volume knob, lower perforated grill area with lower right logo, AM, bat.............$20.00 – 30.00

T-22M, horizontal, 1962, eight transistors, upper front horizontal two-band slide rule dial with thumbwheel tuning, lower perforated grill area with MW/SW switch and battery window, telescoping antenna, AM, SW, bat ....$25.00 – 35.00

T-22U, horizontal, 5x8½x1¾", 1962, eight transistors, upper front hori-

zontal two-band slide rule dial with thumbwheel tuning, lower perforated grill area with MW/SW switch and battery window, telescoping antenna, AM, SW, bat ...$25.00 – 35.00

T-30, horizontal, 6⅝x10x2⅞", 1961, plastic, nine transistors, upper front horizontal two-band slide rule dial with thumbwheel tuning, upper left AM/FM switch, lower perforated grill area, telescoping antenna, handle, AM, FM, bat.$15.00 – 20.00

T-41M, horizontal, 1962, eight transistors, top horizontal two-band slide rule dial with top right thumbwheel tuning, lower right side thumbwheel on/off/volume knob, large perforated grill area with lower right logo, telescoping antenna, AM, SW, bat.........$20.00 – 30.00

T-41U, horizontal, 1962, eight transistors, top horizontal two-band slide rule dial with top right thumbwheel tuning, lower right side thumbwheel on/off/volume knob, large perforated grill area with lower right logo, telescoping antenna, AM, SW, bat.........$20.00 – 30.00

T-50, horizontal, 3¼x5¾x1½", 1962, plastic, six transistors, right front window dial with right side thumbwheel tuning, top left thumb-

wheel on/off/volume knob, large metal perforated grill area, made in Japan, AM, bat.........$25.00 – 35.00

T-66, horizontal, 1962, eight transistors, upper front horizontal three-band slide rule dial, large lower perforated grill area, right side switch, telescoping antenna, handle, AM, 2SW, bat......$20.00 – 25.00

T-70M, horizontal, 1962, eight transistors, right front horizontal two-band slide rule dial with thumbwheel tuning, thumbwheel on/off/volume knob, left grill area with horizontal bars and upper left logo, telescoping antenna, handle, AM, SW, bat..............$20.00 – 30.00

T-70U, horizontal, 1962, eight transistors, right front horizontal two-band slide rule dial with thumbwheel tuning, thumbwheel on/off/volume knob, left grill area with horizontal bars and upper left logo, telescoping antenna, handle, AM, SW, bat..............$20.00 – 30.00

T-92 "Portalarm," vertical/watch radio, 1962, six transistors, upper right side thumbwheel dial knob with wedge-shaped indent, upper left seven-jewel alarm watch face, top left watch stem, top right switch, perforated grill area with lower left logo, AM, bat........$100.00 – 125.00

Mellow-Tone
NR-23 "Boy's Radio," vertical, 4x2½x1¼", plastic, two transistors, rounded upper right corner, upper right front dial knob, left side thumbwheel on/off/volume knob,

lower metal textured and perforated grill area, made in Japan, AM, bat..............................$50.00 – 60.00

Melodic
GT-586, vertical, 1961, six transistors, upper left front round dial knob, upper right front thumbwheel on/off/volume knob, lower perforated grill area, AM, bat..$20.00 – 30.00

MT-69, vertical, 1961, six transistors, upper right front window dial with right side thumbwheel tuning, lower perforated grill area, AM, bat.....................$10.00 – 15.00

Melson
Boy's Radio, vertical, 3¾x2½x1⅛", plastic, two transistors, upper right side thumbwheel dial knob with wedge-shaped indent, left side thumbwheel on/off/volume knob, large metal textured and perforated grill area, lower right logo, made in Japan, AM, bat..........$60.00 – 75.00

Merco

Americall, horizontal, 5½x8¼x2⅞", leatherette, lower right front dial knob, lower left front on/off/volume knob, center grill area with vertical bars, leather handle, made in USA, AM, bat........$20.00 – 25.00

Mercury

2 transistor (no #), horizontal, 2¾x4x1¼", plastic, two transistors, right front dial knob, lower right front thumbwheel on/off/volume knob, left grill area with horizontal bars, made in Japan, AM, bat............$45.00 – 55.00

Metz

Babyphon 102, horizontal/radio-phono, plastic, left front round dial knob, right front on/off/volume knob, horizontal grill bars, lift top, inner phono, handle, made in West Germany.................$35.00 – 45.00

Midland

10-106B, vertical, plastic, six transistors, upper right front window

dial with thumbwheel tuning, thumbwheel on/off/volume knob, lower textured grill area, right side strap, AM, bat............$5.00 – 10.00

10-310, horizontal, 1964, 10 transistors, upper right front window dial with right side thumbwheel tuning, lower right side thumbwheel on/off/volume knob, large perforated grill area, AM, bat.........................$15.00 – 20.00

10-408, horizontal, 1964, eight transistors, right front round dial knob, lower right on/off/volume knob, large left perforated grill area, handle, AM, bat..............$10.00 – 15.00

10-410, horizontal, 1964, leather, 10 transistors, right front round dial, lower right tone switch, upper left on/off/volume knob, large perforated grill area, leather handle, AM, bat.....................$10.00 – 15.00

10-440, horizontal, 1964, 12 transistors, upper front horizontal two-band slide rule dial, two knobs, large lower perforated grill area, telescoping antenna, handle, AM, FM, bat.....................$15.00 – 20.00

10-644, lamp/radio, plastic, radio base with gooseneck lamp shade, right front dial knob, left front on/off/volume knob, AM, bat/AC ....$25.00 – 35.00

11-406, horizontal, 1964, six transistors, right front round dial with thumbwheel tuning, thumbwheel on/off/volume knob, left grill area, AM, bat.....................$10.00 – 15.00

Million

G-601, horizontal, 3x5¼x1½", plastic, six transistors, "mother-of-pearl" right front panel with thumbwheel dial knob, top thumbwheel on/off/ volume knob, left metal perforated grill area, AM, bat......**$65.00 – 80.00**

MTR 201 "Boy's Radio," vertical, 4x2¾x1", plastic, two transistors, upper right front window dial with right side thumbwheel tuning, left side thumbwheel on/off/volume knob, lower metal perforated grill area, swing handle, made in Japan, AM, bat......................**$55.00 – 65.00**

Minute Man

6T-170, vertical, 3⅝x2¼x1⅜", 1960, six transistors, top dial and on/off/volume knobs, two front perforated semicircular wraparound grill areas, made in Japan, AM, bat....................$75.00 – 95.00

Mitchell

1101, vertical, 5x3x1½", 1955, suntan leather, four transistors, upper right front round dial knob and upper left thumbwheel on/off/ volume knob over large perforated grill area, hinged back, AM, bat.......................**$350.00 – 450.00**

1102, vertical, 5x3x1½", 1955, simulated alligator leather, four transistors, upper right front round dial knob and upper left thumbwheel on/off/volume knob over large perforated grill area, hinged back, AM, bat..................**$350.00 – 450.00**

1103, vertical, 5x3x1½", 1955, antique white leather, four transistors, upper right front round dial knob and upper left thumbwheel on/off/volume knob over large perforated grill area, hinged back, AM, bat..................**$350.00 – 450.00**

Mitsubishi

6X-145, vertical, 3¾x2½x1", plastic, six transistors, upper front seethrough panel, right front dial with top right and right side thumbwheel tuning, top left thumbwheel on/off/volume knob, lower metal

perforated grill area with lower left logo, swing handle, made in Japan, AM, bat.................$100.00 – 125.00

6X-148, vertical, 3¾x2⅜x1⅛", plastic, six transistors, upper right front dial with top right and right side thumbwheel tuning, top left thumbwheel on/off/volume knob, lower metal perforated grill area, swing handle, made in Japan, AM, bat.........**$45.00 – 55.00**

6X-720, vertical, plastic, upper right front recessed window dial with thumbwheel tuning, upper left front thumbwheel on/off/volume knob, large vertical metal textured and perforated grill area with lower left logo, AM, bat .....**$45.00 – 55.00**

6X-870 "Elite," vertical, plastic, six transistors, upper front see-through panel with right thumbwheel tuning, upper left front thumbwheel on/off/volume knob, lower metal perforated grill area with lower left logo, AM, bat........**$125.00 – 150.00**

7X-164, vertical, 1965, seven transistors, upper right front round window dial with right side thumbwheel tuning, lower perforated grill area with lower left logo, AM, bat ....**$10.00 – 15.00**

7X-505, vertical, 4⅛x2¾x1¼", plastic, seven transistors, upper front horizontal two-band dial with right side thumbwheel tuning, right side thumbwheel on/off/volume knob, lower metal perforated grill area with lower left logo, left side telescoping antenna, bottom swing-around stand, AM, SW, bat.................**$40.00 – 50.00**

8X-360 "Elite," vertical, 4¼x2¾x1¼", plastic, eight transistors, upper front see-through panel, left front window dial with thumbwheel tuning, thumbwheel on/off/volume knob, lower metal perforated grill area with lower left logo, bottom swing-around stand, made in Japan, AM, bat..........................**$75.00 – 100.00**

8X-678 "Electric," horizontal, 4⅛x6½x1½", plastic, eight transistors, top horizontal two-band slide rule dial with right side thumbwheel tuning & fine tuning knobs, left side thumbwheel on/off/volume knob, large front metal perforated grill area, telescoping antenna, rear band switch, BC, SW..**$25.00 – 35.00**

9X-628, horizontal, 1965, leather, nine transistors, right front vertical slide rule dial with thumbwheel tuning, upper left front knob, horizontal grill bars, leather handle, AM, bat ....**$10.00 – 15.00**

9X-980, horizontal, 1965, nine transistors, right front round dial with right side thumbwheel tuning, left perforated grill area with lower left logo, AM, bat..............$10.00 – 15.00

FX-233 "Three Diamonds," horizontal, 1965, 13 transistors, upper front horizontal three-band slide rule dial, four thumbwheel knobs, MW/SW/FM switch, battery window, perforated grill area, telescoping antenna, AM, FM, SW, bat..............$20.00 – 25.00

FX-412, horizontal, 1965, nine transistors, upper front horizontal two-band slide rule dial with right side thumbwheel tuning, right side thumbwheel on/off/volume knob, large perforated grill area with upper left logo, telescoping antenna, AM, FM, bat..............$10.00 – 15.00

MMA
6TP-317 "High Fidelity," vertical, 1963, six transistors, upper left front window dial with right side thumbwheel tuning, right side thumbwheel on/off/volume knob, lower front perforated grill area, AM, bat..............$10.00 – 15.00

8TP-412 "High Sensitivity," vertical, 1963, eight transistors, upper front window dial with right side thumbwheel tuning, right side thumbwheel on/off/volume knob, lower front perforated grill area with center logo, swing handle, AM, bat..............$40.00 – 50.00

8TP-416, vertical, 1963, six transistors, upper front window dial with

right side thumbwheel tuning, right side thumbwheel on/off/volume knob, lower front perforated grill area, AM, bat..............$10.00 – 15.00

8TP-802M, horizontal, 1962, nine transistors, upper front horizontal three-band slide rule dial with right thumbwheel tuning, two left thumbwheel knobs — one volume, one tone — right side switch, perforated grill area, telescoping antenna, AM, Marine, SW, bat..........$25.00 – 35.00

8TP-905, horizontal, 1963, eight transistors, right front thumbwheel dial, upper left thumbwheel on/off/volume knob, handle, AM, bat..............$15.00 – 20.00

602, vertical, 1963, six transistors, upper right thumbwheel dial, top left thumbwheel on/off/volume knob, lower perforated grill area, AM, bat......................$15.00 – 20.00

F100, horizontal, 1963, 11 transistors, upper front horizontal three-band slide rule dial, two right side knobs, two left front thumbwheel knobs, horizontal grill bars, two telescoping antennas, handle, AM, FM, SW, bat..............$15.00 – 20.00

F-140, horizontal, 1963, 10 transistors, right front thumbwheel dial, upper right AM/FM switch, upper left thumbwheel on/off/volume knob, perforated grill area, telescoping antenna, strap, AM, FM, bat..............................$10.00 – 15.00

TF-52, horizontal, 1963, 11 transistors, upper front horizontal two-band slide rule dial, top knobs, large lower grill area, two telescoping antennas, handle, AM, FM, bat...**$20.00 – 25.00**

Modelux

Boy's Radio, vertical, 3½x2⅜x1¼", plastic, two transistors, upper right front window dial with right side thumbwheel tuning, thumbwheel on/off/volume knob, large round grill area with vertical bars, made in Japan, AM, bat...........**$55.00 – 65.00**

Monacor

RE-3B "Deluxe," horizontal, 1964, eight transistors, upper front horizontal three-band slide rule dial with right thumbwheel tuning, large lower perforated grill area, telescoping antenna, AM, 2SW, bat.................**$25.00 – 30.00**

RE-606, vertical, 1964, six transistors, upper right front window dial with thumbwheel tuning, lower vertical grill bars, right side strap, AM, bat..............................**$5.00 – 10.00**

RE-612, vertical, 1963, six transistors, upper left front window dial with right side thumbwheel tuning, right side thumbwheel on/off/volume knob, large perforated circular grill area, AM, bat.....**$15.00 – 20.00**

RE-613, vertical, 1963, seven transistors, upper front window dial with right side thumbwheel tuning, right side thumbwheel on/off/volume knob, lower perforated grill area, swing handle, AM, bat.**$15.00 – 20.00**

RE-808, vertical, 1964, eight transistors, upper right front window dial

with right side thumbwheel tuning, upper left front on/off/volume window with left side thumbwheel knob, lower perforated grill area, AM, bat......................**$15.00 – 20.00**

RE-1010 "Sportsman," horizontal, 1964, leather, 10 transistors, right front thumbwheel dial, top left on/off knob, large perforated grill area, handle, AM, bat...........................**$10.00 – 15.00**

RE-1200, horizontal, 1965, nine transistors, right front two-band thumbwheel dial, lower right thumbwheel on/off/volume knob, horizontal grill bars, telescoping antenna, AM, FM, bat.......................**$10.00 – 15.00**

RE-1250L, horizontal, 1965, leather, 10 transistors, right front two-band thumbwheel dial, upper right FM/AM switch, upper left thumbwheel on/off/volume knob, perforated grill area, telescoping antenna, handle, AM, FM, bat.....................**$10.00 – 15.00**

RE-1700, horizontal, 1964, 11 transistors, upper front horizontal two-band slide rule dial, large lower grill area with three knobs, telescoping antenna, handle, AM, FM, bat.............................**$10.00 – 15.00**

Monarch

60, vertical, plastic, six transistors, upper front see-through panel with right window dial, top right thumbwheel tuning, top left thumbwheel on/off/volume knob, lower grill area with horizontal bars and lower left logo, AM, bat......**$60.00 – 75.00**

right front window dial with right side thumbwheel tuning, left side thumbwheel on/off/volume knob, lower perforated grill area, made in Japan, AM, bat............$30.00 – 40.00

90, vertical, 4⅝x3x1¼", plastic, nine transistors, upper front see-through panel with center window dial, right side thumbwheel tuning, left side thumbwheel on/off/volume knob, large perforated grill area with lower right logo, rear fold-out stand, made in Japan, AM, bat ...$100.00 – 150.00

RE-760, horizontal, 1964, seven transistors, right front round dial knob, right side knob, feet, handle, AM, bat.....................$10.00 – 15.00

RE-1050, horizontal, 1964, 10 transistors, lower right front dial, upper right on/off/volume knob, large left perforated grill area, handle, AM, bat......................$5.00 – 10.00

Montclaire
Boy's Radio, horizontal/table, plastic, two transistors, right front dial knob/left front on/off/volume knob over vertical grill bars, made in Japan, AM, bat .....$30.00 – 40.00

Morse
131, vertical, 4¼x2⅝x1¼", plastic, six transistors, metal front panel, upper

290, horizontal, 5¼x8¾x2¼", plastic, eight transistors, upper front horizontal three-band slide rule dial with right thumbwheel tuning, top left thumbwheel on/off knob, large lower metal perforated grill area, telescoping antenna, right side band switch, made in Japan, AM, SW, Marine, bat........$25.00 – 35.00

Boy's Radio "Supertone," vertical, 4⅛x2⅝x1¼", plastic, two transistors, upper left front dial knob, upper right side thumbwheel on/off/volume knob, lower metal textured and perforated grill area, made in Japan, AM, bat...........$50.00 – 60.00

Motorola
6X28B, horizontal, 3¼x5¾x1¾", 1959, blue plastic, six transistors, "jet plane" design molded into front panel over vertical grill bars, right window dial with right side thumbwheel tuning, right side thumbwheel on/off/volume knob, AM, bat......................$75.00 – 95.00

6X28N, horizontal, 3¼x5¾x1¾", 1959, mocha plastic, six transistors, "jet plane" design molded into front panel over vertical grill bars, right window dial with right side thumbwheel tuning, right side thumbwheel on/off/volume knob, AM, bat.....................$50.00 – 75.00

**6X28P, horizontal, 3¼x5¾x1¾",
1959, pink plastic, six transistors,
"jet plane" design molded into
front panel over vertical grill bars,
right window dial with right side
thumbwheel tuning, right side
thumbwheel on/off/volume knob,
AM, bat....................$75.00 – 95.00**

6X28W, horizontal, 3¼x5¾x1¾", 1959, antique white plastic, six transistors, "jet plane" design molded into front panel over vertical grill bars, right window dial with right side thumbwheel tuning, right side thumbwheel on/off/volume knob, AM, bat.....................$50.00 – 75.00

6X31C, horizontal, 4x6⅜x1⅞", 1957, blue & beige metal case, right front dial knob, upper right on/off/volume knob, plastic grill area with vertical bars, large swing handle, AM, bat ......$75.00 – 100.00

6X31N, horizontal, 4x6⅜x1⅞", 1957, beige metal case, right front dial knob, upper right on/off/volume knob, plastic grill area with

vertical bars, large swing handle, AM, bat.....................$75.00 – 100.00

6X31R, horizontal, 4x6⅜x1⅞", 1957, red & navy metal case, right front dial knob, upper right on/off/volume knob, plastic grill area with vertical bars, large swing handle, AM, bat ......$75.00 – 100.00

6X32E, horizontal, 4⅛x6½x1¾", 1957, navy metal case, right front dial knob, upper right on/off/volume knob, metal perforated grill area with lower left logo, large plastic swing handle, AM, bat..........................$75.00 – 100.00

6X32E-1, horizontal, 4⅛x6½x1¾", metal case, right front dial knob, upper right on/off/volume knob, metal perforated grill area with lower left logo, large plastic swing handle, AM, bat.............$75.00 – 100.00

**6X39A "Weatherama," 4⅞x6½x2½",
horizontal, 1958, gray metal, six
transistors, right front two-band dial
knob, upper right on/off/volume
knob, left perforated grill area,
large swing handle, AM, LW Bea-
con, bat.................$100.00 – 125.00**

6X39A-1 "Weatherama," 4⅞x6½x2½", horizontal, 1958, six transistors, right front two-band dial knob, upper right on/off/volume knob, left perforated grill area, large swing handle, AM, LW Beacon, bat......$100.00 – 125.00

6X39A-2 "Weatherama," horizontal, 1958, six transistors, right front two-band dial knob, upper right on/off/volume knob, left perforated grill area, large swing handle, AM, LW Beacon, bat......$100.00 – 125.00

7X23E "Power 10," horizontal, 4x 6½x2", 1959, navy blue, seven transistors, metal "jet plane" design molded into front panel over perforated grill area, right window dial with right side thumbwheel tuning, top right on/off/volume knob, large swing handle, AM, bat..........$200.00 – 250.00

7X24S "Power 10," horizontal, 4x 6½x2", 1959, suntan, seven transistors, metal "jet plane" design molded into front panel over perforated grill area, right window dial with right side thumbwheel tuning, top right on/off/volume knob, large swing handle, AM, bat......$200.00 – 250.00

7X24W "Power 10," horizontal, 4x 6½x2", 1959, antique white, seven transistors, metal "jet plane" design molded into front panel over perforated grill area, right window dial with right side thumbwheel tuning, top right on/off/volume knob, back panel has embossed stars, large swing handle, AM, bat..........$250.00 – 300.00

7X25P "Power 9," vertical, 7x4¼x2⅜", 1959, salmon plastic, seven transistors, upper front round dial knob over horizontal grill bars, lower left on/off/volume knob, swing handle, AM, bat......$30.00 – 40.00

7X25W "Power 9," vertical, 7x4¼x2⅜", 1959, antique white plastic, seven transistors, upper front round dial knob over horizontal grill bars, lower left on/off/volume knob, swing handle, AM, bat......$30.00 – 40.00

8X26E "Power 10," vertical, 7x4½x2½", charcoal plastic, eight transistors, upper front round dial knob, lower left on/off/volume knob, horizontal grill bars with logo, swing handle, AM, bat..........$35.00 – 45.00

8X26S "Power 10," vertical, 7x4½x2½", maple sugar plastic, eight transistors, upper front round dial knob, lower left on/off/volume knob, horizontal grill bars with logo, swing handle, AM, bat......$35.00 – 45.00

56T1, horizontal, 3½x5½x1½", 1956, antique white & gold, five transistors, Motorola's first transistor radio, lower right front round dial knob, upper right on/off/ volume knob, perforated grill area with lower left logo, large swing handle with built-in antenna, AM, bat...........$200.00 – 250.00

66T1, horizontal, 3⅛x5x2⅜", 1958, six transistors, lower right front round dial knob, upper right on/ off/volume knob, perforated grill area with lower left logo, large swing handle, AM, bat.....$125.00 – 150.00

76T1, horizontal, 1957, charcoal leatherette, seven transistors, upper right front dial knob, upper left front on/off/volume knob, large metal perforated grill area, rotatable handle, AM, bat ....$45.00 – 55.00

76T2, horizontal, 1957, brown leatherette, seven transistors, upper right front dial knob, upper left front on/off/volume knob, large metal perforated grill area, rotatable handle, AM, bat...............$45.00 – 55.00

AX4B, horizontal, 1961, light blue front/white back, six transistors, large right front round dial and two

knobs over lattice grill area, left logo, AM, bat.............$15.00 – 25.00

AX4G, horizontal, 1961, willow green front/antique white back, six transistors, large right front round dial and two knobs over lattice grill area, left logo, AM, bat...............$15.00 – 25.00

AX4N, horizontal, 1961, sagebrush brown front/antique white back, six transistors, large right front round dial and two knobs over lattice grill area, left logo, AM, bat....................$15.00 – 25.00

CD-XT18B, horizontal, 6⅜x10¼x3⅛", 1962, blue, equipped with Civil Defense antenna terminal to allow emergency reception in fallout shelters, large right front dial knob over large lattice grill area, left on/off/volume knob, pop-up handle, AM, bat.......$15.00 – 20.00

CD-XT18S, horizontal, 6⅜x10¼x3⅛", 1962, tan, equipped with Civil Defense antenna terminal to allow emergency reception in fallout shelters, large right front dial knob over large lattice grill area, left on/off/volume knob, pop-up handle, AM, bat............$15.00 – 20.00

CX1B, horizontal/clock radio, 1961, blue, six transistors, fold-down front, inner right window dial and two knobs, left clock face, center grill area, AM, bat......$20.00 – 25.00

CX1E, horizontal/clock radio, 1961, black, six transistors, fold-down front, inner right window dial and two knobs, left clock face, center grill area, AM, bat......$20.00 – 25.00

CX1W, horizontal/clock radio, 1961, white, six transistors, fold-down front, inner right window dial and two knobs, left clock face, center grill area, AM, bat.......$20.00 – 25.00

CX2N "Tandem," horizontal/clock radio with removable portable radio unit, radio measures 5¼x4x1¾", 1963, plastic, six transistors, radio unit has upper left front half-round dial with right side thumbwheel tuning, right side thumbwheel on/off/volume knob, large round metal perforated grill area, made in USA, AM, bat.
radio only.................$25.00 – 35.00
radio with clock........$50.00 – 60.00

L12G "Power 8," horizontal, 1960, plastic, six transistors, right front round dial, left on/off/volume knob, lower grill area with horizontal bars and lower left logo, handle, AM, bat.....................$10.00 – 15.00

L12N "Power 8," horizontal, 1960, plastic, six transistors, right front round dial, left on/off/volume knob, lower grill area with horizontal bars and lower left logo, handle, AM, bat.....................$10.00 – 15.00

L13S "Power 9," horizontal, 8x9¾x2¾", 1959, maple sugar plastic, seven transistors, right front round dial, left on/off/volume knob, lower grill area with horizontal bars and lower left logo, rotatable handle, AM, bat.............................$20.00 – 30.00

L13W "Power 9," horizontal, 8x9¾x2¾", 1959, antique white plastic, seven transistors, right front round dial, left on/off/volume knob, lower grill area with horizontal bars and lower left logo, rotatable handle, AM, bat..........$20.00 – 30.00

L14E "Ranger 1000," horizontal, 1960, eight transistors, right front round dial, left on/off/volume knob, lower grill area with horizontal bars and lower left logo, rotatable handle, AM, bat..........$20.00 – 30.00

L20E, horizontal, 8¼x9⅝x3", 1960, smoke plastic, right front round dial, left on/off/volume knob, lower grill area with horizontal bars and lower left logo, rotatable handle, AM, bat...............$20.00 – 30.00

TP2EE, vertical, 5¼x3¼x1½", 1968, black, 10 transistors, two upper front horizontal slide rule dial scales with right side thumbwheel tuning, right side thumbwheel on/off/volume knob, lower perforated grill area, telescoping antenna, AM, FM, bat.........$10.00 – 15.00

TP71BE, horizontal, 4½x5¾x2¼", leatherette, off-center large round two-band dial over large textured grill area, two right front knobs and one switch, handle, AM, FM, bat..............................$10.00 – 15.00

X11B, vertical, 4x2¼x1", 1959, six transistors, upper front oval window dial with right side thumbwheel tuning, left side thumbwheel on/off/volume knob, lower metal perforated grill area with "M" logo, rear fold-out stand, AM, bat..............$35.00 – 45.00

X11E, vertical, 4x2¼x1", 1959, plastic, six transistors, upper front oval window dial with right side thumbwheel tuning, left side thumbwheel on/off/volume knob, lower metal perforated grill area with "M" logo, rear fold-out stand, AM, bat.....................$35.00 – 45.00

X11G, vertical, 4x2¼x1", 1959, plastic, six transistors, upper front oval window dial with right side thumbwheel tuning, left side thumbwheel on/off/volume knob, lower metal perforated grill area with "M" logo, rear fold-out stand, AM, bat.....................$35.00 – 45.00

X11R, vertical, 4x2¼x1", 1959, six transistors, upper front oval window dial with right side thumbwheel tuning, left side thumbwheel on/off/volume knob, lower metal perforated grill area with "M" logo, rear fold-out stand, AM, bat.....................$35.00 – 45.00

X12A "Power Eight," horizontal, 1959, plastic, six transistors, lower right front round window dial with lower right side thumbwheel tuning, upper right side thumbwheel on/off/volume knob, left vertical grill bars, AM, bat.....$20.00 – 25.00

X12A-1 "Power Eight," horizontal, 3½x6x1⅞", 1959, gray plastic, six transistors, lower right front round window dial with lower right side thumbwheel tuning, upper right side thumbwheel on/off/volume knob, left vertical grill bars, AM, bat..............................$20.00 – 25.00

X12-E "Power Eight," horizontal, 3½x6x1⅞", 1959, plastic, six transistors, lower right front round window dial with lower right side thumbwheel tuning, upper right side thumbwheel on/off/volume knob, left vertical grill bars, AM, bat..............................$20.00 – 25.00

X12E-1 "Power Eight," horizontal, 3½x6x1⅞", 1959, smoke plastic, six transistors, lower right front round window dial with lower right side thumbwheel tuning, upper right side thumbwheel on/off/volume knob, left vertical grill bars, AM, bat..............................$20.00 – 25.00

X14B, vertical, 4x2¾x1¼", 1960, blue plastic, six transistors, upper left front window dial with right side thumbwheel tuning, right side thumbwheel on/off/volume knob, lower oversized round metal perforated grill area, rear fold-out stand, AM, bat ....$45.00 – 55.00

X14E, vertical, 4x2¾x1¼", 1960, black plastic, six transistors, upper left front window dial with right side thumbwheel tuning, right side thumbwheel on/off/volume knob, lower oversized round metal perforated grill area, rear fold-out stand, AM, bat ....$45.00 – 55.00

X14R, vertical, 4x2¾x1¼", 1960, red plastic, six transistors, upper left front window dial with right side thumbwheel tuning, right side thumbwheel on/off/volume knob, lower oversized round metal perforated grill area, rear fold-out stand, AM, bat.....................$45.00 – 55.00

X14W, vertical, 4x2¾x1¼", 1960, white plastic, six transistors, upper left front window dial with right side thumbwheel tuning, right side

thumbwheel on/off/volume knob, lower oversized round metal perforated grill area, rear fold-out stand, AM, bat ....$45.00 – 55.00

X15A, vertical, 4x2¾x1½", 1960, gray/blue plastic, six transistors, upper left front window dial with right side thumbwheel tuning, right side thumbwheel on/off/volume knob, lower metal perforated grill area, bottom swing-out stand, made in Japan, AM, bat ......$40.00 – 50.00

X15E, vertical, 4x2¾x1½", 1960, black plastic, six transistors, upper left front window dial with right side thumbwheel tuning, right side thumbwheel on/off/volume knob, lower metal perforated grill area, bottom swing-out stand, made in Japan, AM, bat...........$40.00 – 50.00

X15N, vertical, 4x2¾x1½", 1960, brown plastic, six transistors, upper left front window dial with right side thumbwheel tuning, right side thumbwheel on/off/volume knob, lower metal perforated grill area,

bottom swing-out stand, made in Japan, AM, bat..........$40.00 – 50.00

X16B, vertical, 6⅛x3⅞x1½", 1960, blue, seven transistors, upper right front round window dial with right side thumbwheel tuning, right front on/off/volume knob, large grill area with horizontal bars and lower left logo, swing handle, AM, bat..............................$20.00 – 30.00

X16G, vertical, 6⅛x3⅞x1½", 1960, two-tone green, seven transistors, upper right front round window dial with right side thumbwheel tuning, right front on/off/volume knob, large grill area with horizontal bars and lower left logo, swing handle, AM, bat........$20.00 – 30.00

X16N, vertical, 6⅛x3⅞x1½", 1960, brown/tan, seven transistors, upper right front round window dial with right side thumbwheel tuning, right front on/off/volume knob, large grill area with horizontal bars and lower left logo, swing handle, AM, bat..............................$20.00 – 30.00

X17B, vertical, 5¾x4x1½", 1960, blue plastic, eight transistors, upper front window dial with right side thumbwheel tuning, right side thumbwheel on/off/volume knob, large round metal perforated grill area, swing handle, AM, bat..............................$35.00 – 45.00

X17N, vertical, 5¾x4x1½", 1960, brown plastic, eight transistors, upper front window dial with right side thumbwheel tuning, right side thumbwheel on/off/volume knob, large

round metal perforated grill area, swing handle, AM, bat..$35.00 – 45.00

X17R, vertical, 5¾x4x1½", 1960, red plastic, eight transistors, upper front window dial with right side thumbwheel tuning, right side thumbwheel on/off/volume knob, large round metal perforated grill area, swing handle, AM, bat..........$35.00 – 45.00

X19A, vertical, 6¼x4x1¾", 1960, gray blue plastic, eight transistors, upper front horizontal slide rule dial with thumbwheel tuning, lower perforated grill area with lower left logo, bottom swing-out stand, leather handle, AM, bat........................$30.00 – 40.00

X19E, vertical, 6¼x4x1¾", 1960, black plastic, eight transistors, upper front horizontal slide rule dial with thumbwheel tuning, lower perforated grill area with lower left logo, bottom swing-out stand, leather handle, AM, bat................$30.00 – 40.00

X21W, vertical, 3⅛x2⅜x1", 1961, plastic, six transistors, upper right front round dial knob, upper left front thumbwheel on/off/volume knob, lower metal perforated grill area with lower left logo with rhinestone decoration, AM, bat............$40.00 – 50.00

X23B, vertical, 3⅝x2⅜x1⅛", 1961, blue plastic, six transistors, upper right front round dial knob, upper left front thumbwheel on/off/volume knob, lower patterned grill area, AM, bat.............$15.00 – 20.00

X23E, vertical, 3⅝x2⅜x1⅛", 1961, black plastic, six transistors, upper right front round dial knob, upper left front thumbwheel on/off/volume knob, lower patterned grill area, AM, bat............$15.00 – 20.00

X23V, vertical, 3⅝x2⅜x1⅛", 1961, violet plastic, six transistors, upper right front round dial knob, upper left front thumbwheel on/off/volume knob, lower patterned grill area, AM, bat............$15.00 – 20.00

X24N, vertical, 3⅝x2½x1¼", 1961, brown plastic, upper right front round dial knob, upper left front thumbwheel on/off/volume knob, lower perforated grill area with lower left logo, AM, bat........$25.00 – 35.00

X24W, vertical, 3⅝x2½x1¼", 1961, white plastic, upper right front round dial knob, upper left front thumbwheel on/off/volume knob, lower perforated grill area with lower left logo, AM, bat............$25.00 – 35.00

X25E, vertical, 4⅛x2¾x1½", 1960, black plastic, six transistors, upper

left front window dial with right side thumbwheel tuning, right side thumbwheel on/off/volume knob, lower lattice grill area, left side strap, AM, bat............$20.00 – 30.00

X25J, vertical, 1960, jade plastic, six transistors, upper left front window dial with right side thumbwheel tuning, right side thumbwheel on/off/ volume knob, lower lattice grill area, left side strap, AM, bat .$20.00 – 30.00

X26J, vertical, 1961, jade plastic, seven transistors, upper left front round window dial with right side thumbwheel tuning, right side thumbwheel on/off/volume knob, large checkered grill area, left side strap, rear fold-out metal stand, AM, bat....................$20.00 – 25.00

X26W, vertical, 1961, white plastic, seven transistors, upper left front round window dial with right side thumbwheel tuning, right side thumbwheel on/off/volume knob, large checkered grill area, left side strap, rear fold-out metal stand, AM, bat ....$20.00 – 25.00

X27E, horizontal, 3⅛x4x1½", 1961, black plastic, seven transistors, upper right front window dial, two lower right thumbwheel knobs, left metal perforated grill area, left side strap, AM, bat...........$25.00 – 35.00

X27W, horizontal, 3⅛x4x1½", 1961, white plastic, seven transistors, upper right front window dial, two lower right thumbwheel knobs, left metal perforated grill area, left side strap, AM, bat...........$25.00 – 35.00

X28A, horizontal, 4¾x7½x2⅛", 1961, charcoal gray leatherette, seven transistors, lower right front window dial, two upper right thumbwheel knobs, large left grill area with horizontal slots, handle, AM, bat.....................$10.00 – 15.00

X28N, horizontal, 4¾x7½x2⅛", 1961, brown leatherette, seven transistors, lower right front window dial, two upper right thumbwheel knobs, large left grill area with horizontal slots, handle, AM, bat.........$10.00 – 15.00

X29N, vertical, 6⅝x4½x1⅞", 1961, brown plastic, eight transistors, flip-up cover, inner horizontal slide rule dial with two right thumbwheel knobs, lower grill area with horizontal bars, right side strap, AM, bat.....................$25.00 – 35.00

X29W, vertical, 6⅝x4½x1⅞", 1961, white plastic, eight transistors, flip-up cover, inner horizontal slide rule dial with two right thumbwheel knobs, lower grill area with horizontal bars, right side strap, AM, bat.....................$25.00 – 35.00

X31A "Ranger," horizontal, 5x8x3", 1961, charcoal leather, eight transistors, right front vertical slide rule dial, two knobs, left patterned grill area with upper left dial light and lower logo, leather handle, padded leather cover snaps in place to protect the radio front when not in use, AM, bat..............$20.00 – 25.00

X31A-1, horizontal, 5x8x3", 1962, gray leather, eight transistors, right front vertical slide rule dial, two knobs, left patterned grill area with upper left dial light and lower logo, leather handle, padded leather cover snaps in place to protect the radio front when not in use, AM, bat............................$20.00 – 25.00

X31B-1, horizontal, 5x8x3", 1962, blue leather, eight transistors, right front vertical slide rule dial, two knobs, left patterned grill area with upper left dial light and lower logo, leather handle, padded leather cover snaps in place to protect the radio front when not in use, AM, bat............................$20.00 – 25.00

X31E-1, horizontal, 5x8x3", 1962, black leather, eight transistors, right front vertical slide rule dial, two knobs, left patterned grill area with upper left dial light and lower logo, leather handle, padded leather cover snaps in place to protect the radio front when not in use, AM, bat ....$20.00 – 25.00

X31N "Ranger," horizontal, 5x8x3", 1961, brown leather, right front vertical slide rule dial, two knobs, left patterned grill area with upper left dial light and lower logo, leather handle, padded leather cover snaps in place to protect the radio front when not in use, AM, bat ....$20.00 – 25.00

X31N-1, horizontal, 5x7¾x2½", 1962, ginger leather, eight transistors, right front vertical slide rule dial, two knobs, left patterned grill area with upper left dial light and lower logo, leather handle, padded leather cover snaps in place to protect the radio front when not in use, AM, bat..................$20.00 – 25.00

X34B, vertical, 3⅝x2⅜x1", 1962, blue, six transistors, upper right front round dial knob, upper left thumbwheel on/off/volume knob, lower lattice grill area, AM, bat ....$15.00 – 20.00

X34E, vertical, 3⅝x2⅜x1", 1962, black, six transistors, upper right front round dial knob, upper left thumbwheel on/off/volume knob, lower lattice grill area, AM, bat.$15.00 – 20.00

X35B, vertical, 3¾x2½x1⅛", 1962, blue plastic, six transistors, upper right front window dial with right side thumbwheel tuning, upper left front thumbwheel on/off/volume knob, lower perforated grill area with lower left logo, AM, bat ....$10.00 – 15.00

X35E, vertical, 3¾x2½x1⅛", 1962, black plastic, six transistors, upper right front window dial with right side thumbwheel tuning, upper left front thumbwheel on/off/volume knob, lower perforated grill area with lower left logo, AM, bat ....$10.00 – 15.00

X35N, vertical, 3¾x2½x1⅛", 1962, brown plastic, six transistors, upper right front window dial with right side thumbwheel tuning, upper left front thumbwheel on/off/volume knob, lower perforated grill area with lower left logo, AM, bat ....$10.00 – 15.00

X36E, vertical, 4⅛x2¾x1½", 1962, black, six transistors, upper left front dial, right side thumbwheel knobs, lower lattice grill area, AM, bat ....$15.00 – 20.00

X36G, vertical, 4⅛x2¾x1½", 1962, green, six transistors, upper left front dial, right side thumbwheel knobs, lower lattice grill area, AM, bat ....$15.00 – 20.00

X37B, vertical, 4x3½x1½", 1962, blue leather, six transistors, right front window dial with right side thumbwheel tuning, right side thumbwheel on/off/volume knob, front perforated grill area, AM, bat..............................$20.00 – 25.00

X37E, vertical, 4x3½x1½", 1962, black leather, six transistors, right front window dial with right side thumbwheel tuning, right side thumbwheel on/off/volume knob, front perforated grill area, AM, bat ..$20.00 – 25.00

X37S, vertical, 4x3½x1½", 1962, tan leather, six transistors, right front window dial with right side thumbwheel tuning, right side thumbwheel on/off/volume knob, front perforated grill area, AM, bat..$20.00 – 25.00

X38EG, vertical, 5⅜x3¾x1⅝", 1962, black plastic, seven transistors, upper left front window dial with right side thumbwheel tuning, right side thumbwheel on/off/volume knob, large front perforated grill area, AM, bat..............$15.00 – 20.00

X38ES, vertical, 5⅜x3¾x1⅝", 1962, black plastic, seven transistors, upper left front window dial with right side thumbwheel tuning, right side thumbwheel on/off/volume knob, large front perforated grill area, AM, bat..............$15.00 – 20.00

X39E, horizontal, 4⅜x5¾x2", 1962, black leather, seven transistors, upper right front round window dial, lower grill area with vertical bars and lower left logo, leather handle, AM, bat.....................$10.00 – 15.00

X39N, horizontal, 4⅜x5¾x2", 1962, brown leather, seven transistors, upper right front round window dial, lower grill area with vertical bars and lower left logo, leather handle, AM, bat.....................$10.00 – 15.00

X39S, horizontal, 4⅜x5¾x2", 1962, tan leather, seven transistors, upper right front round window dial, lower grill area with vertical bars and lower left logo, leather handle, AM, bat.....................$10.00 – 15.00

X40E, vertical, 6⅝x4½x1¾", 1962, black plastic, eight transistors, foldback top, inner horizontal slide rule dial with thumbwheel tuning, lower perforated grill area, battery life indicator, right side strap, AM, bat..............................$25.00 – 35.00

X40S, vertical, 6⅝x4½x1¾", 1962, sand plastic, eight transistors, fold-back top, inner horizontal slide rule dial with thumbwheel tuning, lower perforated grill area, battery life indicator, right side strap, AM, bat........$25.00 – 35.00

X41E, horizontal, 4¾x7½x2⅜", 1962, black leather, eight transistors, off-center horizontal slide rule dial, two right front thumbwheel knobs, left grill area with horizontal bars and battery life indicator, leather handle, AM, bat ....$10.00 – 15.00

X41E-1, horizontal, 4¾x7½x2⅜", 1962, black leather, eight transistors, off-center horizontal slide rule dial, two right front thumbwheel knobs, left grill area with horizontal bars and battery life indicator, leather handle, AM, bat.........$10.00 – 15.00

X41G, horizontal, 4¾x7½x2⅜", 1962, olive leather, eight transistors, off-center horizontal slide rule dial, two right front thumbwheel knobs, left grill area with horizontal bars and battery life indicator, leather handle, AM, bat ....$10.00 – 15.00

X41G-1, horizontal, 4¾x7½x2⅜", 1962, olive leather, eight transistors, off-center horizontal slide rule dial, two right front thumbwheel knobs, left grill area with horizontal bars and battery life indicator, leather handle, AM, bat ....$10.00 – 15.00

X41N, horizontal, 4¾x7½x2⅜", 1962, brown leather, eight transistors, off-center horizontal slide rule dial, two right front thumbwheel knobs, left grill area with horizontal bars and battery life indicator, leather handle, AM, bat....................$10.00 – 15.00

X41N-1, horizontal, 4¾x7½x2⅜", 1962, brown leather, eight transistors, off-center horizontal slide rule dial, two right front thumbwheel knobs, left grill area with horizontal bars and battery life indicator, leather handle, AM, bat.....$10.00 – 15.00

X42E-1, horizontal, 1963, leather, 10 transistors, right front vertical two-band slide rule dial, two knobs, left grill area with horizontal bars, telescoping antenna, handle, AM, FM, bat...................$10.00 – 15.00

X47B, vertical, 5⅜x3¾x1⅝", 1962, blue plastic, seven transistors, upper left front round window dial with right side thumbwheel tuning, right side thumbwheel on/off/vol-

ume knob, large checkered grill area, AM, bat............$20.00 – 25.00

X47E, vertical, 5⅜x3¾x1⅝", 1962, black plastic, seven transistors, upper left front round window dial with right side thumbwheel tuning, right side thumbwheel on/off/volume knob, large checkered grill area, AM, bat............$20.00 – 25.00

X48E, horizontal, 4⅜x5¾x2", 1962, black leather, seven transistors, upper right front round window dial, lower grill area with vertical bars and lower left logo, battery life indicator, leather handle, AM, bat......$10.00 – 15.00

X48N, horizontal, 4⅜x5¾x2", 1962, brown leather, seven transistors, upper right front round window dial, lower grill area with vertical bars and lower left logo, battery life indicator, leather handle, AM, bat............$10.00 – 15.00

X49B, horizontal, 6¾x7⅞x3¼", 1962, blue leather, six transistors, large right front round dial over perforated grill area, lower right on/off/volume knob, handle, AM, bat..........................$15.00 – 20.00

X49E, horizontal, 6¾x7⅞x3¼", 1962, black leather, six transistors, large right front round dial over perforated grill area, lower right on/off/volume knob, handle, AM, bat..........................$15.00 – 20.00

X49N, horizontal, 6¾x7⅞x3¼", 1962, brown leather, six transistors, large right front round dial over perforated grill area, lower right on/off/volume knob, handle, AM, bat.............................$15.00 – 20.00

X50B, horizontal, 6¾x7⅞x3¼", 1962, blue leather, six transistors, large right front round dial over perforated grill area, lower right on/off/volume knob, handle, AM, bat/AC ....$15.00 – 20.00

X50E, horizontal, 6¾x7⅞x3¼", 1962, black leather, six transistors, large right front round dial over perforated grill area, lower right on/off/volume knob, handle, AM, bat/AC.......................$15.00 – 20.00

X50N, horizontal, 6¾x7⅞x3¼", 1962, brown leather, six transistors, large right front round dial over perforated grill area, lower right on/off/volume knob, handle, AM, bat/AC.......................$15.00 – 20.00

X51N, horizontal, 5⅜x8½x3¼", 1962, brown leather, nine transistors, large right horizontal slide rule dial, two lower knobs, left perforated grill area, padded leather cover snaps in place to protect the radio front when not in use, leather handle, AM, bat ....$10.00 – 15.00

X53EG, vertical, 5⅜x3¾x1⅝", 1962, black plastic, seven transistors, upper left front window dial with right side thumbwheel tuning, right side thumbwheel on/off/volume knob, large front perforated grill area, AM, bat.............$20.00 – 25.00

X53ES, vertical, 5⅜x3¾x1⅝", 1962, black plastic, seven transistors, upper left front window dial with right side thumbwheel tuning, right

side thumbwheel on/off/volume knob, large front perforated grill area, AM, bat.............$20.00 – 25.00

X54B, vertical, 3½x2¼x1", 1962, blue plastic, six transistors, upper right front window dial with right side thumbwheel tuning, upper left thumbwheel on/off/volume knob, lower metal perforated grill area, AM, bat.....................$10.00 – 15.00

X54E, vertical, 3½x2¼x1", 1962, black plastic, six transistors, upper right front window dial with right side thumbwheel tuning, upper left thumbwheel on/off/volume knob, lower metal perforated grill area, AM, bat.....................$10.00 – 15.00

X56G, vertical, 1963, plastic, upper left front window dial with thumbwheel tuning, lower textured grill area, AM, bat.............$10.00 – 15.00

X57E, vertical, 1965, charcoal, seven transistors, large upper front round dial, lower horizontal grill bars with logo, AM, bat.............$10.00 – 15.00

X57N, vertical, 1965, beige, seven transistors, large upper front round dial, lower horizontal grill bars with logo, AM, bat.............$10.00 – 15.00

X58N, vertical, 1965, chocolate plastic, seven transistors, upper left front window dial with right side thumbwheel tuning, right side thumbwheel on/off/volume knob, lower lattice grill area, AM, bat.......$15.00 – 20.00

X58W, vertical, 1965, ivory/white plastic, seven transistors, upper left front window dial with right side thumbwheel tuning, right side thumbwheel on/off/volume knob, lower lattice grill area, AM, bat........$15.00 – 20.00

X60E, vertical, 4¾x3½x1½", 1965, plastic, eight transistors, large upper front horizontal slide rule dial with right thumbwheel tuning, left thumbwheel on/off/volume knob, lower perforated grill area with logo, AM, bat.....$10.00 – 15.00

X60W, vertical, 4¾x3½x1½", 1965, plastic, eight transistors, large upper front horizontal slide rule dial with right thumbwheel tuning, left thumbwheel on/off/volume knob, lower perforated grill area with logo, AM, bat.....$10.00 – 15.00

X61E, horizontal, 4⅛x6x2¾", 1965, black leatherette, nine transistors, upper right front round window dial, two knobs, vertical grill bars with lower left logo, padded leather cover snaps in place to protect the radio front when not in use, leather pull-up handle, AM, bat ....$15.00 – 20.00

X61N, horizontal, 4⅛x6x2¾", 1965, brown leatherette, nine transistors, upper right front round window dial, two knobs, vertical grill bars with lower left logo, padded leather cover snaps in place to protect the radio front when not in use, leather pull-up handle, AM, bat..........$15.00 – 20.00

X80N, horizontal, 1964, 10 transistors, upper front horizontal two-band slide rule dial, large lower grill area with horizontal bars and lower left logo, telescoping antenna, leather handle, AM, FM, bat...$10.00 – 15.00

XP22DE, vertical, 4⅝x2⅞x1⅜", 1968, black, 10 transistors, upper front horizontal slide rule dial with right side thumbwheel tuning, right side thumbwheel on/off/volume knob, large perforated grill area with logo, AM, bat.....$10.00 – 15.00

XP22DL, vertical, 4⅝x2⅞x1⅜", 1968, blue, 10 transistors, upper front horizontal slide rule dial with right side thumbwheel tuning, right side thumbwheel on/off/volume knob, large perforated grill area with logo, AM, bat.....$10.00 – 15.00

XP23DW, vertical, plastic, 10 transistors, upper front horizontal slide rule dial with right side thumbwheel tuning, right side thumbwheel on/off/volume knob, large metal perforated grill area, AM, bat..............................$10.00 – 15.00

XP31FE, vertical, 4½x2¾x1⅜", plastic, upper front dial window and on/off/volume window over large metal perforated grill area, right side thumbwheel tuning, left side thumbwheel knob, made in Taiwan, AM, bat..............$15.00 – 20.00

XP34GN, vertical, plastic, large upper right front dial, left side thumbwheel on/off/volume knob, lower perforated grill area, top vinyl strap, AM, bat .....$5.00 – 10.00

XP42EE, vertical, 4½x2¾x1½", 1968, black plastic, eight transistors, upper front window dial with right side thumbwheel tuning, right side thumbwheel on/off/ volume knob, lower metal perforated grill area, made in Taiwan, AM, bat...................$10.00 – 15.00

XP42EH, vertical, 4½x2¾x1½", 1968, white plastic, eight transistors, upper front window dial with right side thumbwheel tuning, right side thumbwheel on/off/volume knob, lower metal perforated grill area, made in Taiwan, AM, bat..........$10.00 – 15.00

XP64CE, horizontal, leather, large right front round dial, lower right on/off/volume knob, left metal perforated grill area, leather handle, AM, bat...............$10.00 – 15.00

XP69BE, vertical, 4⅝x2⅞x1½", 1965, charcoal plastic, six transistors, large upper front dial, lower grill area with horizontal bars, AM, bat..............................$10.00 – 15.00

XP69BN, vertical, 4⅝x2⅞x1½", 1965, beige plastic, six transistors, large upper front dial, lower grill area with horizontal bars, AM, bat..............................$10.00 – 15.00

XP73BE, vertical, 4⅝x2⅞x1⅝", plastic, large upper front dial, lower grill area with horizontal bars, made in Japan, AM, bat.......$10.00 – 15.00

XT18B "Cordless 1500," horizontal, 1960, blue, six transistors, upper right front large round dial over lattice grill area, left on/off/volume knob and logo, feet, pop-up handle, AM, bat......................$10.00 – 15.00

XT18S "Cordless 1500," horizontal, 1960, tan, six transistors, upper right front large round dial over lattice grill area, left on/off/volume knob and logo, feet, pop-up handle, AM, bat...............$10.00 – 15.00

National

AB-210, horizontal, 5x8½x2", nine transistors, upper front horizontal two-band slide rule dial with right thumbwheel tuning, left thumbwheel on/off/volume knob, large metal perforated grill area with lower left logo, band switch, AM, SW, bat.....................$25.00 – 35.00

T-21, vertical, 4¼x2½x1¼", plastic, seven transistors, two upper front window dials — one MW, one SW — with thumbwheel tuning, lower metal perforated grill area, swing handle, MW, SW, bat.......$20.00 – 30.00

T-40, horizontal, 3⅝x6⅛x1⅜", plastic, eight transistors, top horizontal slide rule dial with top right thumbwheel tuning, lower right side thumbwheel on/off/volume knob, large front metal perforated grill area with three rhinestones, right side SW/MW switch, top left telescoping antenna, made in Japan, SW, MW, bat..............$25.00 – 35.00

T-45, horizontal, 3⅛x5¼x1¼", plastic, seven transistors, upper front horizontal two-band slide rule dial, rounded right side with two thumbwheel knobs, large lower metal perforated grill area with lower right band switch and upper left logo, made in Japan, AM, SW, bat......$25.00 – 35.00

T-98 "Portalarm," vertical/watch radio, 4x2½x1¼", plastic, seven transistors, upper right front window dial with thumbwheel tuning, upper left front Seiko alarm watch face, lower metal perforated grill area, rear stand, AM, bat........$100.00 – 125.00

National Panasonic

R-121, horizontal, 3¼x5½x1⅝", plastic, right front round dial with right side thumbwheel tuning, left front metal perforated grill area, made in Japan, AM, bat...........$20.00 – 30.00

NEC

NT-6B, horizontal, plastic, lower right front horizontal slide rule dial with right side thumbwheel tuning, right side thumbwheel on/off/volume knob, large textured front panel with left checkered grill area, AM, bat.....................$20.00 – 30.00

NT-61, horizontal, 2½x4¼x1¼", 1960, six transistors, right front thumbwheel dial and thumbwheel on/off/volume knob covered by a clear plastic panel, left grill area with textured horizontal bars, made in Japan, AM, bat ..$100.00 – 125.00

NT-620, horizontal, 2¾x4¼x1", 1960, plastic, six transistors, right front see-through V-shaped dial opening with right side thumb-wheel tuning, lower right front thumbwheel on/off/volume knob, left metal perforated grill area with circular indentations, made in Japan, AM, bat...........$65.00 – 85.00

NT-640, vertical, plastic, six transistors, upper right front window dial with right side thumbwheel tuning, upper left front thumbwheel on/off/volume knob, lower metal perforated grill area, AM, bat ....$20.00 – 25.00

NT-730, horizontal, 3⅛x5x1", plastic, seven transistors, upper front see-through panel with right horizontal dial, right side thumbwheel tuning, right side thumbwheel on/off/volume knob, lower front and rear metal perforated grill areas, made in Japan, AM, bat...........$60.00 – 70.00

NEC Galaxie
TN-201 "Boy's Radio," vertical, 4x2½x1¼", plastic, two transistors, rounded upper right corner, upper

right front dial knob, left side thumbwheel on/off/volume knob, lower metal textured and perforated grill area with lower left logo, made in Japan, AM, bat.......$50.00 – 60.00

Nichinan

Boy's Radio, horizontal, 2½x4x1½", plastic, two transistors, right front dial knob, lower right side thumbwheel on/off/volume knob, left grill area with horizontal bars, made in Japan, AM, bat ......$45.00 – 55.00

Nicolet
Boy's Radio, vertical, 4¾x2¾x1¼", plastic, two transistors, upper right front curved window dial with right side thumbwheel tuning, left front on/off/volume window with left side thumbwheel knob, lower grill area with textured horizontal bars, made in Japan, AM, bat.......$55.00 – 65.00

Nobility
832N, vertical, 4¼x2½x1¼", plastic, eight transistors, upper right front square window dial with thumbwheel tuning, lower checkered grill area, AM, bat...............$5.00 – 10.00

1268, vertical, plastic, 12 transistors, upper right front window dial with right side thumbwheel tuning, left side thumbwheel on/off/volume knob, lower checkered grill area, AM, bat....................**$5.00 – 10.00**

Nordmende

Condor, horizontal, 6½x9½x3⅝", 1963, nine transistors, upper right front round two-band dial overlaps checkered grill area, pushbuttons, telescoping antenna, handle, made in Germany, AM, FM, bat..................**$25.00 – 35.00**

Globetraveler, Jr, auto/portable radio, 8x12x3¾", wood grain finish, designed to be used as a car radio as well as a portable, three top horizontal slide rule dial scales, pushbuttons, metal grill with rectangular cut-outs, handle, made in West Germany, bat...................**$60.00 – 75.00**

Mambo, horizontal, 1961, seven transistors, right front round two-band dial, left wedge-shaped lattice grill area, top pushbuttons and thumbwheel on/off/volume knob, handle, AM, LW, bat..**$30.00 – 40.00**

Mambino, horizontal, 1964, six transistors, upper right front round two-band dial overlaps checkered grill area, top pushbut-

tons and thumbwheel on/off/volume knob, handle, AM, LW, bat....................**$25.00 – 35.00**

Mikrobox, horizontal, 1961, plastic, six transistors, right front round two-band dial, top thumbwheel on/off/volume knob, large metal perforated grill area, rear band switch, made in West Germany, AM, LW, bat....................**$20.00 – 30.00**

Mikrobox UKW, horizontal, 1963, plastic, nine transistors, upper front horizontal two-band slide rule dial with large front tuning knob, upper left front thumbwheel on/off/volume knob, lower perforated grill area, pull-up handle, made in West Germany, AM, FM, bat....................**$20.00 – 30.00**

Minibox, horizontal, 1959, plastic, six transistors, right front round two-band dial, top thumbwheel on/off/volume knob, large metal perforated grill area, rear band switch, made in West Germany, AM, LW, bat ....**$25.00 – 35.00**

Starlet, horizontal, 1961, plastic, five transistors, upper right front window dial with right side thumbwheel tuning, lower right front thumbwheel on/off/volume knob, large left perforated grill area, made in West Germany, AM, bat.............**$25.00 – 35.00**

Stradella, horizontal, 6x9¾x3", plastic leatherette, upper front horizontal three-band slide rule dial with top right thumbwheel tuning, lower metal perforated grill area, three top pushbuttons and thumbwheel on/off/volume knob, telescoping antenna, handle, made in West Germany, bat ....**$25.00 – 35.00**

Transita, horizontal, 1961, nine transistors, rounded case, upper right front round three-band dial overlaps checkered grill area, four pushbuttons, telescoping antenna, handle, AM, FM, SW, bat.........**$30.00 – 40.00**

Transita Deluxe K-C, horizontal, 1965, nine transistors, upper front horizontal three-band slide rule dial with top right thumbwheel tuning, lower metal perforated grill area, five top pushbuttons and thumbwheel on/off/volume knob, telescoping antenna, handle, AM, FM, SW, bat ....**$30.00 – 40.00**

Transita Export-C, horizontal, 1964, nine transistors, upper front horizontal four-band slide rule dial with top right thumbwheel tuning, lower metal perforated grill area, five top pushbuttons and thumbwheel on/off/volume knob, telescoping antenna, handle, AM, FM, SW, LW, bat ....**$25.00 – 35.00**

Norelco

L0X95T/62R, horizontal, 1961, seven transistors, right front round dial, lower thumbwheel on/off/volume knob, left perforated grill area, made in Holland, AM, bat....**$20.00 – 30.00**

L1W32T/02G, horizontal, 1965, eight transistors, upper front horizontal three-band slide rule dial, lower perforated grill area with lower right logo, telescoping antenna, AM, FM, LW, bat ....**$20.00 – 25.00**

L1X75T/64R, horizontal, 1960, seven transistors, right front round dial, upper thumbwheel on/off/volume knob, left perforated grill area, made in Holland, AM, bat ....**$20.00 – 30.00**

L1X75T/64RA, horizontal, 3½x6¼x1½", 1959, black plastic, seven transistors, right front round dial, upper thumbwheel on/off/volume knob, left metal perforated grill area, made in Holland, AM, bat ....**$20.00 – 30.00**

L2W54T/54R, horizontal, 1965, 10 transistors, upper front horizontal four-band slide rule dial with thumbwheel tuning, thumbwheel on/off/volume knob, four right band pushbuttons, perforated grill area, telescoping antenna, AM, FM, SW, LW, bat ....**$25.00 – 35.00**

L2X97T, horizontal/clock radio, 1960, seven transistors, right front round dial knob, upper thumbwheel on/off/volume knob, left front round clock face, made in Holland, AM, bat ......**$20.00 – 30.00**

L2X97T/64R, horizontal/clock radio, 1960, plastic, seven transistors, right front round dial knob, upper thumbwheel on/off/volume knob, center grill area, left round clock face, made in Holland, AM, bat ....**$20.00 – 30.00**

L3X09T/54, horizontal, 1962, seven transistors, upper front horizontal three-band slide rule dial with thumbwheel tuning, thumbwheel on/off/volume knob, top pushbuttons, handle, AM, 2SW, bat..............................**$20.00 – 30.00**

L3X19T/97, horizontal, 1964, seven transistors, upper front horizontal three-band slide rule dial with thumbwheel tuning, thumbwheel on/off/volume knob, five top recessed pushbuttons, lower horizontal grill bars, handle, AM, 2SW, bat.....................**$20.00 – 30.00**

L3X76T/07, horizontal, 1961, seven transistors, upper front horizontal two-band slide rule dial with thumbwheel tuning, thumbwheel on/off/volume knob, four top recessed pushbuttons, handle, AM, SW, bat.....................**$20.00 – 25.00**

L3X86T, horizontal, 1960, seven transistors, upper front horizontal two-band slide rule dial with thumbwheel tuning, thumbwheel on/off/volume knob, four top recessed pushbuttons, handle, AM, SW, bat.....................**$20.00 – 25.00**

L3X88T, horizontal, 1960, seven transistors, upper front horizontal two-band slide rule dial with thumbwheel tuning, thumbwheel on/off/volume knob, four top recessed pushbuttons, handle, AM, SW, bat.....................**$20.00 – 25.00**

L3X95T/00E, horizontal, 1961, yellow, seven transistors, right front round three-band dial over large checkered grill area, handle, AM, Marine, SW, bat........**$20.00 – 30.00**

L3X95T/00W, horizontal, 1961, orange, seven transistors, right front round three-band dial over large checkered grill area, handle, AM, Marine, SW, bat........**$20.00 – 30.00**

L3X95T/00X, horizontal, 1961, blue, seven transistors, right front round three-band dial over large checkered grill area, handle, AM, Marine, SW, bat........**$20.00 – 30.00**

L4X05T, horizontal, 1961, seven transistors, upper front horizontal four-band slide rule dial with thumbwheel tuning, thumbwheel on/off/volume knob, seven top pushbuttons, large lower grill area, handle, AM, 3SW, bat.......**$25.00 – 35.00**

L4X25T, horizontal, 1964, seven transistors, upper front horizontal four-band slide rule dial with thumbwheel tuning, thumbwheel on/off/volume knob, seven top pushbuttons, large lower grill area, handle, AM, 3SW, bat.......**$25.00 – 35.00**

L4X95T, horizontal, 1960, brown leatherette with cream plastic front, seven transistors, upper front horizontal four-band slide rule dial with thumbwheel tuning, thumbwheel on/off/volume knob, seven top pushbuttons, large lower grill area, handle, AM, 3SW, bat...............**$25.00 – 35.00**

North American

876, horizontal, 2⅝x4½x1⅜", plastic, eight transistors, upper right front window dial with upper right side thumbwheel tuning, lower right side thumbwheel on/off/volume knob, oval grill area with horizontal bars, top left strap, made in Hong Kong, AM, bat...**$5.00 – 10.00**

1200 "Suburbia," horizontal, 3½x5¾x1⅜", plastic with metal front panel, 12 transistors, rounded upper right corner with dial knob, lower right side thumbwheel on/off/volume knob, left grill area with horizontal slots, made in Japan, AM, bat..........$20.00 – 25.00

1400, horizontal, 1965, 14 transistors, upper front horizontal two-band slide rule dial, right tuning knob and AM/FM switch, left oval perforated grill area, telescoping antenna, handle, AM, FM, bat........**$10.00 – 15.00**

_____

Norwood

MN-1000, horizontal, 1965, 10 transistors, upper front horizontal two-band slide rule dial with thumbwheel tuning, large lower perforated grill area, telescoping antenna, handle, AM, FM, bat.................**$10.00 – 15.00**

NA-1200, horizontal, 1964, 12 transistors, right front dial with upper FM and lower AM windows, right side knob, left perforated grill area, telescoping antenna, handle, AM, FM, bat.....................**$15.00 – 20.00**

NM-600 "HiFi Deluxe," vertical, 1964, six transistors, upper right front window dial with right side thumbwheel tuning, lower perforated grill area, made in Japan, AM, bat............................$10.00 – 15.00

NM-800, horizontal, 1964, eight transistors, upper front horizontal dial with right side thumbwheel tuning, left thumbwheel volume knob, large lower grill area with horizontal slots, AM, bat............................**$10.00 – 15.00**

NS-901, vertical, 1964, nine transistors, upper right front window dial with right side thumbwheel tuning, lower grill area with horizontal slots, AM, bat.............**$10.00 – 15.00**

NT-602, horizontal, 1964, six transistors, upper right front round window dial with upper right side thumbwheel tuning, lower right side thumbwheel on/off/volume knob, left perforated grill area, AM, bat.............................**$15.00 – 20.00**

NRC

6TP-106, vertical, 4¼x2¾x1¼", plastic, six transistors, large upper front dial knob, upper right front thumbwheel on/off/volume knob, lower metal perforated grill area with vertical lines and lower left logo, made in Japan, AM, bat ......**$25.00 – 35.00**

Nuvox

Boy's Radio, vertical, 4⅛x2⅝x1¼", plastic, two transistors, upper right front window dial with right side thumbwheel tuning, left side thumbwheel on/off/volume knob, lower metal perforated grill area, made in Japan, AM, bat ....$40.00 – 50.00

Oldsmobile

Trans-Portable, vertical car/portable radio, 6¾x3½x1¾", 1958, plastic, made to use in or out of the car, chrome front with upper round dial knob, lower vertical grill bars, handle, made for Oldsmobile by Delco, AM ....**$90.00 – 110.00**

Olson

RA-315, vertical, 1960, four transistors, upper left front round dial with thumbwheel tuning, right side thumbwheel knob, lower lattice grill area with lower right logo, AM, bat ....**$50.00 – 60.00**

RA-347, horizontal, 1961, six transistors, right front window dial with right side thumbwheel tuning, right side thumbwheel on/off/volume knob, left perforated grill area, AM, bat ....**$20.00 – 30.00**

Olympic

447, horizontal, 1957, four transistors, top dial and on/off/volume knobs, large front checkered grill area, handle, AM, bat...............**$75.00 – 100.00**

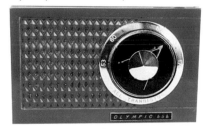

666, horizontal, 1959, plastic, six transistors, off-center large round dial knob overlaps left grill area with diamond cut-outs, top right thumbwheel on/off/volume knob, AM, bat.....................$45.00 – 55.00

766, vertical, 1959, leather, six transistors, upper left large round dial knob overlaps lower perforated grill area, top right thumbwheel on/off/volume knob, leather handle, AM, bat...............**$30.00 – 40.00**

768, horizontal, 1959, six transistors, right front round dial knob, lower right thumbwheel on/off/volume knob, left checkered grill area, handle, AM, bat.........**$35.00 – 45.00**

770, horizontal, 1959, six transistors, right front round dial knob, lower right on/off/volume window with lower right side thumbwheel knob, left grill area with lower left Olympic torch logo, AM, bat....**$45.00 – 55.00**

771, horizontal, 1959, six transistors, right front round dial knob, upper right thumbwheel on/off/volume knob, "wishbone" grill decoration, handle, AM, bat ....**$60.00 – 75.00**

777, vertical, 1960, six transistors, upper front round window dial with thumbwheel tuning, lower perforated grill area with lower right Olympic torch logo, AM, bat ....**$75.00 – 90.00**

778, vertical, 1962, six transistors, upper right front round dial with right side thumbwheel tuning, top left thumbwheel on/off/volume knob, lower perforated grill area, AM, bat ....**$25.00 – 35.00**

779, vertical, 1962, six transistors, upper right front window dial with right side thumbwheel tuning, upper left front on/off/volume window with left side thumbwheel knob, lower round perforated grill area, lower right Olympic torch logo, AM, bat.**$30.00 – 40.00**

780, vertical, six transistors, upper front window dial with right thumbwheel tuning, left thumbwheel on/off/volume knob, lower metal perforated grill area with center Olympic torch logo, metal top and side trim, AM, bat .....**$45.00 – 55.00**

781, vertical, 1962, six transistors, upper right front wedge-shaped window dial with right side thumbwheel tuning, top left thumbwheel on/off/volume knob, lower perforated grill area, AM, bat...............**$25.00 – 35.00**

808, horizontal, 1960, eight transistors, upper right front dial, lower right on/off/volume knob, large lattice grill area, handle, AM, bat ....**$15.00 – 20.00**

859, vertical, 1960, leather, eight transistors, upper front window dial with top thumbwheel tuning, top thumbwheel on/off/volume knob, lower perforated grill area, AM, bat ....**$25.00 – 35.00**

860, horizontal, 3½x5½x1½", 1963, plastic, eight transistors, upper right front round dial with right side thumbwheel tuning overlaps large metal perforated grill area, right side thumbwheel on/off/volume knob, made in Japan, AM, bat ....**$20.00 – 25.00**

861, vertical, 1963, eight transistors, upper right front window dial with right side thumbwheel tuning, left side thumbwheel on/off/volume knob, lower perforated grill area with center Olympic torch logo, AM, bat ....**$25.00 – 35.00**

862, horizontal, 1964, eight transistors, upper right front window dial with upper right side thumbwheel tuning, lower right side thumbwheel on/off/volume knob, large perforated grill area, AM, bat .**$15.00 – 20.00**

1063, horizontal, 1965, 10 transistors, upper right front window dial with right side thumbwheel tuning, lower right thumbwheel on/off/volume knob, left round perforated grill area, Olympic torch logo, AM, bat.............$20.00 – 30.00

1100 "High Fidelity," horizontal, 1963, 11 transistors, two upper front horizontal slide rule dials – one AM/SW, one FM – lower perforated grill area, telescoping antenna, handle, AM, FM, SW, bat..$15.00 – 20.00

1200 "High Fidelity," horizontal, 1963, 12 transistors, two upper front horizontal slide rule dials – one AM, one FM – lower perforated grill area with two knobs, two telescoping antennas, handle, AM, FM, bat......................$15.00 – 20.00

CT999, horizontal/clock radio, 1963, six transistors, upper right front window dial over large perforated grill area with Olympic torch logo, right side thumbwheel tuning and on/off/volume knobs, left clock face, AM, bat....$15.00 – 20.00

Omegas

**AR-1010, horizontal, 3⅞x6x1½",
plastic, 10 transistors, rounded
right side with wrap-around vertical
two-band dial, right side top & bottom thumbwheel knobs, large front**

metal perforated grill area, telescoping antenna, made in Japan, AM, SW, bat.............$30.00 – 40.00

O.M.G.S.
700, vertical, 4¼x2½x1⅜", plastic, seven transistors, upper right front window dial with right side thumbwheel tuning, left side thumbwheel on/off/volume knob, large plastic checkered grill area, made in Hong Kong, AM, bat.............$5.00 – 10.00

1200 "Suburbia," horizontal, 3½x5¾x1⅜", plastic with metal front panel, 12 transistors, rounded upper right corner with dial knob, lower right side thumbwheel on/off/volume knob, left perforated grill area, made in Japan, AM, bat.............$20.00 – 25.00

TRN-8023 "Suburbia," horizontal, 3½x5¾x1⅜", plastic with metal front panel, 12 transistors, rounded upper right corner with dial knob, lower right side thumbwheel on/off/volume knob, left perforated grill area, made in Japan, AM, bat.............$20.00 – 25.00

Onkyo
7TR-800, horizontal, 2¾x5x1¼", plastic, seven transistors, two front window dials – one MW, one SW – with upper right side thumbwheel tuning, lower right side thumbwheel on/off/volume knob, large metal perforated grill area with band switch, can be used with screw-in tripod base, made in Japan, AM, SW, bat.
radio only ....$20.00 – 30.00
with tripod base.........$40.00 – 60.00

Orion

DeLuxe, vertical, 4½x2½x1½", plastic, six transistors, large upper left front dial knob, right side thumbwheel on/off/volume knob, lower metal perforated grill area with lower left logo, AM, bat ...$125.00 – 150.00

JT-602 "Signal-Radio," vertical, 4¼x 2½x1¼", plastic, upper left front round dial knob, right side thumbwheel on/off/volume knob, lower metal perforated grill area, AM, bat ....$20.00 – 25.00

Master, horizontal, 3¾x7⅛x2", plastic, eight transistors, two upper front horizontal slide rule dials, right and left side knobs, right side switch, divided front metal textured and perforated grill area with center logo, telescoping antenna, AM, SW, bat ....$45.00 – 55.00

Orions

Boy's Radio, vertical, 4x2½x1¼", plastic, two transistors, upper front window dial with left side thumbwheel

tuning, rear thumbwheel on/off/volume knob, lower round metal textured and perforated grill area, made in Japan, AM, bat.........$45.00 – 55.00

Oritone

TR-107, vertical, 4¼x2½x1¼", plastic, 10 transistors, upper front window dial over large metal perforated grill area, right side thumbwheel tuning, top left thumbwheel on/off/volume knob, made in Japan, AM, bat .....$20.00 – 30.00

OTL

10TP-904, horizontal, 10 transistors, right front dial with thumbwheel tuning, top left thumbwheel on/off/volume knob, large grill area with vertical slots and "starburst" decoration, bat ....$20.00 – 30.00

Oxford

876, horizontal, 2⅝x4½x1⅜", plastic, eight transistors, upper right front window dial with right side thumbwheel tuning, right side thumbwheel on/off/volume knob, left oval grill area with horizontal bars, top left strap, AM, bat..$5.00 – 10.00

1296 "XII," horizontal, 3¼x6⅛x 1½", plastic, 12 transistors, upper right horizontal slide rule dial with right side thumbwheel tuning, right side thumbwheel on/off/volume knob, large oval metal perforated

grill area, made in Japan, AM, bat.............$20.00 – 30.00

Pacific

FR-601, vertical, plastic, six transistors, upper front window dial with right side thumbwheel tuning, left side thumbwheel on/off/volume knob, round metal perforated grill area, AM, bat.............$25.00 – 35.00

Packard Bell

6RT1, horizontal, 3⅛x6x1⅝", 1957, available in walnut brown, golden tan, or sierra white leather, five transistors, right front round dial knob, right side thumbwheel on/off/volume knob, checkered grill cut-outs with lower left logo, handle, AM, bat ....$45.00 – 55.00

6RT-2, horizontal, 3¼x6½x1⅜", 1958, available in turquoise, red, chalk white, or ebony/white plastic, five transistors, right front round dial knob, left lattice grill area, AM, bat.............$40.00 – 50.00

6RT-6, vertical, 4x2½x1¼", 1964, six transistors, upper front dial with right side thumbwheel tuning, right side thumbwheel on/off/volume knob, lower metal perforated grill area with lower right logo, made in Japan, AM, bat..........$20.00 – 25.00

6RT-7, vertical, 1964, six transistors, upper front dial with thumbwheel tuning, lower perforated grill area with lower right logo, made in Japan, AM, bat..........$20.00 – 25.00

12RT1, horizontal, 1964, 12 transistors, upper left front horizontal two-band slide rule dial, three knobs, lower grill area, telescoping antenna, AM, FM, bat.........$10.00 – 15.00

Pal-F

Boy's Radio, vertical, plastic, two transistors, upper right front window dial with right side thumbwheel tuning, upper left front on/off/volume window with left side thumbwheel knob, lower metal textured and perforated grill area, AM, bat.....................$50.00 – 60.00

Panasonic

DT-495, horizontal/table radio, 5¾x10⅜x3⅛", 1962, ivory/blue plastic, six transistors, step-back top with upper right thumbwheel dial, lower right on/off/volume knob, large grill area with horizontal bars, feet, AM, bat.............$20.00 – 25.00

R-8 "Hide-Away," horizontal/table, 2⅝x7x3", 1964, available in red, blue, white, or black, six transistors, right front horizontal slide rule dial, two knobs, left grill area with lower left logo, top lifts for "secret compartment," feet, AM, bat ....$15.00 – 25.00

R-100, horizontal, 4x7⅝x2⅝", leatherette, nine transistors, right front slide rule dial, two knobs, left metal perforated grill area with lower left logo, handle, AM, bat ....$15.00 – 20.00

R-102, vertical, 1964, six transistors, upper front round dial knob, right side thumbwheel on/off/volume knob, horizontal grill bars with lower logo, AM, bat...$10.00 – 15.00

R-103, vertical, 1964, available in black, white, or blue, six transistors, upper front round dial knob, right side thumbwheel on/off/volume knob, lower grill area with center logo, AM, bat.............$10.00 – 15.00

R-109, horizontal, 1964, leather, nine transistors, upper right front horizontal slide rule dial, two knobs, left perforated grill area with lower left logo, handle, AM, bat ....$10.00 – 15.00

R-111 "Tiny-Tote," vertical, 2¾x1⅞x1", upper right front window dial with right side thumbwheel tuning, right side thumbwheel on/off/volume knob, lower round grill area, AM, bat.......$40.00 – 50.00

R-132, vertical, 1966, textured plastic, eight transistors, narrow front with vertical slide rule dial, right side thumbwheel dial knob and thumbwheel on/off/volume knob, vinyl strap, made in Japan, AM, bat..........$20.00 – 25.00

R-140 "Super Sensitive," horizontal, 1964, leather, six transistors, right front round dial overlaps lattice grill area, left side thumbwheel on/off/volume knob, leather handle, AM, bat ....$10.00 – 15.00

R-141 "Super Sensitive," horizontal, leather, right front round dial overlaps lattice grill area, left side thumbwheel on/off/volume knob, leather handle, AM, bat.........$10.00 – 15.00

R-147 "Super Sensitive," horizontal, 1965, leather, seven transistors, right front round dial overlaps lattice grill area, leather handle, AM, bat ....$10.00 – 15.00

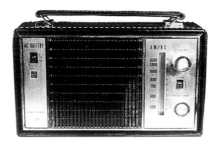

R-159 "Adventurer," horizontal, 5½x8½x3", available in black, red, or white leather, seven transistors, right front vertical slide rule dial, two knobs, off-center textured grill area, upper left AC/battery switch, leather handle, AM, AC/bat ...$10.00 – 15.00

R-505 "Super Sensitive," horizontal, 3⅛x5⅞x1½", 1964, seven transistors, right front window dial with right side thumbwheel tuning, top left thumbwheel on/off/volume knob, perforated grill area with lower left logo, made in Japan, AM, bat.............................$10.00 – 15.00

R-607, vertical, 3½x2½x1", 1965, seven transistors, upper left front window dial with thumbwheel tuning, lower perforated grill area with lower right logo, AM, bat ......$15.00 – 20.00

R-1000 "Radar Matic," horizontal, 1965, 10 transistors, plastic, right front round signal-seeking dial with thumbwheel tuning, top left thumbwheel knob, perforated grill area with left logo, AM, bat.........$35.00 – 45.00

R-1010 "Radar Matic," horizontal, 4x7⅞x1¾", plastic, 10 transistors, right front round signal-seeking dial with right side thumbwheel manual tuning knob and top right auto tuning switch, top left thumbwheel on/off/volume knob, lower metal perforated grill area, handle, made in Japan, AM, bat.......$35.00 – 45.00

R-1014, horizontal, 1966, plastic, upper front horizontal two-band slide rule dial, two right side

thumbwheel knobs, upper left front tone & AC/batt switches, lower grill area with circular cutouts and lower left logo, handle, AM, FM, AC/bat ......$10.00 – 15.00

R-1029, vertical, 4½x3x1⅜", plastic, upper right window dial with right side thumbwheel tuning, left side thumbwheel on/off/volume knob, circular grill cut-outs, vinyl strap, made in Japan, AM, bat.$5.00 – 10.00

R-1052 "Cranford," vertical, available in black, red, white, blue, green, or purple plastic, upper front round dial, right side thumbwheel knob, lower perforated grill area, top vinyl strap, AM, bat..............$5.00 – 10.00

R-1070, vertical, 4½x2¾x1½", plastic, upper front horizontal slide rule dial with right side thumbwheel tuning, left side thumbwheel on/off/volume knob, lower perforated grill area, top strap, made in Taiwan, AM, bat.....................$5.00 – 10.00

R-1076, vertical, 4x2½x1¼", plastic, seven transistors, upper right front window dial with right side thumbwheel tuning, left side thumbwheel on/off/volume knob, lower textured grill area with logo, made in Japan, AM, bat ....**$10.00 – 15.00**

R-1082, vertical, 3¾x2½x1¼", plastic, upper right front window dial with thumbwheel tuning, lower checkered grill area with lower left logo, AM, bat ....**$10.00 – 15.00**

R-1157 "Super 7," "Plainsman," horizontal, 4x6¼x2", black leather, right front round dial, left metal perforated grill area with lower left logo, handle, AM, bat..............................**$10.00 – 15.00**

R-1449, horizontal, 7x4⅝x2¼", leatherette, right front vertical slide rule dial with right side thumbwheel tuning, right side thumbwheel on/off/volume knob, left perforated grill area with upper left high/low tone switch, handle, made in Japan, AM, bat........**$10.00 – 15.00**

RC-7878, folding clock/radio, hinged case with inner right radio controls and perforated grill area with horizontal bars, inner left clock face, made in Japan, AM, FM, bat.......**$30.00 – 40.00**

RF-90 "Tom Thumb," horizontal/table, 3⅛x7⅜x3⅜", simulated wood grain, nine transistors, right front horizontal two-band slide rule dial, two knobs, left grill area with upper left logo, telescoping antenna, top lifts for "secret compartment," AM, FM, bat.**$15.00 – 25.00**

R-1326 "Gadabout," vertical, available in black, tan, or red plastic, eight transistors, narrow front with vertical slide rule dial, right side thumbwheel dial knob and thumbwheel on/off/volume knob, vinyl strap, made in Japan, AM, bat..............$20.00 – 25.00

RF-504, vertical, plastic, upper front horizontal two-band dial, side thumbwheel knobs, lower perforated grill area, top right telescoping antenna, left side strap, AM, FM, bat ....$10.00 – 15.00

RF-626 "Travel Pal," vertical, 5x1½x3¼", plastic, narrow front with vertical two-band slide rule dial, right side thumbwheel dial knob and thumbwheel on/off/volume knob, telescoping antenna, vinyl strap, AM, FM, bat..............................$20.00 – 25.00

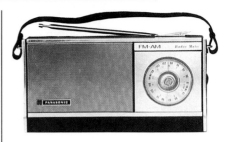

RF-811, vertical, 1965, eight transistors, upper front horizontal two-band slide rule dial with thumbwheel tuning, lower perforated grill area with lower left logo, telescoping antenna, AM, FM, bat.................$10.00 – 15.00

RF-815, horizontal, 1964, eight transistors, top horizontal two-band slide rule dial, front perforated grill area, telescoping antenna, AM, FM, bat.......................$10.00 – 15.00

RF-820, horizontal, 1964, nine transistors, top horizontal two-band slide rule dial with thumbwheel tuning, right side switch, large front perforated grill area with lower left logo, telescoping antenna, AM, FM, bat..............................$10.00 – 15.00

RF-835, horizontal, 7x9x3", 1965, leather, nine transistors, upper front horizontal two-band slide rule dial, lower perforated grill area, telescoping antenna, handle, AM, FM, bat.......................$10.00 – 15.00

RF-3000A "Voyager," horizontal, 11¾x14½x5", six upper front dial scales, bass & treble indicators, right side knobs, lower grill area with horizontal bars, two speakers, telescoping antenna, handle, 6 bands, AC/bat............$50.00 – 60.00

RF-6060 "Radar Matic," "Pacesetter," horizontal, 4⅘x5¾x2", plastic, right front round two-band signal-seeking dial with right side thumbwheel manual tuning knob and top right auto tuning switch, top left thumbwheel on/off/volume knob, lower metal perforated grill area, handle, made in Japan, AM, FM, bat......................$35.00 – 45.00

T-7, vertical, 3¾x2½x1⅛", 1962, seven transistors, available in black or blue plastic, upper front horizontal slide rule dial with right side thumbwheel tuning, right side thumbwheel on/off/volume knob, lower grill area with horizontal slots and lower left logo, AM, bat...............$25.00 – 35.00

T-13, vertical, 4x2⅜x1⅛", 1962, black/ivory plastic, six transistors, upper front horizontal slide rule dial with right side thumbwheel tuning, left front thumbwheel on/off/volume knob, lower perforated grill area with lower right logo, AM, bat.............$20.00 – 30.00

T-13P, vertical, 1964, six transistors, upper front horizontal slide rule dial with right side thumbwheel tuning, left front thumbwheel on/off/volume knob, lower grill area with lower right logo, AM, bat.....$20.00 – 30.00

T-22M, horizontal, 4¾x8½x1⅞", 1962, blue plastic, eight transistors, upper front horizontal two-band slide rule dial, lower perforated grill area with band switch and battery meter, telescoping antenna, AM, Marine, bat.......**$25.00 – 35.00**

T-22U, horizontal, 4¾x8½x1⅞", 1962, blue plastic, eight transistors, upper front horizontal two-band slide rule dial, lower perforated grill area with band switch and battery meter, telescoping antenna, AM, SW, bat...............**$25.00 – 35.00**

T-33, horizontal, 1964, nine transistors, upper front horizontal two-band slide rule dial with thumbwheel tuning, upper left volume window with left side thumbwheel knob, large perforated grill area, band switch, telescoping antenna, handle, AM, FM, bat...........................**$20.00 – 25.00**

T-41M, horizontal, 3½x6x1¼", 1962, ivory/black plastic, eight transistors, top horizontal two-band slide rule dial with top right thumbwheel tuning, lower right side thumbwheel on/off/volume knob, large front perforated grill area with lower right logo, telescoping antenna, AM, Marine, bat........**$20.00 – 30.00**

T-41U, horizontal, 3½x6x1¼", 1962, ivory/black plastic, eight transistors, top horizontal two-band slide rule dial with top right thumbwheel tuning, lower right side thumbwheel on/off/volume knob, large front perforated grill area with lower right logo, telescoping antenna, AM, SW, bat.........**$20.00 – 30.00**

T-50 "Super Sensitive," horizontal, 3½x5¾x1½", 1962, available in salmon or black plastic, six transistors, lower right front window dial with right side thumbwheel tuning, top left thumbwheel on/off/volume knob, metal perforated grill area, made in Japan, AM, bat.........................**$25.00 – 35.00**

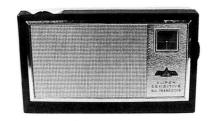

T-50AA "Super Sensitive," horizontal, 3½x6x1¾", 1962, seven transistors, upper right front window dial with right side thumbwheel tuning, top left thumbwheel on/off/volume knob, metal perforated grill area, left side H/L switch, made in Japan, AM, bat.........**$25.00 – 35.00**

T-53, vertical, 3½x2½x1¼", 1962, plastic, six transistors, upper front horizontal slide rule dial with right side thumbwheel tuning, right side thumbwheel on/off/volume knob, lower perforated grill area with lower left logo, AM, bat..**$20.00 – 25.00**

T-59, vertical, 1962, nine transistors, upper front horizontal slide rule dial with right side thumbwheel tuning, right side thumbwheel on/off/volume knob, lower perforated grill area with lower left logo, AM, bat.............**$20.00 – 25.00**

T-70M, horizontal, 1962, eight transistors, large right front horizontal two-band slide rule dial with thumbwheel tuning, thumbwheel on/off/volume knob, right side band switch, horizontal grill bars, telescoping antenna, handle, AM, Marine, bat.................$20.00 – 30.00

T-70U, horizontal, 1962, eight transistors, large right front horizontal two-band slide rule dial with thumbwheel tuning, thumbwheel on/off/volume knob, right side band switch, horizontal grill bars, telescoping antenna, handle, AM, SW, bat......................$20.00 – 30.00

T-81, horizontal, 1962, nine transistors, top horizontal two-band slide rule dial with thumbwheel tuning, thumbwheel on/off/volume knob, right side band switch, oval perforated grill area, telescoping antenna, AM, FM, bat.........$20.00 – 25.00

T-81H, horizontal, 1964, nine transistors, top horizontal three-band slide rule dial with thumbwheel tuning, thumbwheel on/off/volume knob, right side band switch, oval perforated grill area, telescoping antenna, AM, FM, SW, bat.........$20.00 – 25.00

T-92 "Portalarm," vertical watch/radio, 4x2½x1¼", 1962, black plastic, six transistors, right front thumbwheel dial, left side thumbwheel volume knob, top right on/off/auto switch, left Seiko watch face, metal perforated grill area with lower left logo, made in Japan, AM, bat.......$100.00 – 125.00

T-100M, horizontal, 1965, 12 transistors, upper front horizontal four-

band slide rule dial, large lower lattice grill area with lower right logo, telescoping antenna, handle, AM, FM, SW, LW, bat.........$20.00 – 30.00

T-601, vertical, 3½x2¼x1", 1964, plastic, upper left front window dial with thumbwheel tuning, large metal perforated grill area with lower right logo, rear fold-out stand, AM, bat...............................$20.00 – 30.00

T-745, horizontal/table, 1964, wood, 12 transistors, lower slanted horizontal four-band slide rule dial, two knobs, large upper grill area, AM, FM, 2SW, bat .....$20.00 – 30.00

Parlax

P-1000, vertical, plastic, upper right front dial with thumbwheel tuning, thumbwheel on/off/volume knob, perforated grill area, top right vinyl strap, AM, bat.............$5.00 – 10.00

Pateks

Boy's Radio, vertical, 4x2½x1", plastic, two transistors, upper left front window dial with left side thumbwheel tuning, right side thumb-wheel on/off/volume knob, round metal perforated grill area, made in Japan, AM, bat...........$45.00 – 55.00

Pearl

Boy's Radio, vertical 4¼x2⅞x1½", plastic, two transistors, upper left front dial, right side thumbwheel on/off/volume knob, diagonally divided front with lower perforated grill area, made in Japan, AM, bat...............................$65.00 – 75.00

Pearl Tone

T-888, horizontal, plastic, eight transistors, right front dial panel with window dial, right side thumbwheel tuning, lower right front thumbwheel on/off/volume knob, left metal textured and perforated grill area, AM, bat.....$45.00 – 55.00

Peerless

10T-2SP "Twin Speaker," horizontal, 1964, 10 transistors, upper center front horizontal slide rule dial with thumbwheel tuning, right and left grill areas with horizontal slots, twin speakers, AM, bat.......$10.00 – 15.00

630, vertical, 1965, six transistors, upper right front window dial with right side thumbwheel tuning, top left thumbwheel on/off/volume

knob, lower grill area with horizontal slots, AM, bat........$10.00 – 15.00

707, horizontal, 1964, seven transistors, upper front horizontal dial, right and left knobs, lower oval grill area with center "707" emblem, handle, AM, bat ....$15.00 – 20.00

777, vertical, 1965, seven transistors, upper right front round window dial with right side thumbwheel tuning, top left thumbwheel on/off/volume knob, lower round grill area, AM, bat......$10.00 – 15.00

820, vertical, 1965, eight transistors, upper right front window dial with right side thumbwheel tuning, left side thumbwheel on/off/volume knob, lower perforated grill area, AM, bat.....................$10.00 – 15.00

830, vertical, 1965, eight transistors, upper left front round dial, lower round grill area, AM, bat............................$10.00 – 15.00

855, vertical, 4¼x2½x1¼", plastic, eight transistors, upper right front round window dial over front panel with diamond and circular cut-outs, right side thumbwheel tuning, left side thumbwheel on/off/volume knob, made in Hong Kong, AM, bat............................$15.00 – 20.00

880, horizontal, 1965, eight transistors, right front round window dial with thumbwheel tuning, lower right thumbwheel on/off/volume knob, left grill area with horizontal slots, swing handle, AM, bat.....................$10.00 – 15.00

990, horizontal, 1965, leather, nine transistors, upper front horizontal two-band slide rule dial, right and left knobs, lower oval perforated grill area with center "990" emblem, telescoping antenna, handle, AM, FM, bat ......**$15.00 – 20.00**

990-12, horizontal, 6¼x9⅛x3¼", leather, 12 transistors, upper front horizontal two band slide rule dial, right and left knobs, lower oval perforated grill area with center "990" emblem, telescoping antenna, handle, made in Japan, AM, FM, bat ....**$15.00 – 20.00**

1030 "Hi-Fi," vertical, 3⅞x2½x1¼", 1965, 10 transistors, upper front horizontal slide rule dial with right side thumbwheel tuning, right side thumbwheel on/off/volume knob, lower grill area with center logo, strap, made in Japan, AM, bat....................**$10.00 – 15.00**

1033, horizontal, 1965, 10 transistors, upper front horizontal three-band slide rule dial with lower right tuning knob, left grill area with horizontal slots, telescoping antenna, handle, AM, Marine, SW, bat ..**$15.00 – 20.00**

1200, vertical, 4¼x2⅝x1⅜", 1965, 12 transistors, upper right front thumbwheel dial, top left thumbwheel on/off/volume knob, large perforated grill area with center logo, strap, made in Hong Kong, AM, bat.....................**$10.00 – 15.00**

1250, vertical, 4¼x2⅝x1¼", plastic, 12 transistors, upper right front window dial with right side thumbwheel tuning, top left thumbwheel on/off/volume knob, left front perforated grill area, strap, made in Hong Kong, AM, bat.**$10.00 – 15.00**

1333, horizontal, 1965, leather, 13 transistors, upper slanted horizontal three-band slide rule dial, two lower right knobs, left grill area with horizontal slots, telescoping antenna, leather handle, AM, FM, SW, bat.....................**$20.00 – 25.00**

FM-90, vertical, 1965, nine transistors, upper front round two-band dial with thumbwheel tuning overlaps large lower grill area, telescoping antenna, AM, FM, bat.................**$10.00 – 15.00**

Penncrest

1130, horizontal, 2⅝x4½x1⅛", plastic, six transistors, upper right front window dial with upper right side thumbwheel tuning, lower right side thumbwheel on/off/volume knob, large metal grill area with horizontal slots and lower left logo, made in Japan, AM, bat..............**$20.00 – 25.00**

1132, horizontal, 2½x4¼x1", plastic, six transistors, upper right front window dial with upper right side thumbwheel tuning, lower right side thumbwheel on/off/volume knob, large metal perforated grill area with lower left logo, AM, bat.............$20.00 – 25.00

1631, horizontal, 1964, six transistors, upper front horizontal slide rule dial, right and left knobs, large lower perforated grill area with right tone knob and left logo, handle, AM, bat.............$10.00 – 15.00

1871, horizontal, 1964, 10 transistors, two right front dials – upper AM, lower FM – left perforated grill area with upper left logo, telescoping antenna, strap, AM, FM, bat.............$15.00 – 20.00

1896, horizontal, 1963, leather, 12 transistors, two upper front round dials – right AM, left FM – thumbwheel volume and tone knobs, band switch, perforated grill area with logo, telescoping antenna, leather handle, AM, FM, bat..$20.00 – 25.00

1991, horizontal, 1964, 12 transistors, upper front horizontal dial, right and left knobs, lower perforated grill area with lower left logo, two telescoping antennas, handle, AM, FM, SW, bat.......$20.00 – 25.00

Penney's

6TP-243, vertical, plastic, upper front horizontal slide rule dial with large right front tuning knob, left side thumbwheel on/off/volume knob, metal perforated grill area with lower left logo, AM, bat.......$40.00 – 55.00

6TP-322, vertical, 4⅜x2¾x1¼", plastic, upper front window dial with right side thumbwheel tuning, right side thumbwheel on/off/volume

knob, lower metal perforated grill area, rear fold-out stand, made in Japan, AM, bat..........$25.00 – 35.00

41-7TM-285S "Lace," horizontal, 4x6⅞x1¾", plastic, seven transistors, upper front horizontal two-band slide rule dial with top right tuning knob, upper left thumbwheel on/off/volume knob, lower grill area with lace insert, telescoping antenna, AM, SW, bat..........$200.00 – 225.00

41-8TM-360, horizontal, 3¾x6½x1½", plastic, eight transistors, upper front wrap-over dial, right side tuning knob, left side volume knob, metal perforated grill area with "V" decoration, AM, bat.............$30.00 – 40.00

620, horizontal, 1962, leather, 12 transistors, two upper front round dials – one AM, one FM – lower perforated grill area with left logo, thumbwheel volume and tone knobs, band switch, telescoping antenna, leather handle, AM, FM, bat.............$15.00 – 20.00

628, horizontal, 1962, charcoal, seven transistors, wedge-shaped case with large right round dial and thumbwheel knob, left perforated grill area, swing handle, AM, bat.............$15.00 – 25.00

629, horizontal, 1962, leather, eight transistors, off-center round dial over large grill area, right tuning and volume knobs, upper left knob, leather handle, AM, bat ....**$10.00 – 15.00**

1130, horizontal, 2⅝x4½x1⅛", plastic, six transistors, upper right front window dial with upper right side thumbwheel tuning, lower right side thumbwheel on/off/volume knob, large metal perforated grill area with lower left logo, made in Japan, AM, bat...........**$20.00 – 25.00**

1132, horizontal, plastic, six transistors, upper right front window dial with upper right side thumbwheel tuning, lower right side thumbwheel on/off/volume knob, large metal perforated grill area with lower left logo, AM, bat..**$20.00 – 25.00**

1140, square, plastic, right side thumbwheel tuning and on/off/volume knobs, front round metal perforated grill area, top vinyl strap, AM, bat ...**$25.00 – 35.00**

RP-1-124, horizontal, 3⅝x5⅞x1⅝", **1958, plastic, right front thumbwheel dial with V-shaped pointer, center on/off/volume knob, left lattice grill area, made in USA, AM, bat**...........................**$30.00 – 40.00**

Perdio

PC16, horizontal, 4⅛x6⅝x1¾", 1961, leather, seven transistors, left front round brass dial knob, top on/off/volume knob under leather handle, cloth grill area, lower left lion logo, made in England, AM, bat.............................**$25.00 – 35.00**

Pct

Boy's Radio, vertical, 3x2¼x1¼", plastic, two transistors, upper right front window dial with right side thumbwheel tuning, left side thumbwheel on/off/volume knob, round metal perforated grill area, made in Japan, AM, bat...........**$45.00 – 55.00**

Petite

6G620, vertical, plastic, six transistors, upper left front window dial with left side thumbwheel tuning, right side thumbwheel on/off/volume knob, lower metal perforated grill area with lower right triangular logo, AM, bat.............**$20.00 – 25.00**

NTR-120, vertical, 1961, six transistors, upper left front window dial with top left thumbwheel tuning, top right thumbwheel on/off/volume knob, lower perforated grill area with lower left logo, made in Japan, AM, bat...........$30.00 – 40.00

NTR-150, vertical, 1961, six transistors, upper front window dial with thumbwheel tuning, lower perforated grill area with Oriental design, AM, bat ....$40.00 – 50.00

NTR-800, horizontal, 1964, eight transistors, upper front horizontal two-band slide rule dial with right side thumbwheel tuning, perforated grill area with lower right band switch, AM, SW, bat...$20.00 – 25.00

Philco

NT-600BKG, vertical, 3¾x2¼x1", 1964, plastic, six transistors, upper right front window dial with right side thumbwheel tuning, top left thumbwheel on/off/volume knob, metal perforated grill area with lower left logo, AM, bat..$10.00 – 15.00

NT-601BK, horizontal, 6½x10x3¼", 1965, plastic, six transistors, right front round dial knob, lower on/off/volume knob, left grill area with vertical bars, handle, AM, bat....................$10.00 – 15.00

NT-602BK, vertical, 1964, plastic with metal front panel, six transistors, upper front round window dial with right side thumbwheel tuning, right side thumbwheel on/off/volume knob, perforated grill area, AM, bat............$15.00 – 20.00

NT-802WHG, vertical, 1964, eight transistors, upper front round dial over large perforated grill area, right side thumbwheel tuning knob, right side thumbwheel on/off/volume knob, AM, bat ....$15.00 – 20.00

NT-807, horizontal, 1965, eight transistors, upper front horizontal dial with thumbwheel tuning, lower two-section perforated grill area, swing handle, AM, bat ....$10.00 – 15.00

NT-808, horizontal, 1965, leather, eight transistors, upper front horizontal slide rule dial, two knobs, lower grill area with horizontal bars, strap, AM, bat...**$10.00 – 15.00**

NT-814BKG, vertical, 1965, eight transistors, two upper front round dials – one AM, one FM – lower perforated grill area with lower left logo, telescoping antenna, made in Japan, AM, FM, bat...**$10.00 – 15.00**

NT-815BK, horizontal, 1965, leather, ten transistors, off-center vertical three-band slide rule dial, three right knobs, left perforated grill area, telescoping antenna, leather handle, AM, 2SW, bat.................**$15.00 – 20.00**

NT-900, vertical, 1964, nine transistors, upper front round dial over large perforated grill area, right side knob, strap, AM, bat..**$10.00 – 15.00**

NT-903BK, horizontal, 1965, nine transistors, right front round two-band dial overlaps horizontal grill bars, telescoping antenna, handle, AM, FM, bat.............**$10.00 – 15.00**

NT-906BKG, horizontal, 1964, nine transistors, step-back top, two off-center round dials – one FM, one AM – right tone and off/on/volume knobs, right side thumbwheel tuning knob, left perforated grill area, handle, AM, FM, bat.............**$15.00 – 20.00**

NT-912BK, horizontal, 1965, leather, ten transistors, large off-center round two-band dial, three right knobs, left grill area, telescoping antenna, leather handle, AM, FM, AC/bat.............**$10.00 – 15.00**

NT-913BK, horizontal, 8x11x4½", 1965, leather, 11 transistors, two upper left front dials – one FM, one AM – three right knobs, horizontal grill bars, telescoping antenna, leather handle, AM, FM, bat ....**$10.00 – 15.00**

NT-1004, horizontal, 1965, leather, 10 transistors, upper front horizontal slide rule dial, three right knobs, left checkered grill area with lower left logo, telescoping antenna, leather handle, AM, FM, bat..**$10.00 – 15.00**

T-3-130 "Veep," vertical, 3¾x2½x1", 1959, ebony/ivory plastic, three transistors, top window dial with upper front and back double thumbwheel tuning, lower right front thumbwheel on/off/volume knob, front horizontal bars, no speaker, earphone only, AM, bat.....................**$70.00 – 90.00**

T-4-124, horizontal, 3¾x5⅞x1⅞", 1959, plastic, four transistors, right front round dial knob, center on/off/volume knob, left horizontal grill bars, made in USA, AM, bat.............................$45.00 – 55.00

T-4J-124, horizontal, 3¾x5⅞x1⅞", 1959, plastic, four transistors, right front round dial knob, center on/off/volume knob, left horizontal grill bars, made in USA, AM, bat.............................$45.00 – 55.00

T5-124 "500," horizontal, 3½x5⅞x 1¾", plastic, right front window dial over large metal perforated grill area, right side thumbwheel tuning and on/off/volume knobs, AM, bat......................$25.00 – 35.00

T-6-124, horizontal, 6⅛x9¼x3", 1958, leather, six transistors, right front round dial knob, left side on/off/volume knob, front grill area, leather handle, AM, bat...........$15.00 – 20.00

T-7-126, horizontal, 4¼x7x1¾", 1956, plastic, seven transistors, Philco's first transistor radio, two-tone front panel with off-center thumbwheel dial accessible through two triangular openings, lower right thumbwheel on/off/volume knob, left painted metal perforated grill area, AM, bat..............$70.00 – 90.00

T-7X-128, horizontal, 4¼x7x1¾", plastic, seven transistors, two-tone front panel with off-center thumbwheel dial accessible through two triangular openings, lower right thumbwheel on/off/volume knob, left grill area with horizontal bars, AM, bat......................$70.00 – 90.00

T-9 "Trans World," horizontal, 11x 16½x6½", 1958, leather, nine transis-

tors, fold-up front cover, inner right seven-band slide rule dial, left checkered grill area, four knobs, telescoping antenna, bat.......$90.00 – 110.00

T-45-124, horizontal, 3¾x5⅛x1⅝", 1959, available in ivory/terracotta or ivory/aqua plastic, four transistors, large right front dial, center on/off/volume knob, left lattice grill area, AM, bat.....$35.00 – 45.00

T-50, vertical, 4⅝x3⅛x1⅞", 1959, available in ivory/turquoise or ivory/terracotta plastic, five transistors, upper front round dial knob, right side thumbwheel on/off/volume knob, lower horizontal grill bars, AM, bat.............$20.00 – 30.00

T51-124, vertical, 4⅝x3⅛x1⅞", 1961, plastic, five transistors, upper front round dial knob, right side thumbwheel on/off/volume knob, lower horizontal grill bars, AM, bat......................$20.00 – 30.00

T52-124, horizontal, 1961, available in charcoal, ivory, or terracotta, five transistors, right front recessed horizontal slide rule dial with right side thumbwheel tuning, center on/off/volume knob, horizontal grill bars, AM, bat.....$15.00 – 20.00

T-60-124, vertical, 5⅝x3¼x1¾", 1959, available in gold/ebony or charcoal/ivory plastic, six transistors, upper front thumbwheel dial in V-shaped indent, right thumbwheel on/off/volume knob, lower horizontal grill bars, swing handle, AM, bat.....................$25.00 – 35.00

T61-124, vertical, 4⅜x2⅝x1¼", plastic, upper right front window dial with right side thumbwheel tuning, left on/off/volume window with left side thumbwheel knob, lower checkered grill area, AM, bat.....................$15.00 – 20.00

T-62-124, vertical, plastic, upper front thumbwheel dial in V-shaped indent, right thumbwheel on/off/volume knob, lower horizontal grill bars, swing handle, AM, bat.$25.00 – 35.00

T-63-124, vertical, plastic, upper right front dial with right side thumbwheel tuning, left side thumbwheel on/off/volume knob, lower checkered grill area, AM, bat.............................$15.00 – 20.00

T-64, horizontal, 3¾x6x1½", 1963, available in brown or blue plastic, six transistors, upper right front round dial, lower on/off/volume knob, left horizontal grill bars with center logo, AM, bat.$10.00 – 15.00

T-65, horizontal, 6½x8⅞x3", 1959, available in ivory/aqua or ivory/gold plastic, six transistors, right front dial knob, left side on/off/volume knob, left horizontal grill bars, feet, rotatable antenna in handle, AM, bat ....$20.00 – 25.00

T-66-126, vertical, 1961, six transistors, upper right front round dial with right side thumbwheel tuning, left side thumbwheel on/off/volume knob, lower checkered grill area, AM, bat............$15.00 – 20.00

T-67GP, horizontal, 2½x4½x1⅛", 1963, plastic, six transistors, right front window dial over large metal perforated grill area, two right side thumbwheel knobs, made in Japan, AM, bat ....$20.00 – 30.00

T-68BKG, vertical, 4x2½x1½", 1963, plastic, six transistors, upper front round window dial with thumbwheel tuning, lower metal perforated grill area, AM, bat.............................$15.00 – 20.00

T-69WH, horizontal, 1964, six transistors, right front window dial with upper right side thumbwheel tuning, lower right side thumbwheel on/off/volume knob, large perforated grill area, AM, bat ....$15.00 – 20.00

T-70-124, vertical, 5½x3¼x1¾", 1961, plastic, seven transistors, upper front thumbwheel dial in V-shaped indent, right thumbwheel on/off/volume knob, lower horizontal grill bars, swing handle, made in USA, AM, bat........**$25.00 – 35.00**

T-74-124, horizontal, 5⅞x9x3", 1961, leather, seven transistors, off-center horizontal slide rule dial with right side thumbwheel tuning, left side on/off/volume knob, leather handle, AM, bat..............**$15.00 – 20.00**

T-75-124, horizontal, 5½x7⅛x2¼", 1959, leather, seven transistors, off-center round thumbwheel dial overlaps right & left metal perforated grill areas, lower right thumbwheel on/off/volume knob, leather strap, AM, bat.....................**$20.00 – 30.00**

T-76-124, horizontal, 5½x7¼x2½", 1960, leather, seven transistors, off-center round thumbwheel dial overlaps right & left metal perforated grill area, lower right thumbwheel on/off/volume knob, leather strap, AM, bat.....................**$20.00 – 30.00**

T-77-124, vertical, 1962, plastic, seven transistors, upper right front dial overlaps large grill area with horizontal slots, right side thumbwheel tuning, left front on/off/volume window with left side thumbwheel knob, AM, bat..............**$25.00 – 35.00**

T-77BK, vertical, 1962, seven transistors, upper right front dial overlaps large grill area with horizontal slots, right side thumbwheel tuning, left front on/off/volume win-

dow with left side thumbwheel knob, AM, bat............**$25.00 – 35.00**

T-78-124, horizontal, 7⅛x9⅝x4", 1959, leather, seven transistors, right front oblong window dial and tuning knob, left side on/off/volume knob, round metal grill area with triangular perforations, handle, AM, bat..............**$20.00 – 25.00**

T-81GP, **vertical**, **4⅛x2⅝x1⅛"**, **1963, plastic, eight transistors, large upper front dial overlaps metal grill area with horizontal slots, right side thumbwheel on/off/volume knob, made in Japan, AM, bat** ....**$20.00 – 30.00**

T-84BR, horizontal, 1963, leather, eight transistors, right front dial with lower tuning knob and upper on/off/volume knob, large perforated grill area with lower left logo, handle, AM, bat ....**$10.00 – 15.00**

T-88-124, horizontal, 1962, plastic, eight transistors, upper right front/top horizontal slide rule dial with lower front tuning, left lattice grill area, pull-up handle, AM, bat.....................$25.00 – 35.00

T-90, vertical, 1963, nine transistors, upper front round dial knob over large perforated grill area, right side on/off/volume knob, strap, AM, bat............$20.00 – 25.00

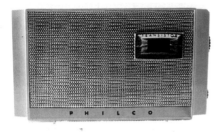

T-500-124 "500," horizontal, 3½x5⅞x1¾", 1957, plastic, right front window dial over large metal perforated grill area, right side thumbwheel tuning and on/off/volume knobs, AM, bat ..$35.00 – 45.00

T-700-124 "700," horizontal, 6¾x9½x4", 1957, leather, seven transistors, lower right front round dial knob overlaps metal grill area, left side on/off/volume knob, leather handle, AM, bat ....$25.00 – 35.00

T-700X, horizontal, 1958, leather, seven transistors, lower right front round dial knob overlaps metal grill area, left side on/off/volume knob, leather handle, AM, bat ......$25.00 – 35.00

T-701-124, horizontal, 1958, plastic, lower right front dial overlaps metal perforated grill area, left side on/off/volume knob, top "Scantenna" antenna/handle, AM, bat ....$25.00 – 35.00

T-702-124 "VII," horizontal, 1960, leather, seven transistors, upper right front window dial with large lower tuning knob, sliding on/off switch next to tuning window, left side volume knob, vertical grill bars, leather handle, AM, bat ....$10.00 – 15.00

T-703-124 "VII," horizontal, 5⅜x9x 3¾", 1963, leather, seven transistors, upper right front window dial with large lower tuning knob, sliding on/off switch next to tuning window, left side volume knob, vertical grill bars, leather handle, AM, bat ....$10.00 – 15.00

T-800-124 "800," horizontal, 1958, 7x10x3½", plastic, seven transistors, large right front round dial, right side on/off/volume knob, left vertical bars, stand/carrying handle, made in USA, AM, bat..........$25.00 – 35.00

T-802-124, horizontal, 1961, leather, eight transistors, right round dial knob over large checkered grill area, leather strap, AM, bat ....$15.00 – 20.00

T-803-124, horizontal, 6⅞x9⅝x3¾", 1961, leather, eight transistors, right front round dial knob overlaps metal horizontal grill bars, left side on/off/volume knob, leather strap, AM, bat............$10.00 – 15.00

T-804, horizontal, 1963, leather, eight transistors, right front round dial knob overlaps horizontal grill bars, leather strap, AM, bat.$10.00 – 15.00

T-902-124, horizontal, 8½x10¼x4⅛", leather, nine transistors, lower front horizontal slide rule dial, three knobs, large upper metal perforated grill area, strap, AM, bat .....$10.00 – 15.00

T-905-124, horizontal, 1962, nine transistors, right front two-band dial over large checkered grill area, AM/FM pushbuttons, telescoping antenna, handle, AM, FM, bat ...$20.00 – 30.00

T-907, horizontal, 1963, available in brown or black, nine transistors, two upper front horizontal dial scales – one AM, one FM – large lower checkered grill area with AM/FM switch, telescoping antenna, handle, AM, FM, bat........$15.00 – 20.00

T-908GY, horizontal, 1964, nine transistors, upper front horizontal two-band slide rule dial, top pushbuttons, lower checkered grill area, telescoping antenna, handle, AM, FM, bat.....................$20.00 – 25.00

T-911, horizontal, 1963, leatherette, nine transistors, upper front horizontal four-band slide rule dial, lower checkered grill area, pushbuttons, two telescoping antennas, handle, AM, FM, SW, LW, bat..$20.00 – 30.00

T1000-124, horizontal/clock radio, 8½x15½x5", 1960, plastic/metal, six

transistors, modernistic design consists of three modules (right/left speakers and center clock face) swivel-mounted on base, thumbwheel tuning and on/off/volume knobs, AM, bat........$75.00 – 100.00

TC-47-124, horizontal/clock radio, 5⅛x10x2½", 1960, leather, four transistors, right front round dial, center round grill area and volume knob, left round clock face, AM, bat.............................$25.00 – 35.00

Philips

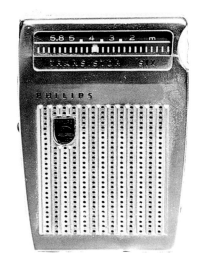

L0X10T, vertical, 1962, plastic, six transistors, upper front horizontal slide rule dial with right side thumbwheel tuning, left side thumbwheel volume knob, top on/off switch, lower metal perforated grill area, made in West Germany, AM, bat...........$20.00 – 25.00

L0X20T "Rosette," vertical, 1964, plastic, six transistors, upper left front horizontal two-band dial with right side thumbwheel tuning, right side thumbwheel on/off/volume knob, lower metal perforated grill area, band switch, made in West Germany, AM, LW, bat.....**$20.00 – 25.00**

L0X25T "Rosette," vertical, 1964, plastic, six transistors, upper left front horizontal two-band dial with right side thumbwheel tuning, right side thumbwheel on/off/volume knob, lower metal perforated grill area, band switch, made in West Germany, AM, SW, bat .....**$20.00 – 25.00**

LOX25T/22G, vertical, plastic, six transistors, upper left front horizontal two-band dial with right side thumbwheel tuning, right side thumbwheel on/off/volume knob, lower metal perforated grill area, band switch, made in West Germany, AM, SW, bat....**$20.00 – 25.00**

L0X90T/L0D90T "Fanette," horizontal, 1960, plastic, seven transistors, right front round two-band dial, lower thumbwheel on/off/volume

knob, upper band switch, left perforated grill area, made in West Germany, AM, LW, bat .....**$30.00 – 40.00**

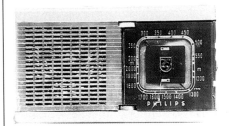

L0X91T "Fanette," horizontal, 1963, plastic, seven transistors, right front square two-band dial with right side thumbwheel tuning, lower front thumbwheel on/off/volume knob, upper band switch, left lattice grill area, made in West Germany, AM, LW, bat......................$30.00 – 40.00

L1D90T "Fanette 190," horizontal, 1959, plastic, seven transistors, right front round dial, just to the left of the dial is the thumbwheel on/off/volume knob, diagonally divided front with lower perforated grill area, made in West Germany, AM, bat......................**$35.00 – 45.00**

L1W22T "Nanette," horizontal, 1962, plastic, eight transistors, upper front horizontal three-band slide rule dial with right side thumbwheel tuning, left side volume knob and on/off switch, lower perforated grill area with lower right logo, band switch, telescoping antenna, made in West Germany, AM, FM, LW, bat ....**$25.00 – 35.00**

L1W22T/64L, horizontal, plastic, eight transistors, upper front horizontal three-band slide rule dial with right side thumbwheel tuning, left side volume knob and on/off switch, lower perforated grill area with lower right logo, band switch, telescoping antenna, AM, FM, LW, bat ....$25.00 – 35.00

L1W30T "Fanette," horizontal, 1965, plastic, six transistors, top horizontal wrap-over two-band dial with top right thumbwheel tuning, large front grill area with lower right thumbwheel on/off/volume knob, made in West Germany, AM, LW, bat......................$20.00 – 30.00

L1W32T "Violette," horizontal, 1965, plastic, eight transistors, upper front horizontal three-band slide rule dial with right side thumbwheel tuning, left side thumbwheel on/off/volume knob, lower perforated grill area with lower right logo, band switch, made in West Germany, AM, FM, LW, bat ....$25.00 – 35.00

L1W40T "Fanette 40," horizontal, 1965, plastic, six transistors, upper front wrap-over horizontal two-band dial with top right tuning, lower right front thumbwheel on/off/volume knob, left metal perforated grill area, made in West Germany, AM, LW, bat ....$25.00 – 35.00

L1W50T "Fanette 50," horizontal, 1965, plastic, six transistors, upper front wrap-over horizontal two-band dial with top right tuning, lower right front thumbwheel on/off/volume knob, left metal checkered grill area, made in West Germany, AM, LW, bat ....$25.00 – 35.00

L1W62T "Fleurette," horizontal, 1966, plastic, eight transistors, upper front horizontal two-band slide rule dial with right side thumbwheel tuning, left side thumbwheel on/off/ volume knob, lower perforated grill area, band switch, made in West Germany, AM, FM, bat......$25.00 – 35.00

L1X15T, horizontal, 1963, plastic, six transistors, upper front horizontal three-band slide rule dial with right thumbwheel tuning, left side thumbwheel on/off/volume knob, lower perforated grill area, telescoping antenna, made in West Germany, AM, 2SW, bat...$25.00 – 35.00

L1X75T "Fanette," horizontal, 1958, plastic, seven transistors, right front round dial, just to the left of the dial is the thumbwheel on/off/volume knob, diagonally divided front with lower perforated grill area, made in West Germany, AM, bat ....$35.00 – 45.00

L1X75T/52, horizontal, plastic, seven transistors, right front round dial, just to the left of the dial is the thumbwheel on/off/volume knob, diagonally divided front with lower perforated grill area, AM, bat ....$35.00 – 45.00

L1X75T/64RA, horizontal, plastic, seven transistors, right front round dial, just to the left of the dial is the thumbwheel on/off/volume knob, diagonally divided front with lower perforated grill area, made in Holland, AM, bat.............$35.00 – 45.00

L1X75T/R, horizontal, plastic, seven transistors, right front round dial, just to the left of the dial is the thumbwheel on/off/volume knob, diagonally divided front with lower perforated grill area, AM, bat ....$35.00 – 45.00

L2D12T "Nicolette," horizontal, 1961, plastic, eight transistors, top horizontal three-band dial with right front thumbwheel tuning, upper left front thumbwheel on/off/volume knob, metal perforated grill area, made in West Germany, AM, FM, LW, bat.....................$30.00 – 40.00

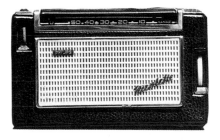

L2D22T "Nicolette 222," horizontal, 1963, padded plastic, eight transistors, top horizontal three-band slide rule dial with right front thumbwheel tuning, upper left front thumbwheel on/off/volume knob, large lower grill area, plastic handle, made in West Germany, AM, FM, LW, bat.......$30.00 – 40.00

L2D42T "Nicolette L," horizontal, 1964, plastic, nine transistors, top horizontal four-band wrap-over slide

rule dial with right front thumbwheel tuning, upper left front thumbwheel on/off/volume knob, large lattice grill area, plastic handle, made in West Germany, AM, FM, LW, SW, bat.........$30.00 – 40.00

L2D52T "Nicolette L," horizontal, 1965, plastic, nine transistors, top horizontal four-band wrap-over slide rule dial with right front thumbwheel tuning, upper left front thumbwheel on/off/volume knob, large lower grill area, handle, made in West Germany, AM, FM, LW, SW, bat ....$30.00 – 40.00

L2X00T/00L, horizontal, plastic, top horizontal three-band slide rule dial, front metal perforated grill area, telescoping antenna, AM, SW, LW, bat.....................$25.00 – 35.00

L2X21T "Suzette," horizontal, 1965, soft plastic, seven transistors, top horizontal two-band dial with top right thumbwheel tuning, lower right front thumbwheel on/off/volume knob, grill area with horizontal bars, plastic handle, made in West Germany, AM, LW, bat......$25.00 – 35.00

Pierpont

The Sportsman, horizontal 4¾x6⅞x2⅞," leather, upper right front dial knob, lower on/off/volume knob, left grill area with horizontal cut-outs, leather handle, made in USA, AM, bat.........$10.00 – 15.00

Plata

8R-34 "High Fidelity Deluxe," horizontal, 1965, leather, eight transistors, upper right front round dial, upper left on/off/volume knob over large perforated grill area, handle, AM, bat ....$10.00 – 15.00

8R-75 "High Fidelity," horizontal, 1965, leather, eight transistors, off-center vertical slide rule dial, three right knobs, left grill area with horizontal bars, leather handle, AM, bat ....$10.00 – 15.00

8S-31, horizontal, 1965, eight transistors, upper front horizontal two-band slide rule dial with right side thumbwheel tuning, lower lattice grill area, telescoping antenna, AM, SW, bat ....$15.00 – 20.00

9TA-370, horizontal, 1962, 10 transistors, upper front horizontal four-band slide rule dial with lower right tuning knob, thumbwheel tone and volume knobs, perforated grill area, telescoping antenna, handle, AM, 2SW, LW, bat......$25.00 – 35.00

10TF-530, horizontal, 4¾x7⅞x2⅛", plastic, upper front horizontal two-band dial with right tuning knob, top left thumbwheel on/off/volume knob, large front metal perforated grill area with center nameplate, right side AM/FM switch, telescoping antenna, made in Japan, AM, FM, bat......................$20.00 – 25.00

Polyrad

KR-6TS43 "Capri," vertical, 3¾x2¼x1", plastic, six transistors, upper left front thumbwheel dial knob, upper right front thumbwheel on/off/volume knob, lower round metal textured and perforated grill area, made in Japan, AM, bat............................$50.00 – 60.00

P-86, vertical, 4⅜x2¾x1⅜", 1961, plastic with metal front panel, six transistors, upper left front round thumbwheel dial knob, upper right thumbwheel on/off/volume knob, lower perforated grill area, AM, bat ....$25.00 – 35.00

PP-T

1 transistor (no #), horizontal, 2⅝x3⅞x1⅝", plastic snap-shut case, one transistor, right front dial knob, no on/off/volume knob, no speaker, earphone only, AM, bat......................$65.00 – 75.00

Primotone

Boy's Radio, vertical, plastic, two transistors, upper right front recessed thumbwheel dial knob, upper left front recessed thumbwheel on/off/volume knob, lower perforated grill area with peacock design and mother-of-pearl accents, AM, bat ....$125.00 – 150.00

Princeton

WTC-610, vertical, 4½x2⅝x1¼", plastic, six transistors, upper right front window dial with right side thumbwheel tuning, left side thumbwheel on/off/volume knob, lower lattice grill area, top right vinyl strap, made in Okinawa, AM, bat....$5.00 – 10.00

Queen

MTR-203 "Boy's Radio," vertical, 4⅛x2½x1¼", plastic, two transistors, upper front see-through panel with right "coat-of-arms" window dial, right side thumbwheel tuning, left side thumbwheel on/off/volume knob, lower textured and perforated grill area, made in Japan, AM, bat...................$50.00 – 60.00

Raleigh

805, vertical, 1965, eight transistors, upper right front oval window dial with thumbwheel tuning, top left thumbwheel on/off/volume knob, lower oval grill area, AM, bat....................$20.00 – 25.00

828, vertical, 1965, eight transistors, upper right front round window dial with thumbwheel tuning, lower perforated grill area, AM, bat....................$10.00 – 15.00

885 "High Sensitivity," horizontal, 1965, eight transistors, right front dial, left grill area with horizontal bars, handle, AM, bat.$15.00 – 20.00

1005, vertical, 1965, 10 transistors, upper right front oval window dial with right side thumbwheel tuning, top left thumbwheel on/off/volume knob, lower oval grill area, AM, bat....................$20.00 – 25.00

FM-925, vertical, 1965, nine transistors, two upper front window dials – one FM, one AM – with thumbwheel tuning, lower horizontal grill bars, telescoping antenna, strap, AM, FM, bat...............$10.00 – 15.00

HT-8057, vertical, 4½x2⅝x1¼", plastic, eight transistors, upper right front oval window dial with thumbwheel tuning, top left thumbwheel on/off/volume knob, lower oval grill area, made in Japan, AM, bat......................$20.00 – 25.00

Ramco

Boy's Radio, vertical, 4x2½x1⅛", plastic, two transistors, upper right front window dial with right side thumbwheel tuning, left side thumbwheel on/off/volume knob, round metal perforated grill area, made in Japan, AM, bat............$45.00 – 55.00

Raytheon

8TP-1, horizontal, 7x9¼x2¾", 1955, tan leather, eight transistors, Raytheon's first transistor radio, top controls – right dial knob, left on/off/volume knob – front and rear metal perforated grill areas, handle, AM, bat ....$150.00 – 175.00

8TP-2, horizontal, 7x9¼x2¾", 1955, brown leather, eight transistors, Raytheon's first transistor radio, top controls – right dial knob, left on/off/volume knob – front and rear metal perforated grill areas, handle, AM, bat ....$150.00 – 175.00

8TP-3, horizontal, 7x9¼x2¾", 1955, beige leather, eight transistors, Raytheon's first transistor radio, top controls – right dial knob, left on/off/volume knob – front and rear metal perforated grill areas, handle, AM, bat ....$150.00 – 175.00

8TP-4, horizontal, 7x9¼x2¾", 1955, red leather, eight transistors,

Raytheon's first transistor radio, top controls – right dial knob, left on/off/volume knob – front and rear metal perforated grill areas, handle, AM, bat ....$150.00 – 175.00

T-100-1, horizontal, 3⅜x6⅜x2", 1956, black/yellow plastic, right front round brass dial over checkered grill area, thumbwheel on/off/volume knob, AM, bat........$275.00 – 350.00

T-100-2, horizontal, 3⅜x6⅜x2", 1956, ivory/yellow plastic, right front round brass dial over checkered grill area, thumbwheel on/off/volume knob, AM, bat........$275.00 – 350.00

T-100-3, horizontal, 3⅜x6⅜x2", 1956, black/red plastic, right front round brass dial over checkered grill area, thumbwheel on/off/volume knob, AM, bat...................$275.00 – 350.00

T-100-4, horizontal, 3⅜x6⅜x2", 1956, ivory/red plastic, right front round brass dial over checkered grill area, thumbwheel on/off/volume knob, AM, bat...................$275.00 – 350.00

T-100-5, horizontal, 3⅜x6⅜x2", 1956, ivory/gray plastic, right front round brass dial over checkered grill area, thumbwheel on/off/volume knob, AM, bat...................$275.00 – 350.00

T-150-1, horizontal, 3⅜x6⅜x2", 1956, black/yellow plastic, right front round brass dial over checkered grill area, thumbwheel on/off/volume knob, right side chain, AM, bat....$275.00 – 350.00

T-150-2, horizontal, 3⅜x6⅜x2", 1956, ivory/yellow plastic, right front round brass dial over checkered grill area, thumbwheel on/off/volume knob, right side chain, AM, bat.......**$275.00 – 350.00**

T-150-3, horizontal, 3⅜x6⅜x2", 1956, black/red plastic, right front round brass dial over checkered grill area, thumbwheel on/off/volume knob, right side chain, AM, bat.....................**$275.00 – 350.00**

T-150-4, horizontal, 3⅜x6⅜x2", 1956, ivory/red plastic, right front round brass dial over checkered grill area, thumbwheel on/off/volume knob, right side chain, AM, bat.....................**$275.00 – 350.00**

T-150-5, horizontal, 3⅜x6⅜x2", 1956, ivory/gray plastic, right front round brass dial over checkered grill area, thumbwheel on/off/volume knob, right side chain, AM, bat.....................**$275.00 – 350.00**

T-2500, horizontal, 9x12½x5¾", 1956, cloth covered with metal trim, seven transistors, top controls – right dial knob, left on/off/volume knob – front and rear metal perforated grill areas, two speakers, handle, AM, bat .....**$90.00 – 110.00**

RCA

1-BT-21 "Transicharg Super," horizontal, 3½x7¼x1¾", 1958, antique white, six transistors, can be used with matching battery charger unit, right front round dial knob, lower thumbwheel on/off/volume knob, left horizontal grill bars, AM, bat.
radio only ....**$35.00 – 45.00**
radio with charger ..**$75.00 – 100.00**

1-BT-24 "Transicharg Super," horizontal, 3½x7¼x1¾", 1958, green/white, six transistors, can be used with matching battery charger unit, right front round dial knob, lower thumbwheel on/off/volume knob, left horizontal grill bars, AM, bat.
radio only ....**$35.00 – 45.00**
radio with charger ..**$75.00 – 100.00**

1-BT-29 "Transicharg Super," horizontal, 3½x7¼x1¾", 1958, two-tone blue, six transistors, can be used with matching battery charger unit, right front round dial knob, lower thumbwheel on/off/volume knob, left horizontal grill bars, AM, bat.
radio only ....**$35.00 – 45.00**
radio with charger...**$75.00 – 100.00**

1-BT-32 "Transicharg Deluxe," horizontal, 3⅝x7½x2", 1958, white/pink, seven transistors, can be used with matching battery charger unit, right front round dial knob, lower thumbwheel on/off/volume knob, left horizontal grill bars, swing handle, AM, bat.
radio only ....**$35.00 – 45.00**
radio with charger ..**$75.00 – 100.00**

1-BT-34 "Transicharg Deluxe," horizontal, 3⅝x7½x2", 1958, white/green, seven transistors, can be used with matching battery charger unit, right front round dial knob, lower thumbwheel on/off/volume knob, left horizontal grill bars, swing handle, AM, bat.

radio only ....$35.00 – 45.00

radio with charger ..$75.00 – 100.00

1-BT-36 "Transicharg Deluxe," horizontal, 3⅝x7½x2", 1958, black/white, seven transistors, can be used with matching battery charger unit, right front round dial knob, lower thumbwheel on/off/volume knob, left horizontal grill bars, swing handle, AM, bat.

radio only ....$35.00 – 45.00

radio with charger ..$75.00 – 100.00

1-BT-41 "Jetstream," horizontal, 5x8x2¼", 1957, antique white leather, six transistors, upper right front round dial knob, top right thumbwheel on/off/volume knob, perforated grill area, leather handle, AM, bat..............$25.00 – 35.00

1-BT-46 "Jetstream," horizontal, 5x8x2¼", 1957, charcoal leather, six transistors, upper right front round dial knob, top right thumbwheel on/off/volume knob, perforated grill area, leather handle, AM, bat....................$25.00 – 35.00

1-BT-48 "Jetstream," horizontal, 5x8x2¼", 1957, russet leather, six transistors, upper right front round dial knob, top right thumbwheel on/off/volume knob, perforated grill area, leather handle, AM, bat ....$25.00 – 35.00

1-BT-58 "Globe Trotter," horizontal, 7x11x4", 1958, leather, seven transistors, upper front horizontal slide rule dial, right and left side knobs,

lower perforated grill area, leather handle, AM, bat ....$20.00 – 25.00

1-MBT-6 "Strato-World III," horizontal, 8x14⅛x5⅜", 1958, leather, nine transistors, fold-up front with world map, inner horizontal seven-band slide rule dial, telescoping antenna, handle, bat.....$75.00 – 90.00

1-RG-11, vertical, 7x4⅛x2⅛", 1962, black/gray plastic, six transistors, upper front round dial knob, lower right side on/off/volume knob, vertical grill bars with lower right Nipper and RCA logos, swing handle, AM, bat..............$15.00 – 20.00

1-RG-14, vertical, 7x4⅛x2⅛", 1962, brown/white plastic, six transistors, upper front round dial knob, lower right side on/off/volume knob, vertical grill bars with lower right Nipper and RCA logos, swing handle, AM, bat..............$15.00 – 20.00

1-RG-15, vertical, 7x4⅛x2⅛", 1962, two-tone green plastic, six transistors, upper front round dial knob, lower right side on/off/volume knob, vertical grill bars with lower right Nipper and RCA logos, swing handle, AM, bat ....$15.00 – 20.00

1-RG-41, horizontal, 1963, six transistors, upper right front round window dial with thumbwheel tuning, left perforated grill area, handle, AM, bat..............$15.00 – 20.00

1-RH-10, vertical, 3⅞x2½x1⅛", 1961, plastic, six transistors, upper front round dial knob, right side thumbwheel on/off/volume knob, lower lattice grill area, made in USA, AM, bat.............$15.00 – 20.00

1-RH-11, vertical, 3⅞x2½x1⅛", 1961, plastic, six transistors, upper front round dial knob, right side thumbwheel on/off/volume knob, lower lattice grill area, made in USA, AM, bat.............$15.00 – 20.00

1-RH-12, vertical, 3⅞x2½x1⅛", 1961, plastic, six transistors, upper front round dial knob, right side thumbwheel on/off/volume knob, lower lattice grill area, made in USA, AM, bat.............$15.00 – 20.00

1-RJ-19, vertical, 4x2½x1¼", 1961, plastic, six transistors, upper front round dial knob, right side thumbwheel on/off/volume knob, lower lattice grill area, AM, bat ....$15.00 – 20.00

1-T-1DJ, vertical, 7x4x2", 1960, plastic, six transistors, upper front round dial, lower right side on/off/volume knob, lower vertical grill bars with lower right Nipper and RCA logos, swing handle, AM, bat.............................$20.00 – 30.00

1-T-1E, vertical, 7x4x2", 1960, plastic, six transistors, upper front round dial, lower right side on/off/volume knob, lower vertical grill bars with lower right Nipper and RCA logos, swing handle, AM, bat.............................$20.00 – 30.00

1-T-1LE, vertical, 7x4x2", 1960, plastic, six transistors, upper front round dial, lower right side on/off/volume knob, lower vertical grill bars with lower right Nipper and RCA logos, swing handle, AM, bat.............................$20.00 – 30.00

1-T-4E "Hawaii," vertical, 6⅞x4x2", 1959, antique white plastic, eight transistors, upper front round dial, lower thumbwheel on/off/volume knob, center perforated grill area, swing handle, AM, bat...........$25.00 – 35.00

1-T-4H "Hawaii," vertical, 6⅞x4x2", 1959, light turquoise plastic, eight transistors, upper front round dial, lower thumbwheel on/off/volume knob, center perforated grill area, swing handle, AM, bat.$25.00 – 35.00

1-T-4J "Hawaii," vertical, 6⅞x4x2", 1959, charcoal gray plastic, eight transistors, upper front round dial, lower thumbwheel on/off/volume knob, center perforated grill area, swing handle, AM, bat...........$25.00 – 35.00

1-T-5J "New Globe Trotter," horizontal, 6¼x9⅜x2⅞", 1959, charcoal, eight transistors, top horizontal slide rule dial, thumbwheel tuning and on/off/volume knobs, front horizontal grill bars, handle, AM, bat..............................$20.00 – 25.00

1-T-5L "New Globe Trotter," horizontal, 6¼x9⅜x2⅞", 1959, aqua, eight transistors, top horizontal slide rule dial, thumbwheel tuning and on/off/volume knobs, front horizontal grill bars, handle, AM, bat..............................$20.00 – 25.00

1-TP-1E, vertical, 1961, champagne white plastic, six transistors, upper front round dial knob, right side

thumbwheel on/off/volume knob, lattice grill area, could be used with optional leather travel/alarm clock case, AM, bat.
radio only ....$20.00 – 25.00
radio with case..........$60.00 – 75.00

1-TP-1HE, vertical, 4x2½x1¼", 1961, Bermuda turquoise/champagne white plastic, six transistors, upper front round dial knob, right side thumbwheel on/off/volume knob, lattice grill area, made in USA, AM, bat.............$20.00 – 25.00

1-TP-1JE, vertical, 4x2½x1¼", 1961, charcoal/champagne white plastic, six transistors, upper front round dial knob, right side thumbwheel on/off/volume knob, lattice grill area, AM, bat.............$20.00 – 25.00

1-TP-2E, vertical, 4x2⅝x1⅛", 1961, champagne white, six transistors, upper front round dial with top thumbwheel tuning, right side thumbwheel on/off/volume knob, lower perforated grill area with lower right Nipper logo, made in USA, AM, bat.............$20.00 – 25.00

1-TP-2J, vertical, 4x2⅝x1⅛", 1961, charcoal, six transistors, upper front round dial with top thumbwheel tuning, right side thumbwheel on/off/volume knob, lower perforated grill area with lower right Nipper logo, AM, bat...........................$20.00 – 25.00

3RG14, vertical, 1962, six transistors, upper front round dial overlaps large lower checkered grill area, swing handle, AM, bat..........$15.00 – 20.00

3RG31, vertical, 6⅜x3⅞x1¾", 1963, plastic, upper front round dial overlaps large lower checkered grill area, right front thumbwheel on/off/volume knob, swing handle, AM, bat..............$15.00 – 20.00

3RG61G, horizontal, 4¾x7¼x2", leather, upper right front dial overlaps large lower metal perforated grill area, lower right front thumbwheel on/off/volume knob, leather handle, AM, bat ....$10.00 – 15.00

3RG81 "Globe Trotter," horizontal, 1963, eight transistors, upper front horizontal slide rule dial, large lower grill area with knob, handle, AM, bat..............................$10.00 – 15.00

3RH10, vertical, 4x2½x1⅛", 1960, plastic, upper front round dial knob, right side thumbwheel on/off/volume knob, lattice grill area, made in USA, AM, bat..............$15.00 – 20.00

3RH21G, vertical, 4x2½x1⅛", 1960, plastic, upper front round dial knob, right side thumbwheel on/off/volume knob, lattice grill area, made in USA, AM, bat..............$15.00 – 20.00

3RH22G, vertical, 4x2½x1⅛", 1960, plastic, upper front round dial knob,

right side thumbwheel on/off/volume knob, lattice grill area, made in USA, AM, bat..............$15.00 – 20.00

3RH31, vertical, 4x2½x1⅜", plastic, upper front dial with top left thumbwheel tuning, right side thumbwheel on/off/volume knob, lower metal perforated grill area, AM, bat....................$20.00 – 25.00

3RH34, vertical, 4x2½x1⅜", plastic, upper front dial with top left thumbwheel tuning, right side thumbwheel on/off/volume knob, lower metal perforated grill area, AM, bat....................$20.00 – 25.00

4RG12, vertical, 1963, plastic, upper front dial knob, right front thumbwheel on/off/volume knob, lower lattice grill area, swing handle, AM, bat..............$15.00 – 20.00

4RG26, horizontal, 4½x6¾x1½", plastic, upper right front round window dial with right side thumbwheel tuning, lower right thumbwheel on/off/volume knob, left metal perforated grill area, pull-up handle, AM, bat ....$15.00 – 20.00

4RG51, vertical, 6½x4⅛x1½", 1963, plastic, eight transistors, upper right front turquoise window dial with thumbwheel tuning, thumbwheel on/off/volume knob, left metal perforated grill area with horizontal lines, pull-up handle, AM, bat ....$20.00 – 30.00

4RG56, vertical, 6½x4⅛x1½", 1963, plastic, eight transistors, upper right front turquoise window dial with thumbwheel tuning, thumbwheel on/off/volume knob, left metal perforated grill area with horizontal lines, pull-up handle, AM, bat ....$20.00 – 30.00

4RG61, horizontal, 1963, plastic, eight transistors, upper right front window dial with thumbwheel tuning, lower right front thumbwheel on/off/volume knob, large left metal perforated grill area with lower left logo, handle, AM, bat.$20.00 – 25.00

4RH11, vertical, 4x2½x1⅜", plastic, upper front dial knob, right side

thumbwheel on/off/volume knob, lower lattice grill area with lower right logo, AM, bat....$10.00 – 15.00

4RM41 "Adonis," horizontal, 7¼x10¾x4½", 1964, black plastic, 12 transistors, three left front vertical dial scales, four knobs, right perforated grill area, telescoping antenna, handle, AM, FM, SW, bat...$15.00 – 20.00

7-BT-9J, horizontal, 3½x5¾x1½", 1955, plastic, RCA's first transistor radio, six transistors, diagonally divided front with right front round dial overlapping perforated grill area, top right thumbwheel on/off/volume knob, AM, bat ....$175.00 – 200.00

7-BT-10K, horizontal, 6½x10x3¾", 1955, leather, seven transistors, upper front horizontal dial, right and left side knobs, horizontal metal grill bars, leather handle, AM, bat......................$40.00 – 50.00

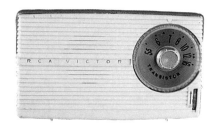

8-BT-7J "Winsome," horizontal, 3¼x5½x1½", 1956, two-tone gray plastic, four transistors, right front round dial knob over horizontal wraparound grill bars, lower right thumbwheel on/off/volume knob, made in USA, AM, bat ....$70.00 – 80.00

8-BT-7LE "Winsome," horizontal, 3¼x5½x1½", 1956, turquoise/

antique white plastic, four transistors, right front round dial knob over horizontal wrap-around grill bars, lower right thumbwheel on/off/volume knob, AM, bat ....$70.00 – 80.00

8-BT-8FE "Stetson," horizontal, 3¼x5½x1½", 1956, pink/antique white plastic, four transistors, right front round dial knob over horizontal wrap-around grill bars, lower right thumbwheel on/off/volume knob, AM, bat............$70.00 – 80.00

8-BT-8JE "Stetson," horizontal, 3¼x5½x1½", 1956, gray/antique white plastic, four transistors, right front round dial knob over horizontal wrap around grill bars, lower right thumbwheel on/off/volume knob, AM, bat............$70.00 – 80.00

8-BT-9E, horizontal, 3½x5¾x1⅜", 1956, antique white plastic, six transistors, diagonally divided front with right front round dial overlapping perforated grill area, top right thumbwheel on/off/volume knob, AM, bat......................$60.00 – 70.00

8-BT-9J, horizontal, 3½x5¾x1⅜", 1956, gray plastic, six transistors, diagonally divided front with right front round dial overlapping perforated grill area, top right thumbwheel on/off/volume knob, AM, bat...............$60.00 – 70.00

8-BT-10K, horizontal, 1956, leather, seven transistors, upper front horizontal dial, right and left side knobs, horizontal metal grill bars, leather handle, AM, bat ....$40.00 – 50.00

9-BT-9E, horizontal, 3½x5⅞x1½", 1957, antique white plastic, six transistors, right front round dial knob overlaps horizontal grill bars, top right thumbwheel on/off/volume knob, AM, bat............$35.00 – 45.00

9-BT-9H, horizontal, 3½x5⅞x1½", **1957, green plastic, six transistors, right front round dial knob overlaps horizontal grill bars, top right thumbwheel on/off/volume knob, AM, bat......................$35.00 – 45.00**

9-BT-9J, horizontal, 3½x5⅞x1½", 1957, gray plastic, six transistors, right front round dial knob overlaps horizontal grill bars, top right thumbwheel on/off/volume knob, AM, bat......................$35.00 – 45.00

PA-5, horizontal, 1964, plastic, six transistors, upper right front window dial with right side thumbwheel tuning, lower right side thumbwheel on/off/volume knob, large left front perforated grill area, AM, bat............$20.00 – 30.00

PT-1 "Havana," vertical, 7x4x2⅛", 1959, moonmist gray plastic, six transistors, upper front round dial knob, lower right side on/off/volume knob, horizontal grill bars, swing handle, AM, bat............................$15.00 – 20.00

RFG 20V, horizontal, 1964, plastic, eight transistors, two upper right front knobs – right tuning, left on/off/volume – lower textured grill area, handle, AM, bat ....$10.00 – 15.00

RFG 25E, horizontal, 5⅝x7¼x2½", 1964, leatherette/plastic, eight transistors, two upper right front knobs – right tuning, left on/off/volume – lower textured grill area, handle, AM, bat ....$10.00 – 15.00

RFG 35, horizontal, 5½x8½x2¾", 1964, leather, eight transistors, right front vertical slide rule dial and two knobs, large left textured grill area, leather handle, AM, bat ....$10.00 – 15.00

RGG 25B "Thor Deluxe," horizontal, 5½x7½x2½", 1965, tan/ivory leatherette/plastic, eight transistors, two upper right front knobs – right tuning, left on/off/volume – lower textured grill area, handle, AM, bat ....$10.00 – 15.00

RGG 25E "Thor Deluxe," horizontal, 5½x7½x2½", 1965, black leatherette, eight transistors, two upper right front knobs – right tuning, left on/off/volume – lower textured grill area, handle, AM, bat ....$10.00 – 15.00

RGG 25G "Thor Deluxe," horizontal, 5½x7½x2½", 1965, olive leatherette, eight transistors, two upper right front knobs – right tuning, left on/off/volume – lower textured grill area, handle, AM, bat ....$10.00 – 15.00

RGG 29E "Globetrotter," horizontal, 6x9x3", 1965, black, eight transistors, upper right front dial knob, lower on/off/volume knob, large left textured grill area, handle, AM, bat ....$10.00 – 15.00

RGH 10E, vertical, 3¾x2½x1", plastic, upper right front window dial with right side thumbwheel tuning, top left thumbwheel on/off/volume knob, large lower metal perforated grill area, made in American Ryukyus, AM, bat ......$10.00 – 15.00

RGH 12A "Goliath," vertical, 4⅝x2⅞x1⅜", 1965, blue/storm gray plastic, eight transistors, upper right front round window dial with right side thumbwheel tuning, right side thumbwheel on/off/volume knob, lower grill area with vertical bars, AM, bat ....$10.00 – 15.00

RGH 12E "Goliath," vertical, 4⅝x2⅞x1⅜", 1965, black/storm gray plastic, eight transistors, upper right front round window dial with right side thumbwheel tuning, right side thumbwheel on/off/volume knob, lower grill area with vertical bars, AM, bat ....$10.00 – 15.00

RGH 12J "Goliath," vertical, 4⅝x2⅞x1⅜", 1965, storm gray plastic, eight transistors, upper right front round window dial with right side thumbwheel tuning, right side thumbwheel on/off/volume knob, lower grill area with vertical bars, AM, bat .... **$10.00 – 15.00**

RGM 19E "Asteroid," vertical, 4⅝x2⅞x1½", 1965, black plastic, nine transistors, two upper front round dials – one AM, one FM – two right side thumbwheel knobs, lower perforated grill area, telescoping antenna, AM, FM, bat .... **$10.00 – 15.00**

RJG 15E "Rogue," vertical, 4x2¾x1¼", 1967, black/white plastic, eight transistors, upper right front square window dial with right side thumbwheel tuning, right side thumbwheel on/off/volume knob, large front metal perforated grill area, AM, bat .... **$15.00 – 20.00**

RJG 15G "Rogue," vertical, 4x2¾x1¼", 1967, olive/ivory plastic, eight transistors, upper right front square window dial with right side thumbwheel tuning, right side thumbwheel on/off/volume knob, large front metal perforated grill area, AM, bat .... **$15.00 – 20.00**

RJG 15Y "Rogue," vertical, 4x 2¾x1¼", 1967, white/blue plastic, eight transistors, upper right front square window dial with right side thumbwheel tuning, right side thumbwheel on/off/volume knob, large front metal perforated grill area, AM, bat .... **$15.00 – 20.00**

RJG 81EK "Amazon," vertical, 4¼x2⅞x1¼", 1967, black/white plastic, eight transistors, upper right front window dial with right side thumbwheel tuning, right side thumbwheel on/off/volume knob, lower grill area, AM, bat .... **$10.00 – 15.00**

RJG 81GK "Amazon," vertical, 4¼x2⅞x1¼", 1967, olive/ivory plastic, eight transistors, upper right front window dial with right side thumbwheel tuning, right side thumbwheel on/off/volume knob, lower grill area, AM, bat .... **$10.00 – 15.00**

RJM 12A, horizontal, 4¾x6x1⅜", blue plastic, two front horizontal slide rule dials – one AM, one FM – with right side thumbwheel tuning, right side thumbwheel on/off/volume knob, lower metal perforated grill area, telescoping antenna, rear band switch, made in Japan, AM, FM, bat....................... **$15.00 – 20.00**

RJM 12N, horizontal, 4¾x6x1⅜", ivory plastic, two front horizontal slide rule dials – one AM, one FM – with right side thumbwheel tuning, right side thumbwheel on/off/volume knob, lower metal perforated grill area, telescoping antenna, rear band switch, made in Japan, AM, FM, bat....................... **$15.00 – 20.00**

RLG 12A, vertical, 4x2¾x1½", blue plastic, upper right front window dial with top right thumbwheel tuning, top left thumbwheel on/off/volume knob, lower grill area with horizontal bars, top left vinyl strap, made in Hong Kong, AM, bat .... **$5.00 – 10.00**

RLG 12E, vertical, 4x2¾x1½", black plastic, upper right front window dial with top right thumbwheel tuning, top left thumbwheel on/off/volume knob, lower grill area with horizontal bars, top left vinyl strap, made in Hong Kong, AM, bat ....$5.00 – 10.00

RLG 12G, vertical, 4x2¾x1½", olive plastic, upper right front window dial with top right thumbwheel tuning, top left thumbwheel on/off/volume knob, lower grill area with horizontal bars, top left vinyl strap, made in Hong Kong, AM, bat................................$5.00 – 10.00

T-1EH "Rio," vertical, 7x4¼x2⅛", 1959, Bermuda turquoise/champagne white plastic, six transistors, upper front round dial knob, lower right side on/off/volume knob, horizontal grill bars, swing handle, AM, bat........................$20.00 – 25.00

T-1EN "Rio," vertical, 7x4¼x2⅛", 1959, Monterey red/champagne white plastic, six transistors, upper front round dial knob, lower right side on/off/volume knob, horizontal grill bars, swing handle, AM, bat......................$20.00 – 25.00

T-1JE "Rio," vertical, 7x4¼x2⅛", 1959, charcoal/champagne white plastic, six transistors, upper front round dial knob, lower right side on/off/volume knob, horizontal grill bars, swing handle, AM, bat..................$20.00 – 25.00

T-2E "Monaco," vertical, 7x4x2⅛", 1959, antique white leatherette, six transistors, upper front round dial

knob, lower right side on/off/volume knob, horizontal grill bars, handle, AM, bat.........$20.00 – 25.00

T-2J "Monaco," vertical, 7x4x2⅛", 1959, charcoal leatherette, six transistors, upper front round dial knob, lower right side on/off/volume knob, horizontal grill bars, handle, AM, bat......................$20.00 – 25.00

T-2K "Monaco," vertical, 7x4x2⅛", 1959, saddle tan leatherette, six transistors, upper front round dial knob, lower right side on/off/volume knob, horizontal grill bars, handle, AM, bat.........$20.00 – 25.00

TX-1JE "Scepter," horizontal/table, 1959, charcoal/champagne white plastic, six transistors, center front vertical dial, right and left grill areas with horizontal bars, upper right thumbwheel on/off/volume knob, dual speakers, AM, bat........$15.00 – 20.00

Realistic

2 transistor (no #), vertical, plastic, two transistors, upper left front window dial with thumbwheel tuning, thumbwheel on/off/volume knob, round metal textured and perforated grill area, AM, bat .$45.00 – 55.00

12-632A, vertical, 4⅜x2⅞x1¾", plastic, two upper front round dials – one AM, one FM – lower metal perforated grill area, telescoping antenna, top left vinyl strap, AM, FM, bat......................$10.00 – 15.00

12-635, vertical, 5x3x1⅝", plastic, upper front horizontal two-band slide rule dial, lower grill area with circular cut-outs, telescoping antenna, left side vinyl strap, AM, FM, bat......................$10.00 – 15.00

12-649 "Diplomat," vertical, 4¼x2½x1¼", plastic, upper right front window dial, left front on/off/volume window, lower metal perforated grill area, AM, bat............................$10.00 – 15.00

12-1290, vertical, 4x2⅝x1⅛", plastic, upper right front window dial with right side thumbwheel tuning, left side thumbwheel on/off/volume knob, lower perforated grill area, right side vinyl strap, AM, bat.......................$5.00 – 10.00

90L611, horizontal, 1962, leather, 10 transistors, upper right front window dial with right side thumbwheel tuning, upper left thumbwheel on/off/volume knob, lower grill area with circular cut-outs and lower left logo, handle, AM, bat .$20.00 – 30.00

90L613, vertical, 4⅝x2⅞x1⅛", plastic, nine transistors, upper front see-

through panel with center window dial, right side thumbwheel tuning, right side thumbwheel on/off/volume knob, metal grill area with horizontal slots and lower left "9" logo, rear fold-out stand, made in Japan, AM, bat..................$125.00 – 150.00

90L665, vertical, 3¼x2¼x⅞", 1962, plastic, six transistors, upper front window dial with right thumbwheel tuning, left thumbwheel on/off/volume knob, lower metal perforated grill area with center logo, made in Japan, AM, bat............$50.00 – 60.00

90L696, horizontal, 1961, leather, eight transistors, off-center front window dial with large right thumbwheel tuning knob, top left thumbwheel on/off/volume knob, square grill cut-outs, handle, AM, bat.....................$15.00 – 20.00

90LX661, horizontal, 1961, nine transistors, upper front horizontal three-band slide rule dial with thumbwheel tuning, lower perforated grill area, right sensitivity/tone/band switches, telescoping antenna, AM, SW, LW, bat................................$20.00 – 25.00

95L-020, horizontal, 3¾x6⅝x1⅝", leather, 10 transistors, upper right front dial with right side thumb-

wheel tuning, upper left front thumbwheel on/off/volume knob, lower grill area with circular cutouts, leather handle, made in Japan, AM, bat ....$20.00 – 25.00

1283K, vertical, 1965, 10 transistors, upper front horizontal two-band slide rule dial with thumbwheel tuning, lower horizontal grill bars, telescoping antenna, strap, AM, FM, bat ....$10.00 – 15.00

1284K, horizontal, 1965, 10 transistors, right front dial with thumbwheel tuning, lower on/off/volume knob, large left grill area, two switches, telescoping antenna, AM, FM, bat................................$10.00 – 15.00

Hi-Fiver, horizontal, 3x5¼x1⅝", plastic, right front thumbwheel dial in wedge-shaped indent, top thumbwheel on/off/volume knob, left metal perforated grill area with upper left logo, made in Japan, AM, bat................................$60.00 – 85.00

Little Six, horizontal, 3x5½x1½", leather, right front dial knob, top thumbwheel on/off/volume knob, left grill area with circular cut-outs, leather strap, AM, bat..$20.00 – 25.00

Petite 6, vertical, plastic, upper right front window dial with right side thumbwheel tuning, left side thumbwheel on/off/volume knob, metal perforated grill area with lower left logo, AM, bat...............$35.00 – 45.00

Realtone

1443-5, vertical, 8x5⅛x2⅞", leatherette, upper front horizontal

slide rule dial, two knobs, lower metal perforated grill area, right side AC/DC switch, handle, AM, bat/AC ....$10.00 – 15.00

TR-501, vertical, plastic, upper left front round dial knob, right side thumbwheel on/off/volume knob, lower metal perforated grill area, made in Japan, AM, bat............................$30.00 – 40.00

TR-555 "Galaxy," vertical, 4x2⅜x1", 1960, plastic, four transistors, upper front window dial with right side thumbwheel tuning, right side thumbwheel on/off/volume knob, metal grill area with horizontal slots, AM, bat........................$60.00 – 75.00

TR-561 "Venus," vertical, 1962, four transistors, upper right front round window dial with right side thumbwheel tuning, left side thumbwheel on/off/volume knob, lower round perforated grill area, AM, bat........................$60.00 – 75.00

TR-801 "Electra," vertical, 4x2½x1", 1960, plastic, six transistors, upper front window dial with right side thumbwheel tuning, right side thumbwheel on/off/volume knob, lower metal perforated grill area, rear fold-out stand, made in Japan, AM, bat........................$50.00 – 60.00

TR-803, vertical, 3⅜x2½x1", plastic with metal side trim, upper front window dial with right front thumbwheel tuning, left front thumbwheel on/off/volume knob, lower round metal perforated grill area, made in Japan, AM, bat............$75.00 – 95.00

TR-804-2, vertical, 1962, six transistors, upper front window dial with right front thumbwheel tuning, left front thumbwheel on/off/volume knob, lower perforated grill area, AM, bat.....................**$45.00 – 55.00**

TR-806-1 "Ultima," horizontal, 1962, six transistors, upper right front window dial with right and left thumbwheel knobs, large lower perforated grill area, AM, bat....................**$40.00 – 50.00**

TR-806B, horizontal, 1963, six transistors, upper right front window dial with right and left thumbwheel knobs, large lower perforated grill area, AM, bat..............**$40.00 – 50.00**

TR-861, vertical, 3⅞x2⅝x1¼", 1962, plastic, six transistors, upper right front round window dial with right side thumbwheel tuning, left side thumbwheel on/off/volume knob, lower round metal perforated grill area, AM, bat..............**$45.00 – 55.00**

TR-861-1, vertical, 3⅞x2⅝x1¼", 1962, six transistors, upper right front round window dial with right side thumbwheel tuning, left side thumbwheel on/off/volume knob, lower metal perforated grill area, made in Japan, AM, bat....................**$45.00 – 55.00**

TR-870 "Satellite," vertical, 4⅝x2¾x1¼", plastic, six transistors, top raised see-through two-band dial with right side thumbwheel tuning, right side thumbwheel on/off/volume knob, left side BC/SW switch, vertical metal grill bars, rear fold-out

stand, made in Japan, AM, SW, bat.....................**$200.00 – 225.00**

TR-970, vertical, 6x4x2", 1963, plastic, nine transistors, case arches backwards, upper front horizontal three-band slide rule dial with right side thumbwheel tuning, right side LW/MW/SW switch, left side thumbwheel volume and tone knobs, lower metal perforated grill area, telescoping antenna, swing handle, made in Japan, SW, LW, MW, bat....................$55.00 – 65.00

TR-1030, horizontal, 1963, leather, 10 transistors, right front window dial, upper left on/off/volume knob, lower horizontal grill bars, leather handle, AM, bat..........**$10.00 – 15.00**

TR-1053, vertical, 1964, 10 transistors, upper front horizontal slide rule dial with thumbwheel tuning, lower vertical grill bars, AM, bat..**$10.00 – 15.00**

TR-1055 "Duo-Fi," horizontal, 1964, leather, 10 transistors, upper right front window dial, two knobs, left grill area with oblong cut-outs, H/L switch, leather handle, AM, bat ....$10.00 – 15.00

TR-1057, horizontal, 1963, 10 transistors, right front dial with thumbwheel tuning, large left perforated grill area, AM, bat .....$15.00 – 20.00

TR-1069, vertical, 4½x3x1½", 1965, 10 transistors, upper right front window dial with right side thumbwheel tuning, left side thumbwheel on/off/volume knob, lower metal perforated grill area, AM, bat ....$5.00 – 10.00

TR-1088 "Comet," vertical, 4¼x2¾x1¼", 1962, plastic, eight transistors, upper front round window dial inside "figure eight" trim, right side thumbwheel tuning & on/off/volume knobs, lower round metal perforated grill area, rear fold-out stand, made in Japan, AM, bat ....$125.00 – 150.00

TR-1256 "Duo-Fi," horizontal, 1963, leather, 12 transistors, upper right front window dial, upper left on/off/volume knob, lower horizontal grill bars, leather handle, AM, bat ....$10.00 – 15.00

TR-1618, horizontal, 1963, six transistors, off-center vertical slide rule dial divides large perforated grill area, right side thumbwheel tuning and on/off/volume knobs, AM, bat ....$15.00 – 20.00

TR-1623, horizontal/watch radio, 1963, six transistors, upper right front window dial with right and left thumbwheel knobs, left round watch face and thumbwheel "auto" knob, lower metal perforated grill area, AM, bat ....$75.00 – 95.00

TR-1623B, horizontal/watch radio, 1963, six transistors, upper right front window dial with right and left thumbwheel knobs, left round watch face and thumbwheel "auto" knob, lower metal perforated grill area, AM, bat ....$75.00 – 95.00

TR-1628, vertical, 1963, six transistors, upper right front window dial with thumbwheel tuning, lower perforated grill area, AM, bat ....$10.00 – 15.00

TR-1645, vertical, 1963, plastic, six transistors, step-back top, upper left front window dial over large grill area with horizontal bars, upper left thumbwheel tuning, right side thumbwheel on/off/volume knob, AM, bat ....$10.00 – 15.00

TR-1660, vertical, 1964, plastic, six transistors, upper right front window dial with right side thumbwheel tuning, large lower grill area with horizontal bars, AM, bat ...**$10.00 – 15.00**

TR-1675, vertical, 1965, six transistors, upper right front window dial with right side thumbwheel tuning, large lower grill area with vertical bars, AM, bat ....**$5.00 – 10.00**

TR-1758, vertical, 1963, seven transistors, upper right front window dial with right side thumbwheel tuning, lower perforated grill area, AM, bat ....**$10.00 – 15.00**

TR-1820, vertical, 4x2½x1¼", 1962, plastic, eight transistors, upper front horizontal slide rule dial with thumbwheel tuning, lower metal perforated grill area, AM, bat ......**$20.00 – 25.00**

TR-1826, vertical, 3⅞x2⅝x1⅛", plastic, eight transistors, upper right front window dial with right side thumbwheel tuning, left side thumbwheel on/off/volume knob, lower metal perforated grill area with right vertical bar, rear fold-out stand, made in Japan, AM, bat ....**$55.00 – 75.00**

TR-1843, vertical, 4¼x2⅝x1¼", 1963, plastic, eight transistors, upper front window dial with right side thumbwheel tuning, right side thumbwheel on/off/volume knob, large metal perforated grill area, made in Japan, AM, bat.....................**$25.00 – 35.00**

TR-1844, horizontal, 1963, eight transistors, right front dial and on/off/volume knobs, left grill area with circular cut-outs, leather handle, AM, bat ....**$10.00 – 15.00**

TR-1859, vertical, 1964, eight transistors, upper front window dial with right side thumbwheel tuning, large lower grill area with horizontal bars, AM, bat ....**$10.00 – 15.00**

TR-1871, vertical, 1965, plastic, eight transistors, upper right front window dial with right side thumbwheel tuning, left side thumbwheel on/off/volume knob, large lower grill area with vertical bars, AM, bat ....$20.00 – 25.00

TR-1887, vertical, 1965, eight transistors, upper right front round window dial with thumbwheel tuning, large lower grill area with vertical bars, AM, bat........**$10.00 – 15.00**

TR-1929, horizontal, 1963, nine transistors, right front dial with right side thumbwheel tuning, right side thumbwheel on/off/volume knob, large left perforated grill area, AM, bat..............$15.00 – 20.00

TR-1946, vertical, 1963, nine transistors, upper right front window dial with right side thumbwheel tuning, large lower grill area with vertical bars, AM, bat..............$10.00 – 15.00

TR-1948, vertical, 1964, nine transistors, upper right front window dial with right side thumbwheel tuning, large lower grill area with horizontal bars, AM, bat.........$10.00 – 15.00

TR-2001, horizontal, 1962, 14 transistors, upper front horizontal two-band slide rule dial with thumbwheel tuning, large lower perforated grill area, two telescoping antennas in handle, AM, FM, bat.................$20.00 – 30.00

TR-2021, horizontal, 1963, ten transistors, upper front horizontal two-band slide rule dial, lower grill area, four knobs, two telescoping antennas, AM, FM, bat.......$20.00 – 30.00

TR-2051, horizontal, 1963, 10 transistors, right front vertical two-band slide rule dial, right and left front thumbwheel knobs, large grill area with horizontal bars, telescoping antenna, AM, FM, bat....$15.00 – 20.00

TR-2076, horizontal, 1965, 10 transistors, upper front horizontal two-band slide rule dial, lower grill area with vertical bars and lower right FM/AM switch, telescoping antenna, AM, FM, bat.........$10.00 – 15.00

TR-2864, horizontal, 1964, eight transistors, upper front horizontal

two-band slide rule dial, large lower grill area with vertical bars, MW/SW switch, telescoping antenna, AM, SW, bat.........$10.00 – 15.00

TR-2884, horizontal, 1965, eight transistors, right front two-band window dial with top thumbwheel tuning and on/off/volume knobs, left grill area with horizontal bars, AM, FM, bat...............$10.00 – 15.00

TR-2925, horizontal, 1963, nine transistors, upper front horizontal two-band slide rule dial, thumbwheel tuning and on/off/volume knobs, round perforated grill area, telescoping antenna, AM, SW, bat ....$20.00 – 25.00

TR-3047, horizontal, 1963, 10 transistors, three right front vertical dial scales, large left grill area with vertical bars, telescoping antenna, AM, SW, LW, bat........$10.00 – 15.00

TR-3422, horizontal, 1963, 14 transistors, upper front horizontal three-band slide rule dial with thumbwheel tuning, large lower perforated grill area, two telescoping antennas in handle, AM, FM, SW, bat...$20.00 – 30.00

TR-4016, horizontal, 1963, 10 transistors, upper front horizontal four-band slide rule dial, large lower perforated grill area, thumbwheel knobs, telescoping antenna, handle, AM, 2SW, LW, bat......$25.00 – 30.00

TR-8611 "Constellation," vertical, 3¾x2½x1", 1963, plastic, six transistors, upper right front round window dial with right side thumbwheel tuning, left side thumbwheel on/off/volume knob, metal perforated grill area, rear fold-out stand, AM, bat................................$45.00 – 55.00

Regency

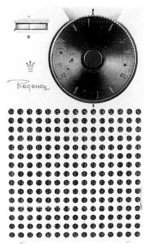

TR-1, vertical, 5x3x1¼", 1954, available in Mandarin red, cloud gray, ivory, black, jade green, and mottled mahogany plastic, four transistors, world's first commercially produced transistor radio, large upper right front round brass dial knob, upper left thumbwheel on/off/volume knob, lower perforated grill area, AM, bat.
Mandarin red........$400.00 – 450.00
cloud gray.............$350.00 – 400.00
ivory.....................$300.00 – 350.00
black.....................$250.00 – 300.00
jade green........................$750.00+
mottled mahogany............$650.00+
• Also produced were limited numbers of clear, see-through plastic cased TR-1s, some with a clear back and a solid colored front, and some with both back and front made of clear plastic.

clear back w/solid front..$1,000.00+
clear back w/clear front..$2,000.00+

• Possibly the rarest of all the TR-1s is the version known among collectors as the "Mike Todd." It is a TR-1 (all known examples to date are jade green) complete with a leather presentation case which looks like a book. On the "spine" of the book is printed "Around the World in 80 Days," and the inside cover of the book contains the names of the recipient, (in this case, Arthur Miller) and Michael Todd.
Mike Todd TR-1.............$4,000.00+

TR-1G, vertical, 5x3x1¼", 1958, available in coral, yellow, black, turquoise, or ivory plastic, four transistors, large upper right front round dial knob with inner concentric circles, upper left thumbwheel on/off/volume knob, lower perforated grill area, AM, bat.

coral ....$325.00 – 375.00
yellow ....$300.00 – 350.00
black.......................$150.00 – 175.00
turquoise ....$300.00 – 350.00
gray........................$275.00 – 325.00

TR-4, vertical, 5x3x1¼", 1957, available in ebony, red, or ivory plastic, four transistors, large upper right front round dial knob with inner concentric circles, upper left thumbwheel on/off/volume knob, lower perforated grill area, AM, bat.

ebony....................$125.00 – 150.00
red.........................$225.00 – 250.00
ivory ....$125.00 – 150.00

TR-5, horizontal, 3½x6½x2", 1958, leather, right front round brass dial knob, lower on/off/volume knob, left grill area with oblong cut-outs

and lower left logo, leather handle, AM, bat ....$45.00 – 55.00

TR-5A, 3½x6½x2", 1958, leather, right front round brass dial knob, lower on/off/volume knob, left grill area with oblong cut-outs and lower left logo, leather handle, AM, bat ....$45.00 – 55.00

TR-5B, 3½x6½x2", 1958, leather, right front round brass dial knob, lower on/off/volume knob, left grill area with oblong cut-outs and lower left logo, leather handle, AM, bat ....$45.00 – 55.00

TR-5C, horizontal, 3½x6½x2", 1958, Briarwood, California saddle, or champagne leather, seven transistors, right front round brass dial knob, lower on/off/volume knob, left grill area with oblong cut-outs and lower left logo, leather handle, AM, bat ....$45.00 – 55.00

TR-6, horizontal, 5¼x7⅛x3⅛", 1957, leather, six transistors, right side dial knob, left side on/off/volume knob, front grill area with circular cut-outs, leather handle, AM, bat ....$50.00 – 60.00

TR-7, vertical, 5¾x3½x2", 1958, available in black or ivory plastic, seven transistors, upper left front round dial knob, upper right front on/off/volume knob, lower perforated random-patterned grill area, swing handle, AM, bat..........$75.00 – 90.00

TR-11, vertical, 5x3x1¼", 1959, available in red, white, or ebony plastic, four transistors, upper front round dial knob over large grill area with horizontal bars, AM, bat..............$75.00 – 90.00

TR-22, horizontal, 1959, leather, four transistors, right side dial knob, left side on/off/volume knob, large front grill area, leather handle, AM, bat ....$35.00 – 45.00

TR-99 "World Wide," vertical, 5⅞x 3⅝x2⅜", 1960, available in white or ebony plastic, seven transistors, upper left front round dial, upper right on/off/volume knob, lower plastic perforated random-patterned grill area with lower right logo, swing handle, AM, bat........$90.00 – 110.00

XR-2A, vertical, 3x2⅛x1⅛", 1958, red plastic, two transistors, large front round dial, top on/off/switch, no volume control, no speaker, earphone is wired in, AM, bat.....$175.00 – 200.00

Rex-Plastic
Bambinetta, horizontal, 1959, plastic, four transistors, lower front dial, right dial knob, left on/off/volume knob, large upper grill area, made in West Germany, AM, bat ....$35.00 – 45.00

Bambino, horizontal, 1958, plastic, two transistors, lower right front dial knob, lower left front on/off knob, large upper grill area with vertical bars, made in West Germany, AM, bat ....$40.00 – 50.00

Rexetta, horizontal, 1959, plastic, four transistors, upper right dial knob over large front perforated grill area, lower on/off/volume

knob, handle, made in West Germany, AM, bat ....$35.00 – 45.00

Sextetta, horizontal, 1959, plastic, six transistors, upper right two-band dial knob over large front perforated grill area, lower on/off/volume knob, handle, made in West Germany, AM, LW, bat ....$35.00 – 45.00

Rhapsody
FA-101, horizontal, 1964, 10 transistors, two upper front horizontal slide rule dials – one AM, one FM – large lower perforated grill area, telescoping antenna, AM, FM, bat ....$15.00 – 20.00

RY-867, vertical, 4¼x2¾x1⅜", **plastic, eight transistors, upper right front window dial with right side thumbwheel tuning, top left thumbwheel on/off/volume knob, lower oval grill area with horizontal bars, made in Hong Kong, AM, bat**..............$5.00 – 10.00

TR8A7 "High Fidelity," vertical, 1963, eight transistors, upper left front round dial knob over large perforated grill area, right side thumbwheel on/off/volume knob, AM, bat......................$20.00 – 25.00

Rincan

KT-605, vertical, plastic, upper front window dial with right side thumbwheel tuning, left side thumbwheel on/off/volume knob, lower metal perforated grill area, swing handle, AM, bat......................$25.00 – 35.00

Riviera

RV62, vertical, 4¼x2¾x1¼", 1962, plastic, six transistors, upper right front window dial with right side thumbwheel tuning, top left thumbwheel on/off/volume knob, lower metal perforated grill area, AM, bat......................$20.00 – 25.00

Robin

TR-605, vertical, 1960, six transistors, upper front see-through panel with left window dial, top left thumbwheel tuning, upper right thumbwheel on/off/volume knob, lower lattice grill area, AM, bat......$75.00 – 95.00

Roland

4TR, horizontal, 4⅞x6⅛x2½", 1959, four transistors, top left dial knob, top right on/off/volume knob, large lower grill area with horizontal bars and lower right logo, handle, made in USA, AM, bat..........$30.00 – 35.00

6TR "All Transistor 66," vertical, 6¼x4¾x2⅝", 1957, leather, six transistors, top right dial knob, top left on/off/volume knob, front grill area with rectangular cut-outs, leather strap, AM, bat ....$40.00 – 50.00

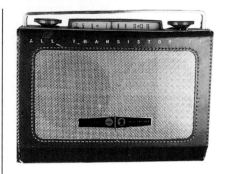

7TL "Twin Speaker," horizontal, 9x11⅜x4⅛", leather, seven transistors, top raised horizontal double-sided slide rule dial, two top knobs, front and back metal perforated grill areas, pull-up handle, AM, bat....................$35.00 – 45.00

51-481 (TW4) "Bi-Fidelity," horizontal, 1960, five transistors, upper front thumbwheel dial knob, large lower grill area with horizontal bars, logo and on/off/volume knob, swing handle, AM, bat.........$20.00 – 30.00

61-482 (5TR), horizontal, 5x6⅜x2⅝", 1959, available in white, ebony, or red plastic, six transistors, top left dial knob, top right on/off/volume knob, large lower grill area with horizontal bars and lower right logo, handle, AM, bat.........$30.00 – 35.00

71-288, horizontal/clock radio, 4¼x6⅝x2½", plastic, lower right front half-round dial, upper lattice grill area, left front alarm clock face, swing handle, AM, bat..........$25.00 – 35.00

71-483 (TW6) "Bi-Fidelity," horizontal, 1959, seven transistors, upper front thumbwheel dial, large lower checkered panel with on/off/volume knob and logo, right and left round grills with horizontal bars, swing handle, AM, bat ....$40.00 – 50.00

71-486 (7TW), horizontal, 9¼x11½x 4⅛", 1959, available in walnut, mahogany, blond, cherry, or ebony wood, seven transistors, top raised slide rule dial, right and left knobs, large lower perforated grill area with twin speakers, wire stand, handle, AM, bat ....$45.00 – 55.00

TC-10, horizontal/clock radio, 1960, seven transistors, lower right front half-round dial, upper lattice grill area, left alarm clock face, handle, AM, bat ....$25.00 – 35.00

TR8 "Bi-Fidelity," vertical, 1960, available in black or tan, seven transistors, top dial and on/off/volume knobs, large front perforated grill area, strap, AM, bat...$25.00 – 35.00

Ronith
101, vertical, 4¼x2¾x1⅜", plastic, 10 transistors, upper front round dial knob, right side thumbwheel on/off/volume knob, lower lattice grill area, made in Hong Kong, AM, bat ....$15.00 – 20.00

Roscon
8TS-33 "Super," vertical, 1962, eight transistors, upper right front round dial knob, upper left front on/off/volume window, lower perforated grill area, AM, bat..$40.00 – 50.00

KR-6TS-40, vertical, 1962, six transistors, upper left front window dial with left side thumbwheel tuning, upper right front

on/off/volume window with right side thumbwheel knob, lower textured and perforated grill area, AM, bat ....$65.00 – 75.00

Ross
1063, vertical, 4x2⅝x1¼", plastic, solid state, upper right front window dial with right side thumbwheel tuning, left side thumbwheel on/off/volume knob, large metal perforated grill area with lower left logo, vinyl strap, made in Hong Kong, AM, bat ....$10.00 – 15.00

1801 "Magnifique," horizontal, 1964, 13 transistors, upper front horizontal three-band slide rule dial, lower grill area with vertical bars, right side knobs, two telescoping antennas, handle, AM, FM, SW, bat ....$20.00 – 30.00

1904 "Adventurer," horizontal, 1965, upper front horizontal three-band slide rule dial with thumbwheel tuning, large lower grill area with vertical bars, two speakers, telescoping antenna, handle, AM, FM, SW, bat ....$15.00 – 20.00

Imperial 76, horizontal, 1964, 11 transistors, right front two-band vertical slide rule dial, three knobs, large left perforated grill area, top pushbuttons, telescoping antenna, handle, AM, FM, bat.$15.00 – 20.00

Imperial 91, vertical, 1964, nine transistors, upper front round two-band dial with center logo, right side thumbwheel knobs, lower lattice grill area, telescoping antenna, AM, FM, bat...............$10.00 – 15.00

Jubilee "Boy's Radio," horizontal, 2¾x4x1¼", plastic, two transistors, right front dial knob, lower right front thumbwheel on/off/volume knob, left checkered grill area, made in Japan, AM, bat........**$60.00 – 75.00**

RE-66, horizontal, 1965, six transistors, upper right thumbwheel dial, lower right thumbwheel on/off/volume knob, left perforated grill area with center logo, strap, AM, bat ....**$20.00 – 25.00**

RE-101 "Dynamic," vertical, 1964, plastic, 10 transistors, upper front round dial knob, right side on/off/volume knob, lower lattice grill area, AM, bat .....**$15.00 – 20.00**

RE-102, horizontal, leather, 10 transistors, upper right front round dial knob, lower right front thumbwheel on/off/volume knob, left round metal perforated grill area with center Ross logo, AM, bat.......**$15.00 – 20.00**

RE-104 "12," horizontal, 1965, leather, 12 transistors, right front round dial knob, left grill area with horizontal bars, leather handle, AM, bat ....**$10.00 – 15.00**

RE-104 "14," horizontal, 1965, leather, 14 transistors, right front round dial knob, left grill area with horizontal bars, leather handle, AM, bat ....**$10.00 – 15.00**

RE-110N "Sportsman," horizontal, 5⅜x9⅛x2½", leather, 12 transistors, right front dial with thumbwheel tuning, right side AC/bat switch, upper left front on/off/volume

knob over grill area, leather handle, made in Hong Kong, AM, AC/bat......................**$10.00 – 15.00**

RE-120, horizontal, 1964, 12 transistors, right front round two-band dial over large perforated grill area, top pushbuttons, telescoping antenna, handle, AM, FM, bat..**$15.00 – 20.00**

RE-125, horizontal, 1964, 12 transistors, large right front round two-band dial, right side knob, left grill area with horizontal slots, telescoping antenna, handle, AM, FM, bat ....**$10.00 – 15.00**

RE-210 "Micro," square, plastic, lower right side dial knob, upper right side on/off/volume knob, front metal perforated grill area with lower left logo, made in Hong Kong, AM, bat ....**$30.00 – 40.00**

RE-510, horizontal, 1964, 10 transistors, upper front horizontal two-band dial with thumbwheel tuning, large lower perforated grill area, telescoping antenna, handle, AM, FM, bat......................**$10.00 – 15.00**

RE-714, square, 1964, seven transistors, right side dial and on/off/volume knobs, front round grill area with center "flower" decoration, left side strap, AM, bat ....**$40.00 – 50.00**

RE-777 "Jubilee," vertical, 1964, plastic, seven transistors, upper front round dial knob, right side thumbwheel knob, lower lattice grill area, AM, bat .....**$10.00 – 15.00**

RE-809N, vertical, 4¼x2½x1¼", plastic, eight transistors, upper right thumbwheel dial knob, top left thumbwheel on/off/volume knob, large front metal perforated grill area with upper logo, made in Taiwan, AM, bat ....**$20.00 – 25.00**

RE-815 "Micro," square, 2¾x2½x1⅛", plastic, eight transistors, right side dial and on/off/volume knobs, front metal perforated grill area with lower left logo, left side metal chain and key ring, made in Hong Kong, AM, bat ....**$30.00 – 40.00**

RE-900 "Micro," vertical, 1965, nine transistors, left front vertical three-band slide rule dial with top thumbwheel tuning, top thumbwheel on/off/volume knob, large perforated grill area, telescoping antenna, strap, AM, FM, SW, bat............................**$20.00 – 25.00**

RE-1112 "Jubilee," horizontal, 1964, leather, 12 transistors, upper front round dial knob, right and left round perforated grill areas, right side thumbwheel on/off/volume knob and switch, leather handle, AM, bat...............**$10.00 – 15.00**

RE-1115 "High Fidelity," horizontal, 1965, leather, 10 transistors, upper right front round dial knob, lower on/off/volume knob, left oval grill area with center logo, handle, AM, bat ....**$10.00 – 15.00**

RE-1202, horizontal, 3⅛x5⅛x1¼", 1966, plastic, 12 transistors, upper right front window dial with right side thumbwheel tuning, lower right front thumbwheel on/off/volume knob, left round metal perforated grill area, rear switch, made in Hong Kong, AM, bat ....**$15.00 – 20.00**

RE-1212, vertical, 1965, 12 transistors, upper right front oval window dial with right side thumbwheel tuning, top left thumbwheel on/off/volume knob, lower oval perforated grill area with center logo, AM, bat.............**$20.00 – 25.00**

RE-1902 "Magnifique," horizontal, 1964, nine transistors, right front dial with thumbwheel tuning, top left thumbwheel on/off/volume knob, oval perforated grill area with center logo, AM, bat..**$15.00 – 20.00**

Royce

FT-620 "Continental," 2½x4⅜x1", plastic, six transistors, top right thumbwheel tuning and on/off/volume knobs, front metal perforated grill area, made in Japan, AM, bat.....................$20.00 – 30.00

Saba

Sabinette 11, horizontal, 1961, plastic, seven transistors, top horizontal wrap-over two-band dial with upper right front tuning knob, lower right front on/off/volume knob, left perforated grill area, made in West Germany, AM, LW, bat ....$35.00 – 45.00

Sabinette 125, horizontal, 1960, plastic, six transistors, top horizontal wrap-over two-band dial with upper right front tuning knob, lower right front on/off/volume knob, left perforated grill area, made in West Germany, AM, LW, bat..............................$35.00 – 45.00

Sampson

BT65, vertical, 1963, six transistors, upper right front window dial with right side thumbwheel tuning, top left thumbwheel on/off/volume knob, large lower perforated grill area with lower left "S" logo, AM, bat..............................$10.00 – 15.00

BT66, vertical, 1963, six transistors, upper right front window dial with right side thumbwheel tuning, top left thumbwheel on/off/volume knob, large lower perforated grill area, AM, bat..............$10.00 – 15.00

BT85, horizontal, 1963, eight transistors, right front window dial with right side thumbwheel tuning, large perforated grill area with lower left "S" logo, AM, bat.......$15.00 – 20.00

S-640, vertical, 1962, six transistors, upper right front round dial knob, upper left front on/off/volume window with top thumbwheel knob, lower perforated grill area, AM, bat.....................$45.00 – 55.00

SC4000 "Super Alarm," horizontal/watch radio, 2¾x4¾x1", plastic, six transistors, upper right front window dial with right side thumbwheel tuning, lower right side thumbwheel on/off/volume knob, right metal perforated grill area, left alarm watch face and "alarm/off/radio" switch, made in Japan, AM, bat.....................$75.00 – 85.00

Sanyo

7S-P6 "Personal All Wave," horizontal, 3¾x6x1⅝", plastic, seven transistors, upper horizontal two-band slide rule dial with right front thumbwheel tuning, top right thumbwheel on/off/volume knob, large lower metal checkered grill area with band switch, telescoping antenna, made in Japan, AM, SW, bat..........................$20.00 – 25.00

8S-P21 "All Wave," horizontal, plastic, eight transistors, two right front oval window dials – one BC, one SW – lower band switch, left metal perforated grill area, BC, SW, bat......................$35.00 – 45.00

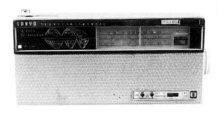

10S-P10N, horizontal, 4½x9⅜x2⅛", plastic, 10 transistors, upper horizontal three-band slide rule dial with right front thumbwheel tuning, top left thumbwheel on/off/volume knob, large lower metal perforated grill area, right side band switch, telescoping antenna, made in Japan, bat......................$40.00 – 50.00

AFT-6N, horizontal, 3¾x6¾x2", plastic, nine transistors, top horizontal three-band slide rule dial, large front metal perforated grill area with lower right switch, LW, MW, UKW, bat...........$30.00 – 40.00

AFT-9S "Transworld," horizontal, 6¾x10½x2½", plastic, nine transistors, step-back top, upper front horizontal three-band slide rule dial with right thumbwheel tuning knob, left thumbwheel on/off/volume knob, large lower metal perforated grill area with center logo, three top pushbuttons, right side fine tuning knob, left side tone switch, telescoping antenna, handle, AM, FM, SW, bat...................$20.00 – 25.00

RP1250, horizontal, 3x4x1¼", plastic, right front dial panel with upper dial scale and two thumbwheel knobs, left grill area with circular cut-outs, vinyl strap, made in Singapore, AM, bat.....$5.00 – 10.00

Satelite
Boy's Radio, vertical, plastic, two transistors, upper front see-through panel, right window dial with thumbwheel tuning, lower metal perforated grill area, made in Japan, AM, bat.............$50.00 – 60.00

Satellite
60N63, vertical, plastic, six transistors, upper right front dial with thumbwheel tuning, left thumbwheel on/off/volume knob, lower perforated grill area, AM, bat..$20.00 – 25.00

Saxony
606, vertical, 4¼x2½x1¼", 1963, plastic, six transistors, upper left front round window dial with left side thumbwheel tuning, right side thumbwheel on/off/volume knob, lower metal perforated grill area, made in USA, AM, bat.............$10.00 – 15.00

Sceptre
Boy's Radio, horizontal, 2¾x4x1¼", plastic, two transistors, upper right front window dial with right side thumbwheel tuning, lower right side thumbwheel on/off/volume knob, left front grill area with horizontal bars, AM, bat..$45.00 – 55.00

STR-217 "Boy's Radio," vertical, 4x2½x1⅛", plastic, two transistors, upper front window dial with left side thumbwheel tuning, right side thumbwheel on/off/volume knob, lower round metal perforated grill area, made in Japan, AM, bat ....$45.00 – 55.00

Schaub-Lorenz

Kolibri T30, horizontal, 1962, plastic, nine transistors, large upper right front round three-band dial, left side thumbwheel on/off/volume knob, metal perforated grill area, top band switch, strap, made in West Germany, AM, FM, LW, bat...............$40.00 – 50.00

Pony KM, vertical, 1961, plastic, eight transistors, upper front horizontal two-band slide rule dial with right side thumbwheel tuning, right side thumbwheel on/off/volume knob, lower metal perforated grill area, rear band switch and fold-out stand, telescoping antenna, made in West Germany, AM, SW, bat ......$25.00 – 35.00

Pony ML, vertical, 1961, plastic, eight transistors, upper front horizontal two-band slide rule dial with right side thumbwheel tuning, right side thumbwheel on/off/volume knob, lower metal perforated grill area, rear

fold-out stand, made in West Germany, AM, LW, bat......$25.00 – 35.00

Selsi

Boy's Radio, vertical, 3⅛x2½x1¼", plastic, two transistors, upper right front window dial with right side thumbwheel tuning, left side thumbwheel on/off/volume knob, front round metal perforated grill area, made in Japan, AM, bat ....$45.00 – 55.00

Seminole

600, vertical, 1962, six transistors, upper front horizontal dial with thumbwheel tuning, lower perforated grill area, AM, bat.$15.00 – 20.00

605, vertical, 1964, six transistors, upper front off-center round window dial with thumbwheel tuning, lower round perforated grill area, AM, bat ....$15.00 – 20.00

800, horizontal, 1963, eight transistors, right front vertical slide rule dial with right side thumbwheel tuning, lower right front on/off/volume window with right side thumbwheel knob, left perforated grill area, AM, bat .....$25.00 – 35.00

801, horizontal, 1963, plastic, eight transistors, right front see-through panel with round dial knob and

decorative "stars," **lower right side thumbwheel on/off/volume knob, left metal perforated grill area, AM, bat**....................$90.00 – 110.00

803, horizontal, 1963, eight transistors, step-down top with horizontal two-band dial, right and left thumbwheel knobs, large lower perforated grill area, telescoping antenna, AM, SW, bat................$20.00 – 25.00

805, vertical, 1964, eight transistors, large recessed and perforated oval front panel with upper "cat's eye" dial, right side thumbwheel knob, AM, bat.....................$25.00 – 35.00

806, horizontal, 1964, eight transistors, upper right front dial with upper right side thumbwheel tuning, lower right side thumbwheel on/off/volume knob, left oval perforated grill area, AM, bat................$20.00 – 25.00

900, horizontal, 2⅞x5x1⅜", 1962, nine transistors, upper front horizontal slide rule dial with upper right side thumbwheel tuning, lower right front round on/off/volume window with right side thumbwheel knob, metal perforated grill area, made in Japan, AM, bat ....$25.00 – 35.00

901, horizontal, 1963, nine transistors, upper front horizontal four-band slide rule dial with thumbwheel tuning, large lower perforated grill area, telescoping antenna, AM, 2SW, LW, bat ....$20.00 – 30.00

1000, horizontal, 1962, 10 transistors, upper front horizontal two-

band slide rule dial with thumbwheel tuning, lower perforated grill area, BC/SW switch, telescoping antenna, AM, SW, bat ....$25.00 – 35.00

1001, horizontal, 3¼x5½x1½", 1963, plastic, 10 transistors, step-down right side, top slide rule dial with top right thumbwheel tuning, lower right side thumbwheel on/off/volume knob, large metal perforated grill area, AM, bat......$35.00 – 45.00

1010, horizontal, 1964, 10 transistors, right front dial over perforated wraparound panel, right side thumbwheel knobs, AM, bat...........$10.00 – 15.00

1011, vertical, 1964, 10 transistors, large recessed and perforated oval front panel with upper "cat's eye" dial, right side thumbwheel knob, AM, bat ....$25.00 – 35.00

1015, horizontal, 1964, 10 transistors, right front round window dial with right side thumbwheel tuning, right side thumbwheel on/off/volume knob, oval grill area, AM, bat.............................$20.00 – 30.00

1020, horizontal, 1964, leather, 10 transistors, right front dial with thumbwheel tuning, large left perforated grill area, handle, AM, bat.............................$15.00 – 20.00

1030, horizontal, 1964, 10 transistors, upper front horizontal three-band slide rule dial, large lower grill area, top pushbuttons, telescoping antenna, handle, AM, FM, SW, bat......................$20.00 – 25.00

1100, horizontal, 1962, 11 transistors, upper front horizontal two-band slide rule dial with upper right thumbwheel tuning, left thumbwheel on/off/volume knob, lower perforated grill area, band switch, telescoping antenna, AM, FM, bat......................**$25.00 – 35.00**

1101, horizontal, 3¼x5½x1⅜", 1963, 11 transistors, step-down right side, top slide rule dial with top right thumbwheel tuning, lower right side thumbwheel on/off/volume knob, large metal perforated grill area, made in Japan, AM, bat.............................**$35.00 – 45.00**

1102, horizontal, 1963, 10 transistors, upper front horizontal two-band slide rule dial, right and left knobs, two lower round perforated grill areas, telescoping antenna, handle, AM, FM, bat.**$15.00 – 20.00**

1205, horizontal, 1964, 12 transistors, upper front horizontal two-band slide rule dial, large lower perforated grill area with two knobs, two telescoping antennas, handle, AM, FM, bat.**$15.00 – 20.00**

KTR-1022, horizontal, 1964, 10 transistors, upper front horizontal two-band slide rule dial with right side thumbwheel tuning, right side thumbwheel on/off/volume knob, large perforated grill area with band switch and lower left logo, telescoping antenna, AM, FM, bat ....**$15.00 – 20.00**

TR-221, horizontal, 1963, six transistors, right front see-through panel

with round dial knob and decorative "stars," lower right side thumbwheel on/off/volume knob, left perforated grill area, AM, bat.....**$90.00 – 110.00**

Sentinel

1E500, horizontal, 3¼x5¾x1¾", plastic, upper right front round thumbwheel dial, lower right on/off/volume window with lower right side thumbwheel knob, large metal grill area with horizontal slots, AM, bat.........**$150.00 – 175.00**

Shalco

M6M, horizontal, 2¾x4¼x1¼", plastic, six transistors, upper right front horseshoe-shaped grill with round dial knob, lower right on/off/volume window with thumbwheel knob, large metal perforated grill area with lower left logo, AM, bat.....**$30.00 – 40.00**

Sharp

BH-352, horizontal, plastic & metal, looks like a rocket complete with fins and metal stand, front perforated grill area, side thumbwheel on/off/volume knob, side switch, AM, bat .....$150.00 – 175.00

BP-374, vertical, 1963, seven transistors, upper right front window dial with thumbwheel tuning, large round perforated grill area, AM, bat.............................$15.00 – 20.00

BP-460, horizontal, 2½x4½x1¼", 1963, plastic, six transistors, upper right front window dial with right side thumbwheel tuning, lower right side thumbwheel on/off/volume knob, left perforated grill area with lower left logo, made in Japan, AM, bat....................$10.00 – 15.00

BP-485, vertical, 1963, nine transistors, upper front horizontal slide rule dial with right side thumbwheel tuning, left front thumbwheel on/ off/volume knob, large lower oval perforated grill area with center logo, swing handle, AM, bat.$15.00 – 20.00

BX-326, horizontal, 1961, 10 transistors, upper front horizontal two-band slide rule dial with upper right thumbwheel tuning, left thumbwheel on/off/volume knob, large perforated grill area, band switch, AM, SW, bat...$25.00 – 35.00

BX-327, horizontal, 3¾x6x1½", plastic, eight transistors, upper front horizontal two-band slide rule dial with upper right thumbwheel tuning, upper left thumbwheel on/off/volume knob, large lower metal perforated grill area with center and lower left logos, telescoping antenna, made in Japan, AM, SW, bat..............$30.00 – 40.00

BX-371, horizontal, 3½x6¼x1⅝", plastic, seven transistors, lower right front two-band horizontal slide rule dial with top right thumbwheel tuning and band switch, right side thumbwheel fine tuning knob, upper left volume window with top thumbwheel knob, large metal perforated grill area, rear raised metal plate with model number and address, telescoping antenna, made in Japan, MW, SW, bat...$20.00 – 30.00

BXS-330, horizontal, 4¾x8¾x1⅞", plastic, upper front horizontal two-band slide rule dial with upper right thumbwheel tuning, left front thumbwheel on/off/volume knob, lower metal perforated grill area, band switch, AM, SW, bat...$25.00 – 35.00

FW-503, horizontal, 1964, 12 transistors, upper front horizontal four-band slide rule dial, large lower perforated grill area with right knob and lower left logo, telescoping antenna, handle, AM, FM, SW, Marine, bat...............$25.00 – 35.00

FX-109, vertical, 1964, 10 transistors, upper front horizontal two-band slide rule dial with thumbwheel tuning, lower perforated grill area with lower left logo, telescoping antenna, AM, FM, bat.....................$10.00 – 15.00

FX-110, vertical, 1965, 10 transistors, upper front horizontal two-band slide rule dial with right side thumbwheel tuning, right side thumbwheel on/off/volume knob, perforated grill area, telescoping antenna, AM, FM, bat....**$10.00 – 15.00**

FX-404, horizontal, 6¾x9⅛x2½", plastic, nine transistors, two upper front horizontal dial scales – one AM, one FM – upper left front thumbwheel on/off/volume knob, two pushbuttons, large metal perforated grill area, telescoping antenna in handle, made in Japan, AM, FM, bat............$20.00 – 25.00

FX-495, horizontal, 1963, 10 transistors, upper front horizontal two-band slide rule dial, lower oval perforated grill area with center logo, telescoping antenna, handle, AM, FM, bat..............**$20.00 – 25.00**

FX-502, horizontal, 1964, 10 transistors, upper front horizontal two-band slide rule dial with right side thumbwheel tuning, large perforated grill area, telescoping antenna, AM, FM, bat..............**$15.00 – 20.00**

FY-151M, horizontal, 1965, leather, ten transistors, upper front horizontal three-band slide rule dial, lower left grill area, lower right tuning knob and thumbwheel on/off/volume knob, right side switch, telescoping antenna, leather handle, AM, FM, Marine, bat..**$15.00 – 20.00**

FYS-151, horizontal, 1965, leather, ten transistors, upper front horizontal three-band slide rule dial, lower left grill area, lower right tuning knob and thumbwheel on/off/volume knob, right side switch, telescoping antenna, leather handle, AM, FM, SW, bat.......**$15.00 – 20.00**

TR-173 "Collie," horizontal, 3¼x 5¾x1½", plastic, six transistors, upper right front round dial knob overlaps large metal grill area with vertical slots, right side thumbwheel on/off/volume knob, AM, bat..............................**$20.00 – 30.00**

TR-182, horizontal, 1959, six transistors, right front window dial over large perforated grill area with upper left logo, two right side thumbwheel knobs – one tuning, one on/off/volume – AM, bat.............**$50.00 – 60.00**

TR-201, horizontal, plastic, six transistors, right front see-through panel with window dial, right side thumbwheel tuning, right side thumbwheel on/off/volume knob, left metal perforated wrap-around grill area, AM, bat.....**$70.00 – 85.00**

TR-202, horizontal, 2½x4¼x1¼", plastic, right front see-through panel with window dial, right side thumbwheel tuning, left metal perforated wrap-around grill area, AM, bat..............................**$70.00 – 85.00**

TR-203, horizontal, 1962, eight transistors, upper front horizontal two-band slide rule dial with upper right thumbwheel tuning, upper left thumbwheel on/off/volume knob, lower perforated grill area, telescoping antenna, AM, SW, bat..**$40.00 – 50.00**

Shaw

6TR6, vertical, 4¼x2⅝x1¼", 1965, plastic, six transistors, upper right front window dial with right side thumbwheel tuning, top left thumbwheel on/off/volume knob, lower checkered grill area, made in Hong Kong, AM, bat ....**$5.00 – 10.00**

8TR8, horizontal, 1965, eight transistors, upper right front window dial with thumbwheel tuning, large oval perforated grill area, AM, bat ....**$15.00 – 20.00**

9FM190, horizontal, 1965, nine transistors, upper front horizontal two-band slide rule dial, large lower perforated grill area with lower right

logo, telescoping antenna, handle, AM, FM, bat...............**$10.00 – 15.00**

10TR10, horizontal, 1965, 10 transistors, upper right front window dial with right side thumbwheel tuning, top thumbwheel on/off/volume knob, large oval perforated grill area, AM, bat......**$15.00 – 20.00**

Shawa

Boy's Radio, vertical, plastic, two transistors, upper right front curved window dial with right side thumbwheel tuning, left side thumbwheel on/off/volume knob, metal perforated grill area, AM, bat...........................**$65.00 – 75.00**

Siemens

RT 10, horizontal, 1960, soft plastic, eight transistors, top horizontal three-band slide rule dial with upper right side thumbwheel tuning, lower right side thumbwheel on/off/volume knob, left grill area with rectangular cut-outs, rear band switch, made in West Germany, AM, FM, LW, bat ....**$20.00 – 25.00**

RT 31, vertical/flashlight radio, 1962, soft plastic, six transistors, upper right front thumbwheel dial knob, upper left front thumbwheel on/off/volume knob, small front flashlight, lower grill area with square cut-outs, made in West Germany, AM, LW, bat....$20.00 – 25.00

T 1, vertical, 1959, plastic, six transistors, upper front large round dial knob, thumbwheel on/off/volume knob, lower grill area with horizontal bars, made in West Germany, AM, bat......................$30.00 – 40.00

T 2, horizontal, 1959, soft plastic, right front flip-up door with two inner window dials, right side thumbwheel tuning knob, right side thumbwheel on/off/volume knob, left grill area with circular cut-outs, top band switch, plastic handle, made in West Germany, AM, LW, bat...............$25.00 – 35.00

Silvertone

19, horizontal/table, 1964, six transistors, top raised horizontal slide rule dial, three knobs, large lower grill area, AM, bat.....$15.00 – 20.00

20, horizontal/table, 1964, six transistors, top raised horizontal slide rule dial, three knobs, large lower grill area, AM, bat.....$15.00 – 20.00

21, horizontal/table, 1964, six transistors, top raised horizontal slide rule dial, three knobs, large lower grill area, AM, bat.....$15.00 – 20.00

22, horizontal/table, 1964, six transistors, top raised horizontal slide rule dial, three knobs, large lower grill area, AM, bat.....$15.00 – 20.00

206, vertical, 1960, four transistors, upper right front quarter-round window dial with right side thumbwheel tuning, upper left thumbwheel on/off/volume knob, lower V-shaped grill bars, AM, bat........$20.00 – 30.00

208 "500," horizontal, 1960, five transistors, upper front round dial knob overlaps left horizontal grill bars, AM, bat.............$10.00 – 15.00

211, vertical, 6¼x3¼x1½", 1959, black plastic, six transistors, upper right front double window dial – upper window shows dial numbers, lower window shows CD marks – right side thumbwheel dial knob, left side thumbwheel on/off/volume knob, lower metal perforated grill area, swing handle, AM, bat..............$30.00 – 40.00

212, vertical, 6¼x3¼x1½", 1959, coral plastic, six transistors, upper right front double window dial – upper window shows dial numbers, lower window shows CD marks – right side thumbwheel dial knob, left side thumbwheel on/off/volume knob, lower metal perforated grill area, swing handle, AM, bat...............**$30.00 – 40.00**

213, vertical, 6¼x3¼x1½", 1959, ice blue plastic, six transistors, upper right front double window dial – upper window shows dial numbers, lower window shows CD marks – right side thumbwheel dial knob, left side thumbwheel on/off/volume knob, lower metal perforated grill area, swing handle, AM, bat.**$30.00 – 40.00**

214, horizontal, 1960, six transistors, upper front window dial with top thumbwheel tuning, upper right thumbwheel on/off/volume knob, left grill area with horizontal bars, handle, AM, bat.........**$20.00 – 30.00**

217 "600," horizontal, 5¼x8½x3⅛", 1960, leather, six transistors, right side dial knob, left side on/off/volume knob, front grill area with rectangular cut-outs, leather handle, AM, bat.................**$15.00 – 20.00**

220 "700," horizontal, 1960, leather, seven transistors, right side

dial knob, left side on/off/volume knob, front lattice grill area, leather handle, AM, bat........**$10.00 – 15.00**

222 "800," horizontal, 1960, leather, eight transistors, upper front horizontal four-band slide rule dial, lower lattice grill area, telescoping antenna, leather handle, bat......**$15.00 – 20.00**

1016, horizontal/table, 1964, ivory, six transistors, wedge-shaped case, upper front horizontal dial, two knobs, large lower grill area, AM, bat....................**$10.00 – 15.00**

1017, horizontal/table, 1964, ivory front/ice blue back, six transistors, wedge-shaped case, upper front horizontal dial, two knobs, large lower grill area, AM, bat......**$10.00 – 15.00**

1018, horizontal/table, 1964, ivory front/coral back, six transistors, wedge-shaped case, upper front horizontal dial, two knobs, large lower grill area, AM, bat......**$10.00 – 15.00**

1019 "Medalist," horizontal/table, 1961, ivory front/brown back, seven transistors, three upper front knobs – volume, tone and tuning – large lower grill area, feet, AM, bat............**$15.00 – 20.00**

1044, horizontal/clock radio, 1961, five transistors, upper right front round dial knob, upper left alarm clock face, lower grill area with horizontal bars, feet, AM, bat....................**$10.00 – 15.00**

1201, vertical, 5⅛x3⅛x1⅝", 1961, plastic, four transistors, upper front thumbwheel dial, right side thumbwheel on/off/volume knob, lower horizontal wrap-around grill bars, AM, bat......................$15.00 – 20.00

1202, vertical, 4x2½x1¼", 1961, black plastic, six transistors, upper right side thumbwheel dial knob, left side thumbwheel on/off/volume knob, metal perforated grill area, AM, bat..............$20.00 – 30.00

1203, vertical, 4x2½x1¼", 1961, mint green plastic, six transistors, upper right side thumbwheel dial knob, left side thumbwheel on/off/volume knob, metal perforated grill area, AM, bat..........$20.00 – 30.00

1205, vertical, 4¾x3x1½", 1961, black plastic, six transistors, upper right front half-round window dial with right side thumbwheel tuning, upper left on/off/volume window with left side thumbwheel knob, metal perforated grill area, swing handle, AM, bat........$20.00 – 30.00

1206, vertical, 4¾x3x1½", 1961, ice blue plastic, six transistors, upper right front half-round window dial with right side thumbwheel tuning, upper left on/off/volume window with left side thumbwheel knob, metal perforated grill area, swing handle, AM, bat........$20.00 – 30.00

1208 "Medalist," horizontal, 3½x7x 1⅝", 1961, black plastic, seven transistors, upper front window dial with top thumbwheel tuning, upper right thumbwheel on/off/volume knob, large metal perforated wrap-around

grill area, swing handle, made in USA, AM, bat..............$20.00 – 25.00

1209 "Medalist," horizontal, 3½x7x 1⅝", 1961, ice blue plastic, seven transistors, upper front window dial with top thumbwheel tuning, upper right thumbwheel on/off/volume knob, large metal perforated wrap-around grill area, swing handle, made in USA, AM, bat..............$20.00 – 25.00

1215 "600," horizontal, 1961, brown leather, six transistors, right side dial knob, left side on/off/volume knob, front perforated grill area, leather handle, AM, bat.........$15.00 – 20.00

1216 "600," horizontal, 1961, gray leather, six transistors, right side dial knob, left side on/off/volume knob, front perforated grill area, leather handle, AM, bat.........$15.00 – 20.00

2016 "Medalist," horizontal/table, 1962, eight transistors, three upper front knobs – volume, tone, and tuning – large lower grill area, feet, AM, bat......................$15.00 – 20.00

1217 "700," horizontal, 1961, leather, seven transistors, right side dial knob, left side on/off/volume knob, large front lattice grill area, leather handle, AM, bat......................$15.00 – 20.00

2201, vertical, 1962, plastic, five transistors, upper right front wedge-shaped window dial with right side thumbwheel tuning, left side thumbwheel on/off/volume knob, lower textured grill area, AM, bat....................**$15.00 – 20.00**

2205, vertical, 3⅜x2⅜x1⅛", 1962, black plastic, six transistors, upper right front wedge-shaped window dial with right side thumbwheel tuning, left side thumbwheel on/off/volume knob, lower "woven" grill area, AM, bat......**$15.00 – 20.00**

2206, vertical, 3⅜x2⅜x1⅛", 1962, gold plastic, six transistors, upper right front wedge-shaped window dial with right side thumbwheel tuning, left side thumbwheel on/off/volume knob, lower "woven" grill area, AM, bat....................**$15.00 – 20.00**

2207, vertical, 3⅜x2⅜x1⅛", 1962, ice blue plastic, six transistors, upper right front wedge-shaped window dial with right side thumbwheel tuning, left side thumbwheel on/off/volume knob, lower "woven" grill area, AM, bat......**$15.00 – 20.00**

2208 "Medalist," horizontal, 3½x7x 1⅝", 1962, black plastic, seven transistors, upper front window dial with top thumbwheel tuning, upper right thumbwheel on/off/volume knob, large metal perforated wrap-around grill area, swing handle, made in USA, AM, bat..............**$20.00 – 25.00**

2209 "Medalist," horizontal, 3½x7x1⅝", 1962, ice blue plastic, seven transistors, upper front window dial with top thumbwheel tuning, upper right thumbwheel on/off/volume knob, large metal perforated wrap-around grill area, swing handle, made in USA, AM, bat............................**$20.00 – 25.00**

2212 "500," horizontal, 1962, brown, five transistors, off-center front dial knob overlaps horizontal grill bars, AM, bat.....**$10.00 – 15.00**

2213 "500," horizontal, 1962, blue, five transistors, off-center front dial knob overlaps horizontal grill bars, AM, bat....................**$10.00 – 15.00**

2214 "Medalist," horizontal, 1962, eight transistors, large off-center round dial area with two window dials – one AM, one Marine – overlaps perforated grill area, two right knobs, telescoping antenna, handle, AM, Marine, bat........**$20.00 – 25.00**

2215 "600," horizontal, 5¼x7¾x3¼", 1961, brown leather, six transistors, right side dial knob, left side on/off/volume knob, large front metal perforated grill area with lower right logo, leather handle, made in USA, AM, bat.........**$15.00 – 20.00**

2216 "600," horizontal, 5¼x7¾x3¼", 1961, gray leather, six transistors, right side dial knob, left side on/off/volume knob, large front metal perforated grill area with lower right logo, leather handle, made in USA, AM, bat.........**$15.00 – 20.00**

2222 "800," horizontal, 6¼x9¾x3¾", 1962, brown leather, eight transistors, right side dial knob, left side on/off/volume knob, large front plastic lattice grill area with round logo, leather handle, AM, bat.......**$15.00 – 20.00**

2223 "800," horizontal, 6¼x9¾ x3¾", 1962, gray leather, eight transistors, right side dial knob, left side on/off/volume knob, large front plastic lattice grill area with round logo, leather handle, AM, bat.....................**$15.00 – 20.00**

2224, horizontal, 1962, eight transistors, three right front vertical slide rule dial scales, three knobs, left perforated grill area, telescoping antenna, handle, AM, 2SW, bat.....................**$15.00 – 20.00**

2226, horizontal, 1962, 10 transistors, upper front horizontal two-band slide rule dial, two knobs, FM/AM switch, large lower perforated grill area, telescoping antenna, handle, AM, FM, bat..**$15.00 – 20.00**

3205, vertical, 3⅜x2½x1⅛", black plastic, six transistors, upper right front window dial with right side thumbwheel tuning, left side thumbwheel on/off/volume knob, metal "woven" grill area, AM, bat........**$15.00 – 20.00**

3206, vertical, 3⅜x2½x1⅛", gold plastic, six transistors, upper right front window dial with right side thumbwheel tuning, left side thumbwheel on/off/volume knob, metal "woven" grill area, AM, bat.......**$15.00 – 20.00**

3207, vertical, 3⅜x2½x1⅛", ice blue plastic, six transistors, upper right front window dial with right side thumbwheel tuning, left side thumbwheel on/off/volume knob, metal "woven" grill area, AM, bat.....................**$15.00 – 20.00**

3208, vertical, 1963, black plastic, seven transistors, upper right front round dial knob, left side thumbwheel on/off/volume knob, metal perforated grill area, AM, bat.....................$15.00 – 20.00

3209, vertical, 1963, blue plastic, seven transistors, upper right front round dial knob, left side thumbwheel on/off/volume knob, metal perforated grill area, AM, bat...**$15.00 – 20.00**

3210, vertical, 1963, rust plastic, seven transistors, upper right front round dial knob, left side thumbwheel on/off/volume knob, metal perforated grill area, AM, bat...................**$15.00 – 20.00**

3229, horizontal, 1963, 13 transistors, upper front horizontal two-band slide rule dial, two knobs, FM/AFC/AM switch, large lower perforated grill area, telescoping antenna, handle, feet, AM, FM, bat............................**$15.00 – 20.00**

4211, horizontal, 3¼x7¼x1¾", 1963, eight transistors, metal flip-up front, inner left horizontal slide rule dial with right thumbwheel tuning and on/off/volume knobs, large lower metal perforated grill area, AM, bat.............**$20.00 – 30.00**

5201, vertical, 1964, six transistors, upper right front round dial knob, large textured grill area, AM, bat......................**$5.00 – 10.00**

5201-A, vertical, 1964, six transistors, upper right front round dial knob, large textured grill area, AM, bat..............................**$5.00 – 10.00**

5202, vertical, 4x2½x1¼", 1965, black plastic, seven transistors, upper right front round dial knob overlaps left textured grill area, left side thumbwheel on/off/volume knob, AM, bat...........**$10.00 – 15.00**

5203, vertical, 4x2½x1¼", 1965, blue plastic, seven transistors, upper right front round dial knob overlaps left textured grill area, left side thumbwheel on/off/volume knob, AM, bat...........**$10.00 – 15.00**

5204, vertical, 4x2½x1¼", 1965, tangerine plastic, seven transistors, upper right front round dial knob overlaps left textured grill area, left side thumbwheel on/off/volume knob, AM, bat...........**$10.00 – 15.00**

5205, vertical, 4x2½x1¼", 1965, olive plastic, seven transistors, upper right front round dial knob overlaps left textured grill area, left side thumbwheel on/off/volume knob, AM, bat...........**$10.00 – 15.00**

5210, vertical, 1964, eight transistors, upper right front round window dial with right side thumbwheel tuning, lower metal perforated grill area, AM, bat.............**$15.00 – 20.00**

5214, vertical, 1965, leatherette and chrome, 10 transistors, right front vertical slide rule dial with right side thumbwheel tuning, upper left on/off/volume window with left side thumbwheel knob, perforated grill area, strap, AM, bat ....**$15.00 – 20.00**

5217, horizontal, 1965, 10 transistors, two upper front horizontal slide rule dials, FM/AFC/AM switch, upper left thumbwheel on/off/volume knob, large lower perforated grill area, telescoping antenna, handle, AM, FM, bat ....**$10.00 – 15.00**

5219, horizontal, 1964, brown leather, eight transistors, upper left front dial, upper right on/off/volume knob, lower lattice grill area, leather handle, AM, bat.........**$10.00 – 15.00**

5220, horizontal, 1964, black leather, eight transistors, upper left front dial, upper right on/off/volume knob, lower lattice grill area, leather handle, AM, bat.........**$10.00 – 15.00**

5221, horizontal, 1964, brown leather, nine transistors, upper right front dial, upper left on/off/volume knob, lower lattice grill area, leather handle, AM, bat ....**$10.00 – 15.00**

5222, horizontal, 1964, black leather, nine transistors, upper right front dial, upper left on/off/volume knob, lower lattice grill area, leather handle, AM, bat ....**$10.00 – 15.00**

5223, horizontal, 7x10¾x4", 1964, tan leather, 10 transistors, upper left front horizontal slide rule dial, three knobs, large lower grill area, leather handle, AM, bat.........**$10.00 – 15.00**

5224, horizontal, 7x10¾x4", 1964, olive leather, 10 transistors, upper left front horizontal slide rule dial, three knobs, large lower grill area, leather handle, AM, bat.........**$10.00 – 15.00**

5225, horizontal, 7x10¾x4", 1964, black leather, 10 transistors, upper left front horizontal slide rule dial, three knobs, large lower grill area, leather handle, AM, bat ....**$10.00 – 15.00**

6201, vertical, 1965, six transistors, upper right front window dial with right side thumbwheel tuning, lower grill area with horizontal bars, AM, bat ....**$5.00 – 10.00**

6214, vertical, 6⅝x3¾x2⅛", brown leatherette and chrome, 10 transistors, right front vertical slide rule dial with right side thumbwheel tuning, upper left on/off/volume window with left side thumbwheel knob, perforated grill area, strap, AM, bat ....**$10.00 – 15.00**

6215, vertical, 6⅝x3¾x2⅛", black leatherette and chrome, ten transistors, right front vertical slide rule dial with right side thumbwheel tuning, upper left on/off/volume window with left side thumbwheel knob, perforated grill area, strap, AM, bat ....**$10.00 – 15.00**

7228, horizontal, 1958, six transistors, lower front horizontal dial, large upper perforated grill area, handle, AM, bat ....**$30.00 – 40.00**

8204, vertical, 6⅜x3x1½", 1957, plastic, upper right front half-round dial with right side thumbwheel tuning, lower grill area with horizontal bars, swing handle, made in USA, AM, bat............$60.00 – 75.00

8220, horizontal, 4½x8x8¾", 1958, plastic, six transistors, right side dial knob, left side on/off/volume knob, front vertical grill bars, top knob rotates antenna inside case, handle, AM, bat........$60.00 – 70.00

8228, horizontal/table, 1958, six transistors, step-down right side, lower right front horizontal dial, three right knobs, large perforated grill area with twin speakers, fold-down handle, AM, bat........$15.00 – 20.00

9014, horizontal/table, 1959, ivory front/brown back, six transistors, raised top dial, three knobs, large lower random-patterned perforated grill area with twin speakers and lower left logo, AM, bat ..$20.00 – 30.00

9015, horizontal/table, 1959, ivory, six transistors, raised top dial, three knobs, large lower random-patterned perforated grill area with twin speakers and lower left logo, AM, bat....................$20.00 – 30.00

9016, horizontal/table, 1959, ivory front/Ming blue back, six transistors, raised top dial, three knobs, large lower random-patterned perforated grill area with

twin speakers and lower left logo, AM, bat....................$20.00 – 30.00

9202, vertical, 1959, four transistors, upper right front half-round window dial with right side thumbwheel tuning, upper left front thumbwheel on/off/volume knob, lower lattice grill area, AM, bat......$30.00 – 40.00

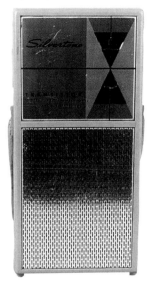

9204, vertical, 6¼x3¼x1½", 1959, gray plastic, six transistors, upper right front double window dial – upper window shows dial numbers, lower window shows CD marks – right side thumbwheel dial knob, left side thumbwheel on/off/volume knob, lower metal perforated grill area, swing handle, AM, bat.............$40.00 – 50.00

9205, vertical, 6¼x3¼x1½", 1959, coral plastic, six transistors, upper right front double window dial – upper window shows dial numbers, lower window shows CD marks – right side thumbwheel dial knob, left side thumbwheel on/off/volume knob, lower metal perforated grill area, swing handle, AM, bat.**$40.00 – 50.00**

9206, vertical, 6¼x3¼x1½", 1959, black plastic, six transistors, upper right front double window dial – upper window shows dial numbers, lower window shows CD marks – right side thumbwheel dial knob, left side thumbwheel on/off/volume knob, lower metal perforated grill area, swing handle, AM, bat..............**$40.00 – 50.00**

9222, horizontal, 6⅞x10¾x3½", 1959, tan leather, six transistors, right and left side knobs, diagonally divided front with circular grill cutouts and upper right logo, leather handle, AM, bat ....**$20.00 – 25.00**

9226, horizontal, 1960, nine transistors, fold-back top with world map, inner multi-band slide rule dial and knobs, telescoping antenna, handle, nine bands, bat.......**$90.00 – 110.00**

Sonata
Royal 400 "Boy's Radio," vertical, 3½x2½x1¼", plastic, two transistors, upper front window dial with top right thumbwheel tuning, top left thumbwheel on/off/volume knob, metal perforated grill area with lower nameplate, made in Japan, AM, bat......................**$50.00 – 60.00**

Sonatone
E-1000, vertical, 4¼x2½x1¼", plastic, 10 transistors, upper right front round window dial with right side thumbwheel tuning, left side thumbwheel on/off/vol-

ume knob, metal perforated grill area, made in Hong Kong, AM, bat...........................**$20.00 – 25.00**

Sonic
TR-500, horizontal, 1958, leather, four transistors, right and left side knobs, large front grill area with rectangular cut-outs, fold-down handle, AM, bat ....**$20.00 – 25.00**

Sonora
610, horizontal, 1958, five transistors, right front round dial knob, top thumbwheel on/off/volume knob, left grill area with rectangular slots, ribbed back, AM, bat.......................**$150.00 – 200.00**

TR-281-B "Power-Mite," vertical, 5⅝x3⅜x1⅝", plastic, six transistors, upper front round metal dial knob, top right on/off/volume knob, lower metal perforated grill area, swing handle, made in USA, AM, bat ....**$75.00 – 100.00**

Sony

1R-81, horizontal, 1¾x2⅜x⅞", 1966, available in black, white, or red, eight transistors, top dial knob, front metal perforated grill area with upper right logo, made in Japan, AM, bat...........$65.00 – 75.00

2F-23W, vertical, 3¼x2¼x1¼", 1969, plastic, nine transistors, solid state, upper front round two-band dial, right side thumbwheel on/off/volume knob, lower metal perforated grill area, rear FM/AM switch, fold-down telescoping antenna, made in Japan, AM, FM, bat..................$35.00 – 45.00

2R-21, square, 3x2¾x1¼", 1965, plastic/metal, eight transistors, upper right front round window dial with right side thumbwheel tuning, right side thumbwheel on/off/volume knob, large front metal circular perforated grill area, lower right side strap, made in Japan, AM, bat...........$30.00 – 40.00

2R-22, vertical, plastic, upper right front dial with right top and side thumbwheel tuning, lower grill area with horizontal bars, AM, bat..................$15.00 – 20.00

2R-26, vertical, 4⅛x2½x1⅛", 1966, plastic, eight transistors, top right manual tuning dial, top left thumbwheel on/off/volume knob, center top switch for four preset stations, four settings on right side are adjustable with key attached to wrist strap, front round metal perforated grill area, made in Japan, AM, bat..................$30.00 – 40.00

2R-27, vertical, 4x2¼x1", plastic, eight transistors, upper front horizontal slide rule dial with right side thumbwheel tuning, large lower metal perforated grill area, AM, bat..................$20.00 – 30.00

2R-30, vertical, 3⅝x2½x1¼", plastic, seven transistors, upper right front window dial with right side thumbwheel tuning, left side thumbwheel on/off/volume knob, metal perforated grill area, AM, bat..................$20.00 – 25.00

2R-31, vertical, 4x2⅞x1¼", 1970, plastic with chromed front, six transistors, upper right front window dial with right side thumbwheel tuning, left side thumbwheel on/off/volume knob, vertical grill bars, made in Japan, AM, bat..................$15.00 – 20.00

3F-61W, vertical, 1967, plastic, top horizontal two-band slide rule dial with thumbwheel tuning, thumbwheel on/off/volume knob, front metal perforated grill area, fold-down telescoping antenna, AM, FM, bat..................$20.00 – 25.00

3F-66W, vertical, 4¼x2¾x1⅜", plastic, upper front round two-band dial over large metal perforated grill area, folding telescoping antenna, rear band switch, made in Japan, AM, FM, bat ...$20.00 – 25.00

3R-67, vertical, 4⅝x3x1⅜", plastic back/chrome front, eight transistors, right front vertical slide rule dial with right side thumbwheel tuning, right side thumbwheel on/off/volume knob, metal perforated grill area, AM, bat...............**$20.00 – 30.00**

6R-33, horizontal, leather, nine transistors, right and left front wood-grain panels, right thumbwheel dial, left thumbwheel on/off/volume, center horizontal grill bars, H/L switch, handle, AM, bat...............................**$15.00 – 20.00**

AFM-152, horizontal, 1965, 15 transistors, automatic tuning, raised top horizontal two-band slide rule dial, pushbuttons, large crisscross grill area, telescoping antenna, handle, AM, FM, bat...............**$40.00 – 50.00**

ICR-100, horizontal, 1¼x2⅜x¾", 1966, world's first integrated circuit radio, top knobs, front grill area, carrying chain, plug-in recharger unit, AM, bat ....**$175.00 – 200.00**

ICR-120, horizontal, 1¼x2x¾", 1968, plastic/metal, integrated circuit radio, three transistors, top knobs & on/off switch, front grill area, plug-in recharger unit, made in Japan, AM, bat ..$135.00 – 150.00

ICR-200, horizontal, 1⅞x4⅜x1", plastic, integrated circuit radio, top left horizontal dial, top right tuning and on/off/volume knobs, front grill area with horizontal bars, lower right side strap, plug-in recharger unit, made in Japan, AM, bat ....**$75.00 – 100.00**

TFM-95, horizontal, 7x10x3⅜", 1963, available in black, cream, or turquoise, nine transistors, top horizontal two-band slide rule dial, pushbuttons, two thumbwheel knobs, large front grill area with center logo, telescoping antenna, handle, AM, FM, bat ....**$25.00 – 35.00**

TFM-96, horizontal, 1964, nine transistors, right front round two-band dial, left perforated grill area, telescoping antenna, AM, FM, bat.....................**$25.00 – 35.00**

TFM-116A, horizontal, 8¼x10¾x3⅜", 1964, 11 transistors, three upper front horizontal dial scales, lower grill area, top pushbuttons, two telescoping antennas, handle, AM, FM, Marine, bat.................**$25.00 – 35.00**

TFM-119A, horizontal, 1965, leather, 11 transistors, upper left front horizontal three-band slide rule dial, lower grill area, top pushbuttons, telescoping antenna, leather handle, AM, FM, Marine, bat ....**$25.00 – 35.00**

TFM-121, horizontal, 6⅜x9¼x2¼", 1961, 12 transistors, upper front horizontal two-band slide rule dial, large lower perforated grill area with tuning knob and switch, two telescoping antennas in handle, AM, FM, bat...............**$40.00 – 50.00**

TFM-121-A, horizontal, 6⅜x9¼x2¼", 1963, plastic, 12 transistors, upper front horizontal two-band slide rule dial, large lower metal perforated grill area with tuning knob and AM/FM switch, two telescoping antennas in handle, AM, FM, bat ...**$40.00 – 50.00**

TFM-151, vertical, 1959, 15 transistors, Sony's first AM/FM transistor radio, top raised horizontal dial, top right and left knobs, front perforated grill area, telescoping antenna, handle, AM, FM, bat..................**$90.00 – 110.00**

TFM-825, vertical, 4½x2⅞x1¼", 1964, eight transistors, left front vertical two-band slide rule dial, step-down top with two thumbwheel knobs, telescoping antenna, AM, FM, bat...............**$25.00 – 35.00**

TFM-834W, horizontal, 3⅜x6½x1½", plastic, eight transistors, upper front horizontal two-band dial, right front tuning knob overlaps large lower perforated grill area with two speakers, left side thumbwheel on/off/volume knob, telescoping antenna, AM, FM, bat.............................**$25.00 – 35.00**

TFM-917W, horizontal, 1965, leather, nine transistors, upper front horizontal two-band slide rule dial, large lower grill area with horizontal bars, telescoping antenna, handle, AM, FM, bat ....**$20.00 – 30.00**

TFM-951, horizontal, 7x10x3⅜", 1964, nine transistors, step-down top with horizontal two-band slide rule dial, pushbuttons, two thumbwheel

knobs, large front grill area with center logo, telescoping antenna, handle, AM, FM, bat..**$20.00 – 30.00**

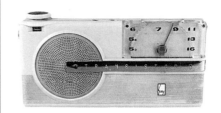

TR-6, horizontal, 1956, plastic, six transistors, upper right front see-through dial area with top thumbwheel tuning, upper left front on/off/volume window with top left knob, left front round metal perforated grill area, AM, bat.....**$500.00+**

TR-33, vertical, 1955, plastic, three transistors, large upper left front dial knob, upper right front on/off/volume knob, lower metallic panel with checkered design and logo, no speaker, earphone only, made in Japan, AM, bat ..**$1,000.00+**

TR-55, horizontal, 1955, plastic, Sony's first commercially produced transistor radio, upper right front dial over large perforated grill area, lower right front tuning knob, lower right side thumbwheel on/off/volume knob, made in Japan, AM, bat..........................**$1,500.00+**

TR-63, vertical, 4¼x2¾x1¼", 1957, available in red, black, green, or yellow plastic, six transistors, the first Sony transistor radio imported to the USA, upper left front round dial knob, right side thumbwheel on/off/volume knob, lower metal perforated grill area, made in Japan, AM, bat........................**$400.00 – 500.00**

TR-72, horizontal, 7x10¼x3¼", 1956, wood, seven transistors, large top right dial knob, top left on/off/volume knob, front metal textured grill area, handle, made in Japan, AM, bat.......**$200.00 – 250.00**

TR-75, horizontal, 4⅜x7⅞x1¾", plastic, seven transistors, upper right front window dial with right side thumbwheel tuning, right side thumbwheel on/off/volume knob, large front grill area with horizontal bars, swing handle, AM, bat.................**$60.00 – 75.00**

TR-84 "Super Sensitivity," horizontal, 4x7¼x1¾", 1959, available in gray, beige, cream, or green plastic, eight transistors, upper right front dial with thumbwheel tuning, lower right front on/off/volume window with thumbwheel knob, left grill area with horizontal bars, made in Japan, AM, bat..........**$30.00 – 40.00**

TR-86, vertical, 4½x2⅞x1⅜", 1959, plastic, eight transistors, upper front see-through panel with right round dial, right side thumbwheel tuning, left front on/off/volume window with left side thumbwheel knob, lower metal perforated grill area, swing handle, made in Japan, AM, bat.................$175.00 – 200.00

TR-510, vertical, 1961, plastic, five transistors, upper front window dial with thumbwheel tuning, thumbwheel on/off/volume knob, round metal perforated grill area, swing handle, AM, bat ....**$100.00 – 125.00**

TR-608, horizontal, 4⅜x7¾x1¾", 1961, six transistors, right front half-round dial with thumbwheel tuning, lower right side thumbwheel on/off/volume knob, left grill area with horizontal bars, AM, bat.............................**$75.00 – 100.00**

TR-609, horizontal, 3¾x6x1½", 1962, plastic, six transistors, right front round dial over large lattice grill area, top left thumbwheel on/off/volume knob, AM, bat.............$60.00 – 75.00

TR-610, vertical, 4¼x2¾x1¼", 1958, available in black, red, green, or ivory plastic, six transistors, upper front window dial with right side thumbwheel tuning, right side thumbwheel on/off/volume knob, lower round metal perforated grill area, swing handle, AM, bat ......**$100.00 – 125.00**

TR-620, vertical, 3½x2⅜x1", 1960, plastic, six transistors, upper left front window dial with right side thumbwheel tuning, right side thumbwheel on/off/volume knob, round metal convex perforated

grill area, left side strap, made in Japan, AM, bat...........**$60.00 – 70.00**

TR-624, horizontal/desktop radio, 4⅜x7¼x1⅜", 1962, available in brown or black, six transistors, flip-up front, inner thumbwheel knobs and grill, radio plays when lid is opened and shuts off when lid is closed, AM, bat..........**$40.00 – 50.00**

TR-627, horizontal, 8⅛x11x3⅜", plastic, six transistors, upper front horizontal slide rule dial, three knobs, horizontal grill bars, handle, feet, made in Japan, AM, bat............................**$20.00 – 30.00**

TR-630, vertical, 3½x2½x1", 1963, plastic, six transistors, upper front window dial with right side thumbwheel tuning, right side thumbwheel on/off/volume knob, perforated grill area, AM, bat.......**$30.00 – 40.00**

TR-650, vertical, 3¾x2⅝x1¼", 1963, six transistors, upper left front window dial with thumbwheel tuning, thumbwheel on/off/volume knob, large round raised grill area, AM, bat............$35.00 – 45.00

TR-710B, horizontal, 3½x6x1¼", cream/brown, seven transistors, upper front horizontal two-band dial with upper right thumbwheel tuning, upper left thumbwheel on/off/volume knob, lower perforated grill area, band switch, AM, SW, bat.......................**$35.00 – 45.00**

TR-710Y, horizontal, 3½x6x1¼", gray, seven transistors, upper front horizontal two-band dial with upper right thumbwheel tuning, upper left thumbwheel on/off/volume knob, lower perforated grill area, band switch, AM, SW, bat....**$35.00 – 45.00**

TR-712 "Handy Personal," horizontal, 4x11½x5¾", 1961, plastic, seven transistors, right front dial, lower right on/off/volume window with right side knob, left checkered grill area, handle, AM, bat.$30.00 – 40.00

TR-712B, horizontal, 4x11½x5¾", 1961, plastic, eight transistors, right front two-band dial, lower right on/off/volume window with right side knob, left checkered grill area, top band switch, handle, AM, SW, bat...............................**$30.00 – 40.00**

TR-714, horizontal, 3x4½x1⅜", 1959, plastic, seven transistors, upper front horizontal two-band dial,

rounded top right with two thumb-wheel knobs, lower metal perforated grill area with switch, telescoping antenna, AM, SW, bat....**$65.00 – 75.00**

TR-716B, horizontal, 3½x6x1⅝", seven transistors, upper front horizontal two-band slide rule dial, two right thumbwheel knobs, top left thumbwheel on/off/volume knob, lower grill area with horizontal bars and band switch, AM, SW, bat ....**$35.00 – 45.00**

TR-716Y, horizontal, 3½x6x1⅝", seven transistors, upper front horizontal two-band slide rule dial, two right thumbwheel knobs, top left thumbwheel on/off/volume knob, lower grill area with horizontal bars and band switch, AM, SW, bat ....**$35.00 – 45.00**

TR-717Y, horizontal, 1962, seven transistors, center front round two-band dial, two right knobs, left lattice grill area, AM, SW, bat ....**$30.00 – 40.00**

TR-724, horizontal, 2½x4⅜x1⅛", plastic, seven transistors, right front round two-band dial over metal perforated grill area, two right side thumbwheel knobs, removable antenna clips onto back and folds up to form a stand, made in Japan, AM, SW, bat...............**$50.00 – 60.00**

TR-725, horizontal, 1963, available in gray or ivory, seven transistors, upper right front window dial with thumbwheel tuning, large left round perforated grill area, telescoping antenna, AM, SW, bat.....**$45.00 – 55.00**

TR-730, vertical, 3x2¼x1⅛", 1963, available in black or bone white plastic, seven transistors, upper left front window dial with right side thumbwheel tuning, right side thumbwheel on/off/volume knob, large metal perforated grill area, made in Japan, AM, bat......................$45.00 – 55.00

TR-733, horizontal, 1964, seven transistors, upper front horizontal two-band slide rule dial, two right side thumbwheel knobs, round grill area, telescoping antenna, AM, SW, bat..............................**$25.00 – 35.00**

TR-750 "High Sensitivity," horizontal, 4⅜x7¾x1⅞", plastic, seven transistors, right round dial overlaps front horizontal grill bars, right side thumbwheel tuning knob, lower right side thumbwheel on/off/volume knob, AM, bat....**$20.00 – 25.00**

TR-752, horizontal, plastic, seven transistors, upper front horizontal slide rule dial with right side tuning knob, upper left front on/off/volume window with left side thumbwheel knob, lower grill area with horizontal bars, AM, bat........................**$20.00 – 25.00**

TR-810, horizontal, 3x5¼x1", 1959, plastic, eight transistors, large front metal textured and perforated grill area with right window dial, two top right thumbwheel knobs, made in Japan, AM, bat...........**$45.00 – 55.00**

TR-812, horizontal, 6⅞x10⅜x3⅞", 1961, eight transistors, upper front horizontal three-band slide rule dial, large lower perforated grill area, telescoping antenna, fold-down handle, AM, 2SW, bat.......**$30.00 – 40.00**

TR-814, horizontal, 7¼x10¾x3", 1961, eight transistors, large right front round three-band dial over lattice grill area, recessed right with upper thumbwheel on/off/volume knob and lower band switch, telescoping antenna, handle, made in Japan, AM, 2SW, bat ....$25.00 – 35.00

TR-817, vertical, 4⅜x2¾x1⅜", 1963, plastic, eight transistors, three upper front round windows – right on/off, center tuning meter, left dial – top on/off button, right side thumbwheel knobs, lower metal perforated grill area with horizontal bars, made in Japan, AM, bat..........$45.00 – 55.00

TR-818, horizontal, 4⅛x7⅞x1¾", 1963, available in gray or cream, eight transistors, upper front horizontal slide rule dial with thumbwheel tuning, lower left grill area with horizontal slots, AM, bat.........................$25.00 – 35.00

TR-826, vertical, 4⅛x2½x1⅛", 1964, eight transistors, upper front horizontal slide rule dial with thumbwheel tuning, upper left front on/off/volume window with left side thumbwheel knob, large lower perforated grill area with lower left logo, AM, bat.............$20.00 – 25.00

TR-881, horizontal, 4¾x7¾x2", plastic, eight transistors, two top horizontal dials, right and left side knobs, large front metal perforated grill area, telescoping antenna, AM, Marine, bat...............$30.00 – 40.00

TR-1811, vertical, 4½x2½x1⅛", 1965, six transistors, upper left front round dial with right side thumbwheel tuning, right front volume window with right side thumbwheel knob, lower perforated grill area, AM, bat.............$25.00 – 35.00

TR-1819, cube-shaped, plastic, large top round dial knob, top on/off/volume knob, side grill perforations, AM, bat.....$20.00 – 25.00

TR-1820, horizontal, 3¼x5⅞x1⅞", plastic, six transistors, right front round dial knob, top left thumbwheel on/off/volume knob, left

horizontal grill bars, made in Japan, AM, bat...........$15.00 – 20.00

TR-1824, vertical, plastic, cylindrical-shaped case with slanted top dial, right and left side knobs, lower base with "fins," AM, bat....$20.00 – 25.00

TR-1829, vertical, 4⅞x2⅞" diameter, plastic, six transistors, cylindrical-shaped case with front window dial, large top thumbwheel dial knob, front thumbwheel on/off/volume knob, lower base with "fins," made in Japan, AM, bat.......$20.00 – 30.00

TR-4100, vertical, 4⅜x2⅝x1¼", 1972, plastic/metal front panel, upper right front round dial with right side thumbwheel tuning, left side thumbwheel on/off/volume knob, large front grill area with circular cut-outs, top right strap, made in Hong Kong, AM, bat ..$20.00 – 25.00

TR-6080, 4⅜x7⅞x1⅞", horizontal, 1963, available in green, red, or ivory plastic, six transistors, upper right front window dial with right side thumbwheel tuning, lower right side thumbwheel on/off/ volume knob, large front grill area with horizontal bars, swing handle, made in Japan, AM, bat............................$25.00 – 35.00

TR-6120, horizontal, 5¾x11½x4", 1963, six transistors, large right front dial, lower right side on/off/volume knob, left grill area with horizontal slots, base, handle, AM, bat.....................$20.00 – 25.00

TR-7120, horizontal, 6¾x11¼x4⅜", 1962, plastic, seven transistors, large right front dial, lower right side on/off/volume knob, left checkered grill area, base, handle, AM, bat.....................$20.00 – 25.00

TRW-621, vertical/watch radio, 4⅛x2⅝x1⅛", 1962, available in black, gray, or beige plastic, six transistors, right window dial with right side thumbwheel tuning, upper right front thumbwheel on/off/volume knob, left watch face with top left winding stem, top right "auto/manu" switch, lower metal perforated grill area with center logo, swing handle, made in Japan, AM, bat.........$90.00 – 110.00

_____

Sorrento

T-666 "Super Powered," vertical, 4¼x2⅝x1¼", plastic, six transistors, two upper front windows – right dial, left on/off/volume – right and left side thumbwheel knobs, lower metal perforated grill area, made in Japan, AM, bat............................$20.00 – 25.00

Soundesign

1177, vertical, 4¾x3x1½," plastic, upper front round dial with top thumbwheel tuning, right side thumbwheel on/off/volume knob, lower front grill area with circular cut-outs, right side strap, made in Hong Kong, AM, bat...$5.00 – 10.00

1276 "Mini," horizontal, plastic, two top knobs, front grill area with horizontal bars, right side vinyl strap, AM, bat..........$10.00 – 15.00

SD-1094, vertical, 1965, 10 transistors, upper right front window dial with thumbwheel tuning, large lower lattice grill area, AM, bat...$5.00 – 10.00

SD-1670, vertical, 1965, six transistors, upper right front window dial with thumbwheel tuning, lower grill area with horizontal bars, AM, bat............................$10.00 – 15.00

SD-2091, horizontal, 1965, 10 transistors, upper front horizontal slide rule dial, large lower perforated grill area with lower right FM/AM switch, telescoping antenna, AM, FM, bat.....................$10.00 – 15.00

_____

Spica

ST-600, horizontal, 3⅜x5x1½", 1965, plastic, six transistors, right front round dial knob, top thumbwheel on/off/volume knob, left horseshoe-shaped grill area with rectangular cut-outs, made in Japan, AM, bat............$40.00 – 50.00

Spice

ST-600, horizontal, 3⅜x5x1½", plastic, six transistors, right front round dial knob, top thumbwheel on/off/volume knob, left horseshoe-shaped metal perforated grill area, AM, bat.............$40.00 – 50.00

SporteAire

2 transistor (no #), vertical, plastic, two transistors, center front dial, no speaker, earphone only, AM, bat............$65.00 – 75.00

Sportmaster

47900, vertical, 1965, six transistors, upper right front window dial with right side thumbwheel tuning, large lower grill area with horizontal bars, AM, bat........$10.00 – 15.00

47915, vertical, 1965, eight transistors, upper right front window dial with thumbwheel tuning, large lower grill area with vertical bars, AM, bat...............$5.00 – 10.00

47920, vertical, 1965, nine transistors, upper right front window dial

with thumbwheel tuning, large lower grill area with horizontal bars, AM, bat......................$5.00 – 10.00

47925, vertical, 1965, 10 transistors, upper right front window dial with thumbwheel tuning, large lower lattice grill area, AM, bat.$5.00 – 10.00

47965, horizontal, 1965, 10 transistors, upper front horizontal slide rule dial, large lower perforated grill area with lower right FM/AM switch, telescoping antenna, AM, FM, bat......................$10.00 – 15.00

Standard

SR-F22, vertical, 4½x2⅞x1¼", 1959, plastic, six transistors, upper front round dial knob, upper right thumbwheel on/off/volume knob, lower metal perforated grill area with vertical divider and lower right logo, made in Japan, AM, bat.....$100.00 – 125.00

SR-F25, horizontal, plastic, six transistors, upper right side dial knob, lower right side thumbwheel on/off/volume knob, large left front metal grill area with circular cut-outs and lower left logo, AM, bat..............................$75.00 – 95.00

SR-F412, horizontal, 2⅜x3⅝x1", plastic, six transistors, right front window dial with upper right side thumbwheel tuning, lower right side thumbwheel on/off/volume knob, large front oval metal perforated grill area, made in Japan, AM, bat..............................$10.00 – 15.00

SR-F415, vertical, 1965, six transistors, upper right front window dial with right side thumbwheel tuning, large lower grill area with vertical slots, AM, bat............**$10.00 – 15.00**

SR-G24, horizontal, 4½x6¾x1⅛", plastic, seven transistors, right front vertical see-through panel with upper thumbwheel dial knob and lower thumbwheel on/off/volume knob, left metal perforated grill area, H/L switch, rear fold-out stand, made in Japan, AM, bat ....**$75.00 – 95.00**

SR-G45 "Micronic Ruby," square, 1⅞x1⅞x⅞", 1966, plastic, two right side knobs – upper on/off/volume, lower tuning – front metal perforated grill area, left side strap, made in Japan, AM, bat..........**$90.00 – 110.00**

SR-G104, horizontal, plastic with chrome "jet plane" front design, upper front horizontal two-band slide rule dial with right side thumbwheel tuning, top left thumbwheel on/off/volume knob, lower grill area with horizontal bars, AM, SW, bat..**$100.00 – 125.00**

SR-G430 "Micronic Ruby," square, 1⅞x1⅝x¾", 1964, plastic, seven transistors, right side tuning and on/off/volume knobs, front metal perforated grill area with center logo, left side strap, AM, bat...........**$110.00 – 125.00**

SR-G433 "Micronic Ruby," square, 1965, plastic, seven transistors, right side tuning and on/off/volume knobs, front grill area with horizontal slots, left side vinyl strap, AM, bat.........**$85.00 – 100.00**

SR-H436 "Micronic Ruby," horizontal, 1⅝x2¼x1", plastic, eight transistors, two right side knobs – upper on/off/volume, lower tuning – front metal perforated grill area, left side strap, made in Japan, AM, bat..................**$100.00 – 125.00**

SR-H437 "Micronic Ruby," square, 2x1⅞x1", 1964, plastic, eight transistors, two right side knobs – upper on/off/volume, lower tuning – lower front metal perforated grill area, left side metal chain and medallion, made in Japan, AM, bat.....**$100.00 – 125.00**

SR-H438, horizontal, 1⅝x2¼x⅞", 1965, eight transistors, right side tuning and on/off/volume knobs, front grill area with horizontal slots, made in Japan, AM, bat......**$85.00 – 100.00**

SR-H501 "Hi-Fi," horizontal, 5⅛x9⅜x1⅞", plastic, eight transistors, upper front horizontal two-band dial, three right front thumbwheel knobs, lower metal textured and perforated grill area, two speakers, right side band switch, telescoping antenna, made in Japan, AM, SW, bat ....$30.00 – 40.00

SR-J100F, horizontal, 5x8¾x2¼", 1962, plastic, 10 transistors, upper front horizontal two-band slide rule dial with right dial knob, upper left thumbwheel on/off/volume knob, large lower metal perforated grill area with left H/L switch and right AM/FM switch, telescoping antenna, made in Japan, AM, FM, bat.....................$25.00 – 35.00

SR-J715F, horizontal, 1964, 10 transistors, upper front horizontal FM slide rule dial, right side thumbwheel knob, lower right AFC switch, telescoping antenna, FM, bat.............................$20.00 – 25.00

SR-J716F, horizontal, 1964, 10 transistors, upper front horizontal two-band slide rule dial, right side thumbwheel knob, lower right AM/FM switch, telescoping antenna, AM, FM, bat........$20.00 – 25.00

SR-J808FA, horizontal, 5x9½x2½", plastic, 10 transistors, upper front horizontal three-band slide rule dial, four right front knobs, left front metal perforated grill area, two telescoping antennas, handle, AM, FM, SW, bat ....$25.00 – 35.00

SR-K71F "Micronic Ruby," vertical, 3x2½x1", plastic, 11 transistors, upper front round two-band

dial with right side thumbwheel tuning, right side thumbwheel on/off/volume knob, lower front metal perforated grill area, rear telescoping antenna and switch, AM, FM, bat..............$65.00 – 75.00

Star

Boy's Radio, vertical, 4x2½x1¼", plastic, two transistors, upper right front round window dial with thumbwheel tuning, thumbwheel on/off/volume knob, metal perforated grill area, made in Japan, AM, bat............................$45.00 – 55.00

Starblazer

2 transistor (no #), vertical, 4x2⅝x1½", plastic, two transistors, upper left front dial knob, upper right front thumbwheel on/off/volume knob, lower metal perforated wrap-around grill area with two oval logos, made in Japan, AM, bat............................$65.00 – 75.00

Star-Lite

AP-642, horizontal, 1964, nine transistors, upper right front round two-band dial with right side thumbwheel tuning, right side thumbwheel on/off/volume knob, perforated grill area, telescoping antenna, strap, AM, FM, bat.................$20.00 – 25.00

Boy's Radio, horizontal/table, plastic, two transistors, upper right front dial, lower on/off knob, left checkered grill area, made in Japan, AM, bat...........$30.00 – 40.00

Boy's Radio "Deluxe," vertical, 4x2½x1¼", plastic, two transistors, upper front see-through panel with right round dial, top thumbwheel tuning, top left thumbwheel on/off/volume knob, lower metal textured and perforated grill area, made in Japan, AM, bat ....$90.00 – 110.00

DE-62 "HiFi Deluxe," vertical, 3½x2¼x1", plastic, six transistors, upper right front window dial with right side thumbwheel tuning, left side thumbwheel on/off/volume knob, metal perforated grill area, AM, bat ....$15.00 – 20.00

DP-118, vertical, 1965, six transistors, upper front window dial with right side thumbwheel tuning, lower lattice grill area, AM, bat ......$10.00 – 15.00

DP-222 "Leatherneck," horizontal, 1965, leather, 12 transistors, right front dial knob, left on/off/volume knob, center grill area with vertical bars, leather handle, AM, bat............................$10.00 – 15.00

FM-500 "Discoverer," horizontal, 1965, 12 transistors, upper front

horizontal five-band slide rule dial with right thumbwheel tuning, large lower lattice grill area with lower right logo, telescoping antenna, handle, AM, FM, 3SW, bat............................$30.00 – 40.00

FM-900, horizontal, 1965, nine transistors, upper front horizontal two-band slide rule dial, large lower perforated grill area with logo, telescoping antenna, AM, FM, bat ....$10.00 – 15.00

GR-3T6, vertical, plastic, six transistors, upper front see-through panel, upper left window dial with top tuning, top right thumbwheel on/off/volume knob, lower grill area with horizontal bars and lower right logo, AM, bat..$85.00 – 110.00

HT-1210 "High Fidelity," vertical, 4¼x2⅝x1¼", plastic with metal front panel, 10 transistors, upper front triangular window dial with right side thumbwheel tuning, top left thumbwheel on/off/volume knob, lower grill area with horizontal slots, made in Japan, AM, bat ....$20.00 – 30.00

MR-777 "Star Ruby," square, 2⅜x2¾x1⅛", **plastic, seven transistors, right side dial knob and on/off/volume knob, front grill area with vertical bars, left side chain with key ring, made in Japan, AM, bat....................$25.00 – 35.00**

PM-714, horizontal, 1965, leather, 10 transistors, upper front horizontal two-band slide rule dial, three right knobs, large perforated grill area with lower left logo, telescoping antenna, AM, FM, bat ....$15.00 – 20.00

T-603, vertical, plastic, six transistors, upper front window dial with right side thumbwheel tuning, upper left front thumbwheel on/off/volume knob, lower metal perforated grill area, AM, bat...............$70.00 – 90.00

TD-660 "Duke," vertical, 1965, 10 transistors, upper front window dial with thumbwheel tuning, lower crisscross grill area, AM, bat ....$10.00 – 15.00

TM-680, vertical, 1965, 10 transistors, upper front window dial with thumbwheel tuning, lower six-section round grill area, AM, bat ....$10.00 – 15.00

TR-21, horizontal, plastic, two right front dial windows with right side thumbwheel tuning, lower right front thumbwheel on/off/volume knob, left lattice grill area with upper left logo, AM, bat........$20.00 – 30.00

TR-24 "Boy's Radio," vertical, 4x2½x1⅛", **plastic, two transistors, upper front window dial with left side thumbwheel tuning, right side thumbwheel on/off/volume knob, round metal perforated grill area, made in Japan, AM, bat............$40.00 – 50.00**

TR-709 "Voyager," vertical, 1965, six transistors, upper right front window dial with right side thumbwheel tuning, lower grill area with concentric square pattern, AM, bat............................$15.00 – 20.00

TR-960 "Rough Rider," horizontal, 1965, leather, 12 transistors, upper right front round dial, lower on/off/volume knob, left lattice grill area, handle, AM, bat.$10.00 – 15.00

TRJ-10 "High Fidelity," vertical, 1965, 10 transistors, upper front triangular window dial with right side thumbwheel tuning, top left thumbwheel on/off/volume knob, lower grill area with horizontal slots, AM, bat..............................**$20.00 – 30.00**

TRN-69 "Celestra," vertical, 4x2⅝x1⅜", 1964, plastic, six transistors, upper front horizontal slide rule dial with thumbwheel tuning, lower metal perforated grill area with lower right nameplate, made in Japan, AM, bat......**$30.00 – 40.00**

TRN-112 "High Sensitivity," horizontal, 1964, 12 transistors, upper right front half-round dial, large lower perforated grill area, handle, AM, bat......................**$20.00 – 25.00**

TS-640 "Skymate," vertical, 1965, 10 transistors, upper front oval window dial with thumbwheel tuning, lower grill area with crisscross pattern, AM, bat.............**$20.00 – 25.00**

Startone
CTR-701, vertical/clock radio, 6x3⅜x1½", plastic, seven transistors, top third of case is removable clock, lower metal textured and perforated grill area, right window dial with right side thumbwheel tuning, left on/off/volume window with left side thumbwheel knob, swing handle, made in Japan, AM, bat.......................**$125.00 – 150.00**

Stat
3 transistor (no #), horizontal, 2¾x3¼x1¼", plastic, three transistors, right front thumbwheel dial/on/off knob, no speaker, earphone only, made in USA, AM, bat.**$85.00 – 95.00**

Sudfunk
K986A, horizontal, 1961, nine transistors, rounded case, right front round two-band dial, three top pushbuttons, left grill area with vertical bars, telescoping antenna, handle, AM, FM, bat.**$35.00 – 45.00**

Summit

FR-601, vertical, plastic, six transistors, upper front window dial with right side thumbwheel tuning, left side thumbwheel on/off/volume knob, lower round metal perforated grill area, AM, bat .....**$40.00 – 50.00**

HS-657 "HiFi," vertical, 4⅛x2½x1⅛", plastic, six transistors, upper right front window dial with right side thumbwheel tuning, left side thumbwheel on/off/volume knob, metal grill area with vertical slots, made in Ryukyu, AM, bat........**$15.00 – 20.00**

S109, vertical, 4½x2½x1⅜", plastic, 10 transistors, upper right front window dial with right side thumbwheel tuning, left side thumbwheel on/off/volume knob, oval metal perforated grill area, made in Ryukyu, AM, bat........**$20.00 – 30.00**

Sunpet

Boy's Radio, vertical, plastic, two transistors, right side thumbwheel dial knob, front round metal perforated grill area, rear clip, AM, bat ....**$85.00 – 100.00**

Suntone

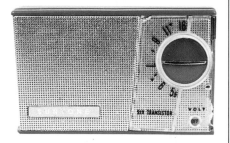

6TR-100, horizontal, plastic, six transistors, right front see-through dial panel over large metal perforated grill area, upper right front dial, lower right front on/off/volume window with right side thumbwheel knob, AM, bat ....$85.00 – 100.00

1112, horizontal, 2⅝x4½x1¼", plastic, solid state, upper right front window dial with right side thumbwheel tuning, lower right front on/off/volume window with right side thumbwheel knob, left textured grill area, made in Hong Kong, AM, bat ....**$15.00 – 20.00**

Super

TR-261 "Boy's Radio," vertical, plastic, two transistors, upper right front window dial with right side thumbwheel tuning, left side thumbwheel on/off/volume knob, metal perforated grill area, made in Japan, AM, bat...........**$45.00 – 55.00**

Superex

TR-66, vertical, 1960, six transistors, upper front round dial knob, lower perforated grill area with small on/off/volume knob, swing handle, AM, bat...............**$40.00 – 50.00**

Supertone

AR800, vertical, 5x3⅜x1", plastic, book-style radio, upper front window dial with "king and queen" pictures, lower grill area with horizontal slots, two thumbwheel knobs – one tuning, one on/off/volume – on left "spine" of book, made in Japan, AM, bat................................**$30.00 – 40.00**

Supre-Macy

M-8 (Macy) "Macy's Own Brand," vertical, 4¼x2⅝x1¼", plastic, eight transistors, upper right front window dial with right side thumbwheel tuning, upper left front on/off/volume window with left side thumbwheel knob, lower metal perforated grill area with vertical lines, AM, bat ....$25.00 – 35.00

Supreme

TR-803, vertical, 3⅜x2½x1", plastic with metal side trim, seven transistors, upper front window dial with right front thumbwheel tuning, left front thumbwheel on/off/volume knob, round metal perforated grill area, AM, bat ....**$75.00 – 95.00**

TR-861, vertical, 3⅞x2⅝x1¼", 1962, plastic, six transistors, upper right front round window dial with right side thumbwheel tuning, left side thumbwheel on/off/volume knob, round metal perforated grill area, made in Japan, AM, bat ....**$45.00 – 55.00**

Sutton

J683, vertical, plastic, seven transistors, upper right front window dial with right side thumbwheel tuning, top left thumbwheel on/off/volume knob, lower oval grill area with vertical bars, AM, bat ..**$5.00 – 10.00**

Sylvania

4P06E, vertical, 1962, four transistors, upper right front window dial with right side thumbwheel tuning, left side thumbwheel on/off/volume knob, lower perforated grill area with lower left logo, AM, bat..............**$35.00 – 45.00**

4P14, horizontal, 3⅞x6⅜x2⅛", 1961, plastic, four transistors, upper left front window dial with top left thumbwheel tuning, lower left on/off/volume knob, horizontal grill bars with right logo, AM, bat..............**$40.00 – 50.00**

4P19W, horizontal, 3½x6½x1¾", 1962, plastic, four transistors, upper right front window dial with right side thumbwheel tuning, lower right side thumbwheel on/off/volume knob, large left grill area with circular cut-outs, AM, bat ..**$20.00 – 25.00**

4P19WD, horizontal, 3½x6½x1¾", 1962, plastic, four transistors, upper right front window dial with right side thumbwheel tuning, lower right side thumbwheel on/off/volume knob, large left grill area with circular cut-outs, AM, bat ..**$20.00 – 25.00**

5P10, horizontal, plastic, five transistors, upper left front window dial with top left thumbwheel tuning, lower left on/off/volume knob, horizontal grill bars with right logo, AM, bat ....**$40.00 – 50.00**

5P11R, horizontal, 1960, five transistors, upper left front window dial with top left thumbwheel tuning, lower left on/off/volume knob, horizontal grill bars with right logo, AM, bat ....**$40.00 – 50.00**

5P16, horizontal, plastic/metal, right front dial knob overlaps large metal perforated grill area with left logo, right side pull-out metal handle, AM, bat..............**$35.00 – 45.00**

6P09T, vertical, 1961, six transistors, upper right front window dial with right side thumbwheel tuning, left side thumbwheel on/off/volume knob, lower perforated grill area with logo, AM, bat .....**$40.00 – 50.00**

7K10, horizontal/clock radio, 1961, seven transistors, lower right front dial knob overlaps lattice grill area, left front alarm clock face and on/off/volume knob, swing handle, AM, bat..............$20.00 – 30.00

7P12, vertical, 6½x4⅛x2", 1959, plastic, seven transistors, upper right front window dial with right side thumbwheel tuning, upper left front on/off/volume knob, large lower metal perforated grill area with lower left logo and right vertical bar, swing handle, AM, bat..........$35.00 – 45.00

7P12T, vertical, 1959, plastic, seven transistors, upper right front window dial with right side thumbwheel tuning, upper left front on/off/volume knob, large lower perforated grill area with lower left logo and right vertical bar, swing handle, AM, bat ....$35.00 – 45.00

7P13, horizontal, 1960, leather, seven transistors, right front dial knob over large perforated grill area with upper left logo, top left knob, leather handle, AM, bat.................$15.00 – 20.00

2700 "Golden Shield," horizontal, 3½x6½x1¾", leather, five transistors, right front round dial knob, large

metal perforated grill area, leather handle, AM, bat.........$20.00 – 25.00

2701 "Golden Shield," horizontal, 3½x6½x1¾", leather, five transistors, right front round dial knob, large metal perforated grill area, leather handle, AM, bat.........$20.00 – 25.00

2808 "Golden Shield," vertical, 6¾x4¼x2", 1960, plastic, upper right round dial with right side thumbwheel tuning, upper left gold shield logo, left side thumbwheel on/off/volume knob, lower metal perforated grill area, pull-up handle, AM, bat ....$35.00 – 45.00

2901 "Golden Shield," vertical, 1960, seven transistors, leather, upper right front round dial knob, upper left front on/off/volume knob, lower metal perforated grill area, leather handle, AM, bat ....$20.00 – 25.00

3102 "Thunderbird," 3½x6½x6½", 1957, plastic, resembles Ford Thunderbird car, two front thumbwheel knobs, lift top, inner clear plastic cover over radio chassis, top built-in speaker, handle, AM, bat ....$325.00 – 350.00

3204TU, horizontal, 1957, plastic, six transistors, right front round see-through dial knob, top left on/off/volume knob, large lattice grill area with lower right "T6" logo, fold-down handle, AM, bat............................$35.00 – 45.00

3204YE, horizontal, 1957, plastic, six transistors, right front round see-through dial knob, top left on/off/ volume knob, large lattice grill area with lower right "T6" logo, fold-down handle, AM, bat ....$35.00 – 45.00

3305BL, horizontal, 6¾x9¼x3¾", 1957, navy/white plastic, six transistors, right front round see-through dial knob, top left on/off/volume knob, large lattice grill area with lower right "T6" logo, fold-down handle, AM, bat ....$35.00 – 45.00

3305TA, horizontal, 6¾x9¼x3¾", 1957, red/white plastic, six transistors, right front round see-through dial knob, top left on/off/volume knob, large lattice grill area with lower right "T6" logo, fold-down handle, AM, bat ....$35.00 – 45.00

3406 Series, horizontal/clock radio, 1959, leather, seven transistors, lower front dial knob and on/off/volume knob overlap woven grill area with upper left logo, right alarm clock face, AM, bat ....$25.00 – 30.00

TH16 Series, vertical, 1963, eight transistors, upper right front dial with right side thumbwheel tuning, upper left front on/off/volume knob, lower right perforated grill area, lower left logo, swing handle, AM, bat ....$35.00 – 45.00

TR-22, horizontal, 1964, seven transistors, right front window dial with right side thumbwheel tuning, left perforated grill area with lower left logo, AM, bat.............$10.00 – 15.00

TR-25, vertical, 1964, eight transistors, upper front horizontal slide rule dial with thumbwheel tuning, lower perforated grill area with lower left logo, AM, bat..$15.00 – 20.00

TR35, horizontal, 1964, nine transistors, right front vertical two-band dial, three knobs, left perforated grill area with lower left logo, two top pushbuttons, telescoping antenna, AM, FM, bat...$15.00 – 20.00

TR50, vertical, 1965, six transistors, upper front round dial with thumbwheel tuning, lower perforated grill area with lower left logo, AM, bat..............................$15.00 – 20.00

TR54, vertical, 4x2½x1¼", 1965, eight transistors, upper front horizontal slide rule dial with right side thumbwheel tuning, lower perforated grill area with lower left logo, AM, bat ....$15.00 – 20.00

TR58, horizontal, 1965, eight transistors, vertical see-through slide rule dial, two right front knobs – upper tuning, lower on/off/volume – left grill area, handle, AM, bat................................**$10.00 – 15.00**

TR62, horizontal, 1965, nine transistors, two right front window dials – upper FM, lower AM – left perforated grill area, telescoping antenna, fold-down handle, AM, FM, bat......**$10.00 – 15.00**

TR102BG "Deluxe Eight," vertical, 4⅜x3x1⅛", plastic, eight transistors, upper front horizontal slide rule dial with right side thumbwheel tuning, lower grill area with horizontal slots, made in Japan, AM, bat........................**$5.00 – 10.00**

Symphonic

S-62, vertical, 1963, six transistors, upper right front round window dial over large perforated grill area, right side thumbwheel tuning knob, top left thumbwheel on/off/volume knob, AM, bat....**$10.00 – 15.00**

S-73, horizontal, 1963, seven transistors, right front window dial with right side thumbwheel tuning, left perforated grill area with lower left logo, AM, bat.............**$20.00 – 25.00**

S-84, vertical, 1963, eight transistors, upper front half-round window dial with thumbwheel tuning, lower perforated grill area with logo, AM, bat.............**$10.00 – 15.00**

S-93, vertical, 1963, nine transistors, upper front window dial over large perforated grill area with lower left logo, AM, bat.............**$15.00 – 20.00**

SF-400, horizontal, 1963, nine transistors, right front three-band dial

knob over large checkered grill area with lower left logo, upper left thumbwheel on/off/volume knob, SW/AM/FM switch, handle, AM, FM, SW, bat...............**$20.00 – 25.00**

Tact

TPR-61 "Phonoradio," vertical, 7x 3¾x1¾", six transistors, combination phonograph and radio, plays 45s and 33s with built-in tone arm, AM, bat......................**$65.00 – 75.00**

Tama-Tone

Boy's Radio, vertical, 3⅞x2½x1¼", plastic, two transistors, upper front see-through panel with right front window dial, right side thumbwheel tuning, left side thumbwheel on/off/volume knob, lower lattice grill area, made in Japan, AM, bat........**$50.00 – 60.00**

Telefunken

Bajazzo Junior, horizontal 7x10¾x3⅛", top dial, knobs and pushbuttons, large front perforated grill area, handle, made in West Germany, bat.............**$35.00 – 45.00**

**Match II, horizontal, 1¼x6½x2⅜",
1965, leather, eight transistors, left
front horizontal slide rule dial, two
right thumbwheel knobs – one tuning, one on/off/volume – leather
strap, made in West Germany, AM,
bat................$20.00 – 25.00**

Mini-Partner 3061, horizontal,
1960, plastic, six transistors, right
front "V" design with upper window
dial, right side thumbwheel tuning
knob, top left thumbwheel
on/off/volume knob, metal perforated grill area, made in West Germany, AM, bat...........$60.00 – 75.00

Partner, horizontal, 1957, plastic, five
transistors, diagonally divided front
with right round dial knob, top left
thumbwheel on/off/volume knob,
vertical grill bars, made in West Germany, AM, bat.............$35.00 – 45.00

Partner II, horizontal, 1958, plastic, six transistors, diagonally divided front with right round dial
knob, top left thumbwheel
on/off/volume knob, vertical grill
bars, made in West Germany, AM,
bat......................$35.00 – 45.00

Partner III 3071, horizontal, 1960,
plastic, seven transistors, diagonally
divided front with right round two-
band dial knob, top left thumbwheel on/off/volume knob, vertical
grill bars, made in West Germany,
AM, LW, bat..............$35.00 – 45.00

Partner IV 3271, horizontal, 1961,
plastic, eight transistors, upper
front horizontal three-band slide
rule dial with right front thumbwheel tuning, left side thumbwheel
on/off/volume knob, perforated
grill area, rear band switch, made
in West Germany, AM, SW, LW,
bat..............$30.00 – 40.00

Ticcolo, horizontal/watch radio,
3x5¼x1½", six transistors, upper
front horizontal two-band slide rule
dial with right and left thumbwheel
knobs, lower right watch face, lower
left metal perforated grill area, AM,
LW, bat.....................$75.00 – 90.00

Ticcolo 3361, horizontal/watch radio, 1962, plastic, six transistors,
upper front horizontal two-band
slide rule dial with right and left
thumbwheel knobs, lower right
watch face, lower left metal perforated grill area, made in West Germany, AM, LW, bat....$75.00 – 90.00

Ticcolo 3461, horizontal/watch radio, 1963, plastic, six transistors,
upper front horizontal two-band
slide rule dial with right and left
thumbwheel knobs, lower right
watch face, lower left metal perforated grill area, made in West Germany, AM, LW, bat....$75.00 – 90.00

Ticcolo 3561, horizontal/watch radio, 1964, plastic, six transistors,
upper front horizontal two-band
slide rule dial with right and left
thumbwheel knobs, lower right
watch face, lower left metal perforated grill area, made in West Germany, AM, LW, bat....$75.00 – 90.00

UKW-Partner, horizontal, 1961, plastic, eight transistors, upper front horizontal two-band slide rule dial with right thumbwheel tuning, left side thumbwheel on/off/volume knob, perforated grill area, telescoping antenna, made in West Germany, AM, FM, bat.....$40.00 – 50.00

UKW-Partner 3081, horizontal, 1960, plastic, eight transistors, upper front horizontal two-band slide rule dial with right thumbwheel tuning, left side thumbwheel on/off/volume knob, perforated grill area, two telescoping antennas, made in West Germany, AM, FM, bat.............$40.00 – 50.00

Tempest

AF-1200, vertical, plastic, upper front horizontal two-band slide rule dial with right side thumbwheel tuning, lower metal perforated grill area, telescoping antenna, left side strap, AM, FM, bat ....$10.00 – 15.00

HT-1251, vertical, 4¼x2⅝x1¼", plastic, 14 transistors, upper right front window dial with right side thumbwheel tuning, top left thumbwheel on/off/volume knob, two oval metal perforated grill areas, made in Japan, AM, bat.......$20.00 – 30.00

HT-8041 "Deluxe," vertical, 4¼x2⅝x1¼", plastic with metal

front panel, eight transistors, upper front oval window dial with right side thumbwheel tuning, top left thumbwheel on/off/volume knob, lower perforated grill area, made in Japan, AM, bat...........$20.00 – 25.00

TR 1200, vertical, 4¼x2⅝x1¼", plastic, upper right front round dial window with right side thumbwheel tuning, upper left front round on/off/volume window with left side thumbwheel knob, lower metal perforated grill area with lower right logo, made in Hong Kong, AM, bat.....................$10.00 – 15.00

Terra

5026, vertical, 4⅜x2¾x1¼", plastic, 12 transistors, upper right front window dial with right side thumbwheel tuning, left side thumbwheel on/off/volume knob, left side strap, made in Japan, AM, bat..............$5.00 – 10.00

Toho

1505, vertical, 7x4x2⅜", leather, 15 transistors, two upper front round dials – one AM, one FM – lower metal perforated grill area, right side band switch, handle, made in Japan, AM, FM, bat .....$5.00 – 10.00

Tokai

FA-951, horizontal, 1963, nine transistors, off-center vertical two-band slide rule dial, two top thumbwheel knobs, two lower switches, left perforated grill area, telescoping antenna, AM, FM, bat.........$15.00 – 20.00

G-202, vertical, 3½x2½x1", plastic, two transistors, upper right front thumbwheel dial knob, upper left front thumbwheel on/off/volume knob, large metal grill area with horizontal slots, rear fold-out stand, made in Japan, AM, bat.........$65.00 – 75.00

HA-911 "Super Sensitivity," horizontal, 1964, nine transistors, upper front horizontal dial, three thumbwheel knobs, large perforated grill area with lower left logo, AM, bat......................$10.00 – 15.00

RA-9, horizontal, 1965, nine transistors, upper right front window dial with right side thumbwheel tuning, lower right side thumbwheel on/off/volume knob, horizontal grill bars, AM, bat .....$10.00 – 15.00

RA-611, vertical, 3x2⅛x1⅛", 1963, plastic, 6 transistors, right side thumbwheel knob, large front round metal perforated grill area, made in Japan, AM, bat..........$25.00 – 35.00

RA-711, vertical, 1963, seven transistors, upper right front dial with

thumbwheel tuning, left side thumbwheel on/off/volume knob, large perforated grill area, AM, bat.............................$30.00 – 40.00

RA-801, horizontal, 1964, plastic, eight transistors, right front window dial with right side thumbwheel tuning, lower right side thumbwheel on/off/volume knob, left perforated grill area with upper left logo, upper right "L/H" switch, AM, bat......................$30.00 – 40.00

Tom Thumb

Boy's Radio, vertical, 4x2½x1", plastic, two transistors, upper right front window dial with right side thumbwheel tuning, left side thumbwheel on/off/volume knob, round metal perforated grill area, made in Japan, AM, bat..........$45.00 – 55.00

Tonecrest

645, vertical, 1965, six transistors, upper left front window dial with thumbwheel tuning, right side thumbwheel on/off/volume knob, large front grill area with horizontal bars, AM, bat..........$5.00 – 10.00

946, vertical, 1965, nine transistors, upper right front window dial with thumbwheel tuning, large lower grill area with vertical bars, AM, bat ....$5.00 – 10.00

1051, horizontal, 1965, 10 transistors, right front vertical two-band slide rule dial with thumbwheel tuning, left grill area with horizontal bars, telescoping antenna, AM, FM, bat.......................$15.00 – 20.00

1094, vertical, 1965, 10 transistors, upper right front window dial with thumbwheel tuning, large lower lattice grill area, AM, bat .$5.00 – 10.00

1670, vertical, 1965, six transistors, upper right front window dial with thumbwheel tuning, lower grill area with horizontal bars, AM, bat ....$10.00 – 15.00

1889, vertical, 1965, eight transistors, upper right front window dial with thumbwheel tuning, left side thumbwheel on/off/volume knob, lower grill area with vertical bars, AM, bat ....$5.00 – 10.00

2091, horizontal, 1965, 10 transistors, upper front horizontal slide rule dial, large lower perforated grill area with lower right FM/AM switch, telescoping antenna, AM, FM, bat.......................$10.00 – 15.00

Tonelux

2 transistor (no #), vertical, 3⅝x2¼x1⅛", plastic, two transistors, upper right front window dial with right side thumbwheel tuning, top left thumbwheel on/off/

volume knob, round checkered grill area, made in Japan, AM, bat ....$50.00 – 60.00

Top-Flight

Boy's Radio, vertical, 4⅛x2⅝x1¼", plastic, two transistors, upper front see-through panel with right round window dial forming open mouth of lion's head decoration, right side thumbwheel tuning knob, left on/off/volume window with left side thumbwheel knob, lower metal perforated grill area, made in Japan, AM, bat.........$50.00 – 60.00

Top Line

Boy's Radio, vertical, 4⅛x2½x1¼", plastic, two transistors, upper right front window dial with right side thumbwheel tuning, left side thumbwheel on/off/volume knob, textured and perforated grill area, made in Japan, AM, bat.............$45.00 – 55.00

Toptone

AR-610, horizontal, 2½x4¼x1⅜", plastic, six transistors, right front thumbwheel dial knob, upper right front thumbwheel on/off/volume knob, metal perforated grill area, made in Japan, AM, bat............$40.00 – 50.00

Toshiba

3TP-315Y, vertical, 1959, three transistors, upper right front thumbwheel dial, upper left thumbwheel on/off/volume knob, lower horizontal grill bars, no built-in speaker, earphone only, AM, bat.................$125.00 – 150.00

5TP-90, vertical, 4x2½x1", 1961, plastic, five transistors, upper right front window dial with right side thumbwheel tuning, left side thumbwheel on/off/volume knob, metal perforated grill area with lower left logo, AM, bat..$30.00 – 35.00

5TR-193 "Lace," vertical, 4⅛x2⅝x1⅜", 1959, plastic, five transistors, upper right front round dial knob, left side thumbwheel on/off/volume knob, lower perforated lace grill area, made in Japan, AM, bat.................$350.00 – 400.00

5TR-193 "Mesh Grill," vertical, 4⅛x2⅝x1⅜", 1959, plastic, five transistors, upper right front round dial knob, left side thumbwheel on/off/volume knob, lower metal perforated grill area, made in Japan, AM, bat......$300.00 – 350.00

5TR-221, vertical, 4x3x1½", plastic, large upper right front dial knob, left front thumbwheel on/off/volume knob, lower grill area with vertical bars and lower left logo, made in Japan, AM, bat..$250.00 – 275.00

6P-10, horizontal, 1963, six transistors, right front window dial with right side thumbwheel tuning, right side thumbwheel on/off/volume knob, left perforated grill area with center logo, AM, bat.$25.00 – 35.00

6P-15, horizontal, 2⅝x4½x1⅛", 1962, plastic, six transistors, upper right front window dial with right side thumbwheel tuning, lower right side thumbwheel on/off/volume knob, left metal perforated grill area with lower left logo, AM, bat ....$35.00 – 45.00

6P-35, horizontal, 2⅝x4⅛x1⅛", plastic, six transistors, upper right front window dial with right side thumbwheel tuning, lower right side thumbwheel on/off/volume knob, left metal perforated grill area, left side strap, made in Japan, AM, bat ....$25.00 – 35.00

6TC-485, vertical/folding-style clock radio, 4¾x2⅞x2¼" (closed), 1963, leatherette, six transistors, inner right round dial/thumbwheel knobs/metal perforated grill area, inner left round alarm clock face and lower knob, AM, bat ....$60.00 – 75.00

6TC-485A, vertical/folding-style clock radio, 4¾x2⅞x2¼" (closed), 1963, leatherette, six transistors, inner right round dial/thumbwheel knobs/metal perforated grill area, inner left round alarm clock face and lower knob, AM, bat ....$60.00 – 75.00

6TP-31, vertical, 4½x2¾x1¼", plastic, six transistors, upper

front half-round dial panel overlaps large metal perforated grill area with lower left logo, right side thumbwheel tuning, lower left logo, rear fold-out stand, AM, bat.......................$200.00 – 225.00

6TP-31A, vertical, 4½x2¾x1¼", 1963, plastic, six transistors, upper front half-round dial panel overlaps large metal perforated grill area with lower left logo, **right side thumbwheel tuning, lower left logo, rear fold-out stand, AM, bat......$200.00 – 225.00**

6TP-304, vertical, 4⅜x2½x1⅛", 1959, six transistors, upper left front vertical slide rule dial with thumbwheel tuning, lower right perforated grill area with lower right logo, AM, bat...................$350.00 – 400.00

6TP-309, vertical, 1959, six transistors, upper front see-through panel, right window dial inside V-shaped trim, right side thumbwheel tuning, left side thumbwheel on/off/volume knob, lower metal perforated grill area with lower left logo, AM, bat ....$175.00 – 200.00

6TP-309A, vertical, 4x2½x1¼", plastic, upper front window dial with right side thumbwheel tuning, left front thumbwheel on/off/volume knob, lower metal perforated grill area, made in Japan, AM, bat ....$100.00 – 125.00

6TP-309Y, vertical, 1959, six transistors, upper front see-through panel, right window dial inside V-shaped trim, right side thumbwheel tuning, left side thumbwheel on/off/volume knob, lower metal perforated grill area with lower left logo, AM, bat.........$175.00 – 200.00

6TP-314, vertical, 4½x2¾x1¼", 1959, available in white, green, or coral plastic, six transistors, upper left front window dial with right side thumbwheel tuning, right side thumbwheel on/off/volume knob, horizontal grill bars with lower right logo, made in Japan, AM, bat......................$20.00 – 30.00

6TP-314A, vertical, plastic, six transistors, upper left front window dial with right side thumbwheel tuning, right side thumbwheel on/off/volume knob, large metal perforated grill area with lower right logo, AM, bat............................$90.00 – 110.00

6TP-354, vertical, 3⅛x2⅜x1", 1960, plastic, six transistors, upper right front thumbwheel dial, upper left thumbwheel on/off/volume knob, lower metal perforated grill area, made in Japan, AM, bat............................$75.00 – 90.00

6TP-357, vertical, 2¾x2⅜x1", 1961, plastic, six transistors, upper right front round dial knob, left side thumbwheel on/off/volume knob, lower metal perforated grill area, made in Japan, AM, bat ....$100.00 – 125.00

6TP-385, horizontal, 2½x4¼x1¼", 1961, plastic, six transistors, right front control panel with window dial and right thumbwheel tuning, metal perforated grill area, telescoping antenna, AM, bat ....$50.00 – 65.00

6TP-394, vertical, 2⅞x2⅜x1⅛", 1961, plastic, six transistors, upper right front round dial knob, upper left side thumbwheel on/ off/volume knob, lower metal perforated grill area, made in Japan, AM, bat.........$55.00 – 70.00

6TR-92 "Rice Bowl," round, 7⅞x7¼" diameter, 1959, six transistors, spherical-shaped set with floral design, top dial, bottom speaker grill, base, handle, AM, bat............$300.00 – 350.00

6TR-186 "Lace," horizontal, 3⅛x5¾x1⅝", 1959, plastic, six transistors, right front thumbwheel dial and thumbwheel on/off/volume knob, left perforated lace grill area, made in Japan, AM, bat....$225.00 – 250.00

7P-45, vertical, plastic, seven transistors, upper right front window dial with right side tuning knob, top left

thumbwheel on/off/volume knob, large metal perforated grill area, left side strap, made in Japan, AM, bat...........................$25.00 – 35.00

7P-70, horizontal, 2¾x5½x1¼", plastic, seven transistors, front round dial overlaps large left metal perforated grill area with upper left logo, lower right front on/off/volume window, two right side thumbwheel knobs, AM, bat..........$25.00 – 35.00

7P-130S, horizontal, 3¼x5⅞x1½", 1963, plastic, seven transistors, upper front horizontal two-band slide rule dial with right side thumbwheel tuning, right side thumbwheel on/off/volume knob, lower right side thumbwheel fine tuning knob, metal perforated grill area, rear SW/MW switch, telescoping antenna, made in Japan, AM, SW, bat...........................$35.00 – 45.00

7TH-425, round, 12x4", 1961, plastic, seven transistors, made to hang on the wall, center round two part dial – the outside is for tuning and the inside is for volume control – on/off switch is a pull-cord at bottom of case, the grill area surrounds the dial and has 48 curved plastic spokes, two speakers, AM, bat..........................$150.00 – 175.00

7TH-425Y, round, 12x4", 1961, plastic, seven transistors, made to hang on the wall, center round two part dial – the outside is for tuning and the inside is for volume control – on/off switch is a pull-cord at bottom of case, the grill area surrounds the dial and has 48 curved plastic spokes, two speakers, AM, bat..........................**$150.00 – 175.00**

7TM-312S, horizontal, 4x7x1¾", 1961, seven transistors, plastic, upper front horizontal two-band slide rule dial with top right tuning knob, upper left front thumbwheel knob, lower left metal perforated grill area with center horizontal bar, telescoping antenna, AM, SW, bat..............................**$50.00 – 60.00**

7TP-21, vertical, 1962, seven transistors, upper right front round window dial with right side thumbwheel tuning, upper left thumbwheel on/off/volume knob, center perforated grill area, AM, bat.....................**$40.00 – 50.00**

7TP-30, vertical, 1962, seven transistors, upper right front round window dial with right side thumbwheel tuning, upper left thumbwheel on/off/volume knob, center perforated grill area, AM, bat..............................**$40.00 – 50.00**

7TP-303, vertical, 4⅜x2¾x1⅜", 1961, plastic, seven transistors, upper front see-through panel with "cat's eye" window dial, right side thumbwheel tuning, right side thumbwheel on/off/volume knob, lower metal perforated grill area with V-shaped decoration, could be used with optional speaker box model 3WX, made in Japan, AM, bat.
radio only..............**$125.00 – 150.00**
with speaker box ...**$175.00 – 200.00**

7TP-352M, vertical, 5x3x1¼", 1961, plastic, seven transistors, upper front horizontal two-band slide rule dial with right thumbwheel tuning, right side thumbwheel on/off/volume knob, lower metal perforated grill area, top left band switch, telescoping antenna, made in Japan, AM, Marine, bat........**$65.00 – 75.00**

7TP-352S, vertical, 5x3x1¼", 1961, plastic, seven transistors, upper front horizontal two-band slide rule dial with right thumbwheel tuning, right side thumbwheel on/off/volume knob, lower metal perforated grill area, top left band switch, telescoping antenna, made in Japan, AM, SW, bat..............**$65.00 – 75.00**

8TH-428R, horizontal/table, 1963, eight transistors, three right front horizontal slide rule dial scales, three knobs, left checkered grill area, feet, AM, 2SW, bat..............**$25.00 – 35.00**

8TM-41, horizontal, 3¾x6½x1½", 1962, plastic, eight transistors, upper front slanted horizontal dial, right side tuning knob, left side on/off/volume knob, metal perforated grill area, AM, bat......**$50.00 – 60.00**

8TM-210S, horizontal, plastic, eight transistors, upper right front two-band window dial with thumbwheel tuning, upper left thumbwheel on/off/volume knob, large lower textured and perforated grill area, AM, SW, bat..............**$70.00 – 85.00**

8TM-294, horizontal, 3¾x6½x1½", 1960, plastic, eight transistors, top horizontal wrap-over dial with right side tuning knob, left side on/off/volume knob, lower metal grill area with rectangular cut-outs, made in Japan, AM, bat......$85.00 – 100.00

8TM-294B, horizontal, 3¾x6½x1½", 1960, plastic, eight transistors, top horizontal wrap-over dial with right side tuning knob, left side on/off/volume knob, lower metal grill area with rectangular cut-outs, made in Japan, AM, bat......$85.00 – 100.00

8TM-300S, horizontal, 4⅝x8x1¾", 1960, plastic, eight transistors, two top horizontal dials, right side tuning knob, left side on/off/volume knob, top MW/SW pushbuttons, large front metal perforated grill area with center logo, telescoping antenna, made in Japan, AM, SW, bat.$35.00 – 45.00

8TM-613, horizontal, 1963, eight transistors, upper front horizontal slide rule dial with top right thumbwheel tuning, lower right thumbwheel on/off/volume knob, perforated grill area, AM, bat...............$25.00 – 35.00

8TP-90, vertical, 4½x2¾x1⅜", 1962, plastic, eight transistors, upper front round window dial with

right side thumbwheel tuning, left side thumbwheel on/off/volume knob, lower round concentric circle grill area, rear fold-out stand, made in Japan, AM, bat ....$700.00+

9TL-365S, horizontal, 5x8½x1¾", 1962, plastic, nine transistors, upper front horizontal two-band dial with upper right thumbwheel tuning, upper left thumbwheel on/off/volume knob, two lower right switches, left metal perforated grill area, top right band switch, telescoping antenna, made in Japan, AM, SW, bat ...$40.00 – 50.00

9TM-40, vertical, 6x3⅝x1¾", 1961, plastic, nine transistors, shouldered case with raised top dial area, right side thumbwheel tuning, left side thumbwheel on/off/ volume knob, large lower metal perforated grill area, rear dial light button, swing handle, made in Japan, AM, bat .....$300.00 – 350.00

10TL-429F, horizontal, 6¼x9⅛x 2⅝", 1961, plastic, 10 transistors, upper right front horizontal two-band slide rule dial with thumbwheel tuning, upper left thumbwheel on/off/volume knob, large metal grill area with horizontal slots, two top pushbuttons, telescoping antenna, handle, AM, FM, bat..............................$45.00 – 55.00

10TL-655F, horizontal, 1963, 10 transistors, upper front horizontal two-band slide rule dial with upper right thumbwheel tuning, upper left thumbwheel on/off/volume knob, large lower perforated grill area, telescoping antenna, handle, AM, FM, bat..............$30.00 – 40.00

10TM-631F, horizontal, 1964, 10 transistors, two right front round dials – upper AM, lower FM – large left grill area, telescoping antenna, strap, AM, FM, bat......$25.00 – 35.00

RP-S5, vertical, 3½x2⅛x½", plastic/metal, left front vertical slide rule dial with top left thumbwheel tuning, top right thumbwheel volume knob, top on/off switch, left side stereo/mono switch, made in Japan, FM, bat..........$45.00 – 55.00

TR-193 "The Reflex," "Lace," vertical, 4x2½x1¼", 1958, plastic, four transistors, upper right front round dial knob, left side thumbwheel on/off/volume knob, lower perforated lace grill area, made in Japan, AM, bat..................$350.00 – 400.00

"Young Mate," horizontal, 2⅝x5x 1¼", plastic, upper right front window dial with right side thumbwheel tuning, right side thumbwheel on/off/volume knob, left grill area with crisscross cut-outs, strap, made in Japan, AM, bat..............................$15.00 – 20.00

_____

Trancel

6TP-348, vertical, 4⅜x2⅝x1¼", plastic, upper front see-through panel with horizontal slide rule dial, right side thumbwheel tuning, left side thumbwheel on/off/volume knob, lower metal perforated grill area with lower left logo, rear fold-out stand, AM, bat....................$100.00 – 125.00

7TM-312S, horizontal, 4x7x1¾", seven transistors, plastic, upper front horizontal two-band slide rule dial with top right tuning knob, upper left front thumbwheel knob, lower left metal perforated grill area with center horizontal bar, telescoping antenna, made in Japan, AM, SW, bat..............................$50.00 – 60.00

T-7, vertical, 1959, six transistors, upper front horizontal slide rule dial with thumbwheel tuning knob, left side thumbwheel on/off/volume knob, lower diagonal grill bars with lower left logo, AM, bat....................$75.00 – 90.00

T-11, horizontal, 2½x4½x1⅛", 1962, plastic, six transistors, right front window dial with right side thumbwheel tuning, lower right side thumbwheel on/off/volume knob, large metal perforated grill area, made in Japan, AM, bat............$25.00 – 35.00

Trans-American

SR-6T60, vertical, 1962, six transistors, upper left front round dial knob, right side thumbwheel on/off/volume knob, lower perforated grill area, made in Japan, AM, bat ....$45.00 – 60.00

Trans-ette

TR 60, vertical, 4⅜x2¾x1¼", plastic, six transistors, upper front see-through panel with horizontal dial, right side thumbwheel tuning, left side thumbwheel on/off/volume knob, lower metal perforated grill area with lower left logo, rear fold-out stand, made in Japan, AM, bat ....$100.00 – 125.00

TR 80, vertical, 4¼x2¾x1¼", plastic, eight transistors, upper front see-through panel with horizontal dial, right side thumbwheel tuning, left side thumbwheel on/off/volume knob, lower metal perforated grill area with lower left logo, rear fold-out stand, AM, bat ....$100.00 – 125.00

TR-81, vertical, 1962, eight transistors, upper front round window dial with thumbwheel tuning, large lower perforated grill area, AM, bat ....$20.00 – 30.00

6YR-21, vertical, plastic, six transistors, upper right front window dial with right side thumbwheel tuning, left side thumbwheel on/off/volume knob, lower round metal perforated grill area, AM, bat.....$85.00 – 100.00

TRN-3, vertical, 1961, three transistors, upper front window dial with left side thumbwheel tuning, lower perforated grill area, swing handle, AM, bat ....$45.00 – 55.00

YRM6, vertical, 1962, six transistors, upper left front round window dial with top thumbwheel tuning, top right thumbwheel on/off/volume knob, lower perforated grill area, AM, bat.............**$35.00 – 45.00**

Transtone

TR-101, vertical, 4x2⅝x1", plastic, six transistors, upper right front window dial with right side thumbwheel tuning, lower round metal perforated grill area, made in Japan, AM, bat..........**$30.00 – 40.00**

Transitone

TR-1645, vertical, 1963, six transistors, step-back top, upper left window dial with thumbwheel tuning, right side thumbwheel on/off/volume knob, large grill area with horizontal bars, AM, bat...**$5.00 – 10.00**

Transonic

9T-641, horizontal, 1964, nine transistors, two right front window dials – one AM, one FM – right side thumbwheel tuning, right side thumbwheel on/off/volume knob, left perforated grill area, telescoping antenna, AM, FM, bat.......................**$10.00 – 15.00**

1095N, vertical, 1964, 10 transistors, upper left front round window dial with thumbwheel tuning, lower grill area with horizontal bars, AM, bat..............................**$10.00 – 15.00**

Trav-Ler

TR-280, vertical, 1958, plastic, six transistors, upper front round dial knob, top right on/off/volume knob, lower metal perforated grill area, swing handle, AM, bat...............**$75.00 – 100.00**

TR-280-B "Power-Mite," vertical, 5¾x3¼x1⅝", 1958, ebony plastic, six transistors, upper front round

dial knob, top right on/off/volume knob, lower metal perforated grill area, swing handle, AM, bat.........................**$75.00 – 100.00**

TR-282-B "Power-Mite," vertical, 5¾x3¼x1⅝",1958, red plastic, six transistors, upper front round dial knob, top right on/off/volume knob, lower metal perforated grill area, swing handle, AM, bat................**$75.00 – 100.00**

TR-283, vertical, 1958, plastic, six transistors, upper front round dial knob, top right on/off/volume knob, lower metal perforated grill area, swing handle, AM, bat................**$75.00 – 100.00**

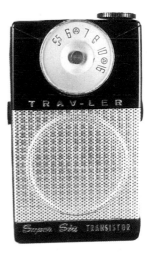

TR-284-B "Power-Mite," vertical, 5¾x3¼x1⅝", 1958, ebony/ivory plastic, six transistors, upper front round dial knob, top right on/off/volume knob, lower metal perforated grill area, swing handle, AM, bat...................$75.00 – 100.00

TR-285-B "Power-Mite," vertical, 5¾x3¼x1⅝", 1958, ebony/ivory plastic, six transistors, upper front round dial knob, top right on/off/volume knob, lower metal perforated grill area, swing handle, AM, bat ....$75.00 – 100.00

TR-286-B "Power-Mite," vertical, 5¾x3¼x1⅝", 1958, red/ivory plastic, six transistors, upper front round dial knob, top right on/off/volume knob, lower metal perforated grill area, swing handle, AM, bat ....$75.00 – 100.00

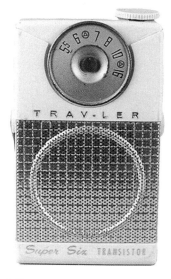

TR-287-B "Power-Mite," vertical, 5¾x3¼x1⅝", 1958, ivory/red plastic, six transistors, upper front round dial knob, top right on/off/volume knob, lower metal perforated grill area, swing handle, AM, bat..................$75.00 – 100.00

TR-601, vertical, 1962, six transistors, upper right side thumbwheel dial, upper left side thumbwheel on/off/volume knob, lower perforated grill area with lower left logo, AM, bat ....$70.00 – 90.00

TR-630, horizontal, 1962, nine transistors, right front dial with right side thumbwheel tuning, lower right side thumbwheel on/off/volume knob, left lattice grill area with upper left logo, AM, bat ....$30.00 – 40.00

_____

Trend
FR-625PH "Super Deluxe," vertical, 1965, six transistors, upper right front window dial with right side thumbwheel tuning, left side thumbwheel on/off/volume knob, lower grill area, AM, bat......$10.00 – 15.00

_____

Truetone
D3614A, horizontal, 1957, plastic, four transistors, right front round dial knob, lower thumbwheel on/off/volume knob, center checkered grill area, left crest, AM, bat.........................$275.00 – 300.00

D3614B, horizontal, 1957, plastic, four transistors, right front round dial knob, lower thumbwheel on/off/volume knob, center checkered grill area, left crest, AM, bat .....$275.00 – 300.00

D3715A, horizontal, 1958, plastic, four transistors, right front round dial knob, lower on/off/volume knob, center checkered grill area, left crest, AM, bat..$275.00 – 300.00

D3716A, horizontal, 1957, leather, five transistors, upper right front dial knob, upper left front on/off/volume knob, lower grill area with rectangular cut-outs, leather handle, AM, bat ....$35.00 – 45.00

D3716B, horizontal, 1957, leather, five transistors, upper right front dial knob, upper left front on/off/volume knob, lower grill area with rectangular cut-outs, leather handle, AM, bat.....**$35.00 – 45.00**

DC1400, horizontal/clock radio, 1964, six transistors, wedge-shaped case, right front dial with upper right thumbwheel tuning, lower right thumbwheel on/off/volume knob, large left grill area, AM, bat..........**$15.00 – 20.00**

DC3050, horizontal, 1959, eight transistors, two upper front horizontal slide rule dials, upper right thumbwheel tuning, upper left thumbwheel on/off/volume knob, lower perforated grill area, telescoping antenna, AM, SW, bat.....................**$30.00 – 35.00**

DC3052, horizontal, 2⅝x4½x1⅜", 1959, plastic, six transistors, right front V-shaped window dial over large perforated grill area, right side thumbwheel tuning, lower right side thumbwheel on/off/volume knob, made in Japan, AM, bat.....................**$40.00 — 50.00**

DC3084A, horizontal, 1960, leather, six transistors, upper right front dial knob, upper left front on/off/volume knob, center grill area with rectangular cut-outs, leather handle, AM, bat................**$15.00 – 20.00**

DC3088A, horizontal, 1960, eight transistors, upper right front dial knob, lower right on/off/volume knob over large perforated grill area with lower left logo, fold-down handle, AM, bat ....**$15.00 – 20.00**

DC3090, vertical, 1960, three transistors, upper front window dial with thumbwheel tuning, lower round perforated grill area, swing handle, AM, bat ....**$60.00 – 75.00**

DC3105, vertical, 3⅞x2½x1⅛", plastic, three transistors, upper left front window dial with left side thumbwheel tuning, thumbwheel on/off/volume knob, metal perforated grill area, swing handle, made in Japan, AM, bat......$45.00 – 55.00

DC3164A, vertical, 1962, six transistors, upper front round window dial with right side thumbwheel tuning, right side thumbwheel on/off/volume knob, lower perforated grill area, AM, bat..............**$25.00 – 35.00**

DC3270, horizontal, 3½x5⅞x1⅞", plastic, nine transistors, right front dial with right side thumbwheel tuning, lower right side thumbwheel on/off/volume knob, left lattice grill area with upper left logo, made in USA, AM, bat........**$30.00 – 40.00**

DC3280, horizontal, 1962, eight transistors, upper front horizontal two-band dial with right thumbwheel tuning, top left thumbwheel on/off/volume knob, lower perforated grill area, AM, SW, bat.**$35.00 – 45.00**

DC3306, horizontal, 1963, six transistors, upper right front window dial with right side thumbwheel tuning, lower right side thumbwheel on/off/volume knob, oval perforated grill area, AM, bat.**$20.00 – 25.00**

DC3316, vertical, 1963, six transistors, upper front horizontal slide rule dial with thumbwheel tuning, large lower perforated grill area, AM, bat......................**$10.00 – 15.00**

DC3318, vertical, 1963, eight transistors, upper front horizontal slide rule dial with thumbwheel tuning, lower perforated grill area, AM, bat......................**$15.00 – 20.00**

DC3338, vertical, 1963, eight transistors, two upper right front windows – one for stations, one for CD marks – lower perforated grill area, strap, AM, bat.............**$15.00 – 20.00**

DC3350, horizontal, 1964, 10 transistors, upper front horizontal two-band dial, right and left side knobs, large lower perforated grill area with lower right and left knobs, telescoping antenna, fold-down handle, AM, FM, bat.**$15.00 – 20.00**

DC3406, vertical, 1963, six transistors, step-back top, upper left front window dial with thumbwheel tuning, right side thumbwheel on/off/vol-

ume knob, large grill area with horizontal bars, AM, bat......**$5.00 – 10.00**

DC3407, vertical, 1964, seven transistors, upper front round dial knob, right side thumbwheel on/off/volume knob, lower lattice grill area with lower left logo, AM, bat..............................**$10.00 – 15.00**

DC3408, vertical, 4¾x3x1¼", 1964, plastic, eight transistors, upper front horizontal slide rule dial with right side thumbwheel tuning, right side thumbwheel on/off/volume knob, lower oval perforated grill area with center logo, AM, bat..**$20.00 – 25.00**

DC3408B, vertical, 4¾x3x1¼", 1964, plastic, eight transistors, upper front horizontal slide rule dial with right side thumbwheel tuning, right side thumbwheel on/off/volume knob, lower oval perforated grill area with center logo, AM, bat.............**$20.00 – 25.00**

DC3416, vertical, 1964, six transistors, upper front horizontal slide rule dial with thumbwheel tuning, large lower perforated grill area, AM, bat......................**$10.00 – 15.00**

DC3426, horizontal watch/radio, 1964, six transistors, upper left front horizontal slide rule dial, three thumbwheel knobs, right round watch face overlaps lower perforated grill area, swing handle, AM, bat......................**$75.00 – 90.00**

DC3429B, horizontal, 1964, nine transistors, right front dial with thumbwheel tuning, upper left on/off/volume knob, large checkered grill area, handle, AM, bat...........**$15.00 – 20.00**

DC3436, horizontal, 1964, six transistors, left front vertical slide rule dial with top left thumbwheel tuning, top right thumbwheel on/off/volume knob, oval perforated grill area with center logo, AM, bat ..**$20.00 – 25.00**

DC3438, vertical, 1963, eight transistors, two upper right front windows – one for stations, one for CD marks – lower perforated grill area, strap, AM, bat............**$15.00 – 20.00**

DC3448, horizontal, 1963, nine transistors, upper front horizontal three-band dial, thumbwheel knobs, lower perforated grill area, swing handle, AM, 2SW, bat..............**$30.00 – 40.00**

DC3459, horizontal, 1963, 10 transistors, upper front horizontal two-band slide rule dial with right tuning knob, top left thumbwheel knob, large lower perforated grill area, telescoping antenna, AM, FM, bat ....**$15.00 – 20.00**

DC3460, horizontal, 1964, 10 transistors, upper front horizontal two-band dial, right and left side knobs, large lower perforated grill area with lower right and left knobs, telescoping antenna, fold-down handle, AM, FM, bat.**$15.00 – 20.00**

DC3506, horizontal, 1964, six transistors, upper right front window dial with right side thumbwheel tuning, lower right side thumbwheel on/off/volume knob, oval perforated grill area, AM, bat.**$20.00 – 25.00**

DC3609 "Hi Fidelity," horizontal, 1965, leather, nine transistors, upper front horizontal slide rule dial, right dial and Hi/Lo switch, left perforated grill area, leather handle, AM, bat ....**$10.00 – 15.00**

DC3610, horizontal, 1965, 10 transistors, right front window dial with upper right side thumbwheel tuning, lower right side thumbwheel on/off/volume knob, large perforated grill area, AM, bat .**$10.00 – 15.00**

DC3612, vertical, 1965, 12 transistors, upper front round dial knob, right thumbwheel on/off/volume knob, lower perforated grill area, AM, bat ....**$10.00 – 15.00**

DC3654, horizontal, 1965, 10 transistors, upper front horizontal two-band slide rule dial with right knob, lower grill area with vertical bars and lower right FM/AM switch, telescoping antenna, AM, FM, bat....................**$10.00 – 15.00**

DC3704 "Jr.," vertical, 3⅞x2½x1¼", plastic, six transistors, upper right front window dial with right side thumbwheel tuning, left side thumbwheel on/off/volume knob, lower grill area with horizontal bars, made in Hong Kong, AM, bat.**$5.00 – 10.00**

DC3754 "Vagabond 10," horizontal, 6⅜x8¼x2⅞", leatherette, upper front horizontal two-band slide rule dial, lower right tuning and on/off/volume knobs, left grill area with horizontal bars, right side band switch, telescoping antenna, pull-up handle, AM, FM, bat..**$10.00 – 15.00**

DC3884, horizontal, 1959, leather, four transistors, upper right front dial knob, upper left front volume knob, center grill area with circular cut-outs, leather handle, AM, bat ....$20.00 – 25.00

DC3886A, horizontal, 1958, leather, six transistors, upper right front dial knob, upper left front volume knob, center grill area with circular cut-outs, leather handle, AM, bat ....$20.00 – 25.00

Tussah

Boy's Radio, vertical, 4x2½x1¼", plastic, two transistors, upper right front round window dial with thumbwheel tuning, thumbwheel on/off/volume knob, metal perforated grill area, made in Japan, AM, bat..............................$50.00 – 60.00

Union

Boy's Radio, horizontal/table radio, 4¼x7x4", plastic, two transistors, upper right front dial, lower right on/off/volume knob over horizontal grill bars, left side

switch, can be used with matching intercom/external speaker, made in Japan, AM, bat.

radio only ....$30.00 – 40.00
with speaker..............$55.00 – 65.00

United Royal

801, horizontal, plastic with metal front panel, eight transistors, upper right front window dial with right side thumbwheel tuning, left side thumbwheel on/off/volume knob, large perforated grill area with lower left logo, AM, bat ....$25.00 – 35.00

802, horizontal, 3⅝x5⅞x1½", plastic, eight transistors, upper front horizontal two-band dial with right side thumbwheel tuning, right side thumbwheel on/off/volume knob, right side BC/SW switch, large metal perforated grill area, made in Japan, AM, SW, bat ...$20.00 – 30.00

1050, horizontal, 5⅞x10¼x2½", plastic, top raised two-band horizontal slide rule dial, top right tuning knob, top left volume/tone knob, large front perforated grill area with lower right logo, three pushbuttons, telescoping antenna, handle, made in Japan, AM, FM, bat ....$30.00 – 40.00

"Ten Hundred," horizontal, 3½x6x 1½", 1964, plastic, nine transistors, upper right front window dial with right side thumbwheel tuning, right side thumbwheel on/off/volume knob, large metal perforated grill area with lower left logo, made in Japan, AM, bat...........$30.00 – 40.00

Universal

713B, horizontal, 2⅝x4⅝x1¼", plastic, upper right front round window dial with right side thumbwheel tuning, lower right side thumbwheel on/off/volume knob, left front textured grill area, top right braided strap, made in China, AM, bat...............................$20.00 – 25.00

PTR-62B, vertical, 4¼x2¾x1¼", 1963, plastic, six transistors, upper right front thumbwheel dial, upper left front thumbwheel on/off/volume knob, lower metal perforated grill area, made in Japan, AM, bat....................$20.00 – 30.00

PTR-81B, vertical, 4⅜x2¾x1¼", 1962, plastic, eight transistors, upper right front thumbwheel dial, upper left front thumbwheel on/off/volume knob, lower metal perforated grill area with lower left logo, made in Japan, AM, bat.......$30.00 – 40.00

RE-64 "Deluxe," vertical, 4x2⅝x1", 1964, plastic, six transistors, upper right front window dial with right side thumbwheel tuning, left side thumbwheel on/off/volume knob, lattice grill area, made in Taiwan, AM, bat.....................$10.00 – 15.00

SM-888 "Big 8," horizontal, 3x5⅛x1⅛", plastic, eight transistors, upper right front window dial with right side thumbwheel tuning, lower right side thumbwheel on/off/volume knob, large metal perforated grill area, made in Hong Kong, AM, bat ....$10.00 – 15.00

YT-161, vertical, 4⅛x2½x1⅜", plastic, six transistors, upper right thumbwheel dial knob, left on/off/volume window with left side thumbwheel knob, lower metal perforated grill area, made in Japan, AM, bat..........$25.00 – 35.00

Usalite

Boy's Radio, vertical, 3⅞x2½x1¼", plastic, two transistors, upper front window dial with left side thumbwheel tuning, right side thumbwheel on/off/volume knob, lower metal textured and perforated grill area, made in Japan, AM, bat ....$45.00 – 55.00

Valiant

655 "Hi-Fi," vertical, plastic, six transistors, upper right front window dial with right side thumbwheel tuning, top left thumbwheel on/off/volume knob, lower grill area with horizontal bars, AM, bat.................$5.00 – 10.00

AM1400 "Hi Power," vertical, upper left front round dial knob, upper right on/off/volume knob, lower grill area with vertical bars, AM, bat......................$20.00 – 30.00

Boy's Radio, vertical, 3⅞x2½x1⅛", plastic, two transistors, upper front window dial with left side thumbwheel tuning, right side thumbwheel on/off/volume knob, round metal perforated grill area, made in Japan, AM, bat...........$40.00 – 55.00

Boy's Radio "Deluxe," vertical, 4x2½x1¼", plastic, two transistors, upper left front window dial with left side thumbwheel tuning, thumbwheel on/off/volume knob, right front vertical textured panel, left front vertical grill bars, made in Japan, AM, bat...........$55.00 – 65.00

HT-1200 "High Fidelity," vertical, 4¼x2⅝x1¼", plastic with metal front panel, 10 transistors, upper right front triangular window dial with right side thumbwheel tuning, top left thumbwheel on/off/vol-

ume knob, lower perforated grill area with crisscross pattern, made in Japan, AM, bat......$25.00 – 35.00

HT-1221, vertical, plastic with metal front panel, 10 transistors, upper right front window dial with right side thumbwheel tuning, top left thumbwheel on/off/volume knob, large oval grill area, AM, bat ....$20.00 – 25.00

HT-6043 "Deluxe HiFi," vertical, 4¼x2½x1¼", plastic with metal front panel, six transistors, upper right front square window dial with right side thumbwheel tuning, top left thumbwheel on/off/volume knob, lower perforated grill area with vertical lines, AM, bat........$20.00 – 25.00

V-666-A "DeLuxe," vertical, 4¼x2⅝x1¼", plastic, six transistors, upper right front window dial with right side thumbwheel tuning, left side thumbwheel on/off/volume knob, vertical grill bars, made in Hong Kong, AM, bat...$5.00 – 10.00

VRC-12, vertical, 6⅛x2½x1⅜", plastic with metal front panel, 12 transistors, upper right front window dial with right side thumbwheel tuning, top left thumbwheel on/off/volume knob, large oval grill area, AM, bat .....**$20.00 – 25.00**

VEB Stern-Radio

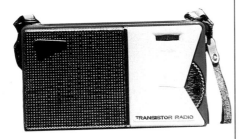

Sternchen, horizontal, 1959, plastic, six transistors, lower right front dial knob in V-shaped indent, upper thumbwheel on/off/volume knob, left metal perforated grill area with upper left logo, made in East Germany, AM, bat ....$65.00 – 100.00

T100, horizontal, 1962, plastic, six transistors, right front vertical three-band slide rule dial with top right thumbwheel tuning, top left thumbwheel on/off/volume knob, large lattice grill area, made in East Germany, AM, SW, LW, bat.........**$30.00 – 40.00**

Vesper

G-1110, horizontal, 1963, nine transistors, right front vertical two-band slide rule dial with thumbwheel tuning, lower FM/AM switch, left perforated grill area, telescoping antenna, AM, FM, bat ....**$10.00 – 15.00**

Victor

8TA-7, horizontal, 3⅞x6⅜x1⅝, plastic, eight transistors, upper front horizontal two-band slide rule dial with right side thumbwheel tuning, lower right side thumbwheel fine tuning knob and MW/SW switch, left side thumbwheel on/off/volume knob, large front metal perforated grill area with Nipper logo, telescoping antenna, made in Japan, AM, SW, bat ...**$20.00 – 30.00**

TH-2770, horizontal, 6½x11¾x4", wood, top horizontal two-band slide rule dial with right tuning knob and band switch, left on/off/volume knob, front grill area with vertical bars, telescoping antenna, handle, made in Japan, AM, SW, bat ....**$40.00 – 50.00**

Victoria

TR-650, vertical, 1961, six transistors, upper front horizontal dial with thumbwheel tuning, lower perforated grill area, AM, bat .**$30.00 – 40.00**

Viscount

6TP-102, vertical, 4¼x2⅝x1¼", plastic, six transistors, upper front see-through

window dial with top thumbwheel tuning, upper right front thumbwheel on/off/volume knob, lower metal textured and perforated grill area, made in Japan, AM, bat.....$115.00 – 135.00

6TP-103, vertical, 4¼x2¾x1¼", plastic, six transistors, upper front see-through window dial with top thumbwheel tuning, upper right front thumbwheel on/off/volume knob, lower metal textured and perforated grill area, AM, bat....$125.00 – 150.00

601, vertical, 1965, six transistors, upper right front window dial with right side thumbwheel tuning, left side thumbwheel on/off/volume knob, lower horizontal grill bars, strap, AM, bat..............$5.00 – 10.00

602 (several variations), vertical, 4⅜x2¾x1¼", 1962, plastic, six transistors, upper front thumbwheel dial knob, upper right thumbwheel on/off/volume knob, lower metal perforated grill area, made in Japan, AM, bat.
see-through panel .$125.00 – 150.00
metal dial panel........$50.00 – 60.00

616, vertical, plastic, six transistors, upper right front window dial with right side thumbwheel tuning, top left thumbwheel on/off/volume knob, lower metal perforated grill area, AM, bat..............$20.00 – 25.00

712, vertical, 1965, seven transistors, upper front round dial knob, right side thumbwheel on/off/volume knob, lower horizontal grill bars, AM, bat..............$5.00 – 10.00

725 "Tiny Pal," horizontal, plastic with metal front panel, right front horizontal two-band slide rule dial with right side thumbwheel tuning, right side thumbwheel on/off/volume knob, large metal perforated grill area, rear band switch, AM, SW, bat......................$25.00 – 35.00

815, vertical, 4¼x2½x1½", plastic, eight transistors, upper front round dial knob, right side thumbwheel on/off/volume knob, lower horizontal grill bars, made in Hong Kong, AM, bat ....$5.00 – 10.00

820, horizontal, plastic, eight transistors, two right front window dials – one AM, one FM – left metal perforated grill area, telescoping antenna, AM, FM, bat ....$25.00 – 35.00

833, horizontal, 4¾x8½x1¾", plastic, eight transistors, upper front horizontal three-band slide rule dial with right tuning, upper left thumbwheel on/off/volume knob, top right switch, lower metal perforated grill area with two switches, AM, SW, Marine, bat ....$40.00 – 50.00

909, square, 2⅛x2x1", plastic, nine transistors, right side tuning and on/off/volume knobs, front metal perforated grill area, left side metal chain and fob, made in Japan, AM, bat ....$60.00 – 75.00

1022, vertical, 1965, 10 transistors, upper right front window dial with right side thumbwheel tuning, lower perforated grill area, AM, bat ....$10.00 – 15.00

1030, horizontal, 3½x6⅜x1⅛", plastic, 10 transistors, large right front window dial with right thumbwheel tuning, top left thumbwheel on/off/volume knob, left metal perforated grill area, made in Japan, AM, bat...........$25.00 – 35.00

Vision
TR-102 "Boy's Radio," "Deluxe," vertical, plastic, two transistors, upper front diamond shaped window dial with top left thumbwheel tuning,

right side thumbwheel on/off/volume knob, metal perforated grill area, AM, bat...............$60.00 – 70.00

Vista

8TS33 "Super," vertical, 4⅜x2⅞x 1⅜", plastic, eight transistors, upper right front dial knob, upper left front on/off/volume window with left side thumbwheel knob, checkered grill area, made in Japan, AM, bat.........$30.00 – 40.00

10, horizontal, 1965, 10 transistors, right front vertical two-band slide rule dial, large left perforated grill area, telescoping antenna, strap, AM, FM, bat...............$10.00 – 15.00

G-1050, horizontal, 1964, 10 transistors, right front two-band thumbwheel dial, upper AM/FM switch, upper left thumbwheel on/off/volume knob, left grill area with horizontal slots, telescoping antenna, AM, FM, bat...............$15.00 – 20.00

NTR-800, horizontal, 2⅞x4⅞x1¼", 1964, plastic, eight transistors, upper front horizontal two-band slide rule dial with right side thumbwheel tuning, right side thumbwheel on/off/volume knob, metal perforated grill area with MW/SW switch, telescoping antenna, can be used with matching speaker box, made in Japan, AM, SW, bat.
radio only .... $35.00 – 45.00
with speaker box .... $75.00 – 90.00

NTR-850, horizontal, 1963, eight transistors, upper front horizontal slide rule dial with right side thumbwheel tuning, oval perforated grill area, AM, bat .... $20.00 – 30.00

NTR-966, vertical, 1964, upper front window dial with right side thumbwheel tuning, lower round perforated grill area, AM, bat. $40.00 – 50.00

Vogel-Elektronik
TR 3 "Junior," vertical, 1960, plastic, upper front window dial with thumbwheel tuning, thumbwheel on/off/volume knob, round metal perforated grill area, swing handle, AM, bat .... $40.00 – 50.00

TS 60, horizontal, 1960, leather, six transistors, right front window dial in the shape of a crown overlaps large metal perforated grill area, right side thumbwheel tuning knob, right side thumbwheel on/off/volume knob, made in West Germany, AM, LW, bat .... $35.00 – 45.00

TS 8758, horizontal, 1958, leather, seven transistors, right front window dial in the shape of a crown over-

laps large metal perforated grill area, right side thumbwheel tuning knob, right side thumbwheel on/off/volume knob, made in West Germany, AM, bat ..... $35.00 – 45.00

TS 8759/L, horizontal, 1959, leather, seven transistors, right front window dial in the shape of a crown overlaps large metal perforated grill area with bird logo, right side thumbwheel tuning knob, right side thumbwheel on/off/volume knob, made in West Germany, AM, LW, bat .... $35.00 – 45.00

Volt

Boy's Radio, vertical, 4⅛x2½x1¼," plastic, two transistors, upper right front window dial with thumbwheel tuning, thumbwheel on/off/volume knob, metal textured and perforated grill area, crown logo, made in Japan, AM, bat .... $50.00 – 60.00

Vornado
V-700, vertical, 1965, eight transistors, upper front window dial with right side thumbwheel tuning, large

lower tear drop-shaped perforated grill area, AM, bat......**$20.00 – 25.00**

V-820, vertical, 1965, eight transistors, upper front horizontal slide rule dial with right side thumbwheel tuning, lower perforated grill area, AM, bat.............**$15.00 – 20.00**

V-1670, vertical, 1965, six transistors, upper right front window dial with right side thumbwheel tuning, lower grill area with horizontal bars, AM, bat.............**$15.00 – 20.00**

V-2091, horizontal, 1965, 10 transistors, upper front horizontal two-band slide rule dial, large lower perforated grill area with lower right FM/AM switch, AM, FM, bat....**$10.00 – 15.00**

Vulcan

6T-160, horizontal, 2¾x4½x1¼", 1960, plastic, six transistors, upper right front thumbwheel dial behind see-through panel, upper left thumbwheel on/off/volume knob, lower metal perforated grill area, made in Japan, AM, bat...........**$65.00 – 80.00**

Wales

6YR-15A, vertical, 3½x2¼x1", plastic, six transistors, upper right front thumbwheel dial, upper left front thumbwheel on/off/volume knob, lower round metal perforated grill area, made in Japan, AM, bat ....**$85.00 – 100.00**

Waltham

WA1001, vertical, 1965, six transistors, upper right front window dial with right side thumbwheel tuning, lower grill area, right side strap, AM, bat ....**$5.00 – 10.00**

WA3201L, horizontal, 1965, leather, eight transistors, right front vertical slide rule dial with right side tuning, right side on/off/volume knob, left perforated grill area, leather handle, AM, bat................**$10.00 – 15.00**

WA5001, vertical, 1965, 10 transistors, upper right front window dial with right side thumbwheel tuning, top left thumbwheel on/off/volume knob, left vertical perforated grill area, AM, bat.....**$10.00 – 15.00**

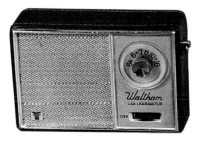

WA5102L, horizontal, 3¼x4⅞x1⅝", 1965, leather, 10 transistors, upper right front dial knob, lower right thumbwheel on/off/volume knob, left metal perforated grill area with lower left logo, handle, AM, bat............................**$10.00 – 15.00**

WA5303L, horizontal, 1965, leather, 10 transistors, upper front horizontal slide rule dial, three right knobs, left grill area with horizontal bars, leather handle, AM, bat ....**$10.00 – 15.00**

WB4101, horizontal, 1965, nine transistors, upper right front round two-band dial, right side thumbwheel knobs, left grill area with horizontal bars, telescoping antenna, strap, AM, FM, bat.....**$10.00 – 15.00**

WB5201L, horizontal, 1965, leather, 10 transistors, right front vertical two-band slide rule dial with right side tuning, right side on/off/volume knob, left perforated grill area, leather handle, AM, FM, bat......................$15.00 – 20.00

WB7303L, horizontal, 1965, 12 transistors, upper front horizontal two-band slide rule dial, four right knobs, left grill area with horizontal bars, telescoping antenna, leather handle, AM, FM, bat.$15.00 – 20.00

Watterson

601, horizontal/table, 1958, wood, six transistors, right front dial, three knobs, left grill area, feet, AM, bat.....................$15.00 – 20.00

Webcor

310, horizontal, 1961, 10 transistors, off-center vertical two-band slide rule dial over large perforated grill area with lower left logo, top thumbwheel tuning and on/off/volume knobs, telescoping antenna, AM, FM, bat......................$25.00 – 35.00

B-308, horizontal, 1962, plastic with two "leatherette" front panels, eight transistors, upper front horizontal slide rule dial with top thumbwheel tuning, lower right thumbwheel on/off/volume knob, textured metal grill area with horizontal slots, AM, bat.............$50.00 – 60.00

E306, horizontal, 1961, seven transistors, upper front horizontal two-band slide rule dial with top thumbwheel tuning, lower right thumbwheel on/off/volume knob,

perforated grill area, telescoping antenna, AM, SW, bat....$50.00 – 60.00

E307, vertical, 4⅛x2½x1⅛", 1964, six transistors, upper front slanted horizontal slide rule dial with thumbwheel tuning, large lower metal textured and perforated grill area with center logo, made in Japan, AM, bat...........$20.00 – 30.00

E-312, horizontal, 1962, eight transistors, upper front horizontal three-band slide rule dial, lower left grill area with horizontal slots, telescoping antenna, AM, SW, LW, bat.............................$15.00 – 20.00

E313, horizontal, 1964, six transistors, upper right front round window dial with right side thumbwheel tuning, right side thumbwheel on/off/volume knob, large left perforated grill area, AM, bat ....$10.00 – 15.00

E314, vertical, 1964, eight transistors, upper front horizontal slide rule dial with right side thumbwheel tuning, right side thumbwheel on/off/volume knob, perforated grill area with lower left logo, AM, bat.............$10.00 – 15.00

E316 "Patio," horizontal, 1964, nine transistors, upper front horizontal two-band slide rule dial, four right knobs, large lower checkered grill area, telescoping antenna, handle, AM, FM, bat.$10.00 – 15.00

G-309, horizontal, 1962, eight transistors, upper front horizontal two-band slide rule dial with right side thumbwheel tuning, top left thumbwheel on/off/volume knob, perforated grill area, battery window, AM, Weather, bat......$30.00 – 40.00

R305, vertical, 1961, six transistors, upper left front window dial with left side thumbwheel tuning, upper right thumbwheel on/off/volume knob, lower perforated grill area, swing handle, AM, bat.........$50.00 – 60.00

Wendall-West

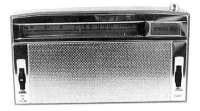

CR-18, horizontal, 3¾x7x1⅞", plastic with metal front panel, eight transistors, upper front horizontal slide rule dial with lower right front thumbwheel tuning, lower left front thumbwheel on/off/volume knob, large perforated grill area, telescoping antenna, made in Japan, bat..............$25.00 – 35.00

Westclox

80002, horizontal/clock radio, 1962, six transistors, upper right front window dial over perforated grill area, right side thumbwheel tuning and on/off/volume knobs, left front clock face, AM, bat ....$45.00 – 55.00

80004, horizontal/clock radio, 1962, six transistors, upper right front window dial over perforated grill area, right side thumbwheel tuning and on/off/volume knobs, left front clock face, AM, bat ....$45.00 – 55.00

80006, horizontal/clock radio, 1962, six transistors, upper right front window dial over perforated grill area, right side thumbwheel tuning and on/off/volume knobs, left front clock face, AM, bat ....$45.00 – 55.00

Westinghouse

H-587P7, horizontal, 3⅛x6x1¾", 1957, gray plastic, seven transistors, large right front round dial knob, lower right thumbwheel on/off/volume knob, left checkered grill area, AM, bat......................$75.00 – 85.00

H-588P7, horizontal, 3⅛x6x1¾", 1957, black/pearlescent gray plastic, seven transistors, large right front round dial knob, lower right thumbwheel on/off/volume knob, left checkered grill area, AM, bat......................$75.00 – 85.00

H-589P7, horizontal, 3⅛x6x1¾", 1957, red/black plastic, seven transistors, large right front round dial knob, lower right thumbwheel on/off/volume knob, left checkered grill area, AM, bat.......$75.00 – 85.00

H-602P7, horizontal, 7½x9⅜x4⅛", 1957, tan leather, seven transistors, upper right front dial knob, upper left front on/off/volume knob, lower metal perforated grill area, leather handle, AM, bat ....$30.00 – 40.00

H610P5, horizontal, 1957, charcoal gray plastic, five transistors, large right front round dial knob, lower right thumbwheel on/off/volume knob, left checkered grill area, AM, bat .... $75.00 – 85.00

H611P5, horizontal, 1957, blue plastic, five transistors, large right front round dial knob, lower right thumbwheel on/off/volume knob, left checkered grill area, AM, bat .... $75.00 – 85.00

H612P5, horizontal, 1957, yellow plastic, five transistors, large right front round dial knob, lower right thumbwheel on/off/volume knob, left checkered grill area, AM, bat .... $75.00 – 85.00

H617P7, horizontal, 3⅛x6x1¾", 1957, gray plastic, seven transistors, large right front round dial knob, lower right thumbwheel on/off/volume knob, left checkered grill area, AM, bat .... $65.00 – 75.00

H618P7, horizontal, 3⅛x6x1¾", 1957, black plastic, seven transistors, large right front round dial knob, lower right thumbwheel on/off/volume knob, left checkered grill area, AM, bat .... $65.00 – 75.00

H619P7, horizontal, 3⅛x6x1¾", 1957, red plastic, seven transistors, large right front round dial knob, lower right thumbwheel on/off/volume knob, left checkered grill area, AM, bat .... $65.00 – 75.00

H621P6 "Cordless," horizontal, 6½x9¼x3½", 1958, charcoal plastic, six transistors, right front round dial knob, left front round on/off/volume knob, top raised lattice grill area, swing handle, AM, bat .... $45.00 – 55.00

H622P6 "Cordless," horizontal, 6½x9¼x3½", 1958, yellow/white plastic, six transistors, right front round dial knob, left front round on/off/volume knob, top raised lattice grill area, swing handle, AM, bat .... $45.00 – 55.00

H-651P6, horizontal, 3x6x1½", 1958, charcoal plastic, six transistors, right front round dial knob overlaps top checkered grill area, lower left perforated grill area, lower right thumbwheel on/off/volume knob, AM, bat.... $30.00 – 40.00

H-652P6, horizontal, 3x6x1½", 1958, turquoise plastic, six transistors, right front round dial knob overlaps top checkered grill area, lower left perforated grill area, lower right thumbwheel on/off/volume knob, AM, bat.... $30.00 – 40.00

H-653P6, horizontal, 3x6x1½", 1958, off-white plastic, six transistors, right front round dial knob overlaps top checkered grill area, lower left perforated grill area, lower right thumbwheel on/off/volume knob, AM, bat.... $30.00 – 40.00

H655P5, vertical, 7x4x1⅞", 1959, white/charcoal plastic, five transistors, lower front round dial knob overlaps upper checkered grill area, right side on/off/volume knob, swing handle, AM, bat...................... $30.00 – 40.00

H656P5, vertical, 7x4x1⅞", 1959, white/red plastic, five transistors, lower front round dial knob overlaps upper checkered grill area, right side on/off/volume knob, swing handle, AM, bat.........**$30.00 – 40.00**

H-657P5, vertical, 7x4x1⅞", 1959, white/turquoise plastic, five transistors, lower front round dial knob overlaps upper checkered grill area, right side on/off/volume knob, swing handle, AM, bat..........**$30.00 – 40.00**

H-685P8, horizontal/clock radio, 4⅛x9⅝x3", 1959, white/brown plastic, eight transistors, right front round dial over large perforated grill area, lower thumbwheel alarm/volume knob, left alarm clock face, feet, AM, bat.....................**$20.00 – 25.00**

H-686P8, horizontal/clock radio, 4⅛x9⅝x3", 1959, white/pink plastic, eight transistors, right front round dial over large perforated grill area, lower thumbwheel alarm/volume knob, left alarm clock face, feet, AM, bat.....................**$20.00 – 25.00**

H-690P5, horizontal, 6⅝x7¾x2¾", plastic, five transistors, large right front round dial knob overlaps grill area with circular cut-outs, left side on/off/volume knob, handle, AM, bat............................**$20.00 – 25.00**

H-693P8, horizontal, 3⅛x6x2", 1959, brown plastic, eight transistors, right front round convex dial knob overlaps top checkered grill area, lower left perforated grill area, lower right thumbwheel on/off/volume knob, AM, bat....**$30.00 – 40.00**

H-694P8, horizontal, 3⅛x6x2", 1959, green plastic, eight transistors, right front round convex dial knob overlaps top checkered grill area, lower left perforated grill area, lower right thumbwheel on/off/volume knob, AM, bat....**$30.00 – 40.00**

H-695P8, horizontal, 3⅛x6x2", 1959, pink plastic, eight transistors, right front round convex dial knob overlaps top checkered grill area, lower left perforated grill area, lower right thumbwheel on/off/volume knob, AM, bat...**$30.00 – 40.00**

H-697P7, vertical, 7x4¼x2⅛", 1959, charcoal gray/white plastic, seven transistors, lower front round dial knob overlaps upper checkered grill area, right side on/off/volume knob, swing handle, AM, bat.............**$25.00 – 35.00**

H-698P7, vertical, 7x4¼x2⅛", 1959, yellow/white plastic, seven transistors, lower front round dial knob overlaps upper checkered grill area, right side on/off/volume knob, swing handle, AM, bat.....................**$25.00 – 35.00**

H-699P7, vertical, 7x4¼x2⅛", 1959, green/white plastic, seven transistors, lower front round dial knob overlaps upper checkered grill area, right side on/off/volume knob, swing handle, AM, bat.............................$25.00 – 35.00

H-707P6GP, vertical, 3¾x2½x1⅛", green plastic, six transistors, upper right front window dial with right side thumbwheel tuning, top left thumbwheel on/off/volume knob, lower metal perforated grill area with lower left logo, made in Japan, AM, bat.....................$15.00 – 20.00

H-707P6GPA, vertical, 3¾x2½x1⅛", green plastic, six transistors, upper right front window dial with right side thumbwheel tuning, top left thumbwheel on/off/volume knob, lower metal perforated grill area with lower left logo, made in Japan, AM, bat.....................$15.00 – 20.00

H-712P9, horizontal, 1960, charcoal/white plastic, nine transistors, two upper front horizontal slide rule dial scales, large lower grill area, telescoping antenna, handle, AM, SW, bat..............$15.00 – 20.00

H-713P9, horizontal, 1960, dove gray/white plastic, nine transistors, two upper front horizontal slide rule dial scales, large lower grill area, telescoping antenna, handle, AM, SW, bat..............$15.00 – 20.00

H725P6, horizontal, 6½x7¾x2¼", 1960, white/flame plastic, six transistors, large right front round dial knob overlaps grill area with circular cut-outs, left side on/off/volume knob, handle, AM, bat.............$20.00 – 25.00

H-725P6A, horizontal, 1961, white/flame plastic, six transistors, large right front round dial knob overlaps grill area with circular cut-outs, left side on/off/volume knob, handle, AM, bat ....$20.00 – 25.00

H-726P6, horizontal, 6½x7¾x2¼", 1960, white/aqua plastic, six transistors, large right front round dial knob overlaps grill area with circular cut-outs, left side on/off/volume knob, handle, AM, bat.............................$20.00 – 25.00

H-727P6, horizontal, 6½x7¾x2¼", 1960, mist green/white plastic, six transistors, large right front round dial knob overlaps grill area with circular cut-outs, left side on/off/volume knob, handle, AM, bat.............................$20.00 – 25.00

H-728P6, horizontal, 6½x7¾x2¼", 1960, charcoal/white plastic, six transistors, large right front round

302

dial knob overlaps grill area with circular cut-outs, left side on/off/volume knob, handle, AM, bat.............................$20.00 – 25.00

H-729P7, horizontal, 1960, suntan leather, seven transistors, right front round dial with right side tuning knob, left side on/off/volume knob, left front grill area, leather handle, AM, bat ....$10.00 – 15.00

H-730P7, horizontal, 1960, gray leather, seven transistors, right front round dial with right side tuning knob, left side on/off/volume knob, left front grill area, leather handle, AM, bat ....$10.00 – 15.00

**H-732P7, vertical, 4⅜x2⅝x1⅜",
1961, chestnut brown plastic, seven transistors, upper left front round window dial with right side thumbwheel tuning, right side thumbwheel on/off/volume knob, metal perforated grill area, rear fold-out stand, made in USA, AM, bat...........................$15.00 – 20.00**

H-733P7, vertical, 4⅜x2⅝x1⅜", 1961, shadow white plastic, seven transistors, upper left front round window dial with right side thumbwheel tuning, right side thumbwheel on/off/volume knob, metal perforated grill area, rear fold-out stand, made in USA, AM, bat ....$15.00 – 20.00

H-737P7, horizontal, 1960, harvest gold plastic, seven transistors, upper front horizontal slide rule dial with right side tuning, left side on/off/volume knob, lower grill area with horizontal bars, AM, bat....................$10.00 – 15.00

H-738P7, horizontal, 1960, turquoise plastic, seven transistors, upper front horizontal slide rule dial with right side tuning, left side on/off/volume knob, lower grill area with horizontal bars, AM, bat....................$10.00 – 15.00

H769P7, horizontal, 1960, tan leather, seven transistors, right front round dial with right side tuning knob, left side on/off/volume knob, left checkered grill area, leather handle, AM, bat ....$10.00 – 15.00

H769P7A, horizontal, 1960, tan leather, seven transistors, right front round dial with right side tuning knob, left side on/off/volume knob, left checkered grill area, leather handle, AM, bat ....$10.00 – 15.00

H-770P7, horizontal, 1960, gray leather, seven transistors, right front round dial with right side tuning knob, left side on/off/volume knob, left checkered grill area, leather handle, AM, bat ....$10.00 – 15.00

H770P7A, horizontal, 1960, gray leather, seven transistors, right front round dial with right side tuning knob, left side on/off/volume knob, left checkered grill area, leather handle, AM, bat ....$10.00 – 15.00

H-771P6, horizontal, 6½x7¾x2¼", 1961, charcoal/white plastic, six transistors, large right front round dial knob overlaps grill area with circular cut-outs, left side on/off/volume knob, handle, AM, bat ....$20.00 – 25.00

H-772P6, horizontal, 6½x7¾x2¼", 1961, ivory/white plastic, six transistors, large right front round dial knob overlaps grill area with circular cut-outs, left side on/off/volume knob, handle, AM, bat ....$20.00 – 25.00

H-772P6GP, horizontal, 1961, plastic, six transistors, large right front round dial knob overlaps grill area with circular cut-outs, left side on/off/volume knob, handle, AM, bat ....$20.00 – 25.00

H-773P6, horizontal, 6½x7¾x2¼", 1961, vermilion/white plastic, six transistors, large right front round dial knob overlaps grill area with circular cut-outs, left side on/off/volume knob, handle, AM, bat ....$20.00 – 25.00

H-790P6, vertical, 7x4¼x2", 1962, plastic, six transistors, lower front round dial overlaps upper horizontal grill bars, lower right side on/off/volume knob, swing handle, AM, bat ....$25.00 – 35.00

H-790P6GP, vertical, 7x4¼x2", 1962, plastic, six transistors, lower front round dial overlaps upper horizontal grill bars, lower right side on/off/volume knob, swing handle, AM, bat ....$25.00 – 35.00

H-791P6, vertical, 7x4¼x2", 1962, plastic, six transistors, lower front round dial overlaps upper horizontal grill bars, lower right side on/off/volume knob, swing handle, AM, bat ....$25.00 – 35.00

H-791P6GP, vertical, 7x4¼x2", 1962, plastic, six transistors, lower front round dial overlaps upper horizontal grill bars, lower right side on/off/volume knob, swing handle, AM, bat ....$25.00 – 35.00

H-793P6GP, horizontal, 1962, white/charcoal plastic, six transistors, large right front round dial knob overlaps grill area with circular cut-outs, left side on/off/volume knob, handle, AM, bat ....$20.00 – 25.00

H-795P6, vertical, 4½x2½x1½", 1962, plastic, six transistors, upper left front round window dial with thumbwheel tuning, lower round metal perforated grill area, AM, bat.............................$15.00 – 20.00

H-796P6, vertical, 4½x2½x1½", 1962, plastic, six transistors, upper left front round window dial with thumbwheel tuning, lower round metal perforated grill area, AM, bat ....$15.00 – 20.00

H-798P7, vertical, 1962, black plastic, seven transistors, upper left front round window dial with right side thumbwheel tuning, right side thumbwheel on/off/volume knob, large metal perforated grill area, AM, bat ....$15.00 – 20.00

H-798P7GP, vertical, 1962, black plastic, seven transistors, upper left front round window dial with right side thumbwheel tuning, right side thumbwheel on/off/volume knob, large metal perforated grill area, AM, bat ....$15.00 – 20.00

H-812P8, horizontal, 1962, black leather, eight transistors, flip-up top with cut-outs for right and left top knobs, inner three-band slide rule dial, front perforated grill area with lower right logo, telescoping antenna, strap, AM, 2SW, bat .....$45.00 – 55.00

H-841P6, horizontal, 2⅝x4⅞x1¼", 1963, beige plastic, six transistors, large right front round dial knob, top left thumbwheel on/off/volume knob, left front grill area with horizontal bars, AM, bat..................$10.00 – 15.00

H-842P6, horizontal, 2⅝x4⅞x1¼", 1963, charcoal plastic, six transistors, large right front round dial knob, top left thumbwheel on/off/volume knob, left front grill area with horizontal bars, AM, bat ....$10.00 – 15.00

H-842P6GP, horizontal, 2⅝x4⅞x1¼", 1963, charcoal plastic, six transistors, large right front round dial knob, top left thumbwheel

on/off/volume knob, left front grill area with horizontal bars, AM, bat ....$10.00 – 15.00

H-868P12, horizontal, 7x9½x3½", 1963, leather, 12 transistors, two upper front pointer dials – right AM, left FM – center band switch, lower right thumbwheel knobs, lower left perforated grill area, telescoping antenna, handle, AM, FM, bat ....$20.00 – 25.00

H-901P7GP, vertical, 4¼x2⅝x1½", 1964, charcoal gray/white plastic, seven transistors, large upper left front round dial knob overlaps lower grill area with horizontal bars and lower right logo, right side thumbwheel on/off/volume knob, AM, bat...................$15.00 – 20.00

H-902P6GP, vertical, 1965, plastic, six transistors, upper right front window dial with right side thumbwheel tuning, top left thumbwheel on/off/volume knob, lower perforated grill area with lower left logo, AM, bat ....$10.00 – 15.00

H-902P6GPA, vertical, 3¾x2⅜x1", 1967, plastic, six transistors, upper right front window dial with right side thumbwheel tuning, top left thumbwheel on/off/volume knob, lower metal perforated grill area with lower left logo, made in Japan, AM, bat.....................**$10.00 – 15.00**

H-903P8GP, vertical, 1964, plastic, eight transistors, large upper left front dial knob, thumbwheel on/off/volume knob, large metal perforated grill area, AM, bat........**$15.00 – 20.00**

H-908PN9GP, vertical, 1965, nine transistors, two upper front horizontal slide rule dial scales – one FM, one AM – right side thumbwheel knobs, lower perforated grill area with lower right logo, telescoping antenna, AM, FM, bat.**$15.00 – 20.00**

H-914P8GP, vertical, 4¼x2⅝x1¼", 1965, black plastic, eight transistors, upper right front window dial with right side thumbwheel tuning, upper left front on/off/volume window with left side thumbwheel knob, lower metal perforated grill area, made in Japan, AM, bat........**$10.00 – 15.00**

H-939P8GP, vertical, 4¼x2⅝x1¼", white plastic, eight transistors, upper right front window dial with right side thumbwheel tuning, upper left front on/off/volume window with left side thumbwheel knob, lower metal perforated grill area, made in Japan, AM, bat..........**$10.00 – 15.00**

H968PLA, horizontal/travel alarm clock radio, plastic outer case snaps

open, inner thumbwheel dial and volume knobs, off/on/auto switch, right alarm clock face, left metal perforated grill area, AM, bat..**$15.00 – 20.00**

H-969P6GP, vertical, 3¾x2½x1", green plastic, upper right front window dial with right side thumbwheel tuning, top left thumbwheel on/off/volume knob, metal perforated grill area with lower left logo, can be used with combination lamp/speaker box base (Lumina Series Convertible #H-969CA), AM, radio-bat, lamp base-AC.
radio only ....**$15.00 – 20.00**
with lamp/speaker....**$30.00 – 40.00**

RG11P28A, square, 3⅛x3⅛x1", plastic, eight transistors, rounded corners, top right corner window dial with thumbwheel tuning, top left corner thumbwheel on/off/volume knob, large front metal perforated grill area with center logo, made in Japan, AM, bat ....$15.00 – 20.00

RS11P28-A "Escort," horizontal/radio flashlight, 3¼x4¼x1¼", plastic, upper right front window dial, lower metal perforated grill area, left side flashlight, built-in recharger, AM, bat ....**$15.00 – 20.00**

RS21P08A "Escort," horizontal/radio flashlight/watch/cigarette lighter, 3¼x4¼x1¼", plastic, upper right front window dial, upper left watch face, lower metal perforated grill area, left side flashlight and cigarette lighter, built-in recharger, AM, bat.....................**$60.00 – 75.00**

Wilco

ST-6, horizontal, 1962, six transistors, right front V-shaped window dial with right side thumbwheel tuning, lower right round on/off/volume window with right side thumbwheel knob, left perforated grill area with upper left logo, AM, bat.....................**$70.00 – 90.00**

ST-88, horizontal, 1963, eight transistors, right front dial with right side thumbwheel tuning, lower right round on/off/volume window with right side thumbwheel knob, left perforated grill area with upper left logo, AM, bat.......**$50.00 – 60.00**

Windsor

2 transistor (no #), vertical, 3⅝x2½x1¼", plastic, two transistors, upper front window dial with top right thumbwheel tuning, top left thumbwheel on/off/volume knob, lower metal textured and perforated grill area, made in Japan, AM, bat.....................**$45.00 – 55.00**

15064 "Boy's Radio," vertical, 4⅛x2½x1¼", plastic, two transistors, upper front see-through panel with right window dial inside crown design, right side thumbwheel tuning, left front on/off/volume window with left side thumbwheel knob,

metal textured and perforated grill area with lower right logo, made in Japan, AM, bat............**$55.00 – 65.00**

15066 "Boy's Radio," vertical, 4⅛x2½x1¼", plastic, two transistors, upper front see-through panel with right window dial inside crown design, right side thumbwheel tuning, left front on/off/volume window with left side thumbwheel knob, metal textured and perforated grill area with lower right logo, made in Japan, AM, bat............**$55.00 – 65.00**

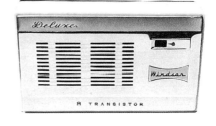

16002, horizontal, 3¼x5½x1⅜", plastic with metal front panel, eight transistors, upper right front window dial with thumbwheel tuning, left grill area with horizontal slots, AM, bat.....................$20.00 – 30.00

Boy's Radio (several variations), vertical, plastic, two transistors, all have thumbwheel tuning and on/off/volume knobs and metal perforated grill areas, made in Japan, AM, bat...........**$55.00 – 65.00**

Coronet "Boy's Radio," vertical, 4⅛x2½x1¼", plastic, two transistors, upper front see-through panel with right window dial inside crown design, right side thumbwheel tuning, left front on/off/volume window with left side thumbwheel knob, metal textured and perforated grill area with lower right logo, made in Japan, AM, bat...........$55.00 – 65.00

Superior Deluxe "Boy's Radio," vertical, 4⅜x2¾x1¼", plastic, two transistors, upper front see-through panel with left window dial, top left thumbwheel tuning, right side thumbwheel on/off/volume knob, metal textured and perforated grill area, made in Japan, AM, bat...........$55.00 – 65.00

Winston

W111, vertical, 1965, 11 transistors, upper left front window dial with thumbwheel tuning, large lower perforated grill area, AM, bat ....$15.00 – 20.00

W700, vertical, 1965, seven transistors, right side tuning and on/off/volume knobs, front perforated grill area, left strap, AM, bat...............$30.00 – 40.00

Yaecon

YTR-58, vertical, 4x2½x1½", 1960, plastic, six transistors, upper left

front window dial with left side thumbwheel tuning, right side thumbwheel on/off/volume knob, lower metal perforated grill area with lower right logo, made in Japan, AM, bat...........$75.00 – 90.00

YTR-721, horizontal, plastic, seven transistors, two right front square window dials – one BC, one SW – with right side thumbwheel tuning, lower right front round on/off/volume window with right side thumbwheel knob, band switch, left metal perforated grill area with lower left logo, BC, SW, bat..............................$20.00 – 30.00

Yashica

YT-100, vertical, 4½x2¾x1½", 1961, plastic with metal front panel, six transistors, upper right front round dial knob overlaps large lower perforated grill area with vertical lines and lower left logo, swing handle, AM, bat ....$25.00 – 35.00

YT-300, horizontal, 1961, plastic, nine transistors, upper front horizontal two-band slide rule dial with top right thumbwheel tuning, top left thumbwheel on/off/volume knob, battery window, large lower perforated grill area with lower right logo, right side switch, telescoping antenna, AM, SW, bat.....................$20.00 – 30.00

York

TR-65, vertical, 1965, six transistors, upper right front window dial with right side thumbwheel tuning, lower textured grill area, AM, bat..............................$5.00 – 10.00

TR-89, vertical, 1965, eight transistors, upper right front window dial with right side thumbwheel tuning, lower patterned grill area, AM, bat ....**$5.00 – 10.00**

TR-100, horizontal, 1963, leather, 10 transistors, right front thumbwheel dial, top left thumbwheel on/off/volume knob, large grill area with horizontal slots, handle, AM, bat ....**$10.00 – 15.00**

TR-101, horizontal, 1965, 10 transistors, right front window dial with right side thumbwheel tuning, large left perforated grill area, AM, bat ....**$10.00 – 15.00**

TR-103, vertical, 4½x2⅞x1½", **1965, plastic, 10 transistors, large** **round upper front dial knob, upper right thumbwheel on/off/volume knob, lower metal perforated grill area, made in Japan, AM, bat ....$10.00 – 15.00**

TR-105, horizontal, 1965, 10 transistors, right front two-band thumbwheel dial, lower on/off/volume

knob, upper FM/AM switch, large left grill area, telescoping antenna, AM, FM, bat ....**$10.00 – 15.00**

TR-121, horizontal, 1965, leather, 12 transistors, right front two-band thumbwheel dial, upper FM/AM switch, upper left thumbwheel on/off/volume knob, round perforated grill area, telescoping antenna, AM, FM, bat ....**$15.00 – 20.00**

TR-122, vertical, 1965, 12 transistors, large round upper front dial knob, upper right thumbwheel on/off/volume knob, lower perforated grill area, AM, bat ....**$10.00 – 15.00**

TR-123, horizontal, 1965, leather, 12 transistors, right front two-band thumbwheel dial, lower on/off/volume knob, upper FM/AM switch, large left perforated grill area, telescoping antenna, handle, AM, FM, bat ....**$10.00 – 15.00**

Zenith

Zenith "Royal" model numbers can be confusing at times. For example, a set that is marked on the front of the case "Royal 41" can have a paper label inside the case with a model number "R41W." Because most transistor collectors use the "Royal" number from the front of the case for identification purposes (rather than the model number from the inside label), to keep Zenith identification as simple as possible we have decided to use the common practice of referring to the "Royal" number from the case front when listing the following sets.

Royal 10, vertical, 4½x2¾x1½", plastic, eight transistors, upper front window dial with top thumbwheel tuning, right side thumbwheel on/off/volume knob, metal perforated grill area, AM, bat..**$15.00 – 20.00**

Royal 13, vertical, 3⅞x2⅝x1¼", plastic, upper front window dial over vertical grill bars, right side thumbwheel tuning knob, left side thumbwheel on/off/volume knob, made in Hong Kong, AM, bat.............**$15.00 – 20.00**

Royal 15, vertical, plastic, eight transistors, left front vertical slide rule dial overlaps lower perforated grill area, two right side thumbwheel knobs, AM, bat..........$15.00 – 20.00

Royal 16, vertical/billfold-style, 5⅜x 3½x1⅜" (closed), plastic outer case with perforated front cover, inner metal perforated grill area with upper right window dial, two right side thumbwheel knobs, made in Japan, AM, bat..........**$20.00 – 25.00**

Royal 20, vertical, 3x2⅜x1¼", plastic, eight transistors, upper front window dial with top thumbwheel tuning, left side thumbwheel

on/off/volume knob, chrome front grill area with vertical bars, made in Hong Kong, AM, bat.**$25.00 – 30.00**

Royal 32, horizontal, plastic, eight transistors, step-down top with right on/off/volume knob, lower right dial knob overlaps large front grill area with horizontal slots, handle, AM, bat.....................**$10.00 – 15.00**

Royal 40, vertical, 4¼x2¾x1¼", 1963, plastic, large upper front round dial knob with center pointer arrow, right side thumbwheel on/off/volume knob, lower grill area with vertical bars, AM, bat........**$20.00 – 25.00**

Royal 41, horizontal, 4⅝x5¼x1¾", 1966, plastic, upper front horizontal dial with sliding pointer, right side thumbwheel tuning knob, left side thumbwheel on/off/volume knob, lower metal grill area with horizontal bars, AM, bat........**$20.00 – 30.00**

Royal 50 (several variations), vertical, 4¼x2¾x1½", 1962, plastic, upper front round dial knob overlaps lower grill area with vertical slots and lower right logo, right side thumbwheel on/off/volume knob, made in USA, can be used with optional "Converta" speaker box, AM, bat.
radio only ....**$20.00 – 30.00**
with speaker box .....**$75.00 – 100.00**

Royal 56 "Sun Charger," horizontal, 4⅝x5¼x1¾", 1966, plastic, upper front horizontal dial with sliding pointer, right side thumbwheel tuning, left side thumbwheel on/off/volume knob, lower metal grill area with horizontal bars, swing handle with built-in solar panel, AM, bat......**$175.00 – 200.00**

Royal 59, vertical, 4½x2¾x1⅜", plastic, eight transistors, upper front round dial with top thumbwheel tuning, right side thumbwheel on/off/volume knob, lower metal perforated grill area, AM, bat...... $25.00 35.00

Royal 60, vertical, 4⅜x2¾x1½", plastic, upper front round dial knob over large metal perforated grill area, right side thumbwheel on/off/volume knob, made in USA, AM, bat............**$20.00 – 30.00**

Royal 70, horizontal, leather, upper front horizontal slide rule dial, right and left knobs overlap large lower metal perforated grill area with lower right logo and lower left tone switch, leather handle, AM, bat............**$20.00 – 30.00**

Royal 74, horizontal, 6½x9½x3¾", leather, upper front horizontal slide rule dial, lower metal checkered grill area with right and left knobs, lower right tone switch, pull-up handle, AM, bat...**$20.00 – 25.00**

Royal 80, vertical, 4⅜x2½x1⅜", plastic, eight transistors, recessed right panel with thumbwheel tuning and on/off/volume knobs, large front textured/perforated grill area with logo, AM, bat............**$30.00 – 40.00**

Royal 85, vertical, 4⅜x2⅞x1½", plastic, eight transistors, upper front dial with semicircular pointer and right side thumbwheel tuning,

right side thumbwheel on/off/volume knob, lower metal perforated grill area with lower left logo, AM, bat............**$25.00 – 35.00**

Royal 90, vertical, 4¼x2⅝x1¼", plastic, upper front round dial knob overlaps large textured and perforated grill area, right side thumbwheel on/off/volume knob, AM, bat............**$25.00 – 35.00**

Royal 97 "Super Navigator," horizontal, 7½x10¼x4½", leather, upper front horizontal three-band slide rule dial, lower metal perforated grill area with three knobs, top directional antenna and compass, handle, BC, SW, LW, bat.........**$45.00 – 55.00**

Royal 100 "Zenette," vertical, 1961, six transistors, upper right front round dial knob overlaps large lower crisscross grill area with lower right logo, rear fold-out stand, AM, bat............**$30.00 – 40.00**

Royal 130, vertical, plastic, upper front horizontal slide rule dial with thumbwheel tuning, thumbwheel on/off/volume knob, metal perforated grill area, AM, bat ..**$25.00 – 35.00**

Royal 150, vertical, 1962, plastic, six transistors, upper right front round dial knob over large perforated grill area, lower left logo, left side thumbwheel on/off/volume knob, AM, bat......................$25.00 – 35.00

Royal 185, vertical, plastic, left front vertical slide rule dial over large metal perforated grill area with upper right logo, two right side thumbwheel knobs, AM, bat.$20.00 – 30.00

Royal 200, vertical, 1959, plastic, seven transistors, upper front round dial knob, lower on/off/volume knob over checkered grill area with lower right logo, swing handle, AM, bat......................$40.00 – 50.00

Royal 250, vertical, 5⅞x3¾x1¾", 1959, plastic, six transistors, upper right front dial knob, upper left front on/off/volume knob over left grill area with horizontal bars, swing handle, made in USA, AM, bat..............$25.00 – 35.00

Royal 270, vertical, 5¾x3½x1½", 1965, plastic, upper right front round dial knob, upper left front round on/off/volume knob, large lower grill area with lower right logo, swing handle, AM, bat...........$30.00 – 40.00

Royal 275, vertical, 1960, plastic, seven transistors, upper right front round dial knob, upper left front on/off/volume knob, large lower lattice grill area with lower right logo, swing handle, AM, bat ....$30.00 – 40.00

Royal 280, vertical, 5¾x3¾x1¾", plastic, upper right front round

dial knob, upper left front on/off/volume knob, lower metal perforated grill area, swing handle, AM, bat......................$30.00 – 35.00

Royal 285, vertical, plastic, upper right front round dial knob, upper left front on/off/volume knob, lower metal perforated grill area, swing handle, AM, bat.........$25.00 – 30.00

Royal 300, vertical, 5¾x3⅝x1½", 1958, plastic, upper right front round window dial with right side thumbwheel tuning, left side thumbwheel on/off/volume knob, lower grill area with horizontal bars and lower right logo, swing handle, AM, bat......................$30.00 – 40.00

Royal 400, vertical, 5⅞x3⅝x1⅞", 1963, plastic, seven transistors, upper right front round dial knob over large metal perforated grill area with lower right logo, left side thumbwheel on/off/volume knob, swing handle, made in USA, AM, bat..............$20.00 – 30.00

Royal 450, horizontal, plastic, upper left front round dial, lower on/off/volume knob, large right checkered grill area with lower right logo, handle, AM, bat.$25.00 – 35.00

Royal 475, horizontal, 1962, seven transistors, upper left front round dial knob, lower left on/off/volume knob, perforated grill area with lower right logo, AM, bat .....$25.00 – 35.00

Royal 500

The following six models are only part of the "Royal 500" family. As with other

Zenith "Royal" models, the "500" family has areas of confusion in identification because of differences in model numbers, chassis numbers, and numbers of transistors – sometimes found in sets that appear to be the same on the outside. These are six of the most popular models with the average collector.

Royal 500 "Hand-Wired," vertical, 5¾x3½x1½", 1955, available in maroon or black plastic, seven transistors, hand-wired chassis (chassis numbers 7XT40, 7XT40Z, 7XT40Z1), the earliest of the Royal 500s, identifiable by its recessed upper front tuning and on/off/volume "owl-eye" knobs – each with a center bar across its diameter – lower round metal perforated grill area, swing handle, AM, bat ....**$125.00 – 150.00**

Royal 500, in 1956 three other colors were added to the Royal 500 line – pink, tan, and white – along with the introduction of a printed circuit.
pink..............................**$300.00+**
tan..............................**$150.00 – 200.00**
white ....**$75.00 – 100.00**

Royal 500D, vertical, 5¾x3½x1½", 1959, available in maroon, black, or white plastic, eight transistors, recessed upper front tuning and on/off/volume "owl-eye" knobs with see-through plastic marking protectors, lower round metal perforated grill area, swing handle, AM, bat ....**$65.00 – 75.00**

Royal 500E, vertical, 1960/61, available in maroon, black, white, or two-tone plastic, eight transistors, upper right front round dial knob,

upper left front round on/off/volume knob, lower round metal perforated grill area, swing handle, AM, bat ....**$45.00 – 55.00**

Royal 500H, vertical, 6x3½x1¾", 1962/63, available in black, white, and two-tone gray plastic, eight transistors, step-back top with right thumbwheel dial knob and left thumbwheel on/off/volume knob, large lower oval metal perforated grill area with center logo, swing handle, AM, bat.
black ....**$90.00 – 110.00**
white ....**$125.00 – 150.00**
two-tone gray..........**$175.00 – 200.00**

Royal 500L, vertical, 1964, plastic, upper front horizontal slide rule dial with right side thumbwheel tuning, left side thumbwheel on/off/volume knob, lower metal perforated grill area with lower right logo, swing handle, AM, bat..........**$25.00 – 35.00**

Royal 500N, horizontal, 4⅝x 5¼x1¾", 1965, plastic, upper front horizontal dial with sliding pointer, right side thumbwheel tuning, left side thumbwheel on/off/volume knob, lower metal grill area with horizontal bars, swing handle, AM, bat..............**$35.00 – 45.00**

Royal 555 "Sun Charger," horizontal, 4⅝x5¼x1¾", 1966, plastic, upper front horizontal dial with sliding pointer, right side thumbwheel tuning, left side thumbwheel on/off/volume knob, lower metal grill area with horizontal bars, swing handle with built-in solar panel, AM, bat.......**$175.00 – 225.00**

Royal 645, horizontal, 6½x7⅞x3¾", 1963, leatherette, large right dial knob over front patterned grill area, thumbwheel on/off/volume knob, handle, AM, bat ....$20.00 – 25.00

Royal 650, horizontal, 5⅛x7¼x3", leather, upper left front round dial knob, lower left on/off/volume knob, right leather checkered grill area with lower right logo, leather handle, AM, bat ....$15.00 – 20.00

Royal 675, horizontal, 5x8½x3⅜", 1960, leather, upper right front round dial knob, upper left on/off/volume knob over large grill area with vertical bars, handle, AM, bat ....$20.00 – 25.00

Royal 700, horizontal, 5¼x8⅜x3¼", 1958, leather, seven transistors, upper right front dial knob, upper left front on/off/volume knob, large lower checkered chrome grill area with center logo, leather handle, AM, bat ....$30.00 – 35.00

Royal 710, horizontal, 1960, leather, upper right front dial knob, upper left front on/off/volume knob, large lattice grill area with lower right logo, leather handle, AM, bat ....$20.00 – 25.00

Royal 750, horizontal, 5⅝x8⅞x3¾", 1958, leather, upper right front dial knob, upper left front on/off/volume knob, large lower metal checkered grill area with center logo, leather handle, AM, bat ....$25.00 – 30.00

Royal 755 (several variations), horizontal, leather, upper front hori-

zontal slide rule dial, lower metal grill area, two knobs, handle, AM, bat ....$20.00 – 30.00

Royal 760 "Navigator," horizontal, 5½x9x4", 1959, leather, eight transistors, upper right front dial knob, upper left front on/off/volume knob, large metal lattice grill area with lower right and left knobs and center logo, top "compass," leather handle, AM, bat ....$30.00 – 40.00

Royal 780 "Navigator," horizontal, 5⅝x9¼x4¼", 1960, leather, eight transistors, upper front horizontal two-band slide rule dial, large lower grill area with four knobs and center logo, leather handle, AM, LW, bat ....$35.00 – 40.00

Royal 800, horizontal, 6½x9¾x2⅝", 1957, plastic, seven transistors, right side dial knob, left side on/off/volume knob, front circular metal perforated grill area with center logo, pop-up handle, AM, bat ....$175.00 – 225.00

Royal 810, horizontal, plastic, large right round two-band dial over front metal perforated grill area, two right side thumbwheel knobs, AM, FM, bat...............$20.00 – 25.00

Royal 820, horizontal, 6⅜x11x4½", 1964, leatherette, left front two-band slide rule dial with lower tuning knob, right metal checkered grill area with lower right on/off/volume knob, right side telescoping antenna, pull-up handle, AM, FM, bat....**$20.00 – 25.00**

Royal 850, horizontal clock radio, 4⅝x10x2¾", 1959, plastic, seven transistors, front control panel with knobs and clock face overlaps vertical grill bars with right logo, feet, AM, bat ....**$40.00 – 50.00**

Royal 880, horizontal, 6½x10x5", leatherette, left front vertical two-band slide rule dial, large right cloth grill area, telescoping antenna, handle, AM, FM, bat..**$20.00 – 25.00**

Royal 950 "Golden Triangle," vertical/three-sided triangular-shaped clock radio, 9x6", 1960, metal and plastic, seven transistors, first side: round dial with two knobs, second side: round alarm clock face with lower on/off/alarm switch, third side: round perforated metal grill and logo, bottom three-legged base, top handle, clock made in Switzerland, AM, bat ....**$175.00 – 200.00**

Royal 1000 "Trans-Oceanic," horizontal, 10⅛x12¾x5", 1958, leatherette/metal/plastic, fold-down front with world map, inner eight band dial and metal perforated grill area, right side band switch, folding handle with built-in telescoping antenna, AM, 7SW, bat.....**$75.00 – 100.00**

Royal 1000-1 "Trans-Oceanic," horizontal, 10⅛x12¾x5", 1958, leather-ette/metal/plastic, nine transistors, fold-down front with world map, inner multi-band dial and metal perforated grill area, right side band switch, folding handle with built-in telescoping antenna, eight bands, bat ....**$75.00 – 100.00**

Royal 1000-D "Trans-Oceanic," horizontal, 10⅛x12¾x5", 1958, leatherette/metal/plastic, fold-down front with world map, inner multi-band dial and metal perforated grill area, right side band switch, folding handle with built-in telescoping antenna, nine bands, bat ....**$75.00 – 100.00**

Royal 2000, horizontal, 10x11⅝x5¼", 1961, 11 transistors, two upper left round dials – one FM, one AM – upper right band and tone knobs, large lower grill area with lower right tuning and on/off/volume knobs, two telescoping antennas, handle, AM, FM, bat ....**$45.00 – 55.00**

Royal 2000-1, horizontal, 10x11⅝x5¼", 1961, 11 transistors, two upper left round dials – one FM, one AM – upper right band and tone knobs, large lower grill area with lower right tuning and on/off/volume knobs, two telescoping antennas, handle, AM, FM, bat ....**$45.00 – 55.00**

Royal 3000 "Trans-Oceanic," horizontal, 1963, 12 transistors, fold-down front with world map, inner multi-band dial and metal perforated grill area, right side band switch, folding handle with built-in telescoping antenna, AM, FM, LW, 6SW, bat.................**$100.00 – 125.00**

Royal 3000-1 "Trans-Oceanic," horizontal, 10¼x12½x5⅜", 1963, 12 transistors, fold-down front with world map, inner multi-band dial and metal perforated grill area, right side band switch, folding handle with built-in telescoping antenna, nine bands, bat...............$100.00 – 125.00

Royal 7000 "Trans-Oceanic," horizontal, 9x13⅜x6⅜", fold-down front, inner multi-band slide rule dial and metal perforated grill area, fold-back top with world map, folding handle with built-in telescoping antenna, bat.
made in America...$175.00 – 200.00
made in Taiwan.....$200.00 – 250.00

Zephyr

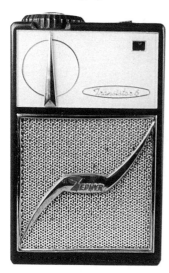

AR-600, vertical, 4⅛x2½x1¼", plastic, six transistors, upper front see-through panel, top left dial knob, upper right front on/off/volume window with top right thumbwheel knob, lower metal textured and

perforated grill area with center bar and logo, made in Japan, AM, bat........................$175.00 – 200.00

ZR-620, vertical, 4¼x2½x1¼", 1962, plastic, six transistors, upper right front window dial with right side thumbwheel tuning, left side thumbwheel on/off/volume knob, lower metal perforated grill area, made in Japan, AM, bat ......$125.00 – 150.00

ZR-930, vertical, 4⅝x3x1¼", plastic, nine transistors, upper front see-through panel with window dial, right side thumbwheel tuning, left side thumbwheel on/off/volume knob, lower metal perforated grill area, rear fold-out stand, AM, bat ......$175.00 – 200.00

Zohar

MTR-201 "Boy's Radio," vertical, 2½x4x1", plastic, two transistors, upper right front window dial with right side thumbwheel tuning, left side thumbwheel on/off/volume knob, lower metal perforated grill area, swing handle, AM, bat.............$60.00 – 85.00

Radio Clubs

The following is a list of antique radio clubs throughout the country. They are always happy to supply potential members with information about their activities and publications. The first club listed is a national organization; the rest are regional.

Antique Wireless Association
P.O. Box E
Breesport, NY 14816

Alabama Historical Radio Society
2413 Old Briar Trail
Birmingham, AL 35226

Antique Radio Club of Illinois
Carolyn Knipfel
RR3, 200 Langham
Morton, IL 61550

Antique Radio Collectors Club of Ft. Smith, Arkansas
Wanda Conatser
7917 Hermitage Drive
Ft. Smith, AR 72903

Antique Radio Collectors & Historians of Greater St. Louis
Gloria Juedemann
2015 Hickory Ridge Road
Union, MO 63084

Antique Radio Collectors of Ohio
ARCO
P.O. Box 292292
Kettering, OH 45429

Arkansas Antique Radio Club
Tom Burgess
P.O. Box 191117
Little Rock, AR 72219

Arizona Antique Radio Club
Art Heikkila
4002 W. Beryl Lane
Phoenix, AZ 85051

Belleville Area Antique Radio Club
Charles Haynes
219 W. Spring
Marissa, IL 62257

Buckeye Antique Radio & Phonograph Club
Steve Dando
4572 Mark Trail
Copley, OH 44321

California Historical Radio Society
CHRS
P.O. Box 31659
San Francisco, CA 94131

North Valley Chapter, CHRS
Chris Galantine
15853 Ontario Place
Redding, CA 96001-9785

Carolina Antique Radio Society
Carl Shirley
824 Fairwood Road
Columbia, SC 29209

Central PA Radio Collectors Club
Frank Hagenbuch
1440 Lafayette Parkway
Williamsport, PA 17701

Cincinnati Antique Radio Collectors
Tom Ducro
6805 Palmetto
Cincinnati, OH 45227

Colorado Radio Collectors
Larry Weide
5270 E. Nassau Circle
Englewood, CO 80110

Connecticut Area Antique Radio Collectors
Walt Buffinton
500 Tobacco Street
Lebanon, CT 06249

Delaware Valley Historic Radio Club
DVHRC
P.O. Box 41031
Philadelphia, PA 19127-0031

East Carolina Antique Radio Club
Bill Engstrom
218 Bent Creek Drive
Greenville, NC 27834

Florida Antique Wireless Group
Paul Currie
Box 738
Chuluota, FL 32766

Greater Boston Antique Radio Collectors
Richard Foster
12 Shawmut Avenue
Cochituate, MA 01778

Greater New York Vintage Wireless Assoc.
Bob Scheps
12 Garrity Avenue
Ronkonkoma, NY 11779

Hawaii Chapter/ARCA
Leonard Chung
95-2044 Waikalani Place, C-401
Mililani, HI 96789

Hawaii Historical Radio Club
Kevin Dooley
45 Ala Kimo Drive
Honolulu, HI 96817-5221

Houston Vintage Radio Association
HVRA
P.O. Box 31276
Houston, TX 77231-1276

Hudson Valley Antique Radio and
Phonograph Society
John Gramm
P.O. Box 1, Rt 207
Campbell Hall, NY 10916

Indiana Historical Radio Society
IHRS
725 College Way
Carmel, IN 46032

Iowa Antique Radio Club & Historical
Society
Gerald Lange
2191 Graham Circle
Dubuque, IA 52002

Kentucky Chapter/ARCA
John Caperton
3114 Boxhill Court
Louisville, KY 40222

Michigan Antique Radio Club
Bruce Eddy
2590 W. Needmore Highway
Charlotte, MI 48813

Mid-America Antique Radio Club
Monty Greenstreet
220 Bayview
Lee's Summit, MO 64064

Mid-Atlantic Antique Radio Club
Roy Morgan
P.O. Box 1362
Washington Grove, MD 20880

Mid-South Antique Radio Collectors
Linda Ramirez
811 Maple Street
Providence, KY 42450-1857

Mississippi Historical Radio &
Broadcasting Society
Randy Guttery
2412 C Street
Meridian, MS 39301

Mountains 'n' Plains Radio Collectors'
Association
MPRCA
1249 Solstice Lane
Fort Collins, CO 80525-1239

Music City Vintage Radio & Phonograph
Society
P.O. Box 22291
Nashville, TN 37202

Nebraska Antique Radio Collectors Club
Steve Morton
905 West First
North Platte, NE 69101

New England Antique Radio Club
Greg Thompson
P.O. Box 298
Newtonville, MA 02160

New Jersey Antique Radio Club
Kathleen Flanagan
92 Joysan Terrace
Freehold, NJ 07728

New Mexico Radio Collectors Club
Bill Schultz
11605 Versailles Avenue NE
Albuquerque, NM 87111

Niagara Frontier Wireless Association
Gary Parzy
135 Autumnwood
Cheektowaga, NY 14227

Northland Antique Radio Club
NARC
P.O. Box 18362
Minneapolis, MN 55418

Northwest Vintage Radio Society
P.O. Box 82379
Portland, OR 97282-0379

Oklahoma Vintage Radio Collectors
   Club
OKVRCC
P.O. Box 72-1197
Oklahoma City, OK 73172

Pittsburgh Antique Radio Society
Richard Harris, Jr.
407 Woodside Road
Pittsburgh, PA 15221

Puget Sound Antique Radio
   Association
PSARA
P.O. Box 125
Snohomish, WA 98291-0125

Radio History Society, Inc.
Steve Snyderman
4147 Lenox Drive
Fairfax, VA 22032

Rhode Island Antique Radio
   Enthusiasts
Len Arzoomanian
61 Columbus Avenue
North Providence, RI 02911

Sacramento Historical Radio Society
P.O. Box 162612
Sacramento, CA 95816-9998

E. H. Scott Historical Society, Inc.
John Meredith
P.O. Box 1070
Niceville, FL 32588-1070

Society for the Preservation of Antique
   Radio Knowledge
Harold Parshall
2673 So. Dixie Drive
Dayton, OH 45409

Southeastern Antique Radio Society
Charles Milton
P.O. Box 500025
Atlanta, GA 31150

Southern California Antique Radio
   Society
Clarence Hill
6934 Orion Avenue
Van Nuys, CA 91406

Southern Vintage Wireless Association
Bill Moore
3049 Box Canyon Road
Huntsville, AL 35803

South Florida Antique Radio
   Collectors
Thomas Valenti
Suite 315, 172 West Flagler Street
Miami, FL 33130

SPARK/Cincinnati Chapter
Tim Kaiser
P.O. Box 81
Newport, KY 41071

SPARK/Columbus Chapter
Sharon or Kenney Fullerton
2327 E. Livingston Avenue
Columbus, OH 43209

Tidewater Antique Radio Association
Phil Stroud
2328 Springfield Avenue
Norfolk, VA 23523

Vintage Audio Listeners & Valve
 Enthusiasts
Dan Schmalle
1127 NW Bright Star Lane
Poulsbo, WA 98370

Vintage Radio & Phonograph Society
Larry Lamia
P.O. Box 165345
Irving, TX 75016

Vintage Radio Unique Society
Jerryl Sears
312 Auburndale Street
Winston-Salem, NC 27104

Western Wisconsin Antique Radio
 Collectors Club
Dave Wiggert
1611 Redfield Street
La Crosse, WI 54601

West Virginia Chapter, ARCA
Geoff Bourne
405 - 8th Avenue
St. Albans, WV 25177

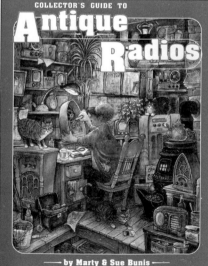